First published in Great Britain in 2015
by Wymer Publishing
www.wymerpublishing.co.uk
Tel: 01234 326691
Wymer Publishing is a trading name of Wymer (UK) Ltd

First edition. Copyright © 2014 Alan Hewitt / Wymer Publishing.

ISBN 978-1-908724-19-9

Edited by Phil Syphe at Grammar Eyes

The Author hereby asserts his rights to be identified
as the author of this work in accordance with sections
77 to 78 of the Copyright, Designs & Patents Act 1988.

All rights reserved. No part of this publication may be
reproduced or transmitted in any form or by any means,
electronic or mechanical, including photocopying, or any
information storage and retrieval system, without written
permission from the publisher.

This publication is sold subject to the condition that it shall not,
by way of trade or otherwise, be lent, re-sold, hired out or
otherwise circulated without the publishers prior consent in any
form of binding or cover other than that in which it is published
and without a similar condition including this condition
being imposed on the subsequent purchaser.

Every effort has been made to trace the copyright holders of the
photographs in this book but some were unreachable. We would
be grateful if the photographers concerned would contact us.

Typeset by Wymer.
Printed and bound in England by Mixam.

A catalogue record for this book is available from the British Library.

Cover design by Wymer.
Front cover photo © Alan Perry

A Selection Of Shows

Genesis
(& Solo)

Live Guide 1976-2014

Alan Hewitt

A Selection Of Shows

Genesis
(& Solo)

Live Guide 1976-2014

Alan Hewitt

WP
WYMER
PUBLISHING
Bedford, England

CONTENTS

INTRODUCTION	8
THE PROS & CONS OF COLLECTING	9
FOREWORD BY PHIL COLLINS	12
FOREWORD BY STEVE HACKETT	13

PART ONE: GENESIS

CHAPTER ONE - "DOES MY BUM LOOK BIG IN THIS?" A TRICK OF THE TAIL TOUR 1976	15
CHAPTER TWO - "WHERE'S HEATHCLIFF?" WIND & WUTHERING TOUR 1977	21
CHAPTER THREE - "FOLLOW YOU FOLLOW ME" AND THEN THERE WERE THREE TOUR 1978	29
CHAPTER FOUR - "ENTER THE DUKE" DUKE TOUR 1980	41
CHAPTER FIVE - "LEIDEN? WHERE THE ***K IS LEIDEN?" ABACAB TOUR 1981	51
CHAPTER SIX - "IT'S BEEN A LONG TIME… HASN'T IT?" ENCORE/THREE SIDES LIVE TOUR 1982	59
CHAPTER SEVEN - "I CAN SEE YOU MAMA" THE MAMA TOUR 1983-84	71
CHAPTER EIGHT - "INVISIBLE STRINGS" THE INVISIBLE TOUCH TOUR 1986/87	77
CHAPTER NINE - "FAR FROM 'FADING LIGHTS' " THE WE CAN'T DANCE TOUR 1992	83
CHAPTER TEN - "NOT ABOUT US" THE CALLING ALL STATIONS TOUR 1998	93
CHAPTER ELEVEN - "A SELECTION OF SHOWS" THE TURN IT ON AGAIN TOUR 2007	103

PART TWO: PETER GABRIEL

CHAPTER TWELVE - "EXPECTING THE UNEXPECTED" 1977	115
CHAPTER THIRTEEN - "CASTING A WHITE SHADOW" 1978-79	119
CHAPTER FOURTEEN - "TOURING WITHOUT FRONTIERS" 1980	123
CHAPTER FIFTEEN - "THE RHYTHM OF THE HEAT" 1982-83	126
CHAPTER SIXTEEN - "A CONSPIRACY OF HOPE ON MERCY STREET" 1986-87	131
CHAPTER SEVENTEEN - "HUMAN RIGHTS IN THE SECRET WORLD" 1988-94	134
CHAPTER EIGHTEEN - "GROWING UP" 1998-2009	137
CHAPTER NINETEEN - "AN INFUSION OF NEW BLOOD" 2010-2012	144
CHAPTER TWENTY - "GETTING THINGS BACK TO FRONT" 2012-14	146

PART THREE: STEVE HACKETT

CHAPTER TWENTY-ONE - "THE ACOLYTE STEPS OUT OF THE SHADOW OF THE HIEROPHANT" 1978	151
CHAPTER TWENTY-TWO - "GREETING THE SPECTRAL MORNING" 1979	153
CHAPTER TWENTY-THREE - "WELCOMING THE DEFECTOR" 1980	157
CHAPTER TWENTY-FOUR - "TAKING THE CURE" 1981	159
CHAPTER TWENTY-FIVE - "HIGHLY STRUNG" 1982-83	162
CHAPTER TWENTY-SIX - "YOU CAN'T BEAT A PAIR OF NYLONS" 1983	164
CHAPTER TWENTY-SEVEN - "TUNING THE GTR" 1986	167
CHAPTER TWENTY-EIGHT - "GAINING MOMENTUM" 1988-90	168
CHAPTER TWENTY-NINE - "TOUR NOIR" 1992-93	171
CHAPTER THIRTY - "NOT NECESSARILY ACOUSTIC" 1994-1998	174
CHAPTER THIRTY-ONE - "DARKTOWN RIOTS" 2000-2002	175
CHAPTER THIRTY-TWO - "WATCHING THE STORMS" 2003-2004	179
CHAPTER THIRTY-THREE - "ACOUSTIC METAMORPHOSES" 2005-2007	182
CHAPTER THIRTY-FOUR - "OUT OF THE TUNNEL'S MOUTH" 2009-2011	184
CHAPTER THIRTY-FIVE - "MAKING TRACKS AROUND THE WORLD" 2011-2012	189
CHAPTER THIRTY-SIX - "REVISITING OLD FRIENDS & SMOKING HOGWEED" 2013 -14	192

PART FOUR: PHIL COLLINS

CHAPTER THIRTY-SEVEN - "BRAND LOYALTY WITH BRAND X" 1976-79	199
CHAPTER THIRTY-EIGHT - "FOR PERVERTS ONLY" 1982-1983	201
CHAPTER THIRTY-NINE - "NO JACKET REQUIRED" 1985	203
CHAPTER FORTY - "A SERIOUS BUSINESS" 1990	205
CHAPTER FORTY-ONE - "BOTH SIDES AND FAR SIDES" 1994-1995	206
CHAPTER FORTY-TWO - "BUSKING WITH THE BIG BAND & SEEING THE LIGHT" 1996-1998	210
CHAPTER FORTY-THREE - "I WANT TO TESTIFY" 1998-2002	212
CHAPTER FORTY-FOUR - "FAREWELL, ADIEU, AUF WIEDERSEHEN" 2004 - 2010	214

PART FIVE: MIKE RUTHERFORD

CHAPTER FORTY-FIVE - "THE MIRACLE TOUR" 1986	217
CHAPTER FORTY-SIX - "A CALL T0 ARMS" 1989	220
CHAPTER FORTY-SEVEN - "HITS ON A BEACH OF GOLD" 1995-1996	223
CHAPTER FORTY-EIGHT - "TRAVELLING ON THE M6" 1999	225
CHAPTER FORTY-NINE - "GETTING REWIRED" 2004	227
CHAPTER FIFTY - "HITTING THE ROAD" 2010-13	228
CHAPTER FIFTY-ONE - "REVISITING THE LIVING YEARS" 25th ANNIVERSARY TOUR 2014	233

PART SIX: RAY WILSON

CHAPTER FIFTY-TWO - "NOT NECESSARILY ACOUSTIC" 1999 -2003	235
CHAPTER FIFTY-THREE - "VISITING THE WORLD OF GENESIS" 2003 - 2006	237
CHAPTER FIFTY-FOUR - "STILTSKIN AND OTHER STORIES" 2006 - 2013	239

PART SEVEN: AFTERGLOW

CHAPTER FIFTY-FIVE - WHAT THEY SAID...	247
ACKNOWLEDGEMENTS	254
ABOUT THE AUTHOR	254

INTRODUCTION

I am sure that I was not the only one taken by surprise by the announcement on 6 November 2006 that Genesis, the band which had effectively split up after the end of the *Calling all Stations* tour in May 1998, were reuniting with former frontman Phil Collins, for, as he put it: "A selection of shows" in Europe and the USA in the summer and autumn of 2007. The news was surprising and exciting for all of us who had carried a torch for some form of reunion by the band since '98. The resulting shows were an encapsulation of everything that fans of the band had loved about them: drama, lyricism; a stage show that defied description and above all: a self-effacing sense of humour.

The band's live story had not ceased with the departure of former frontman and self-confessed hogweed abuser Peter Gabriel, despite what certain elements of the fan base have maintained ever since! When Phil Collins decided to take the risk and "wiggle his bum" as the singer, the band achieved what many had thought impossible. They returned with a massively successful album, a fresh and invigorated sound, which flew in the face of the new wave discord that was currently the vogue here in the UK. They managed to increase their fan base into the bargain and sell-out arenas and theatres both here and overseas – no cancellations owing to poor ticket sales here, guys!

The departure of Peter Gabriel and the arrival of Phil Collins is effectively where my story with Genesis begins. The first albums I ever heard by the band were *Selling England By the Pound* and *A Trick of the Tail* both on the same magical evening at a friend's house in the summer of 1976. The rest of my story has been revealed through the pages of *The Waiting Room (TWR)*. However, the band's live story during those years since 1976 has not been told in detail, which is really the purpose of this project. Both Paul Russell and Yashima Tsukamoto's books have given fans an excellent grounding in the minutiae of live recordings by the band up to and including the *Calling all Stations* tour of 1998.

As if that wasn't enough, the band's story has expanded to encapsulate the burgeoning and incredibly successful solo careers of several of the incumbents and the story of their live performances is also told here in detail for the first time. If your favourite show isn't included within these pages then I hope you will forgive me. With so many performances to choose from I had by necessity to be somewhat selective – a "selection of shows" indeed! And, if recent reports are to be believed, perhaps we night yet still have more gigs for an update to this volume! Anyway, I hope you enjoy this excuse for me to wander down Memory Lane before old age sets in!

Alan Hewitt, Liverpool, 2014.

"The Pros and Cons of Collecting"
Your author plays Devil's Advocate
on the subject of live recordings...

This subject is one that raises almost as many hackles as some religious disputes. Indeed, to many fans, bootlegs are a religion of their very own.

My own first encounter with bootlegs and the shady world they inhabited, occurred on an MGP coach (dear old MGP, remember them?), making its way home to England from a Genesis concert in Germany back in September 1982, and yes, that concert *is* featured in this book before you ask, dear reader! I still vividly remember a member of our coach party approaching the driver and thrusting the treasured C120 cassette into his hands with the injunction, "play this!" And so barely half an hour after the gig I had attended had finished, there I was listening to a recording that was barely audible over the chatter on board the coach. I was determined to find out more about these mysterious objects and if possible start to acquire these gems for myself and, more importantly, try to find out if recordings of any other gigs I had attended over the years were available. That, simply put, was my entire rationale for entering the fractious world of bootleg collecting. I still think that it is the main rationale for any fan doing likewise even to this day.

Bear in mind that back in 1982 fans did not have the luxury of the Internet. All communication was done via letters and telephone calls or word of mouth, so finding people prepared to indulge my new hobby was not all that easy. The Genesis fan base, however, seemed to be as indulgent of newbies then as it is nowadays and I was lucky to find a few fans who were prepared to get my own collection started.

Ah yes, I still remember those first parcels of cassette tapes delivered by a bemused postman. In fact the large number of brown paper packages that arrived at our house might have made him (a Genesis fan himself, by the way) suspect that I was either a terrorist or a pornographer on a truly massive scale. Neither of which was the case, I hasten to add, folks! Finally getting to hear such delights as 'From the Mouth of the Monster', 'Living Revelations', and 'Awed Man Out' for the first time was a thrill that hasn't dimmed with the passage of thirty years.

The difficulty then, as now, was to get a collection of material suitably varied as to be able to entice other collectors into parting with their salubrious goodies. Strangely enough, this did not prove to be as difficult a proposition as I had expected. Within a few months I had sturdy and growing collection, thanks to the help of a few dedicated but clearly insane fans, several of whom are still collecting today and whom I am proud to call friends of mine. I was blissfully unaware of the "darker" side to collecting, that is those obsessive fans who for reasons of their own opt to keep recordings "rare" or "hidden" and unavailable to the general collecting public. This was a side of collecting I only really became aware of once the Internet had taken off and thankfully, even then, the "sharers" outnumbered the "hoarders" and that is precisely the way it should be in my opinion!

The fascination of this subject is something that can only be confusing to someone from outside the collecting arena, and the only way I can really describe it, which might make sense to such an individual who might be reading this, is to refer to it as "Musical Archaeology". That analogy is not entirely without merit either. With a band that has as long a history as Genesis and its solo members, there is much that has not been properly documented, stored, or indeed lost. The band's own archive of recordings is as we have only recently begun to find out, sadly lacking in many areas, which is where the existence of bootlegs can plug the gaps. A case in point is the compilation by the band, which has yet to gain an official release, of all their session recordings for the BBC. A double CD was pressed up in very limited numbers at the time of the release of the band's second *Genesis Archive* boxed set and I was fortunate enough to receive one of these, which of course made for very exciting listening even if its contents do fall outside of the remit of this book.

What surprised me was the quality, or rather the lack of quality, of the final session on the discs, which sounded as if it had been recorded in a biscuit tin! Apparently the original master tape for this session could not be located at the time that this compilation was made, so an extremely low-fi bootleg version was substituted for the sake of completeness. Fortunately for all concerned, the original master of this session has since been located and is safe and sound in the BBC sound archive should the band ever decide to give these recordings an official release.

More recently still, the last of Steve Hackett's *Live Archive* series of albums featured his first acoustic tour, back in 1983. Surprisingly enough, this was sourced from an audience bootleg recording padded out to completion by the inclusion of tracks taken from a closed microphone soundboard recording of another gig. Without the existence of that audience recording, this album would never have seen the light of day and fans would have been deprived of another slice of Hackett history. From a personal viewpoint my own collection of recordings has proven to be a vital resource in the writing of the several books I have written on the band and solo members.

The lack of care with which parts of the band's heritage has been treated was also brought forcibly home to me whilst I was working on the *Genesis Songbook* project back in 2000 and one small instance might suffice to illustrate the point. The production company were tasked with finding available footage of various songs, etc.., and contacted the TV companies not only here in the UK but throughout Europe and further afield. One of those companies had recorded a news feature about the band's gig at Roundhay Park back in 1987 and when I enquired as to the whereabouts of that footage I was informed that it had been wiped! Fortunately for me at least, I have a broadcast copy of that footage in my own collection. Even the extra unused interview footage, etc.. from the *Songbook* project itself has been wiped or scrapped since that project was completed – so I will never get to hear what I said about the *Abacab* album – criminal, really! Sadly, TV companies are only just waking up to the inherent value (commercial and historical) of their own archives, although in many cases it is too little too late.

That is the argument in favour of the humble bootleg. Of course, there are equally valid arguments against them. Many artists have no desire to air their "bad hair days" to the scrutiny of the public and Genesis in particular have been notorious for their quality control of releases. Many TV appearances are embarrassing in the extreme as anyone who has watched their various slots on the UK TV show *TISWAS* will testify. Of course the artist has the right not to have their mistakes aired in public and indeed, studio outtakes and demos are another fertile field for collectors. Much of that material would most likely only be of interest to extremely diehard fans anyway.

From a commercial standpoint, bootlegs take on an extremely different context. Record companies view them as a legitimate threat to their activities. The sale of bootlegs deprives both a record company and their artists of royalties; monies that could be invested in the record company's case into new and exciting artists and development. Or in the case of the artists themselves, new studio recording equipment, instruments, or a brand new sports car depending on where their interests lie.

Both record companies and artists make their living from the sale of albums/CDs, etc.., which is the commercial reality that eludes many fans. Genesis themselves have often been accused of being "commercial". Of course they were! Genesis began life as a songwriters' collective determined to sell their songs to others who would record them, and when that didn't happen decided to record and sell them themselves. Musicians make music as their way of putting bread and butter on the table, pure and simple, and the sale of recordings, etc., is how that is done. Anything that threatens that ability to make a living has been frowned upon and has been dealt with, with an increasingly heavy hand by record companies.

This has especially become the case ever since the advent of the Internet and the arrival of commercial concerns such as Napster, which have brought the whole issue into the light of day for all to see. Napster's downfall, however, was their failure to see that sharing files of commercially available music without paying either the record company or artists for the privilege would only bring down the wrath of the gods upon them, which in due course it did!

The Internet has been a positive godsend for collectors, especially for new fans with so many trading groups springing up than can easily be counted. The ethos behind most of them seems to be a simple one of getting previously unheard music out to fans free of charge, which in itself is not illegal (not in the UK, at least). The days of having crappy recordings in deceptively well packaged sleeves for which you were charged extortionate amounts of money are over. Witness the demise of such "companies" as Highland in Japan as proof of the power that these new trading groups have. This is much more effective than periodic raids by the likes of the BPI for instance, who should be focussing their attentions on the bootleggers of commercially available product, in my humble opinion.

The efforts that ordinary fans or groups of fans have expended on investing in the technology to not only clean up the sound of recordings but also package them in such a fashion that in many cases it is easy to mistake them for official product is breathtaking and in many cases puts the record companies to shame. Sad to say, not all fans are aware of the existence of such groups and are still ripped off by rogue traders on the likes of Ebay when they should be looking elsewhere.

The sad thing is that the record companies, and indeed bands/artists themselves, seem unlikely to relinquish their control of exactly the sort of material that the fans are interested in and which is the subject matter of this book. Great examples of where this kind of material has been made available include both Peter Gabriel and Steve Hackett's official live bootleg series of recordings and latterly Genesis' own series of recordings from the 2007 *Turn it on Again* tour, which go some way to proving that there is a marketplace for such product out there if they are prepared to indulge it. It would be even more remarkable if the two areas of this field could actually work together without the usual mistrust that is the norm at present. For example, where no archival recording exists in the band's own archive, the gap could be plugged by the use of the very resources that the fans have been carefully archiving for many years, and instead of seeing each other as a threat, actually work together to ensure that the band's remarkable legacy is preserved for future generations, as well as putting money back into the hands of both record company and artist into the bargain.

Maybe I am dreaming here but the potential that could be harnessed for the mutual benefit of all involved is huge. I for one am thankful for all of those musical "archaeologists" who have kept my own musical box so full of wonderful music over the years!

FOREWORD

Alan Hewitt has been a longstanding and loyal Genesis fan over the last thirty-plus years. The books he's produced so far have been informative and useful for Genesis fans everywhere. Even the band has found them interesting, listing all the shows we've played over our long career. It is no easy task and I congratulate him for his detailed endeavours. Thanks for all the hard work, Alan!

Phil Collins

FOREWORD

As Alan Hewitt hails from the first British home of real Rock & Roll, Liverpool, he's already qualified to extend his pen down along the M6 in the direction of us Southerners. Genesis is fortunate to have a persistent biographer who operates with a tenaciousness that rivals Darwin. Many interviews later his stealth approach has worked wonders. Good for him! His down to earth 'Fifty Sheds of Grey' style has caught many of us napping ... It's his ability to put his interviewee at ease that gets him called back for an encore. He is also a first-class 'archaeologist', often digging in unexplored cupboards and precarious attics whilst discovering forgotten Genesis gems.

Alan is foremost a great friend and a father confessor rather than interrogator. He'll usher you in gently but surprise you with his insights.

Steve Hackett

A Selection Of Shows: Genesis & Solo Live Guide 1976-2014

PART ONE: GENESIS

CHAPTER ONE
"DOES MY BUM LOOK BIG IN THIS?"
A TRICK OF THE TAIL TOUR 1976

By the time that Peter Gabriel's departure and the band's decision to continue as a recording/performing entity had become public knowledge in the summer of 1975, the band had already been ensconced in rehearsal rooms for several months. Steve Hackett had already taken advantage of the uncertainty about the future of the band to try his hand at recording a solo album and it was this recording – Voyage of the Acolyte – that was to prove that interest in the band was still high when, upon its release in the summer of 1975, it went silver. The band themselves had no problems with having sufficient material in their arsenal to record, and the resulting album, *A Trick of the Tail*, released on 13 February 1976, took everyone who had written the band off by surprise. Here was a band sounding fresh, invigorated, and above all, in the light of the new wave revolution sweeping the UK, melodic! The presence of Phil as singer no doubt prevented the backlash that might have greeted an outsider. After all, Phil was part of the "family" and he was accepted with minimal fuss.

The album became the band's biggest seller and demand was high for them to tour to promote it. One problem remained to be resolved, however. If Phil was to be singer, who was going to take his place as drummer? Only one name leaped to Phil's mind: his long-time hero and occasional sparring partner in Zox and the Radar Boys, Bill Bruford. Bruford's credentials in the world of Progressive rock and Jazz were impeccable. His time with King Crimson where effectively that band created the "Prog" genre and subsequent time with Yes lent him enough clout to silence any doubters out there.

With a stable and contented line up all that remained was to organise a tour and decide upon the material that was going to form the basis for the new live show. Whereas with the Lamb the band had been effectively tied to a stage production and set that revolved around the album and precious little else, with the new album there was no such problem and a set could accurately reflect more of a résumé of the band's career in total, although obviously with a healthy emphasis on the new material. The resulting shows were a revelation for everyone; fans, critics, and band members alike.

The tour opened on 25 March 1976 at the Civic Centre in London, Ontario in Canada to an audience that was expected to be merely a few hundred but was in fact over 2,000 strong – a great indicator that the band's popularity was certainly not on the wane. Sadly, this gig does not appear to have been documented by either a soundboard recording by the band or a bootleg from the audience, so the story of this tour begins with the next show on the tour...

THE AUDITORIUM, KITCHENER, ONTARIO, CANADA, 27 MARCH 1976

Set List: Dance on a Volcano/The Lamb Lies Down on Broadway/Fly on a Windshield/Carpet Crawlers/Cinema Show/Robbery, Assault & Battery/White Mountain/Firth of Fifth/Entangled/Squonk/I Know What I Like/Los Endos/It/Watcher of the Skies//
Source: Soundboard recording.

An essential recording, especially when you remember that the first gig that Phil performed as frontman is missing from the archives. This recording had been rumoured to exist for many years but was in the hands of a private collector who restricted its circulation. Sadly, this behaviour has meant that fans have been deprived of hearing so many wonderful recordings from the band. However, thanks to the activities of a dedicated group of fans, this situation has begun to change, and much previously unheard material is beginning to reach the wider fan base.

This recording is a fascinating listen. Phil's onstage patter sounds somewhat stilted but musically the band are right on the money here. Opening with their brand new signature tune, 'Dance on a Volcano', what is apparent from the very start is exactly how much Phil's delivery sounds like his predecessor's! The band, and particularly Phil, do sound somewhat nervous, and his between songs banter here is at times a little mannered almost as if he is still unsure about how the audience will react to him. Musically, however, there are no such problems. The 'Lamb Stew' section follows and it is delivered tasty and piping hot. Bill Bruford's licks are impeccable and drive the rest of the band along nicely whilst Phil delivers a wonderful vocal performance. 'Fly on a Windshield' really gives Steve a chance to shine as well. He takes it with both hands and blows everyone away.

'Cinema Show' tests the depping drummer's percussive skills and it has to be said he sounds a little out of his depth here. The rest of the band, however, execute a near flawless rendering of this classic with kudos to both Tony and Steve who obviously relish their individual moments.

'Robbery, Assault & Battery' follows and here we get to hear Phil's corny introduction for the first time and it is interesting to hear that not only did the music evolve as the tour progressed but so did Phil's stories! From the outset, it is obvious that Mr Bruford's percussive skills aren't necessarily on the same wavelength as the rest of the band and his playing sounds somewhat disjointed here as well, which is a pity because the rest of the band put in another excellent performance. Mike's introduction to 'White Mountain' appears to fall on deaf ears if the lack of audience response is anything to go by. The song itself is glorious, however, and it makes me wonder why this track was seldom (if ever) performed live during the Gabriel era. Anyway, it is here now and for once Bruford's percussion is tastefully understated and greatly augments the marvellous playing from everyone, especially Tony and Steve.

'Firth of Fifth' is always a delight to hear and here we have another opportunity to hear Phil put his own stamp on the track for the first time. Both Steve and Tony accompany him in fine style and Mike and Bill underpin the whole with an understated but tasteful rhythm section. The perils of a psychiatrist's couch are explored next in 'Entangled' and what a joy it is to hear this underrated classic. 'Squonk' proves that Genesis always knew how to rock with the best of 'em and tonight the performance threatens to tear the roof off the auditorium, with special kudos here to Bill and Mike whose rhythms drive the whole song along.

'I Know What I Like' takes us back a little bit with the entire band letting their hair down and having some fun on this one – I can even imagine Tony breaking into a smile during it before the show proper is ended by 'Los Endos', which certainly showcases the combined talents of Collins and Bruford, while the rest of the band rampage round them. The encore is a truncated version of 'It' coupled with an instrumental segue of 'Watcher of the Skies', which wraps things up rather nicely.

CENTURY THEATRE, BUFFALO, NEW YORK, USA, 28 MARCH 1976
Set List: Dance on a Volcano/The Lamb Lies Down on Broadway/Fly on a Windshield/Carpet Crawlers/Cinema Show/Robbery, Assault & Battery/White Mountain/Firth of Fifth/Entangled/Squonk/I Know What I Like/Los Endos//
Source: Soundboard recording.

The third gig into the tour and still the band are working things out. Once again, no 'Supper's Ready' but gone are the nerves so evident in the preceding night's recording. The opener, 'Dance on a Volcano', is unleashed upon an evidently enthusiastic crowd who lap it up. Phil's voice sounds full of confidence and excitement as he begins to get used to this lead singer lark. Tony and Steve do a fair imitation of molten lava, while Chester and Mike chug along as a rock solid rhythm section. Phil still sounds a little uncertain as he introduces the 'Lamb Stew' section of the show but there is no similar uncertainty from the band during the performance. 'The Lamb' itself is delivered piping hot to the exuberant crowd whilst 'Fly on a Windshield' and 'Carpet Crawlers' demonstrate why they are acknowledged as classics by fans. Steve has seldom sounded better than he does on the latter!

Why Phil decided to put on a cod Yorkshire accent whilst introducing the torrid antics of 'The Cinema Show' is beyond me but the audience don't seem to mind – they probably don't even recognise it! Musically, this is another assured performance with honours being shared equally between Steve and Tony. Phil's Music Hall influences are to the fore in the corny intro to 'Robbery, Assault & Battery', which once again is a fine ensemble performance in which Mr Bruford puts in some fine jazzy percussion.

'White Mountain' is another underrated gem and tonight everyone is on fine form and I have to wonder why this song wasn't performed much more often because it is superb! The echoey acoustics of the hall even add to the drama as it plays out on stage. Unfortunately there is a rather savage edit in the recording in my possession, which is quite disappointing. 'Firth of Fifth', surprisingly enough, sounds a little flat tonight but I think that might be the acoustics of the hall rather than anything wrong with the band's playing.

We get to hear Mr Hackett's dulcet tones as he introduces 'Entangled', another masterpiece from the band's current album. Mike, Steve, and Tony combine their respective instruments to make a truly glorious sound, while Phil's vocals sound suitably angelic and Bill's percussion is tasteful but never invasive. The band rock-out the end of this recording with sterling renditions of 'Squonk', 'I Know What I Like', and 'Los Endos'. Unfortunately, the encore of 'It'/'Watcher of the Skies' is missing, which is a shame, but nonetheless this is another excellent recording from the early part of the tour.

SYRIA MOSQUE, PITTSBURGH, PENNSYLVANIA, USA, 13 APRIL 1976

Set List: Dance on a Volcano/The Lamb Lies Down on Broadway/Fly on a Windshield/Carpet Crawlers/The Cinema Show/Robbery, Assault & Battery/White Mountain/Firth of Fifth/Entangled/Squonk/Supper's Ready/I Know What I Like/Los Endos/It/Watcher of the Skies//
Source: FM Radio Broadcast.

This is another justly famous bootleg. This one has been in circulation for a great many years under various titles, including *The Bubble Will Burst*. Taken from the FM radio broadcast of the show by a local radio station, this is an excellent rendering of the 1976 shows. By now the nerves that had been so plain during the first few shows have been replaced by a confidence that shines through in this gig.

Once again, the opening track, 'Dance on a Volcano', gives the lie to those who doubted that Phil could deliver the "epic" vocal. His performance here is faultless, no signs of the strain that would appear at later shows and on later tours. Tony's keyboard simmers and Steve's guitar sears the air whilst the percussion section of Rutherford and Bruford bubble away like lava – quite appropriate, really! "Good evening, Baltimore" heralds probably the only cock-up all night as Phil humorously sends himself up whilst introducing tonight's offering of 'Lamb Casserole'. Tony's arpeggio hovers over the auditorium whilst Mike and Steve battle away. to my ears, the only weak link here is Bruford, whose percussion sounds both tinny and disjointed. 'Fly on a Windshield' is much better, with Steve riffing away like a banshee and Mike's dirty bass threatening to tear the roof down. 'Carpet Crawlers' is already a bona fide classic and tonight we have a stunning performance. Phil's voice has seldom sounded better and he even manages to sound suspiciously like Mr G. at times. Tony and Steve augment his performance with some fine ensemble playing and Bill's percussion is tasteful and restrained.

The lurid tale of the happenings at 'The Cinema Show' hasn't got any better but the performance itself seems to get better with each and every show, tonight opening by some absolutely lovely playing from Tony and Steve, over which Phil lays down an incredible vocal performance. The real star tonight though is Steve. His playing is absolutely incredible and he dominates the proceedings throughout.

With the show now set as a standard one, and with 'Supper's Ready' now firmly ensconced as the centrepiece of the set, this recording has all of the usual highlights, although is always the case, some songs come across better on different nights and tonight 'White Mountain' certainly seems to tick all the right boxes both with the band and the audience. Steve and Mike manage to recreate the shimmering guitar intro that Mike and Steve's predecessor had made so famous. Tony, as usual, underpins everything with some impeccable chords and Phil's vocal contains just the right combination of angst and bathos – wonderful stuff!

The old favourites retain their special place, but tonight the crowning glories are the new material, 'Entangled', 'Squonk', and 'Los Endos' really bring home the goods. 'Squonk' threatens to bring the room down about our ears, while 'Entangled' is an almost balletic delight, in which Tony and Steve weave musical patterns around us whilst Phil sings like his life depended on it. All in all, an essential recording for any collector to have.

WILL ROGERS AUDITORIUM, FORT WORTH, TEXAS, USA, 7 MAY 1976

Set List: Dance on a Volcano/The Lamb Lies Down on Broadway/Fly on a Windshield/Broadway Melody of '74/Carpet Crawlers/The Cinema Show/Robbery, Assault & Battery/White Mountain/Firth of Fifth/Entangled/Squonk/Supper's Ready/I Know What I Like/Los Endos/It/Watcher of the Skies//
Source: Soundboard recording.

Despite being reported on in the music press, this festival never took place.
Even back in the seventies, the local council had too many issues concerning health and safety to grant a licence for the event to be staged.

This is another fine recording from the final show of the US tour. By the time this gig was performed the band had obviously honed their performance to a fine art and the end result is a polished show. Sound quality is at times a bit echoey, no doubt owing to the size of the auditorium. It is crystal clear throughout, however. Phil's earlier nerves are not at all in evidence here, and his between song banter is in fine form, especially his Vaudeville hawker introduction to the 'Lamb Stew' section of the gig.

Musically, the band are all in excellent form. Bruford batters seven shades out of his kit during several tracks and the rhythm section is always augmented by Mike's meaty and tasteful bass playing. In fact this show serves to emphasise again just how good a bass player Mike really is. Tony too is on good form; impeccable and at times understated. Steve too comes into his own on several tracks. His playing on 'Fly on a Windshield' is absolutely awesome. He lifts the track to ethereal heights and is obviously having a great time. Other musical highlights include another stunning performance by the entire band on 'White Mountain'. Tony and Steve share equal honours on yet another rousing version of 'Firth of Fifth'. 'Supper's Ready', though, remains the real jewel in the crown of these shows and by this, the final show, the band are truly at their peak with everyone playing their hearts out – a great ending to a fantastic tour and another excellent recording to boot!

HAMMERSMITH ODEON, LONDON, ENGLAND, 10 JUNE 1976

Set List: Dance on a Volcano/The Lamb Lies Down on Broadway/Fly on a Windshield/Carpet Crawlers/The Cinema Show/Robbery, Assault & Battery/White Mountain/Firth of Fifth/Entangled/Squonk/Supper's Ready/I Know What I Like/Los Endos/It/Watcher of the Skies//
Source: Soundboard recording.

For many years the only recording from the band's run of gigs at the Hammersmith Odeon was the hour-long British Biscuit radio broadcast. Excellent as that was, it was obviously missing many highlights from the show. Fortunately, a very recently unearthed soundboard recording finally gives us one of these shows in its glorious entirety.

This is without doubt one of the best, if not the best, recording I have ever heard from the band (any line up, any era) and what a truly wonderful celebration it is! From the opening salvo of 'Dance on a Volcano' it is obvious that we are listening to a band at the very peak of their powers. Phil's nerves, so evident on earlier recordings, are replaced here by the confident cheeky chappy we have come to know and he hams it up in fine style throughout the gig. 'The Lamb' selection is astonishing, simply astonishing. Phil's vocals are impeccable, while Steve and Tony in particular augment them with a whole gamut of effects. Messrs Bruford and Rutherford are the glue that holds everything together. Steve threatens to rip the roof off the Odeon with his riffs during 'Fly on a Windshield', restating his position as one of the most inventive guitarists in rock, while Mike certainly gives his all in the bass department.

Phil is in fine form with his Vaudevillian introduction to 'Cinema Show', which raises a laugh from the audience. Performance wise, this is another impeccable offering, with Steve and Mike opening the piece in glorious unison augmented by Tony before Phil joins in with an absolutely flawless vocal performance, which, I am sorry to say, absolutely wipes the floor with any Gabriel version I have heard. The only downside to this performance is Bruford's percussion, which sounds disjointed here. This is a recurring problem throughout the gig. Bill's Jazz sensibilities don't really fit within Genesis' more Progressive music. The same can be said of the drumming during 'Robbery, Assault & Battery', which follows and is far too rigid for an otherwise fluid performance by the rest of the band. Tony in particular lays down one of the finest solos I have ever heard him play, which redeems things somewhat.

The performance of 'White Mountain' was always the surprise of this tour, and here it is in truly wonderful fashion, although I do miss Mike's story about "One Eye". This has always been my favourite track from the Trespass album and to have it here in such quality is fantastic. Phil's vocals here are magnificent whilst both Steve and Mike are obviously revelling in the opportunity to "go acoustic" for a while. Tony's performance here is impeccably understated and even Bruford's percussion lends a certain majesty to the proceedings. This really is a show of highlights and every track in the set is a classic and this is an essential addition to any collection of recordings by the band. My only question is why on earth wasn't it released officially?!

CHAPTER TWO
"WHERE'S HEATHCLIFF?"
WIND & WUTHERING TOUR 1977

By the summer of 1976 Genesis had done what twelve months before would have seemed impossible. They had survived the departure of Peter Gabriel, produced an album that cemented and increased their popularity, and toured extensively both at home and abroad to rapturous receptions. Now came the difficult bit: following up on that success. All was not rosy within the Genesis camp, however, although outward appearances were deceptive. Steve Hackett was becoming increasingly disillusioned with things within the band and eventually decided to check out at the end of the massive tour which the band undertook in support of their new album, *Wind & Wuthering*, which was released on 23 December 1976. An altogether more dramatic affair than its predecessor, *Wind & Wuthering* harked back more to the days of Foxtrot in terms of the content.

With the music world setting its face firmly against music such as what Genesis were creating, the band were on the receiving end of some harsh criticism for their new work, even from long-time supporters like Chris Welch. That did not prevent the subsequent tour being a huge success both at home and abroad. In fact, such was the demand to see the band that they returned to the UK in late June to perform three sold-out nights at the 19,000-seater Earls Court Arena in London after having toured the UK at the start of the year, including prestigious shows at the Rainbow Theatre in London, which until the advent of Wembley Arena and Earls Court, had been the biggest venue that a band could play in the capital, and one that Genesis had graced on several previous outings. As if that was not enough, Genesis also performed a string of sold-out shows at the massive stadia in several cities in Brazil – a first for the band and indeed one of the first visits by a Western artist to South America.

As always with Genesis, the emphasis was on presenting the music in the best possible light and no expense was spared in bringing the latest technology including lasers and a multitude of lights to bear on a show that musically was crammed full of highlights, including several tracks that had not been played before, including the unheard of step of promoting a track from the band's current EP (Inside & Out), as well as a visit back to *Trespass* days with a truncated version of 'The Knife' rounding off later shows on the tour. Interestingly enough, for each territory a slightly different set list was performed, making this tour a particular favourite with collectors. Fortunately, this tour is also probably the best documented by FM Radio and soundboard recordings out of any tour by the band until the most recent tour last year.

RAINBOW THEATRE, LONDON, ENGLAND, 3 JANUARY 1977
Set List: Eleventh Earl of Mar/The Carpet Crawlers/Robbery, Assault & Battery/Your Own Special Way/Squonk/One for the Vine/Firth of Fifth/All in a Mouse's Night/Supper's Ready/I Know What I Like/Dance on a Volcano/Los Endos/The Lamb Lies Down on Broadway/Musical Box (Closing Section)//
Source: Soundboard recording.

This is one of the best soundboard recordings to have emerged from this or any other tour by the band to date. This was only the band's third gig of the tour and consequently things are still a little haywire at times and nerves are still showing. It is interesting to hear that the experimental inclusion of 'Lilywhite Lilith' on the opening night has been dropped and the set has yet to become firm. 'All in a Mouse's Night', for instance, has yet to meet its demise and appears here in all its glory for the first (or third) time.

Opening with the truly glorious and majestic 'Eleventh Earl of Mar', the band are certainly intent on not taking any prisoners. Phil is in fine form and the interplay between Steve and Tony is a joy to listen to. Mike and Chester give sterling service in the rhythm department too, giving a keen edge to this dramatic opener. The pace changes next with a superb performance of 'Carpet Crawlers', in which Tony and Phil really shine, while Chester's understated percussion drives the whole song on.

The story of Harry is next, giving Phil a chance to mug up to the audience with his tale of crime and injustice. A Victorian "Penny Dreadful" for the ears this one, a delightfully tongue-in-cheek romp that everyone seems to be enjoying immensely – especially Steve, whose jaunty guitar playing creates the image of Harry confidently striding towards his goal – or should that be gaol? A simple love song at a Genesis gig? Oh, the horror of it! Nah, 'Your Own Special Way' remains one of the underrated gems from this period of the band's story and tonight's performance is pristine and delicate, like the jewel it is.

Back to the Rock 'n' Roll à la Genesis with 'Squonk' and a damn fine version too. Mike's bass threatens to raise the roof whilst Steve and Tony's intricate and delicate playing gilds a truly beautiful performance topped off by a meaty vocal from Phil. Epic storytelling has always been a Genesis trademark, and nowhere is it more dramatically demonstrated than in Tony's glorious tale of the leadership principle gone wrong; 'One for the Vine', which is given a truly remarkable performance tonight. Phil's anguished vocal is accompanied by a barrage of instrumental accompaniment from the rest of the band turning a rock song into an overture – stunning!

Really, this show, and indeed this tour, firmly drew a line under the Gabriel-era and, with the show becoming effectively a résumé of the band's finest moments up to this point, you are spoiled for choice here, and this show is another essential for collectors.

WINTERLAND BALLROOM, SAN FRANCISCO, CALIFORNIA, USA, 25 FEBRUARY 1977

Set List: Squonk/One for the Vine/Robbery, Assault & Battery/Your Own Special Way/Firth of Fifth/Carpet Crawlers/In That Quiet Earth/Afterglow/I Know What I Like/Eleventh Earl of Mar/Supper's Ready/Dance on a Volcano/Drum Duet/Los Endos/The Lamb Lies Down on Broadway/Musical Box (Closing Section)//
Source: Soundboard recording.

This one is another relatively recent find and another excellent soundboard recording. Having completed an extremely successful UK tour, the band were at the top of their game as they set off to continue their conquest of the USA, which they had begun in earnest the previous year.

Beginning what became a tradition of opening the show with a track from the preceding album, the band unleashed the raw power of 'Squonk' to open the show – definitely announcing that they meant business. Phil's vocals are crystal clear, while new boy Chester Thompson rattles the traps in fine style, belying Chris Welch's damning comments in the UK Press. Then on to the new album, and the epic that is 'One for the Vine', in which Steve and Tony really demonstrate why they made such a marvellous partnership. Steve underpins Tony's classical chords throughout whilst Mike and Chester make an impeccable rhythm section. The dramatic middle section has seldom if ever sounded better. Steve's guitar wails like a soul in torment against Phil's equally impassioned vocals – stirring stuff indeed!

'Robbery, Assault & Battery' is approaching the end of its live shelf life here. Phil's introductory story, complete with local references hasn't got any better, but the song itself is delivered in suitably tongue-in-cheek fashion, with Tony's jaunty keyboards setting the tone for this mini mock-operetta, joined in equally humorous fashion by Steve, whose guitar adds a slightly more earthy quality to the proceedings. Phil sounds perfectly at home in this setting, bringing his "Artful Dodger" style vocals to bear throughout. Mike's tale of 'Myrtle the Mermaid' heralds 'Your Own Special Way', preceded by yet another example of Mr Collins' finest percussive gyrations. Without doubt, this is one of the most underrated songs in the Genesis catalogue and on this recording it is truly delightful. Once again, Steve and Tony perform a stately dance over which Phil delivers a charming vocal tinged with just the right amount of bathos.

Steve delivers his intro to 'Firth of Fifth' in suitably tongue-in-cheek fashion: "A short one for us, about seven minutes …" There's nothing tongue-in-cheek about the performance though. This classic is given the full treatment tonight. Once again, Tony and Steve share the honours with two of their finest moments. Mike too augments the ensemble with some extremely tasteful playing. Phil's vocal has seldom if ever sounded better – he really shines here but the real star is Steve whose solo simply steals the show! A trio of classics, old and new, round off the first half of this recording. 'Carpet Crawlers' is sedate and serene, while 'In That Quiet Earth' and 'Afterglow' simply beggar belief – the band at their creative apogee and the ensemble playing on this recording simply knocks the recordings used for the subsequent Seconds Out live album into a cocked hat – nuff said!

Some light relief next, opening with Phil's now famous tarantella and the whirr of Tony's keyboards, with Steve's guitar announcing the arrival of the "Cosmic Lawnmower" in the shape of 'I Know What I Like'. Once again, the entire band seem to be having an absolute ball here. I can even imagine Tony cracking a rare smile. Even the sing-along chorus incorporating Mike (and Tony?) can be heard here. 'Eleventh Earl of Mar', complete with brief intro by Mike, is next. Once again, it is Steve and Tony who vie for the honours, both evoking the windswept Scottish highlands through their respective instruments. Mike soon joins the fray with some combative bass lines and we're off for another classic slice of Genesis story telling with Phil as a suitably impressive narrator. 'Supper's Ready', by now firmly ensconced as the centrepiece of the set, brings the show to a suitably dramatic climax.

IBIRAPUERA STADIUM, SAO PAOLO, BRAZIL, 21 MAY 1977

Set List: Squonk/One for the Vine/Robbery, Assault & Battery/Inside & Out/Firth of Fifth/The Carpet Crawlers/In That Quiet Earth/ Afterglow/I Know What I Like/Eleventh Earl of Mar/Supper's Ready/Dance on a Volcano/Drum Duet/Los Endos/The Lamb Lies Down on Broadway/Musical Box (Closing Section)//
Source: Soundboard recording.

For years the existence of soundboard or soundboard recordings from this tour were known about by only a handful of fans lucky enough to have access to them. Thankfully, the advent of the Internet has broadened not only that access but the sheer number of such recordings now available to the general fan base. Here is a case in point, another soundboard recording that catalogues one of the band's shows from their inaugural (and so far only) tour of South America.

Opening as usual with 'Squonk' we have a workmanlike performance here. Phil sounds in good form though and it is nice to hear Steve's ethereal chords battling away with Mr Banks' symphonic keyboards. 'One for the Vine' and 'Robbery, Assault & Battery' are given similar workouts and it is amusing to hear Phil's cod Portuguese introduction to the latter. Musically the band are tight and seem to be having a good time. Mike and Steve in particular are evidently having a ball trading some fearsome licks throughout both songs. 'Your Own Special Way' has been replaced by 'Inside & Out', another underrated classic from the band's catalogue. The band put in a great performance on this tale of injustice with Steve and Mike accompanying Tony with some delightful acoustic playing over which Phil puts in an impressive vocal. The instrumental end section roars off like a jet plane with Tony and Steve leading the chase in a fantastic performance. Steve then introduces 'Firth of Fifth' in word-perfect Portuguese, not surprising with him having a Brazilian girlfriend at the time! No need for translation as far as the music is concerned, and once again, Tony and Steve are the heart of the song. Take advantage of hearing Steve's wonderful playing with the band for one of the last times and here he really takes the song to new heights.

'Carpet Crawlers' introduced as a "samba" by Phil. Well, I'm not sure if that appellation is accurate or not, but what isn't in doubt is the sheer majesty of this song. Tony conjures almost

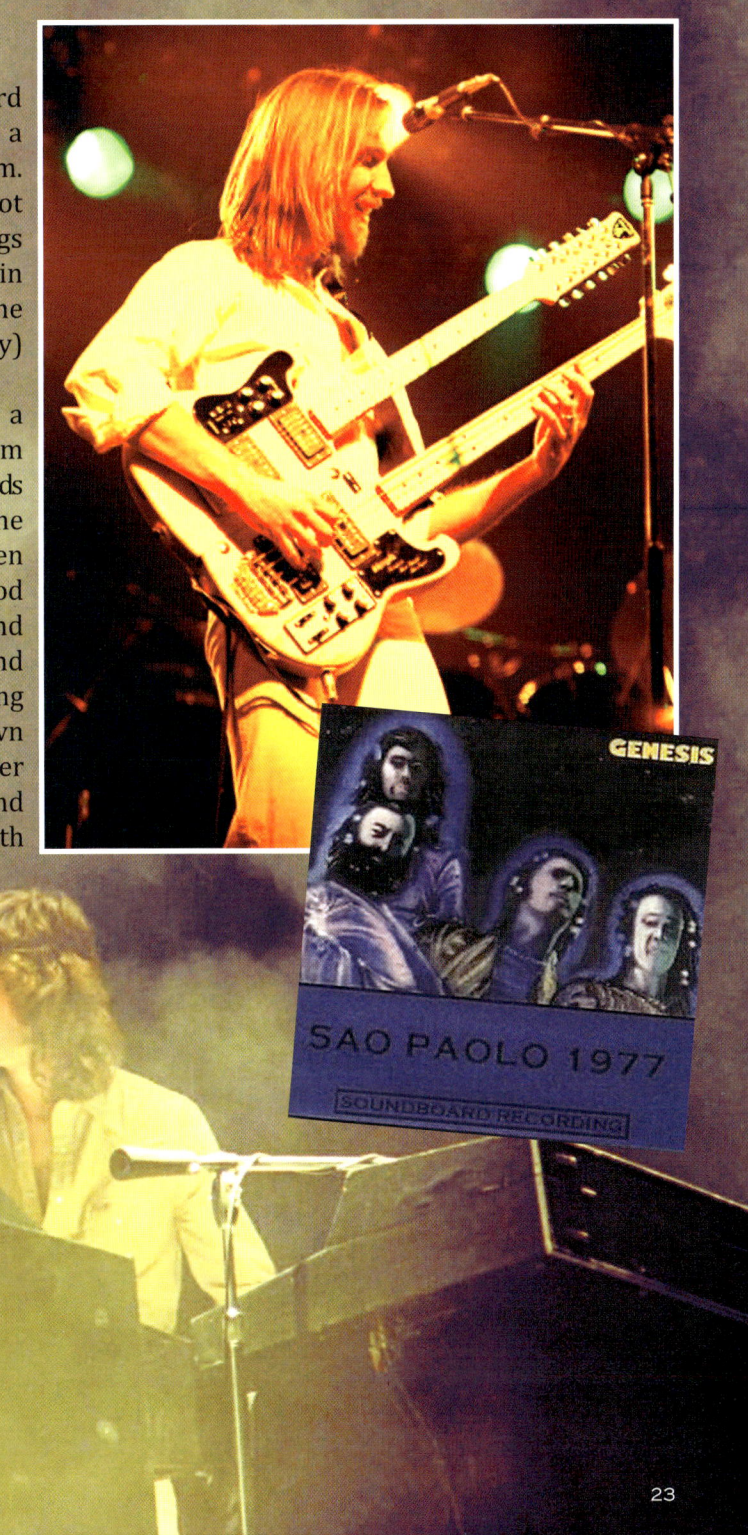

A Selection Of Shows: Genesis & Solo Live Guide 1976-2014

harpsichord-like sounds from his keyboard, while Steve indulges in another of his ethereal flights of fancy. Phil's voice is suitably angelic throughout and he certainly outdoes Peter in his performance of this song. New boy Chester is introduced to the appreciative crowd by Phil before 'In That Quiet Earth', which gives everyone a chance to stretch their musical legs and everyone obviously relishes the opportunity to do just that. Once again, Steve and Tony battle away with each other, but Chester gives them a run for their money with some ferocious drumming and Phil puts in yet another sterling performance as they reach the climactic 'Afterglow'.

Firecrackers are in evidence as the band rev up the Cosmic Lawnmower to introduce 'I Know What I Like'. Phil leads the band through this one and you can hear Mike and Tony helping out on the choruses. Steve and Mike lay down some solid riffs and Chester proves his worth with a tasty percussive backing. From the vaguely ridiculous, to the sublime as 'Eleventh Earl of Mar' and its tale of a failed Scottish uprising takes the stage. Always one of Genesis' best "pictorial" songs and here tonight you can almost hear the skirl of the bagpipes and the smell of the heather thanks to Tony and Steve's imaginative playing. Rhythmically, Mike and Chester fire off some cannonades between them and Phil puts in a typically dramatic vocal performance.

From a new classic-in-the-making to an established one, as the epic 'Supper's Ready' blows all before it. Even on this recording with an audience way down in the mix, you can just about hear the crowd going nuts (pun intended) as the band commence their extended epic of the struggle of good over evil. Words

Brazil goes nuts for Genesis
(Groan. — Ed.)

GENESIS are literally causing riots on their current South American tour. They report RIOTS in Puerto Allegro, where the band played two shows for a 50,000 audience. The band then proceeded to play six shows in Rio de Janeiro to 100,000 people. Brazilian fervour was so — uhh, *fervent* — that in Sao Paulo they cancelled a proposed 100,000-seater stadium gig for fear of further rioting in the streets. Instead the band played additional shows at a small venue Over-exuberant fans have driven Gensis to move hotels repeatedly; each band member is accompanied by an *armed bodyguard* each time they venture out of the hotel. Fans travelled from Bolivia, Paraguay, Uruguay and Argentina in bus-loads to attend the Porto Allegro gig — Genesis' lasers, light and sound equipment had to be flown in by a specially chartered Boeing 707. After the last Sao Paulo date all the band except Mike Rutherford flew back to the comparative calm of England. Rutherford decided to cool out in the sanctuary of Africa.

really cannot describe the impact that this song has in the live context – infinitely superior to the recorded version and growing in stature. Phil does not have the sense of the obscure that imbued Peter's version, but he makes up for that with fire and passion throughout. The rest of the band also deliver in spades, and it is on recordings such as this and the other soundboards available from this tour, that you get the sense of the sheer scale of the performance, which was lacking from Seconds Out until the 5.1 remastered version redressed the balance.

'Dance on a Volcano' and the drum duet leading into 'Los Endo' close the show proper as usual. Again, Tony's keyboards chime away like an alarm and Steve's guitar, augmented by the fearsome percussion of Mike and Chester are suitably explosive too. Phil is evidently in character and his vocal packs an awesome punch. 'The Lamb Lies Down on Broadway' heralds the band's return to the stage for the encores and once again you can just about hear the crowd in the distance. This and an impressive closing section from 'Musical Box' bring this fine recording to a suitably emphatic close. It is only a pity that the TV footage that was filmed at some of these gigs has yet to be rediscovered but in the meantime here is another fine representative of the band at what many fans consider to be their peak.

EARLS COURT ARENA, LONDON, ENGLAND, 24 JUNE 1977

Set List: Squonk/One for the Vine/Robbery, Assault & Battery/Inside & Out/Firth of Firth/The Carpet Crawlers/In That Quiet Earth/Afterglow/I Know What I Like/Eleventh Earl of Mar/Supper's Ready/Dance on a Volcano/Drum Duet/Los Endos/The Lamb Lies Down on Broadway/Musical Box (Closing Section)/The Knife//
Source: FM Radio broadcast.

Unusually for a band of Genesis' stature at this time, this recording is one of only a handful of available radio broadcasts from the *Wind & Wuthering* tour. Broadcast initially by Capitol Radio in London and subsequently bootlegged in various forms, this has become one of the most commonly available recordings from the period.

Coming almost at the end of a six month tour that had literally taken the band around the world, what you have here is a band at the peak of match fitness, opening as usual with 'Squonk', which is delivered in typically feisty form. Phil's voice still has the power to satisfy and none of the problems that were to dog him on subsequent outings. Steve Hackett also sounds sublime, delivering ethereal chords to rival Tony's orchestral keyboards, while once again Mike and Chester provide a meaty rhythm backing. Unlike many radio broadcasts, though, the audience are fully in evidence and sound as if they are relishing the performance.

Another latter-day classic next – 'One for the Vine' – one of the band's finest mini epics and one that is performed flawlessly here. Tony has seldom sounded better, leading the band from behind his keyboards. Steve also delivers the goods with some magnificent rock riffs that threaten to tear the roof down – if that doesn't then the awesome percussion of Chester might just do it instead. If anyone ever thought that Genesis did not have a sense of humour, then 'Robbery, Assault & Battery', the tale of a bungled burglary, should set them straight (pardon the pun). Phil is obviously in his element here acting out the sordid character of Harry. Tony's jaunty intro sets the tone for a tongue-in-cheek romp that owes as much to Benny Hill as it does to Prog Rock!

Sadly, the next number was destined not to outlast the tour. 'Inside & Out' has to be one of the most underrated songs in the Genesis catalogue – a tale of a miscarriage of justice; an unusual topic for Genesis but told in typical fashion. Tony, Steve, and Mike interweave their playing into a marvellous ensemble, lush and deceptively calm as the story unfolds. Phil's voice is simply angelic here and this is one of his best performances. The storm breaks though as the band drag us from our reveries with a rampaging instrumental climax, which gives us one of our last chances to hear Steve's playing at his very best with the band – brilliant stuff! 'Firth of Fifth', too, is greeted like an old friend by the crowd. The combination of Steve and Tony's playing still astonishes me every time I listen to this recording.

A Jim Reeves epic next (well according to Phil, anyway). 'Carpet Crawlers' simply gets better with age. This performance is simply wonderful. The combination of Tony's keyboards and a pure vocal delivery from Phil, augmented by some soaring guitar work from Steve, takes this one to new heights. Speaking of soaring, Steve and Tony do it again as they rampage through a stunning 'In That Quiet Earth', with Mike, Chester, and Phil all battling along as well. Phil doesn't even seem to have broken sweat, though as the piece climaxes with 'Afterglow', which ... well if you've ever heard it live, need I say any more?

A rather savage edit leads us further westward as the 'Cosmic Lawnmower' rattles along once more, heralding 'I Know What I Like'. Once again, it is Steve and Tony that really take the honours here. Their combination of sounds is unique in rock and will never be bettered and here you have them both at their best. Mike and Chester also deliver the goods with some impeccable rhythm playing, and Phil sounds as if he is having a blast, hamming it up for the audience.

'Eleventh Earl of Mar' is another one of those underrated Genesis tracks, replete with fantastic instrumental passages and some wonderful lyrics. Tonight, introduced by Mr Rutherford, it is given a sterling performance. Steve rampages his way throughout the song in fierce hand-to-hand combat with an equally feisty Tony Banks. Mike and Chester augment the performance with some explosive percussion although Phil sometimes struggles to reach the notes, which in itself adds enormously to the atmosphere and passion of the performance.

'Supper's Ready' has had enough superlatives thrown at it over the years. I doubt if I can add any more to the list but it has to be said that the decision to reinstate this epic to the live set was an inspired one. Gigantic, thrilling, and at times apocalyptic, tonight's performance has to rate as one of the best. Maybe it is the sense of occasion, the final UK shows of the year, or perhaps simply the sheer scale of the track itself. Either way, the band deliver a reverential performance here, which is lapped up by the crowd.

In the old days 'Supper's Ready' would have closed the show. How can you follow something as magnificent as that? Well, with something equally as magnificent of course. 'Dance on a Volcano', coupled with 'Los Endos' proves that 'Supper's Ready' was no fluke. Explosive percussion from Chester and some equally fiery guitar playing from Steve sets the tone and Tony quickly joins in the fray. Phil's anguished vocal captures the spirit of the song whilst Mike underpins everything with some fine bass playing.

Leaving themselves and their audience breathless, I certainly don't know where the band got their energy from but they aren't long in returning for a string of encores, beginning with the timeless 'Lamb Lies Down on Broadway', and Tony's introduction still sends shivers down the spine. Phil is joined on the refrain by Mike and Tony whilst Steve's guitar sounds like an angry wasp. This segues nicely into the closing section of 'Musical Box', where once again Steve and Tony conjure up the sound of the subject of the song. The calm is soon shattered as Phil's voice implores the audience to "touch me" whilst the rest of the band expand the musical angst of the song. Surely that would be enough for anyone? Well, not tonight, as the band return (badly edited on this recording though) for a storming rendition of 'The Knife', which gives the Punks a run for their money in terms of thrash music, bringing this superb concert to a suitably dramatic if not say downright exhausting end.

HALLENSTADION, ZURICH, SWITZERLAND, 2 JULY 1977

Set List: Squonk/One for the Vine/Robbery, Assault & Battery/Inside & Out/Firth of Fifth/The Carpet Crawlers/In That Quiet Earth/Afterglow/I Know What I Like/Eleventh Earl of Mar/Supper's Ready/Dance on a Volcano/Drum Duet/Los Endos/The Lamb Lies Down on Broadway/Musical Box (Closing Section)//
Source: Soundboard recording.

Without doubt, this is one of the best recordings of the band from this or any other tour. Taken from the penultimate gig of a massive tour, here we have Genesis at their peak. Opening with 'Squonk' as usual, here we have a great example of Mike's bass playing, he fills the track with some incredibly thunderous playing, over which Steve and Tony float in fine style. Phil hams it up again with his introductions and for once, the audience are clearly audible in the mix. 'One for the Vine' follows and it is here that Steve really shines. His playing throughout is impeccable. Phil's vocals are clear and almost angelic. Chester underpins the whole with some delightful percussion and once again Mike's bass thunders along at a ferocious pace.

Another comic operetta follows with the tale of 'Harry' and 'Robbery, Assault & Battery'. Phil's introductions in a mixture of French and German are absolutely hilarious but the crowd seem to appreciate them.

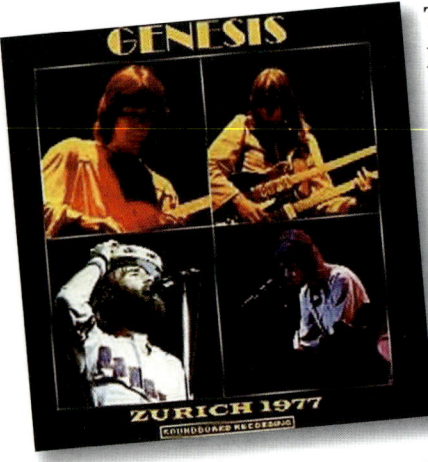

Tony leads the pack here with a jaunty keyboard arpeggio over which Steve plays some handy riffs. Phil's delivery is suitably corny, while Mike and Chester bring some beef to the proceedings with an impressive rhythm section. The tale of injustice that is 'Inside & Out' is next, a firm favourite of mine and a marvellous performance here. Mike, Steve, and Tony give the song a deceptively simple beginning with Phil's almost choral vocal belying the anguish and anger to come later. By the middle of the song, however, you can clearly hear that Phil is struggling to reach the high notes. Then the entire band take the final part of the song off at a searing pace with everyone clearly enjoying the chance to stretch their musical legs.

Then the band takes a couple of trips back in time, beginning with a Hackett-introduced 'Firth of Fifth', which simply gets better with age. Steve and Tony battle away magnificently whilst Mike and Chester deliver the goods once again with some impeccable playing. Even Phil's tambourine can be clearly heard in what is an incredibly clear mix – if this is what it sounded like onstage then the audience must have had a real treat at this gig! 'Carpet Crawlers' quietens things down a bit, although sadly the tape op obviously forgot to turn the tape over because this is a truncated version, which is a shame really because what we have of it sounds magnificent.

'Eleventh Earl of Mar' sounds superb. Tony's ethereal keyboards are mimicked by some fine playing from Steve, while Chester gives the lie to Chris Welch's comments about his percussive skills with a marvellous performance, which, alongside Mike's tasty bass playing, underpins the whole song. Phil then tries out his best French to deliver the story of "two virgins", which leads us into... 'Supper's Ready', of course! And what a wonderful version it is, too. Crystal clear and full of surprises, this remains the jewel in the crown of Genesis live performances.

CHAPTER THREE
"FOLLOW YOU FOLLOW ME"
AND THEN THERE WERE THREE TOUR 1978

The band wasted little time in reconvening in the aftermath of Steve Hackett's departure in the autumn of 1977. Working again at Relight Studios in Holland, the now three-piece-band were faced with the same dilemma that many of their contemporaries were facing. The music scene in the UK had changed forever in the preceding two years. The New Wave/Punk revolution had created many casualties and bands that were the darlings of public and critics alike back in 1976 were cast aside in favour of the new flavour of the month.

Several bands, however, managed to ride out the new wave tidal wave. Pink Floyd and Yes, for example, carried on seemingly regardless for the trends that were surrounding them. Genesis, however, were very much a horse of a different colour. They had been imbued with a new sense of realism and the albums which had followed Peter Gabriel's departure had one thing in common: they were *accessible*. Gone was the deliberate obscurantism of the past in favour of an altogether more direct and forthright approach. One thing remained from the old regime, however: the band's penchant for storytelling. True, the need for extended metaphors on Greek Mythology had gone and quite rightly so. After all, that was a field that Genesis had ploughed assiduously during their formative period.

The new-look Genesis took a head-on approach to their song writing, admitting that they needed to learn the art of self-editing. This they achieved remarkably well on their first post-Hackett album, 1978's ironically titled, *And Then There Were Three*. An unheard of eleven songs were to appear on that album along with numerous single B-sides. The album also gave them a – shock horror – *hit* single in the shape of 'Follow You Follow Me'; an infectious three-minute number that gained the band their first actual appearance on BBC's prestigious *Top of the Pops* show! However, look beyond the apparent simplicity of some of the songs and there was a depth to many that was inspiring. Say 'It's Alright, Joe', for instance. A wonderful observation of the life of one of life's casualties. Joe lives his life through the bottom of a whiskey glass and the portrayal gave Phil a genuine chance to "act" during the subsequent tour where he adapted Joe's persona to perfection. Then there is 'Down And Out', a song rarely performed in concert but a brilliantly evocative look at the situation the band found themselves in with regard to how they were viewed both by the critics and the fans alike …

"There's people out there who can take your place/A more commercial view, a fresher face!"

All of which was indeed true! Genesis were no longer the critics' darlings and they had realised that to retain and expand their audience they were going to offer them something fresher and different. This they did on *And Then There Were Three* without sacrificing that innate sense of "quality" that marks Genesis' music out from so many other bands.

For the tour (or should that be tours?) that followed in the wake of the album's release, Genesis went to town in terms of the kind of show they were to present. Visually, every available piece of technological kit was used: lasers, jumbo landing lights, and other lighting galore accompanied by six computerised revolving mirrors and lasers. The result was quite spectacular. Musically too, the band gave the fans a show built on the solid foundations of their heritage. True, many of the epics such as 'Supper's Ready' had been laid to rest but in the surprising inclusion of 'In the Cage', the band had found another suitable peg on which to hang the epic and dramatic elements of their show. The tour began in April in the USA, which was to see no less than three separate tours during the course of the year in a final attempt to break the band over there. Europe too was visited on two separate occasions and even Japan finally got a taste of the Genesis magic. The poor old UK, however, had to make do with one gig, albeit in the surroundings of the massive Knebworth Park. Nonetheless, many here in the UK felt that the band were abandoning them for success Stateside. Anyone who saw the 1978 tour (myself included) was blown away by the sheer scale of both the stage show and the music itself. Genesis don't really need a light show when you have musical pyrotechnics of the calibre of 'Afterglow' and 'In the Cage' and it was all here on display.

LAS COLINAS, TEXAS USA, (REHEARSALS), MARCH 1978

Tracks: Eleventh Earl of Mar/In the Cage/Burning Rope/Ripples/Fountain of Salmacis/Deep in the Motherlode/Down and Out/One for the Vine/Squonk/Follow You Follow Me/Follow You Follow Me (Take Two)/Apocalypse in 9-8//
Source: Audience recording.

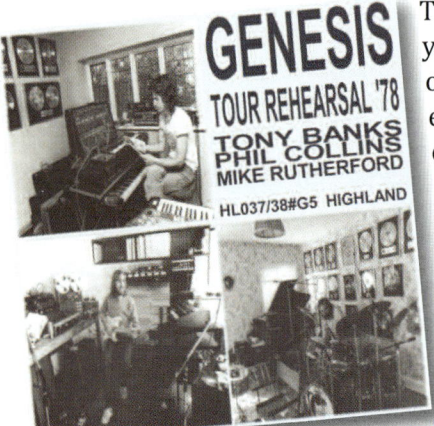

This one has an interesting variation on the theme. Available to fans for many years this recording gives a peek behind the scenes of a tour with a selection of songs from the 1978 shows. Opening with 'Eleventh Earl of Mar', it is evident from the start just how much of his own stamp Daryl Stuermer put on this, and indeed on may other established classics. It is strange to hear the band without an audience going nuts in the background but once you get used to it the results are fascinating. 'In the Cage' taken out of its context for the first time is next. Once again, Daryl's lead playing and Mike's beefy bass lines make this the new beating heart of the stage show.

Now for the new stuff, opening with the magnificently symphonic 'Burning Rope', in which Tony's keyboards lay down a suitably impressive introduction before the rest of the band get down to the nitty gritty. There are a few moments of hesitation here, which isn't really anything to be surprised at, but what is surprising is the magnificently emotional vocal that Phil puts in when there are only the road crew there to witness it!

Among the remaining tracks on this two-disc set perhaps the most interesting are the ancient (by Genesis standards) 'Fountain of Salmacis' getting its first (and last) airing under the aegis of Mr Collins. Mike's bass playing here is impressive augmented by some tasteful percussion from Chester and once again Daryl nails the guitar part to perfection. 'Follow You Follow Me' sounds completely different in this setting as the band try out a variety of sound effects and Daryl is evidently trying out different guitar styles, but the end result is equally satisfying, especially the second take, which is more of an informal jam but fascinating to hear. Without doubt though the biggest surprise on these discs is the final track; the awesome 'Apocalypse in 9/8', which in the end only got its chance to shine at one solitary gig (reviewed elsewhere in this book) and which leaves me wondering why it was not performed more than once. Either way, this one is a fascinating document for any fans interested in how the live sets for tours are put together.

PART ONE: GENESIS

COLISEUM, OAKLAND, CALIFORNIA, USA, 14 APRIL 1978

Set List: Eleventh Earl of Mar/In the Cage/Burning Rope/Ripples/Deep in the Motherlode/Down and Out/Fountain of Salmacis/Dance on a Volcano/Drum Duet /Los Endos/I Know What I Like//
Source: Audience recording.

The 1978 tour was so extensive that the band decided to split the US leg into not one but three separate tours during the course of the spring, summer, and autumn, fitting Europe and Japan around them. As such, the set differed slightly on each leg and what we have here is an above average audience recording of one of the shows from the inaugural leg of the tour.

Beginning with what by now had become a Genesis "tradition" the band opened the show with a track of their last album, in this case the glorious 'Eleventh Earl of Mar'. A truly marvellous show opener and here you have the entire band in what was evidently fine form. Daryl and Tony trade licks throughout whilst Mike and Chester put down a pretty impressive rhythm section. Even Phil sounds in fine fettle here. He even has the audience in the palm of his hand as he announces 'In the Cage', without doubt the surprise inclusion in the 1978 set, destined to remain there throughout the remainder of Genesis's live career. Here we have a fine version too. Tony lays down a suitably dramatic keyboard part whilst the rest of the band sound in fine form.

New stuff next as 'Burning Rope' roars out of the traps. Tony's symphonic keyboards are almost a paean of triumph soaring over the top of everything before Daryl, Mike, and Chester take up the cudgels and augment what is a truly impressive performance. Phil's voice too manages to capture the sheer emotion that the song's character must be feeling. Sadly the song is marred by several dropouts, which spoils the effect somewhat, but that's the downside of bootlegs I suppose.

Why Phil mentions Maurice Chevalier to an American audience, who probably have no idea who he is, is anyone's guess, but his rather chauvinistic intro to 'Ripples' is quite entertaining in its own way. Always a joy to hear, even in the obviously enormous setting of the Coliseum, the song still manages to bring a lump to your throat. 'Deep in the Motherlode' and 'Down and Out' are next, both of which throw the focus back on to the new album. The former gets off with an ambling gate highly suggestive of the covered wagons meandering slowly across the prairie, while 'Down and Out' without doubt features one of Phil's strangest introductions, mainly centred around the problems associated with short people (you're not that short, Phil!). For a band that at the time didn't really do social commentary, 'Down and Out' is an acidic observation on the manipulation of the little man by big business – a reflection on the current state of affairs in the music biz, perhaps? Either way, Phil delivers one of his fieriest vocals on this one in an all too rare performance of a greatly underrated track.

'Fountain of Salmacis' takes us right back to the band's formative years. Not the most obvious choice for performance in such a massive setting but it works. Daryl's guitar is to the fore again here, battling away against Tony's equally symphonic keyboards, while Phil puts in an emotional performance. A somewhat shorter set than usual here as Phil announces the last song, the explosive 'Dance on a Volcano', which simply gets better with age. Chester rattles the traps while the rest of the band seethe and simmer like a veritable lava flow before Phil joins Chester for what by now had become the standard five minutes of thunder leading into an equally fiery 'Los Endos' brining the show to an emphatic close.

Of course, an encore is demanded and the band return to the stage for a slowed down 'I Know What I Like'. The audience obviously know what's coming and behave accordingly, while Phil takes evident delight in winding them up with his Mockney accent and general hamming up for the crowd. The band are evidently in good spirits here and this confident and exuberant performance closes the recording in enjoyable fashion.

PALAIS DES SPORTS, DIJON, FRANCE, 3 JUNE 1978

Set List: Eleventh Earl of Mar/In the Cage/Burning Rope/Ripples/Deep in the Motherlode/The Fountain of Salmacis/Ballad of Big/One for the Vine/Squonk/Say it's Alright, Joe/The Lady Lies/Cinema Show/Afterglow/Follow You Follow Me/Dance on a Volcano/Drum Duet/Los Endos/I Know What I Like//
Source: Soundboard recording.

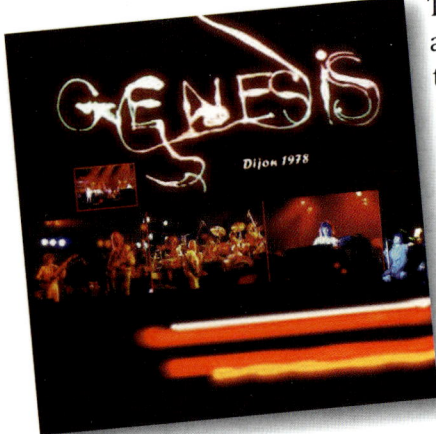

The band had opted to split their touring duties into chunks for this year's activities and they finally reached Europe in the middle of May. By the time they arrived they had perfected their new live show and it is captured here in another previously "hidden" soundboard recording.

The recording is crisp and clear from the outset with the audience well down in the mix. As such, this recording gives us ample opportunity to hear each and every member of the band. 'Eleventh Earl of Mar' is a prime example. Phil's wonderful vocal is accompanied by some fine playing from Tony and it is obvious that Daryl has settled into Steve's shoes quite nicely. As usual, Chester and Mike form the underpinning backbone to the ensemble. Phil's attempt at French falls rather flat but the audience, who sound as though they are miles away in the mix, seem to like it though, as he introduces the pre-medley rendering of 'In the Cage'. For those of us now used to hearing this as part of a medley, hearing it as a stand-alone track is a treat and once again the band deliver it in fine form. Tony's stabbing keyboards and Mike's meaty bass greatly augment Phil's impassioned vocals before Daryl delivers a storming guitar part. The only disappointment is that Chester's percussion is greatly reduced in the mix and sounds irritatingly tinny here.

With a new album to promote, the band are not long in introducing it to the audience, opening with 'Burning Rope'. An underrated classic this, as far as I am concerned, and this recording shows exactly why. Tony opens with a spine-tingling keyboard introduction, augmented by Chester, whose percussion has suddenly come up in the mix and deservedly so, too! Phil puts in another sterling performance on vocals here, as well and both Daryl and Mike embellish the song with great panache.

Phil's attempts at "Franglais" don't get any better but he does try. 'Ripples' "un chanson tres triste," however, is impeccable. Phil's vocal has lost none of its impact and is greatly augmented by some fine ensemble playing from Daryl and Tony. 'Deep in the Motherlode also features some fine playing by the entire band, with

Mike and Chester laying down an incessant rhythm, which Tony and Daryl embroider with some fine licks. Phil's voice has yet to show any of the signs of strain that would appear on later recordings and he gives the song a fine treatment throughout.

It is fun to hear Phil trying to explain the story of 'Hermaphroditus' in cod French, even alleging that Mr Banks is a Hermaphrodite doesn't affect his keyboard playing though! Genesis at their symphonic best here. Tony lays down a lush orchestral patina, over which Chester battles away like the frustrated character the song depicts. Daryl too, takes Mr Hackett's part and makes it definitively his own here. A rarity follows this, with a performance of 'Ballad of Big', another underrated song from the new album. An epic in miniature and one that certainly deserved to be played more often than it was on this tour. From the outset, this is a percussion-driven beast with both Mike and Chester driving the song along like a herd of cattle on the plains. Daryl conjures up a country and western style guitar refrain while Phil is obviously relishing getting into character once again.

Other highlights from this fine recording include yet another hilarious attempt by Phil to explain the proceedings going on during 'Say it's Alright, Joe'. Genesis don't do social conscience songs, do they? Well, this is a brilliantly observed tale of a drunk from his viewpoint and here Phil's acting credentials work to the song's advantage. 'Cinema Show' is greeted by a cheer, although once again you would almost miss it because the audience are almost out of the mix. Musically, this is yet another gem of a performance. Tony and Daryl's delicate introduction is overlaid by a suitably angelic vocal from Phil before the rhythm section of Mike and Chester lead the charge through the frantic instrumental section that, as usual, culminates with 'Afterglow'.

By the time we reach "la derniere chanson" (that's the last song to those of you who don't parlez vous) the band are pulling out all the stops. A hard rockin' version of 'Dance on a Volcano', in which Daryl, Mike, and Chester have some fun swapping licks and paradiddles with each other, before Phil gets back where he belongs – behind the drum kit – for an equally impressive 'Los Endos', which closes the show proper. 'I Know What I Like' is the only encore tonight bringing another excellent show to a suitably emphatic close.

WESTFALENHALLE, DORTMUND, GERMANY, 14 JUNE 1978

Set List: Eleventh Earl of Mar/In the Cage/Burning Rope/Ripples/Deep in the Motherlode/The Fountain of Salmacis/Down and Out/One for the Vine/Squonk/The Lady Lies/The Cinema Show/Afterglow/Follow You Follow Me/Dance on a Volcano/Drum Duet/Los Endos/I Know What I Like/Apocalypse in 9/8//
Source: Audience recording.

This one is something of a rarity, as you can see from the set list. Sadly, such a unique recording is only available to us in a rather enjoyable audience recording. Who knows, maybe the soundboard for this one is lurking in the band's now fully digitised tape archive?

Anyway, on with the show... As usual, the band open with a number from the previous album – 'Eleventh Earl of Mar' – which is greeted with cheers from the crowd. Once again, it is Daryl and Tony who scoop the musical honours here with some fine playing, although Mike's bass at times threatens to raise the roof. Phil sounds in good voice too and we are off to a good start. Strangely enough, the sound quality alters halfway through the song, as if the taper moved to avoid being caught by security, perhaps?

As Phil introduces 'In the Cage' you get something of a flavour of the echoey nature of some of the halls the band were playing. That echo certainly adds to the atmosphere as Chester and Mike set up a throbbing rhythm section, while Daryl and Tony's frantic playing and Phil's anguished vocal conjure up just the right combination of paranoia and claustrophobia. 'Burning Rope' is the first offering from the new album and it sounds suitably majestic as it echoes round the hall. Tony and Chester really set the pace here and Chester's percussion is a delight to hear, tasteful as always and never overstated.

'Ripples', prefaced by Phil's usual phonetic introduction, is as beautiful as ever. Mike and Daryl create a really lovely atmosphere with their acoustic playing, Phil's voice still has that pure quality that excessive use was soon to spoil but tonight he is in good voice. He really puts it to the test with the next two songs though. 'Deep in the Motherlode' really requires a lot from the singer but Phil delivers here over a suitably energetic performance from the rest of the band. A real trip back in time next with 'Fountain of Salmacis' opening with the usual church

PETTY WON THE DAY...

GENESIS/Jefferson Starship/Devo: Knebworth Festival.

Although the Knebworth bill also included Atlanta Rhythm Section, Roy Harper and Brand X none of these inspired enough enthusiasm from either me or the audience to be worth writing about.

A large amount of horseshit has been written about Devo in the Music Press. I personally reckon them as some kind of intellectual in-joke. I mean how can you take a band seriously when they appear dressed up like the local skateboard team?

Their music takes the form of hard metallic riffing overlaid with a bubbling synthesised hook that won't let go. Best numbers—their cover version of Satisfaction, Mongoloid and the cybernetic looning of Jocko Homo.

Predictably enough they evoked zero response from a puzzled audience. Pity—they rather appealed to my warped sense of humour.

Tom Petty and The Heartbreakers were the first band to receive a positive reaction. Hardly surprising as they were, for me anyway, the best act of the day.

They pulled out some white hot rock 'n' roll from the new album, You're Gonna Get It plus ballsy versions of Anything That's Rock'n'Roll and Fooled Again.

Naturally they were called back for an encore—a steaming rendition of Route 66... pretty damn good.

Wish I could say the same about Jefferson Starship. Minus Grace Slick it fell to Marty Balin to be Starship Pilot—a position that doesn't seem to suit him—his vocals bearing all the conviction of Boney M.

There may be life in the old dog yet, but they're going to have to watch Balin carefully to make sure he doesn't pilot The Starship into the black hole of MOR.

And so to Genesis in whom I've long since lost interest.

However there were some very tasteful special effects including the use of lasers.

Follow You Follow Me was the prelude to their final number The Cinema Show. Rapturous applause brought them back for one encore I Know What I Like.

The accent on this year's Knebworth leant more towards competent professionalism than rock'n'roll. Still OK for a day out I suppose.

Steve Chaos, Brighton

---

like chords from Tony. Mike and Chester soon pick up the chase with a thundering rhythm section and Daryl rips the hair off the back of your neck with some awesome playing.

'Down and Out' is making one of its last appearance in the set tonight. No messing about intro-wise, Phil just tells us what the song is called and then Tony's ethereal chords and Daryl's rhythm guitar take over. Strangely enough, Chester's percussion sounds very disjointed here which spoils the drama somewhat but we can't have everything. In many ways this song marks the way that Genesis would evolve over the coming years as they emerged from cult status to superstardom and the future blueprint is there to read in the lyrics.

'One for the Vine' and 'Squonk' contrast the epic and rock elements in the band's repertoire quite nicely. The former is a worthy successor to 'Supper's Ready', although obviously more concise, while the latter definitely shows the influence of Zeppelin on the band. Mike and Chester lay down an incredibly heavy rhythm, over which Daryl and Tony gild the lily in fine style. Poor old Phil has his work cut out trying to sing over the top of such a rowdy ensemble. No Vaudeville intro for 'The Lady Lies' but that's okay. The song speaks for itself. Yet another delightful example of Genesis' storytelling. It's tongue-in-cheek but with some seriously good playing, particularly from Mike, whose bass rampages like a giant on the loose.

The rest of the show comprises the usual fare, which fans had come to expect from the band, but the real surprise was still to come, as the band returned to the stage after the usual encore of 'I Know What I Like' to please the fans who take up the 'Supper's Ready' chant by launching straight into the 'Apocalypse in 9/8' finale to that very song, which, as far as I am aware, makes this recording unique and a must for collectors.

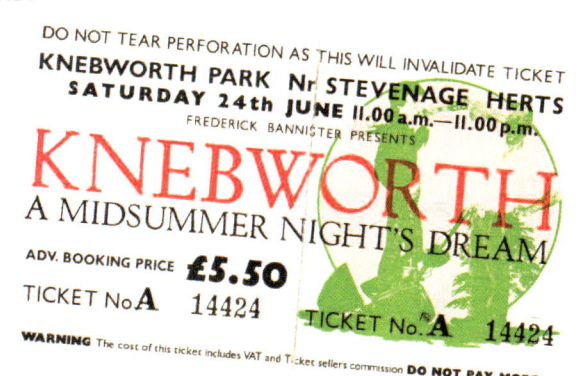

KNEBWORTH PARK, STEVENAGE, ENGLAND, 24 JUNE 1978

Set List: Squonk/Burning Rope/Ripples/The Fountain of Salmacis/ One for the Vine /Deep in the Motherlode/The Lady Lies/Afterglow/Follow You Follow Me/Dance on a Volcano/Drum Duet/Los Endos/ I Know What I Like//
Source: Pre-FM recording.

Aaah yes, the memories! This is where yours truly can begin to state "I was there!" Knebworth was my first encounter with the "Genesis Experience" and what a way to start! Everything about the day is ingrained on my memory. The first experience of being "adopted" into a family of Genesis fans, encounters with "zoider" and not a hogweed in sight! Oh, and yes, as you would expect at an open air gig by the band, it rained but no one seemed to care!

As the band's only UK gig of the year, the atmosphere was electric and the recording now available manages in some form to capture that excitement. Sadly, no complete broadcast of the gig exists, although the show itself was a slightly shorter one than normal because the band were headlining a festival. Originally broadcast in truncated form as a mere hour-long show, it has been re-broadcast regularly ever since and each time with different tracks! However, it is only recently that the Pre-FM broadcast tapes have become available and what a delight they are.

Introduced by Brian Matthews, the band open with 'Squonk' and proceed to tear through their back catalogue with alarming speed. With a new album to promote, there is a healthy dose of new material including a

A Selection Of Shows: Genesis & Solo Live Guide 1976-2014

PART ONE: GENESIS

PART ONE: GENESIS

superb rendering of 'Burning Rope' where Tony really shines. As my first experience of a Genesis gig, hearing the likes of 'Ripples' and 'One for the Vine' live for the first time was truly unforgettable. I have to give Daryl special kudos for stepping into Steve's shoes so convincingly that I could not see the join, so to speak.

The show was simply full of highlights, but when Phil begins his introduction to 'Fountain of Salmacis', my laughter is still accompanied by shivers down the spine even after thirty years! How can anyone forget Phil's Vaudevillian routine exhorting the audience to boo the villain during 'The Lady Lies'?!

The only disappointment is the presence of the radio commercials, which really are irritating and spoil the flow of an otherwise near perfect recording. However, I will forgive their presence if only for the truly magnificent final triptych of 'Dance on a Volcano'/'Los Endos', and 'I Know What I Like' where audience participation took on a whole new meaning for me on the night – and still does every time I listen to the recording!

The light show was awe-inspiring too but it is the music that counts and it is here in spades on this truly amazing recording.

UPTOWN THEATRE, CHICAGO, ILLINOIS, USA, 13 OCTOBER 1978

Set List: Eleventh Earl of Mar/In the Cage/Burning Rope/Dancing with the Moonlit Knight/Musical Box/Ripples/Deep in the Motherlode/One for the Vine/Squonk/Say it's Alright, Joe/The Lady Lies/ Cinema Show/Afterglow/Follow You Follow Me/Dance on a Volcano/Los Endos/I Know What I Like//
Source: Pre-FM recording.

Without doubt, this is one of the most famous recordings by Genesis from any era. Originally released at the time of the performance under the title From the Mouth of the Monster as an extortionately priced but highly sought after vinyl bootleg, this recording has been re-packaged in various forms ever since. However, with the advent of the Internet, and fans with the technology and dedication to do so, what we now have is without doubt one of the finest recordings available by any band.

Sourced this time form the Pre-FM broadcast tapes, this is the entire show from that famous performance in superb quality and for once, including all the between-song stories!

The band open the show with a blistering version of 'Eleventh Earl of Mar', always a favourite, and tonight they are taking no prisoners! Daryl's guitar threatens the roof whilst Tony and Mike battle away against each other like the protagonists of the story. Phil is in superb form whilst Chester, as usual, provides the musical backbone to everything. The '78 tour saw the arrival of 'In the Cage' as the new jewel in the Genesis crown, replacing 'Supper's Ready'. Placing it as merely the second song of the show, however, meant that the band might be in danger of peaking too early, as Phil might say! No such worries tonight though. Right from the start, the entire band are at the top of their game. Tony leads the pack, with Mike and Daryl battling away with some blistering riffs. Mike's bass has seldom sounded dirtier!

By the time the band got to the US on what was their third tour there, the newer material had been honed down to a fine art. 'Burning Rope' is a fine case in point. An epic "short" song and one that was given a superb treatment by the entire band tonight. A real surprise next though, an all too rare performance of 'Dancing with the Moonlit Knight', segued into the closing section of 'Musical Box', which served as a delightful replacement for 'Fountain of Salmacis', which had been exhumed for earlier shows.

'Ripples' also takes up the mantle of some of the older songs in terms of epic status and is a truly glorious affair tonight. Daryl really shines here with a wonderful performance, which, dare I say it, outshines Mr Hackett! A "Genesis history lesson" follows as Phil gives us another potted (or should that be potty?) history of the American gold rush whilst introducing another underrated gem from the new album, 'Deep in the Motherlode', which is one of the rockiest numbers that Genesis had written up to that point in their career. Tonight, Mike and Chester drive the song along with a dynamic rhythm section, over which Tony and Daryl allow their respective instruments to soar over them.

'One for the Vine' and 'Squonk' both manage to showcase two sides of Genesis that would certainly seem at odds with each other. The former a glorious epic in the true Genesis style, orchestral in magnitude and scope, and 'Squonk' an out and out heavy rocker that once again is driven by the impressive rhythmic talents of Mike and Chester and given added passion by a marvellous vocal performance by Phil.

Anyone bemoaning the lack of theatricality in Genesis shows after Peter's departure must surely have been delighted by Phil's adoption of the only "costume" he ever wore during his time with the band during 'Say it's Alright, Joe'. Okay, so it's a flasher mac and trilby, but used to great effect during the pathos-ridden tale of 'Joe' who sees life from the bottom of a whiskey glass. Another underrated classic from the new album.

Phil is obviously in his element here, as he continues the trip into Vaudeville with his intro to the next track, 'The Lady Lies', by exhorting the audience to boo, hiss, or make alternative noises whilst stroking his moustaches like some silent movie villain. Pantomime stuff for sure but the track itself is anything but. Phil puts on his best Anthony Newley voice and generally overacts, but that's the fun of it! This really is a classic slice of Genesis humour – even the music has me thinking of the Keystone Kops!

The emphasis turns from melodrama to high drama next for an impressive rendering of Cinema Show replete with yet another example of Phil's corny acting. The story of "two virgins" doesn't get any better but it wouldn't be a show without it, now, would it? Daryl really is the hero of this performance, he puts his own indelible stamp on the solos and this recording still sends shivers down my spine while hearing it. The extended instrumental section leading up to the climacteric 'Afterglow' simply defies description and how I envy the audience who saw this show!

Time for us all to catch our breath again with the new "hit" single. 'Follow You Follow Me' almost single-handedly gave the band an entirely new audience, especially here in the USA. Older fans might decry it as being "commercial". So what? It's a brilliant song, catchy, deeply infectious, and tonight the band deliver it in fine style and it is greeted by obvious enthusiasm by the crowd.

No rest for the wicked though, as 'Dance on a Volcano' and 'Los Endos' herald the end of the show proper. What a glorious finale, and this recording beggars belief in terms of sound quality, every note is there in stereophonic glory! Phil has seldom, if ever, sounded as passionate as he does here. Tony and Daryl trade formidable licks whilst Mike and Chester (and latterly Phil as well) lay down a rhythm section that would leave many a so-called "heavy" rock band floundering in their collective wake.

It was never in doubt that after a performance of such magnificence as this one that the band would not return for the obligatory encore. Sure enough, once again, the 'Cosmic Lawnmower' heralds the arrival of the final chance for the audience to indulge in some serious audience participation and sing their hearts out. Phil certainly does and you can even hear Mike on the chorus as well! From the evidence on display here, it is obvious that the band have relished this performance as much as the audience and there are few recordings around that equal this one for the sheer excitement, dynamism, and quality.

GENESIS SELL OUT MADISON

GENESIS LEFT Britain last weekend for an extensive tour of North America, which runs through until Christmas. They open with a string of dates in Canada, then move on to the United States, where they undertake their first headlining coast-to-coast tour. Already their concert at the vast Madison Square Garden is sold out — this takes place on November 23, which is Thanksgiving Day and generally recognised as a poor day for concert bookings.

Proof that you can't believe what you read in the papers. The date is incorrect as they played Madison Square Garden on 29 July. Peter Gabriel made a guest appearance for 'I Know What I LIke'. The last date of the 1978 US tour was on 22nd November in Houston.

HOFHEINZ PAVILION, HOUSTON TEXAS, USA, 22 NOVEMBER 1978
Set List: Deep in the Motherlode/In the Cage/The Lady Lies/Follow You Follow Me/Cinema Show/In That Quiet Earth/Afterglow/Dance on a Volcano/Los Endos//
Source: FM Radio broadcast.

This one is something of a rarity. Despite the band's growing popularity and the enormity of the tours to support the new album, radio broadcasts from gigs on the 1978 tour still appear to have been few and far between.

This show was the band's last one in the USA and a mere five days before their inaugural visit to Japan. After almost eight months on the road the band have their performance down to a fine art. Opening with a magnificent version of 'Deep in the Motherlode', Phil's voice betrays no signs of the strain, which was evident at earlier gigs, although given the demands that he placed on it, it would have been quite natural.

Sadly, as is the nature with radio broadcasts, time limitations mean that the between-songs banter has been edited out, which rather spoils the flow of the performance. Nonetheless, the version of 'In the Cage' here is a magnificent one. Tony's opening keyboard arpeggios are suitably menacing and Phil's impassioned vocals give a suitably paranoid aura to the performance.

'The Lady Lies' lacks the element of audience participation that really kick-starts it even though you can hear some audience booing down in the mix. The whole band really gel on this performance. Mike's bass pedals reverberate throughout augmenting Chester's thoughtful but understated percussion, while Tony is the lord of all he surveys as he lays down a masterful keyboard performance to accompany Phil's story of unrequited lust!

The hit single is next and what a belter it is. It is amazing how such an ostensibly simple three-minute piece of music can change the fortunes of a band. 'Follow You Follow Me' is a classic, pure and simple. Daryl's guitar playing augmenting Tony's lush keyboards give this track a wonderful bed into which Phil's angelic vocals fit perfectly in a delightful performance all round.

'Cinema Show' is once again one of the highlights of the show. A truly magnificent performance, panoramic in scope, yet tinged with moments of whimsical delight. Tony's playing accompanied by the rhythm department is truly superb here whilst Daryl's interpretation of one of Steve's finest riffs is a joy to behold, and the segue into 'Afterglow' lifts the performance to truly ethereal heights. 'Dance on a Volcano' and 'Los Endos' round out this performance in a suitably explosive style. As an edited broadcast this show certainly seems to focus upon the band's finest moments and this is another essential addition to any collection.

SHINJUKA KOSEI NENKIN HALL, TOKYO, JAPAN, 2 DECEMBER 1978
Set List: Eleventh Earl of Mar/In the Cage/Burning Rope/Ripples/Deep in the Motherlode/One for the Vine/Squonk/Say it's Alright, Joe/The Lady Lies/Cinema Show/Afterglow/Follow You Follow Me/Dance on a Volcano/Drum Duet/Los Endos/I Know What I Like//
Source: Audience recording.

These shows were ones which, by his own admission, Phil hated, owing to the problems within his own personal life at this time. Not that he would ever let that show to the audience – consummate professional that he is!

This is the recording of the band's penultimate gig in Japan with the same set as the band had been performing at their last handful of gigs in America scarcely a week before. The recording we have here is an above average audience one, which certainly manages to bring a flavour of the gig to us. Phil's between-song patter seems to fall not so much on deaf ears as completely non-comprehending ones. Even his phonetic song intros don't seem to elicit much response from the crowd, apart from some polite applause and occasional giggle

'Eleventh Earl of Mar' gets things off to a suitably dramatic start with Daryl and Tony battling away aided and abetted by Chester and Mike who put in a formidable rhythm section. Phil's announcement of 'In the Cage' brings a suitably retrained but enthusiastic response. Here Chester and Tony build up a claustrophobic atmosphere before Daryl chimes in with some frantic chords over which Phil delivers an impassioned vocal. From the sound of the recording this must have been a comparatively small hall. The acoustics are comparatively flat but clear nonetheless.

'Burning Rope' is the first offering from the new album and it is as majestic as ever. Tony and Daryl lay down an orchestral backdrop against which Chester provides an emphatic rhythm section. It's almost like the old days next when Chester has to do a couple of minutes' drumming whilst someone tunes up. Nothing daunted, the band then launch into 'Ripples', which sounds spot on tonight. Tony, Mike, and Daryl are impeccable in their playing, each augmenting rather than competing with the others.

With the set remaining the same as it had been on the final leg of the US tour, the Japanese audience is treated to the same mix of old and new making a fine showcase for what were probably many fans unfamiliar with the band's back catalogue. Not that you would know it from their responses, which are always enthusiastic, and this recording is an enjoyable document of the band's first trip to the Land of the Rising Sun.

PART ONE: GENESIS

CHAPTER FOUR
"ENTER THE DUKE"
DUKE TOUR 1980

The final drive for success in the US may have brought the band the financial security that they had striven for, for so long. For one band member, however, the cost was enormous. Phil Collins' marriage was the casualty and indeed the band itself came close to folding as Phil, determined to save his marriage, moved temporarily to Vancouver. This gave Tony and Mike the opportunity to try their hand at long overdue solo albums whilst Phil concentrated on his personal life. The resulting albums, *A Curious Feeling* and *Smallcreep's Day*, were well received by the fans, and the experience gave both Mike and Tony a heightened appreciation of each other and Phil, which they were to bring to bear on their next group album.

Phil eventually returned to the UK after having failed to save his marriage and immediately threw himself into writing as his own therapy. The band reconvened in the autumn of 1979 and work began on the follow up to 1978's *And Then There Were Three* album. Returning to the group written format, the new album took Genesis even further away from the epics of old. Phil's writing contributions now started to impinge on the contents of Genesis' albums and it must have given him no end of satisfaction when his composition, 'Misunderstanding', became the band's first US top ten hit.

The rest of the album, titled *Duke*, is very much a transitional effort. The commercial sensibilities of Phil were still married to the more Progressive influences of Tony and Mike. Tracks such as 'Cul de Sac' and 'Heathaze' are still cast in the mould of early '70s' numbers, such as 'Can-Utility' & 'The Coastliners', while 'Misunderstanding' and 'Turn it on Again' have their roots firmly embedded in modern Pop. For longstanding fans, *Duke* was probably a confusing album. The band were definitely at a crossroads in terms of which direction their music was going to take.

There were no such doubts where the live presentation was concerned. Having concentrated on the USA and Europe in 1978, this time the band gave their UK fans a long overdue treat. The tour schedule, when announced, took in over thirty gigs in *theatres* up and down the UK. Many of these places had not seen the band since the early 1970s. In addition to this, there was an extensive tour of the USA, where the mix was between theatres and arenas to cope with the still growing demand by US fans to see the band.

Continuing the trend of gradually phasing out many of the older songs and weaning the audience on to the newer material, the band once again presented a glorious showcase. The emphasis of the show firmly on the new album as evidence by the opening salvo of tracks which gradually became referred to as 'The Duke Suite' as the tour progressed along, with a healthy selection of material from the 1976-78 period the audience lapped the new show up giving healthy respect to old and new alike, although of course older favourites such as 'Dancing with the Moonlit Knight' and 'I Know What I Like' were accorded more applause on occasions.

Scaling the visual side of the show down in order to fit the show within the confines of the older halls the band were playing in the UK, there was no such reduction in terms of the length of the show, which usually lasted for an exhausting two and a half hours. By the end of the UK leg, Phil's voice was beginning to show signs of strain, which is hardly surprising given the demands that he placed upon it nightly. In the UK, the tour was an unprecedented success with over one and a half million applications for the eighty thousand tickets that were available. In fact, an additional show was eventually added to the schedule at the grand old Theatre Royal in Drury Lane, London, on 5 May, but that scarcely dented the amazing demand for tickets to see the band.

The US tour was similarly successful, with the band wisely mixing venues between larger scale arenas and smaller theatres in order to present the show to as many people as possible. The show at the 500-seater Roxy Theater in West Hollywood was as intimate as you could get and the band sat in the sales kiosk selling the fans tickets for the show – a nice touch! By the end of the summer of 1980 there was little doubting Genesis' position among the top acts in the UK; a position they were to consolidate and expand upon during the rest of the 1980s.

FESTIVAL HALL, PAIGNTON, ENGLAND, 17 MARCH 1980

Set List: Back in NYC/Dancing with the Moonlit Knight/Carpet Crawlers/ Squonk/ One for the Vine/Behind the Lines/Duchess/Guide Vocal/Turn it on Again/Duke's Travels/Duke's End/Say it's Alright, Joe/The Lady Lies/Ripples/In the Cage-Raven-Afterglow/Follow You Follow Me/Dance on a Volcano/Drum Duet/Los Endos/I Know What I Like//
Source: Audience Recording.

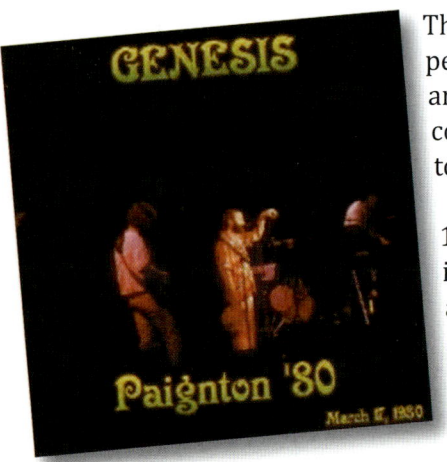

There has always been some confusion over the exact number of concerts performed during the UK leg of this tour, mainly owing to the re-scheduling and eventual cancellation of several of the early gigs, owing to Phil having contracted a severe bout of laryngitis just prior to the commencement of the tour.

So, eventually after re-jigging the schedule, the band officially opened their 1980 tour with two nights at the seaside in Paignton and what we have here is the only known extant recording of the first night. Sadly, it does not appear that a soundboard recording of this show survives and this recording was made by a member of the audience.

The band take us on a little trip back with the opening trio of songs. 'Back in NYC' gets things off to a fine start before the band repeat the formula that had so famously worked in Chicago back in 1978 and treat us to a delightful version of 'Dancing with the Moonlit Knight'. Though even here you can tell that Phil's voice is still affected by the laryngitis that had forced the rescheduling of the tour. 'Carpet Crawlers' is much better though and Phil's voice rises to the occasion although he does forget some of the words!

'Squonk' and 'One for the Vine' really test Phil's mettle and even with a recording of such average quality as this one you can hear the strain at times. Musically though, there are no such problems, as the rest of the band give both songs impeccable renderings. Here we have the first telling of the "Story of Albert", which continues to evolve throughout the tour, but the bare bones of it are here tonight. The now famous 'Duke Suite' kicks off with 'Behind the Lines' and you can almost imagine the band eager and keen to unleash their new opus. Even here, the dynamism of the performance is plain to hear. Daryl and Tony tear away like greyhounds in the slips, but once again Phil's voice is showing signs of strain and he fluffs the words again – opening night and all that, eh? 'Duchess' too benefits in a strange way from Phil's ragged vocals although his plaintive delivery on 'Guide Vocal' is extraordinary. 'Turn it on Again' gets a good work out, with Mike and Daryl trading some rock 'n' roll licks and Tony gallops along with a will. Poor Phil, though, is really struggling here and it shows. The rest of this recording manages to give a glimpse into the genuine excitement that these shows generated. If only a better quality recording of it existed then I would be very happy.

PART ONE: GENESIS

GREAT HALL, EXETER UNIVERSITY, ENGLAND, 19 MARCH 1980

Set List: Back in NYC/Dancing with the Moonlit Knight/Carpet Crawlers/Squonk/One for the Vine/Behind the Lines/Duchess/Guide Vocal/Turn it on Again/Duke's Travels/Duke's End/Say it's Alright, Joe/The Lady Lies/In the Cage-Raven-Afterglow/Follow You Follow Me/Dance on a Volcano/Drum Duet/Los Endos/I Know What I Like//
Source: Audience Recording.

This is another early recording that manages to capture much of the excitement and drama of the band's 1980 show. Once again, the show opens with a marvellous version of 'Back in NYC', in which Phil really manages to deliver the song with every bit as much passion as Peter ever did. The demands this placed on his voice, however, ensured that the song was soon dropped from the set. As usual, the recording quality is not great but nonetheless, it is clear throughout the bulk of the recording. Daryl's playing threatens to take the roof off. 'Dancing with the Moonlit Knight' and 'Carpet Crawlers' calm things down for a while. Tony's playing on the latter is superb. Phil, though, sounds as if he is struggling with the vocals and his voice is increasingly ragged as the song progresses.

No rest for the wicked though, as 'Squonk' kicks off an increasingly demanding series of songs. The audience get stuck right in with some seriously out of time clapping to accompany Chester's thudding percussion. Mike and Daryl trade off some searing licks. Phil's vocal once again betrays the strain he is placing on his voice and the effects of the recent severe flu/laryngitis that led to the rescheduling of several shows on this tour. Phil's introduction to One for the Vine even acknowledges that he is having problems with his voice. Nonetheless, like the trooper he is, he persists in fine style.

The "story of Albert" is still in its evolutionary stages but it still manages to raise a few laughs from the crowd. There's nothing to laugh about in the music, however, as the band launch into a ferocious rendition of the 'Duke Suite', opening with 'Behind the Lines', which gives the entire band a chance to shine. 'Guide Vocal' features a wonderful trio between Daryl, Tony, and Chester, where the interplay between them is a delight to hear. Sadly, there is some distortion on the tape here, which spoils the effect somewhat. The problem is rectified for 'Turn it on Again' though, which opens with some more of Mike's incredible bass playing before he is joined by the rest of the band at full throttle.

'Duke's Travels' and 'Duke's End' round out the 'Duke Suite', as it has since become known in fine style with some marvellous drumming from both Phil and Chester, while the rest of the band let their hair down as well.

Phil's Vaudeville routine leads us nicely into 'Say it's Alright Joe', one of the most underrated songs from *And Then There Were Three*, and definitely one in the old storytelling tradition of the band. The melodramatic theme continues with Phil's lead introduction to 'The Lady Lies', exhorting the audience to "boo, hiss or make alternative noises ..." Tony is at his most magnificent here and his introduction is akin to the opening of an opera, which I suppose this song is – in miniature, thankfully! Mike and Chester create a solid rhythmic backbone to the song whilst Phil delivers the vocal in suitably over the top form.

The now ubiquitous 'In the Cage' medley was still something of a novelty back in 1980 and it is ecstatically received by the audience here. The band seem to be energised by that reaction and they turn in a dynamic and thrilling performance, which, despite the average quality of the recording, still manages to capture the excitement that these shows generated. 'Follow You Follow Me' quietens the atmosphere down as the band no doubt prepare themselves for the onslaught that follows it.

'Dance on a Volcano' erupts with all the suitable energy and drama upon the audience with Phil delivering a particularly passionate vocal, which is augmented by some fine playing from Tony, but the stars of the show here are Chester and Daryl who battle away like troopers. The ensemble playing reaches a peak with 'Los Endos' where everyone has the chance to really flex their collective muscles to bring the musical bacon home at the end of the show proper. After putting in so much effort, the band would have been within their rights not to return for an encore, but there was no way that this was going to happen, and after a short break the whirr of the 'Cosmic Lawnmower' signals the start of 'I Know What I Like' and cue the audience going nuts! it is only a pity that the existing recording from this gig is of average quality because from the evidence the band were on top form here.

LYCEUM BALLROOM, LONDON, ENGLAND, 7 MAY 1980

Set List: Deep in the Motherlode/Dancing with the Moonlit Knight/Carpet Crawlers/Squonk/One for the Vine/Behind the Lines/Duchess/Guide Vocal/Turn it on Again/Duke's Travels/Duke's End/Say it's Alright, Joe/The Lady Lies/Ripples/In the Cage-Colony of Slippermen-Raven-Afterglow/Follow You Follow Me/Dance on a Volcano/Drum Duet/Los Endos/I Know What I Like/The Knife// Source: FM and Pre-FM Broadcasts.

This, along with the Uptown Theatre recording from 1978, is probably one of the most famous Genesis recordings of all time. Originally broadcast at the time of the gig, and subsequently re-broadcast in various edited forms, it is only recently that the entire show has been restored to us – including all the between-song patter from Phil. And what a joy it is to have it in its entirety!

Coming at the culmination of an almost two-month tour of the UK, the band were in peak form at this show. Once again, the deceptive heartbeat intro leads you to think that 'Back in NYC' will herald the start of the show but you would be wrong as the band emerge on stage to a full throated cheer from the crowd and launch into 'Deep in the Motherlode'. The laryngitis that led to the cancellation of several gigs on this tour has obviously had an effect on Phil's voice, which from the start sounds raspy and harsh – which all adds to the drama of course! 'Dancing with the Moonlit Knight', which was such a surprise on the 1978 tour, has settled into the set quite nicely, although even here Phil's voice sounds slightly strained. Daryl and Tony deliver a perfect accompaniment that is obviously relished by the crowd. Tony's piano intro to 'Carpet Crawlers' also gets a cheer from the crowd and it is a delightful version here tonight. Phil manages to give just the right amount of emphasis to the song, while once again Daryl takes on Mr Hackett's part admirably.

'Squonk' simply gets better with age. Here Phil's strained vocals definitely add to the atmosphere of the song. Mike's bass pedals threaten to rip the roof off the Lyceum, while Daryl and Tony once again throw caution to the winds with some inspired playing. One for the Vine too, has by this stage of the tour evolved into an epic tour de force worthy of the epics of yore. Tony conducts the proceedings from behind his keyboards with some extremely tasteful playing. Daryl and Mike augment him, while Chester underpins everything with a flawless rhythm, over which Phil delivers yet another ballsy vocal performance.

Now on the new stuff prefaced by Phil's increasingly corny "story of Albert", which, from the audience reaction, has become very well known as, unlike previous shows, it is obvious they know what is coming next – probably because they were all at the Hammersmith shows earlier on the tour! The 'Duke Suite', as it has since come to be known, strings together over half of the new album in a rip roaring extravaganza in which each and every band member

Genesis in doubt

GENESIS had to pull out of two gigs early this week because Phil Collins contracted laryngitis and at press time there was some doubt about their Hammersmith dates, which are due to start on Thursday.

The cancelled dates were at Portsmouth Guildhall on Monday (which was an unannounced warm-up date) and Bournemouth Winter Gardens on Wednesday. A decision on the Hammersmith concerts will be taken on Wednesday and ticket holders should check local radio stations or the Odeon itself.

Arrangements to reschedule the Portsmouth and Bournemouth dates are being made and ticket holders should keep their tickets for the time being.

A Selection Of Shows: Genesis & Solo Live Guide 1976-2014

PART ONE: GENESIS

has a chance to shine. Opening with 'Behind the Lines', in which Daryl and Chester deliver some ferocious playing, and leading us through 'Duchess', 'Guide Vocal', 'Turn it on Again', which was destined to survive in the set right the way through until the band's final tour in 2007, and culminating with the extended instrumental romp that is 'Duke's Travels' and 'Duke's End' performed with a frenetic energy that leaves the listener breathless.

Sadly this tour was to see the final performances of much of the material from the *And Then There Were Three* album, which is a pity because 'Say it's Alright, Joe' and 'The Lady Lies' have both gained enormously in performance, even if Phil's stories haven't! 'Ripples' also is due to exit stage left after this tour, not to be revived again until 2007, so relish the performance on this recording, as it is one of the best available. 'In the Cage', though, is now ensconced in the central position it is to enjoy through what remains of Phil's tenure with the band. Surely this has to be one of the most inspired choices by the band. Separated from some of the frippery that surrounded it on "The Lamb" this song really does shine like a polished diamond and the attached medley leading up to the orgasmic 'Afterglow' is, perhaps, the only one that I have any lasting affection for – anything else would be unforgivable. Tonight, with the band's penultimate UK show, the urgency of this performance is almost tangible.

The rest of the set remains the same as it was for the previous tour, culminating with another emphatic rendering of 'Dance on a Volcano' and 'Los Endos'. Anyone who says that Genesis don't do "Rock" should do themselves a favour and listen to this recording as I have seldom heard the band as feisty as they are here. Even the encores contain a surprise, opening with the now standard 'I Know What I Like' and the show closes with a frantic version of 'The Knife', on which Phil's ragged vocals evoke the drama of the song in ways that I doubt even Peter could have done! Like the recording from Chicago in 1978, this one stands as a testament to the very best of Genesis.

GREEK THEATRE, LOS ANGELES, CALIFORNIA, USA, 27 MAY 1980
Set List: Deep in the Motherlode/Dancing with the Moonlit Knight/Squonk/Behind the Lines/ Duchess/Guide Vocal/Turn it on Again/Duke's Travels/Duke's End/The Lady Lies/Ripples/ Misunderstanding/In the Cage-Raven-Afterglow/Follow You Follow Me/Dance on a Volcano/Drum Duet/Los Endos/I Know What I Like//
Source: Audience Recording.

This is one of the handful of theatre shows that the band squeezed in between their increasingly arena dominated tours of the USA and Canada. The sound quality is average and the acoustic is very flat, suggesting that this was recorded somewhere either in the rear of the stalls or the balcony. Sound is clear, however, and the vocals are clearly discernible.

Once again, the band perform a selection of oldies leading up to the presentation of the new album in what has since become known as the 'Duke Suite'. 'Deep in the Motherlode', 'Dancing with the Moonlit Knight', and 'Squonk' get the audience in the mood, not that they need encouraging by the sound of it – a very enthusiastic audience this one! Phil's story about their "good friend Albert" is augmented by the cardboard cut-out of a lady with rather large breast, which Phil apparently had on stage with him – dirty boy! The jokes don't get any better and the audience take the piss quite freely with catcalls and jeers. By this stage of the tour the new material is well bedded into the show and the band are on fine form here. It is only a pity that the sound quality of this recording is not better, but nonetheless this is an interesting recording for collectors.

FORUM, MONTREAL, QUEBEC, CANADA, 19 JUNE 1980

Set List: Deep in the Motherlode/Dancing with the Moonlit Knight/Squonk/One for the Vine/ Behind the Lines/Duchess/Guide Vocal/ Turn it on Again/Duke's Travels/Duke's End/The Lady Lies/Ripples/Misunderstanding/In the Cage-Raven-Afterglow/Follow You Follow Me/Dance on a Volcano/Drum Duet/Los Endos/I Know What I Like//
Source: Soundboard Recording.

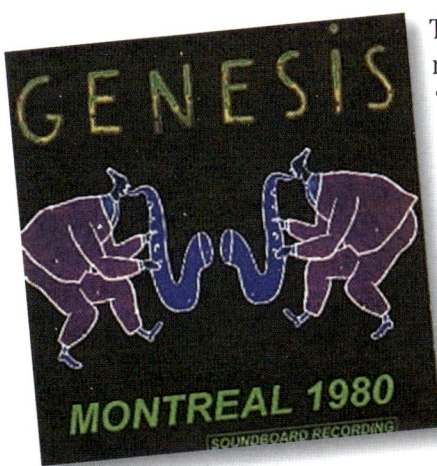

This is another rarity. This recording is one of only a handful of soundboard recordings available to fans from the 1980 tour. Opening once again with 'Deep in the Motherlode', it is obvious from the outset that Phil's voice is beginning to suffer from the incredible strain placed on it by each night's performance. He struggles manfully with the show opener, but recovers his composure somewhat with 'Dancing with the Moonlit Knight', in which both Tony and Daryl accompany him beautifully. 'Squonk' is next, and a fine version is delivered here, with some tasty playing by both Mike and Chester in the rhythm department. Once again, Phil's vocal sounds ragged but strangely in keeping with the drama of the song.

The epic tale of misguided loyalty and treachery that is 'One for the Vine' is given a fine delivery here with Tony revelling in one of his finest creations. Phil, however, is definitely struggling here and his voice falls flat at several points throughout the track. "L'histoire d'Albert" is next and Phil's Franglais is embarrassing to hear but the audience, which you can hear (just about), seem to like it. The 'Duke Suite' follows and sounds marvellous. Chester and Daryl in particular take the opening salvo of 'Behind the Lines' and kick the living daylights out of it before they are joined by the rest of the band. Mike's meaty bass lines underpin the entire thing whilst Tony augments things with some impeccable chords. Phil's vocal, however, is definitely getting worse and he really struggles with some of the vocal melodies throughout this and the subsequent tracks.

More of Phil's awful Franglais next with the rather camp story leading us into 'The Lady Lies' but he has incredible difficulty in getting any kind of reaction out of the audience who probably haven't got a clue what he is going on about! Strangely enough, Phil sounds more like Dudley Moore here than anything else but the rest of the band are typically Genesis, thank goodness! A wonderful performance of 'Ripples' follows, in which kudos must go to Mike, Tony, and Daryl, who deliver the goods in spades. Phil's voice still sounds strained but he soldiers on regardless.

By the time we reach the grand finale of 'Dance on a Volcano' and 'Los Endos', Phil's voice is in tatters and his thanks to the audience sound as if his throat has been cut. to be honest, struggling as he was, I am surprised that the show continued but that's how much of a trouper he is! A ragged 'I Know What I Like' ends the performance where the rest of the band battle on through whilst poor Phil tries to retain what little voice he has left – plenty of cough linctus was taken after this show, methinks!

PART ONE: GENESIS

CHAPTER FIVE
"LEIDEN? WHERE THE ***K IS LEIDEN?"
ABACAB TOUR 1981

Genesis did not take their feet off the pedals during the early 1980s. No sooner had they completed the hugely successful *Duke* tour in the summer of 1980, than they were back in the studio; their own recently acquired one, this time. The Farm Studio gave the band the freedom to experiment without having to watch the ever expensive studio clock count out the time (pardon the pun!). There were even bigger changes afoot this time around. The band opted to produce themselves rather than have an outsider doing the job and with their own studio, they were obviously much more at ease with their experiments.

The resulting album, *Abacab*, was released in August 1981 and is perhaps the most divisive album by the band since the *Lamb Lies Down On Broadway*. Older fans, already finding the band's increasing slide towards commerciality – as they saw it – hard to take, were horrified to hear a horn section on several tracks on the album and one track in particular – 'Who-Dunnit?' – has been the subject of universal revulsion ever since. Perversely, this track is one of Tony Banks' favourites, although heaven alone knows what might have happened if this track had been released as a single, which allegedly was on the cards. Fortunately, wiser heads prevailed in the end!

Abacab is an abstract album in more ways than one. The band's sound is pared down to a bare minimum. The glorious lush sounds of old are gone and replaced by a dryer, harsher sound. The album is a bona fide Rock album however, tracks such as 'Abacab' and 'Dodo' are among the heaviest that Genesis have ever produced. Sandwiched in between them were several much more accessible tracks. Once the initial shock of hearing the horns on 'Man on the Corner' and 'No Reply at All' has receded, the tracks themselves are instantly recognisable as Genesis. Storytelling is still as strong as ever, especially on the story of a man's experience with aliens in 'Keep it Dark'. 'Man on the Corner' and 'Another Record' are second cousins to 'Say it's Alright, Joe' and 'Dodo'/'Lurker', with its gnomic riddle lyrics is every bit as obscure as any of Mr Gabriel's previous efforts.

The new-look live show once again took in new technology. The band had invested in the new Vari Lite, which was a computerised lighting system that could change the colour of lights and move them to varying angles, giving many different lighting configurations. This system was to come into its own on subsequent tours but certainly looked impressive enough on its debut in 1981. Musically too, it was "all change". The emphasis firmly placed on the new album and its immediate predecessor and the beginning of a trend to compress the older material into a series of medleys. The new show did not go down too well with everyone, and at one show in Holland the band were subjected to ferocious booing from the crowd whenever any new material was played, which must have been an interesting experience for the band. Fortunately, the reaction to the show was not as antagonistic elsewhere, and as a whole the new show was a great success, continuing the band's rise toward superstardom.

AMPHITHEATRE, FREJUS, FRANCE, 27 SEPTEMBER 1981
Set List: Behind the Lines/Duchess/The Lamb Lies Down on Broadway/Dodo-Lurker/Abacab/Misunderstanding/Firth of Fifth/No Reply at All/Me and Sarah Jane/In the Cage-Cinema Show-Afterglow/Turn it on Again/Los Endos/Man on the Corner/Who-Dunnit?/I Know What I Like//
Source: Audience Recording.

This is another of those wonderful vinyl boots that you used to find under the counter at so many record fairs – those were the days! Taken from one of the first shows on the band's 1981 *Abacab* tour, this is evidently an audience recording but quite an enjoyable one.

The name of the venue would seem to suggest that it was an open air gig but the acoustics on the recording suggest otherwise. In fact, this recording sounds as if it took place in a small club. There's no doubt that the audience are up for it on this one, they are behind the band from the start as they open the show with a storming version of 'Behind the Lines' and 'Duchess', continuing the tradition of opening a show with a song (or songs) from the previous album. Phil sounds in top form here as he rampages through the songs. Daryl also plays his heart out. Chester and Mike put down another impressive performance from the rhythm section.

'The Lamb Lies Down on Broadway' makes a welcome return to the set on this tour and tonight Tony steals the show with an impeccable performance. Phil is in his element here and he seems to be having a great time. Sadly, any between song patter has been cut out on this recording so I don't know how Phil introduced the first of this evening's new songs. However, neither 'Dodo-Lurker' nor 'Abacab' that follow it are greeted with anything other than enthusiasm from the very vocal crowd. Musically the new album comes over far better live than it does on record. 'Dodo' has an incredibly edgy feel to it whilst 'Abacab' takes care of any doubts that Genesis can rock out with the best of 'em. Once again, Mike and Chester deliver a solid rhythmic foundation, over which Daryl and Tony some formidable playing. Tony's chords stab like a knife at times. Phil also has seldom sounded in better form and he grabs the audience by the scruff of the neck with a powerful performance that is greeted by cheers from the crowd.

Unusually, Phil introduces 'Misunderstanding' in another amusing attempt at French, which the crowd seem to appreciate. Daryl really shines here with some brilliant playing. More savage cuts omit the intro to 'Firth of Fifth' but the song itself is as brilliant as ever. Daryl has by now stamped his own signature on the solo although that doesn't stop one member of the audience crying out "Steve!" at one point. Unusually for an audience recording the rhythm section is high up in the mix and once again Mike's bass rattles the speakers.

It is during both 'No Reply at All' and 'Me and Sarah Jane' that Phil's voice starts to show signs of strain and he is reaching for the notes at times. Musically, the rest of the band put in workmanlike performances here. 'In the Cage', introduced in French again, is much better. Tony's arpeggios and Daryl's stabbing chords induce just the right atmosphere of claustrophobia and fear in which Phil's impassioned, and at times strained, vocal adds to the tension of the song, while Mike's bass sounds like someone trying to batter down a wall (or cage). Quite appropriate, really!

'Turn it on Again' continues the hard-rocking element of the show. In fact, the *Abacab* tour was to be the rockiest that Genesis ever performed. 'Dance on a Volcano' and 'Los Endos' also throw everything including the musical equivalent of the kitchen sink into the mix, although I would imagine that by now Phil was really beginning to feel the strain. He sounds tired here, which isn't really surprising, given the effort it has taken to deliver a performance such as this. The rest of the band take up the slack though, with excellent performances throughout.

For reasons best known to the makers of the original LP, we next have a pair of tracks that should appear in the middle of the set. 'Man on the Corner', which has never been a favourite of mine, and here even taken out of its proper context within the live set does nothing for me, I'm afraid. This segues into the song that most Genesis fans love to hate: 'Who-Dunnit?' – a song that was to get the band into a small degree of trouble elsewhere on this tour. No trouble tonight, though. The audience seem to indulge this aberration with a modicum of enthusiasm. Me? I still hate it!

Encore time brings us to 'I Know What I Like', which is greeted by the usual round of audience participation, and a workmanlike performance rounds out another interesting document from this early stage of the tour.

GROENOORDHAL, LEIDEN, NETHERLANDS, 3 OCTOBER 1981

Set List: Behind the Lines/Duchess/The Lamb Lies Down on Broadway/Dodo-Lurker/Abacab/Misunderstanding/Man on the Corner/Who-Dunnit?/No Reply at All/Firth of Fifth/Me and Sarah Jane/In the Cage-Cinema Show-Raven-Afterglow/Turn it on Again/Dance on a Volcano/Drum Duet/Los Endos/I Know What I Like//
Source: Audience Recording.

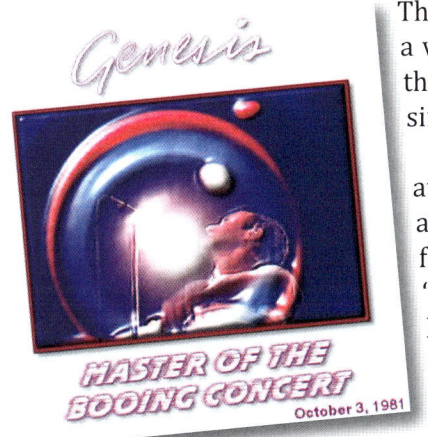

This is the famous (or should that be infamous?) gig where the band received a very rough reception and were booed! Yes, *booed* at several points during the show. *Abacab*, as I have already mentioned, has divided most Genesis fans since its release in a way that no other Genesis album has since "The Lamb."

Taken from an audience recording, this effort gives an authentic feel of the atmosphere during the gigs on the *Abacab* tour, coupled with an above average sound quality, although still a little treble-heavy at times. Things are fine with the opening salvo of 'Behind the Lines'/Duchess and especially 'The Lamb', which gets a riotous reception from the partisan Dutch crowd. Despite this being an early show in the tour, the band are in fine form. 'Duchess' is inspired and Tony is in great shape. Daryl and Mike trade off some fine licks backed by both Phil and Chester. Phil's voice is in fine form too.

Phil winds up the crowd with his introduction to 'Dodo' and this is where the trouble starts with the first batch of booing, which Phil responds to in good humour: "Oh you playful things." As for the performance, 'Dodo' and 'Abacab' here are storming rock versions that grab you by the scruff of the neck and shake you and Phil's sneeringly cod punk delivery is priceless. The trouble really starts after 'Who-Dunnit' where booing takes on an unheard of element. My own feelings on the subject of this track are quite negative but I would never dream of booing a performance by the band! 'Firth of Fifth' is surprisingly lacklustre here, perhaps the audience's lack of enthusiasm for the new stuff was rubbing off on the band. Who knows? Sadly, the audience's enthusiasm can clearly be heard here with the rent-a-crowd chorus! Once again, Daryl really shines here with a magnificent rendering of this Hackett classic. 'Me and Sarah Jane' is another underrated classic and gets a respectful response and the rest of the show, which is drawn from pre-*Abacab* material, escapes any further incidents.

The performance by the band, however, was undoubtedly affected by the response of the audience towards the new album and is one of the more average performances on the tour. I do have sympathy with the band. Such negative responses as are evident here really serve no useful purpose. After all, the band were on tour to promote a new album, for goodness' sake! Nevertheless, this is an interesting recording of one of the more unusual Genesis moments. And to think, while all of this was going on, I was at the Empire Theatre Liverpool watching Mr Hackett get a rapturous reception for his new album on stage with a new band – nowt as strange as folk, eh?!

SPORTSHALLE, COLOGNE, GERMANY, 17 OCTOBER 1981
Set List: Behind the Lines/Duchess/The Lamb Lies Down on Broadway/Dodo-Lurker/Abacab/Carpet Crawlers/Me and Sarah Jane/Misunderstanding/No Reply at All/Firth of Fifth/Man on the Corner/Who-Dunnit?/In the Cage-Cinema Show-Raven-Afterglow/ Dance on a Volcano/Drum Duet/Los Endos/I Know What I Like//
Source: Audience Recording.

Coming a couple of weeks after the previous gigs, it is refreshing to hear an audience that is genuinely enthusiastic about the band's newer material. An above average recording documents another vibrant performance from the band.

The hall's acoustics make for a very vibey performance from the outset with 'Behind the Lines' rattling along at a frantic pace. Tony and Daryl's playing is assured and confident throughout and Chester has seldom sounded in better form. Phil sounds in good voice too, with none of the vocal problems that had been so evident on the previous year's tour.

'Duchess' gets off to a good start too, aided by some serious audience participation. Once again, Daryl and Tony lead the pack but augmented by some impressive playing from Mike. 'The Lamb' completes the opening trio and everyone is obviously having a great time. The audience are in fine voice and the band are evidently feeding off the excitement and perform accordingly. There is evidently a strong English contingent among the audience here tonight and they make their presence felt throughout the show.

Their presence is acknowledged by Phil in the introductions to the first batch of new stuff in the show, although once again the "stuckes" are everywhere. The new material, opening with a stunning version of 'Dodo', is greeted warmly by the crowd, with no repetitions of the now famous booing earlier in the tour. Here Mike lets loose some truly terrifying bass work and Tony's keyboards slash the air like a maniac. A rather swift tape change ensures that we do not miss a note of 'Abacab' and just as well because tonight's version rocks out with a vengeance. Mike and Tony trade off some ferocious licks – call and response isn't in it! Phil sings like his life depends on it and Chester indulges in some more wanton cruelty to his drum kit.

'Carpet Crawlers' calms things down for a while and the audience, once again, show their appreciation with some applause and a fine impromptu chorus. Daryl is absolutely amazing here. His playing lifts the song to new heights. 'Me and Sarah Jane' is introduced in a mixture of German and cod Yorkshire, which goes down well with everyone, although I am sure it must have bemused the Germans! Another underrated Genesis song this one, and one destined not to survive into subsequent tours, which is a shame because it is a fine showcase for the entire band. Chester really grabs the percussion by the scruff of the neck and Tony's penchant for the odd jazz chord is evident here too.

Back to *Duke* for 'Misunderstanding', which is given a workmanlike treatment here but the audience seem to like it. The taper obviously forgets his timings though, as a tape change means we miss about half of 'No Reply at All', but that doesn't spoil what there is of it. Phil sounds like he is having as good time and Daryl again puts in some fine guitar work augmented by Chester's jazzy percussion and some more of Mike's driving bass lines.

Phil then takes great delight in winding the crowd up before announcing 'Firth of Fifth', and once again cue the crowd going wild. Tony's church organ-like chords lead the sermon, with Phil delivering an impassioned vocal, before brothers Mike and Daryl join the chorus with some amazing playing. Once again, Chester threatens to tear down the roof of the hall with some ferocious percussion before Tony calms things down for a while by delivering a delightful piano solo, aided by some fervent clapping from the crowd, before Daryl takes the lead with a stunning solo, in which he really makes this classic his own.

The calls for 'Supper's Ready' are answered by an impromptu vocal rendering by Phil, which is appreciated, before he announces the arrival of another "good song", 'Man on the Corner'. Cue audience participation again. The difference in atmosphere between this show and Leiden is almost tangible here, as this is a crowd ready to give the new material a fair hearing, and the band are obviously reacting to their enthusiasm. This is tested next though as the band launch into the song that Genesis fans the world over love to hate: 'Who Dunnit?' Sorry, but even after all these years, I still can't find a kind word to say about this aberration, but here it seems to go down quite well, actually.

Not as well as the next song though, namely the evergreen 'In the Cage', which reached new heights on this tour. From its beginnings as a stand-alone track, back in 1978, it has evolved into the one medley that all Genesis fans are completely happy with as you can hear from the reaction tonight even when Phil forgets some of the words! Mike takes control here and bombards us with some amazingly beefy bass chords, over which Tony's keyboard executes almost balletic arpeggios and Daryl's soloing really beggars belief. Rampaging through 'In the Cage', the extended instrumental medley gives everyone a chance to shine and the crowd lap up each and every note, and no wonder, because tonight's performance ascends to the heavens, with a divine performance of 'Afterglow' bringing it to a suitably sublime close.

You would think that everything after this would be an anti-climax, but Genesis are masters of their craft, and 'Turn it on Again' races out of the traps like a champion boxer. A bona fide crowd pleaser and tonight Phil is determined to drag the audience along with him. His voice punches through the raucous musical accompaniment from the band and the audience are simply swept along in their wake. 'Dance on a Volcano' heralds the end of the show proper and once again it is a stunning ensemble performance from the entire band. Phil delivers a suitably dramatic vocal over a simmering musical accompaniment from Daryl and Tony. The fireworks continue with the now legendary five minutes of thunder between Chester and Phil, which simply knocks any other drum solo/duet you may hear into a cocked hat. Tonight, in keeping with the atmosphere that has been generated throughout the gig, we have a ferocious, no holds barred performance that leads ultimately into 'Los Endos' itself and a frantic, almost demonic version, which threatens to rip the hall apart.

Of course, the band were never going to be allowed to get away without an encore. It isn't long before the 'Cosmic Lawnmower' makes its presence known and the crowd simply go wild. It's party time à la Genesis and both band and audience combine making this another one of those magical nights that fans who were there always talk about with a mixture of amazement and awe. I am sure that there are better recordings than this one available, but seldom have I heard a recording that manages to really capture the sheer exhilaration that Genesis bring to their audiences as this one does.

FESTHALLE, FRANKFURT, GERMANY, 30 OCTOBER 1981

Set List: Behind the Lines/Duchess/The Lamb Lies Down on Broadway/Dodo-Lurker/Abacab/Carpet Crawlers/Me and Sarah Jane/Misunderstanding/No Reply at All/Firth of Fifth/Man on the Corner/Who-Dunnit?/Turn it on Again/In the Cage-Cinema Show-Raven-Afterglow/Dance on a Volcano/Drum Duet/Los Endos/I Know What I Like//
Source: Soundboard Recording.

As far as I know, this is the only soundboard recording from the *Abacab* tour to be in circulation and only recently at that! And what a recording it is too. By the time of this gig the band were firing on all cylinders and this fantastic recording manages to bring all of the excitement, drama, and humour of the shows vividly to life.

After the experimentation of the first couple of gigs, the set had settled down to a more or less standard two-hour show, which catalogued pretty much most areas of the band's back catalogue. Of course, the emphasis is very much on the new album, *Abacab*, and six out of the nine tracks on it are performed at this gig. The opening salvo, as usual, however, takes us a little further back to Duke, with 'Behind the Lines' and 'Duchess' both performed even better than on the 1980 tour. On the latter, Mike's meaty bass playing is plainly evident, while Daryl trades off some tasty licks of his own, too. Phil's voice is in fine form too, delivering the latter in fine angst-driven style, while Tony and Chester augment the picture with some elegant playing of their own.

'The Lamb Lies Down on Broadway' takes us even further down memory lane, opening with Tony's arpeggios flawlessly executed. Always a dramatic and exciting track it is exactly that here, once Mike recovers from a couple of bum notes. Once again, his dirty bass lines are high up in the mix for a change, giving us a chance to hear how good a player he really is. Chester is the heart of this performance. His playing is simply awesome. He never misses a beat whilst the rest of the band quietly (!) rage around him. Daryl also takes one of Steve's finest moments and makes it his own in an astonishing rendering of the track.

And so to the new stuff. Over half the new album follows in almost a "suite" opening with 'Dodo'/'Lurker', but not before Phil indulges in his now traditional mangling of the local lingo and generally winding the audience up in a gently teasing way. 'Dodo' serves notice that Genesis *are* a rock band and, indeed, *Abacab* is without doubt the heaviest Genesis album to date. Tony's staccato keyboards are once again to the fore but this track and 'Abacab' itself are both prime examples of Genesis as a band. Daryl takes the lead on 'Abacab' riffing away like crazy, while Tony and Chester augment his playing and Phil delivers another extremely powerful vocal performance – I hated this track on the album, but *live* …

'Carpet Crawlers' interrupts the flow of new material, but we won't hold that against it, will we?! Always a favourite Genesis track, and one which evidently the band themselves enjoy, it is delivered here in magnificent style. Phil's voice is uncannily similar to Peter's at times. The rhythm section of Mike, Daryl, and Chester pull off a sterling performance, while Tony's nicely-out-of-tune keyboard rounds out the picture delightfully. The rest of the show is equally crammed full of highlights. 'In the Cage' is as magnificent as usual, leading to the triumphant finale that is 'Afterglow'. Other classics include a marvellous rendering of 'Turn it on Again' and both 'Dance on a Volcano' and 'Los Endos' close the show in marvellous style. The show is rounded off with the perfect closer, 'I Know What I Like', which gets better every time and is obviously appreciated by the enthusiastic crowd.

If any recording could possibly be nominated as the one that represents the 1981 tour best, it is this one without doubt – a magnificent performance captured by an equally magnificent recording.

SAVOY THEATRE, NEW YORK, USA, 28 NOVEMBER 1981

Set List: Behind the Lines/Duchess/The Lamb Lies Down on Broadway/Dodo-Lurker/Abacab/Carpet Crawlers/Me and Sarah Jane/Misunderstanding/No Reply at All/Firth of Fifth/Man on the Corner/Who-Dunnit?/In the Cage-Cinema Show-Raven-Afterglow/Turn it on Again/Dance on a Volcano/Drum Duet/Los Endos/I Know What I Like/ Like it or Not/The Knife//
Source: Soundboard recording.

This is one of only a handful of theatre gigs that the band performed on the 1981 tour and one that was used for the subsequent *Three Sides Live* album. The more intimate setting is obviously one that the band enjoy, and from the start they are intent on having a blast. 'Behind the Lines' races out of the slips like a greyhound, the charge being led by some wonderful percussion by Chester. Meanwhile, Daryl and Tony take out their respective territories with some impeccable playing. Phil is in fine voice, no trace of the problems that were evident at some other shows on this tour. 'Duchess' also is delivered impressively and segues nicely into 'The Lamb Lies Down on Broadway', which sends the crowd into collective apoplexy. The band are firing on all cylinders here, perhaps it is the realisation that they "ain't got that many gigs left". I don't know, but they deliver a piping hot 'Lamb' for the crowd tonight.

Phil then exhorts the crowd to write to their local DJ if they like the show before the usual wind up about "old songs" and "new songs" and even threatening if the crowd are lucky they "might hear me play the trumpet". Thankfully we are spared that but not from the aural nightmare that is 'Dodo-Lurker'. A track designed for the arenas but equally at home in the smaller confines of the Savoy tonight. Daryl, Mike, and above all Chester, threaten to tear the theatre down with some fearsome playing. Chester's percussion in particular is tight and meaty. The acoustics of the room make for a much brighter 'Abacab' too, with Daryl and Tony swapping salvoes of chords, under which Mike and Chester are having their very own percussive battle too. Phil is in excellent voice and is obviously enjoying playing up to the decidedly partisan crowd.

'Carpet Crawlers' sounds absolutely superb here. Phil has seldom put in a better performance of this one than he does here tonight. Musically understated but impeccably played, especially by Tony and Daryl, who weave a beautiful web of sound, which the crowd obviously enjoy immensely. "A sordid tale of incest and bondage with bestiality overtones" next. 'Me and Sarah Jane' brings the focus back on to the band's new album. Whether the song is about all those things that Phil mentioned, I don't know, but either way it is a brilliant example of the new Genesis. Phil hammers the hell out of his tambourine whilst Tony puts a little jazz into the proceedings. Anyone missing the old Genesis "sound" should give the instrumental section of this one a listen – seriously good stuff!

'Misunderstanding' and 'No Reply at All' are given a mannered performance here, although the crowd are enthusiastic for the newer stuff unlike the crowds at some of the earlier European shows! There are shouts for 'Supper's Ready' but Phil translates from the original rubbish and relates the hilarious age old story of Cindy Lou and her enormous breasts, but oh no, we are not leading up to the torrid missive of sexual naughtiness that is 'Cinema Show', but instead 'Firth of Fifth', which once again leaps out at you from the speakers. It sounds as if the entire band have swallowed this one with a heap of collective glee and it is without doubt one of the finest performances I have ever heard.

'Man on the Corner' and 'Who-Dunnit?' pale into insignificance after what had preceded them but the crowd seem to enjoy this slice of Genesis perversity and their indulgence is rewarded by another amazing performance of 'In the Cage', which has blossomed into the centrepiece of the band's live show, and doing the unthinkable: replacing 'Supper's Ready'! Here on this crystal clear recording, every note and every nuance of the drama unfolds perfectly. Phil has never sounded better and he wrings every last bit of emotion from a superb vocal performance, while Daryl, Tony, Chester, and Mike create the aural "cage" from which he is trying to escape. The extended medley leading into 'Afterglow' simply beggars belief!

'Turn it on Again' gives notice that we are in the final straight and gets the party into full swing – not that this crowd needed any encouragement from the evidence here. The rest of the show is the typical fare that had delighted audiences across Europe and the USA and was soon to do so again in the UK and this is without doubt one of the best recordings available from this tour. Interestingly enough, tagged on to the end of it are rare live performances of 'Like it or Not' and 'The Knife', although no indication is given as to the location where they were recorded. Received wisdom has it that the former was recorded two days after the Savoy gig at the Capitol Centre in Largo NY. As for 'The Knife' ... well, it is definitely from the 1981 tour and the only gig at which I know it was performed was the band's final gig at the NEC in Birmingham on 23 December, so that is where I am putting my money. Another fantastic recording and one that belongs in any serious collector's archive.

Gabriel rejoins Genesis

PETER GABRIEL teams with Phil Collins, Tony Banks, Mike Rutherford, Daryl Stuermer and Chester Thompson to play a special benefit show at Milton Keynes Bowl on Saturday, October 2.

All the musicians will be giving their services free of any payment and profits from the show will be donated to Music, Arts And Dance Expo Ltd, the company set up to organise the musically successful but financially disastrous WOMAD Festival, recently held at Shepton Mallet.

The event, which teams Gabriel and Genesis for the first time since 'The Lamb Lies Down On Broadway' tour of Spring 1975 (though it's the first time that this set of musicians have all worked together) is a one-off gig and never likely to be repeated. Tickets for the show, which runs from 2.00 till 8.00pm, are therefore likely to be in considerable demand and these can be obtained in advance from NJF/Marquee, PO Box 4SQ, London W1A 4SQ, price £9.00. Please enclose an SAE with your cheques and postal orders which should be made out to NJF/Marquee.

A supporting bill will be announced shortly.

PART ONE: GENESIS

CHAPTER SIX
"IT'S BEEN A LONG TIME ... HASN'T IT?"
ENCORE/THREE SIDES LIVE TOUR 1982

Capitalising on the enormous success of the *Abacab* tour, the band soon announced a series of shows for the summer of 1982, covering many territories which had been missed on the previous tours. Mixing open air shows in Europe and the US along with indoor shows in the UK, the band brought their brand of magic to fans in droves.

Ostensibly as a continuation of the 1981 tour, and one to promote the recently released live album, *Three Sides Live*, the set list was quite a surprise. The oldies were back and none more welcome than 'Supper's Ready', performed here in its entirety for the first time since 1977. The juxtaposition of this and 'Misunderstanding' in the set gave the greatest possible demonstration of Genesis evolution possible. There were no repetitions of the unruly behaviour by the fans that had been seen on the 1981 tour at any of these gigs.

Whilst the set list saw the band maintain momentum, the live show continued to develop new technology. The *Vari Lites*, which had first appeared during the *Abacab* tour the year before, were put to far greater use during the 1982 tour. They certainly came into their own at the open air gigs that formed a greater proportion of the shows played on this tour. Indeed, perversely enough, thanks to the *Vari Lites*, the track universally reviled by Genesis fans – 'Who-Dunnit – became a visual (but definitely not musical) highlight of the show!

What makes 1982 a veritable *annus mirabilis* among Genesis fans, however, was the announcement of a reunion show with former frontman Peter Gabriel. This event took place on a rain-sodden Saturday 2 October 1982 in the presence of 60,000 fans at Milton Keynes Concert Bowl. The band had spent the afternoons prior to their three gigs at London's Hammersmith Odeon in rehearsal with Peter for this show, and I suppose the entire tour could be viewed as an exorcism of the band's past, for it was to be the last time such a large amount of older material was included in their set. The Milton Keynes gig itself was a shambolic affair with missed cues and forgotten lyrics but nobody really cared, and when Steve Hackett was announced onstage for the encores, I doubt if there was a dry eye in the crowd.

TENNIS CENTRE, FOREST HILLS, NEW YORK, USA, 22 AUGUST 1982

Set List: Dance on a Volcano/Behind the Lines/Follow You Follow Me/Dodo-Lurker/Abacab/ No Reply at All*/ Paperlate*/Supper's Ready/Misunderstanding/Man on the Corner/Who-Dunnnit?/In the Cage- Cinema Show-Raven-Afterglow/Turn it on Again/Drum Duet/Los Endos/The Lamb Lies Down on Broadway/Watcher of the Skies/I Know What I Like//
*Tracks performed with the Earth, Wind & Fire horn section.
Source: Audience Recording.

Genesis do open air and it doesn't rain shock! Yes, the 1982 tour saw the band putting in their fair share of open air gigs including this one, which comes towards the end of the American leg of the tour. An audience recording again, and one which gives some idea of the size of the venue in question, but surprisingly clear nonetheless.

Fundamentally an extension of the previous year's tour, the set still has most of the same elements that made that show such an exciting one for fans. There are some major changes as well though. 'Dance on a Volcano' has been promoted to set opener for one and it is delivered at a rapid pace here. 'Behind the Lines' also races out of the traps and here Daryl really lets rip with some fearsome riffs racing along with some wonderful playing from Tony as well. Phil's voice seems to be holding up well thus far and the audience sound suitably enthusiastic. 'Follow You Follow Me' also receives a warm welcome from the crowd.

Phil then announces that the band are in fact the opening act for the tennis, which raises a laugh, and the usual tease of playing some old songs and some not so old songs, which leads nicely into 'Dodo-Lurker-Abacab'. Lumbering along like some ungainly giant, this unlikely trio proves that the band can really rock. Daryl and Mike sound as if they are having a great time and Mike can even be heard on the chorus.

The evening then takes a slightly surprising turn as Phil announces the Phoenix Horns on stage to a mixed reaction from the crowd. This is only the second time in the band's history that additional musicians have played onstage with them – the other having been the preceding night's concert at the same venue! The drum machine intro to 'No Reply at All' gets things going and the horns certainly do add something to the performance and Mike certainly delivers the goods on bass making this an entirely funkier version than we had seen on the previous year's tour. Phil's voice certainly takes a battering on this one though, but he seems to be having fun. An unannounced 'Paperlate' takes everyone by surprise and certainly livens up the crowd with Chester putting in some fine licks on his kit. Phil's voice is evidently feeling the strain here, which might be why the song was dropped from the set after tonight's performance.

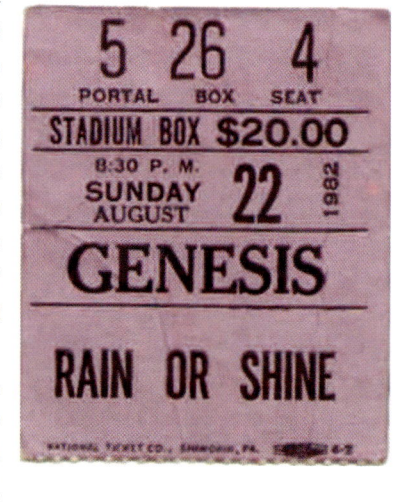

Now to the "old shit" that Phil had mentioned earlier in the evening, celebrating the tenth anniversary of this song and we even get the story of "two virgins", which Phil certainly seems to be enjoying almost as much as the crowd. Of course, it doesn't lead into 'Cinema Show' but instead … 'Supper's Ready', which sends the crowd into hysterics –at this and just about every other show the reaction was the same. The twelve strings have been well and truly dusted off and the opening is a delight even over the cheers of the crowd. Phil's voice, which sounded so strained earlier, is in fine form here. The song as usual has several peaks and troughs but always the musicianship is impeccable. Mike's bass rumbles along like an avalanche, while Tony and Daryl execute some almost balletic pirouettes on their respective instruments, and Chester is the back bone of the ensemble who delivers a truly remarkable percussive performance during the 'Apocalypse in 9/8' section – even on this average sounding audience recording you can almost feel the tension and excitement.

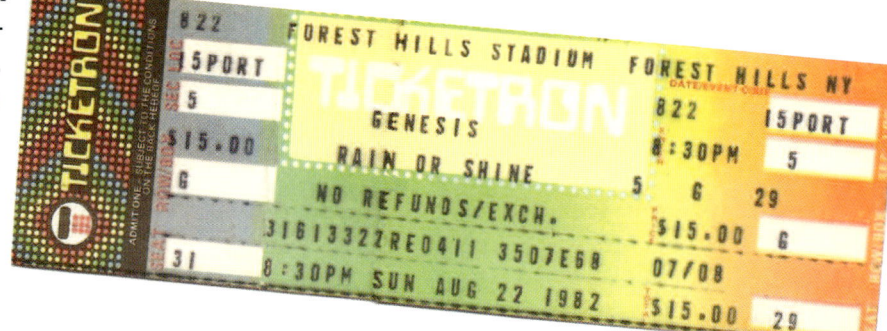

As has become the norm by now, the band contrast the epic with the concise. 'Misunderstanding', the band's first proper American hit, is greeted like an old friend here. More recent material goes down well too. 'Man on the Corner' and even 'Who-Dunnit?' are greeted with cheers, although the performance of either can best be described as studied rather than exceptional. With 'Supper's Ready' in the set, it is surprising that the band opted to retain 'In the Cage', which had taken its place as the beating heart of the show on the last three tours, especially with its ever evolving medley. Even up against its predecessor, however, it manages to more than hold its own tonight with a fine performance by everyone, which is greeted by enthusiastic cheers from the crowd. 'Turn it on Again' is also greeted by wild cheers from the audience. The other half of the duo, namely 'Dance on a Volcano', finally appears here with the ubiquitous drum duet between Chester and Phil, leading into a bracing performance of 'Los Endos', which closes the show proper.

Phil then asks, "If you know this one then you will sing along, won't ya?" as a snappy drum intro from Chester leads into a marvellous rendering of 'The Lamb Lies Down on Broadway'. Tony and Daryl share the honours here with some incredible playing, and Phil sounds in his element, obviously hamming it up for the crowd. A neat segue leads into the finale, a nifty combination of 'It' and the instrumental section from 'Watcher of the Skies', in which Daryl and Chester battle away against each other for poll position. The fun isn't over though, as the band take to the stage again for a sing-along version of 'I Know What I Like', which even on this evidence must have had the audience in hysterics. Phil puts on his usual rogues gallery of character voices, and you can even hear Mike and Tony on the chorus! A magnificent ending to what was evidently a great night.

PERFORMING ARTS CENTER, SARATOGA SPRINGS, NEW YORK, USA, 26 AUGUST 1982

Set List: Dance on a Volcano/Behind the Lines/Follow You Follow Me/Dodo-Lurker/Abacab/Supper's Ready/Misunderstanding/Man on the Corner/Who-Dunnit?/In the Cage-Cinema Show-Raven- Afterglow/Turn it on Again/Drum Duet/Los Endos/The Lamb Lies Down on Broadway/Watcher of the Skies/I Know What I Like//
Source: Soundboard recording.

Almost a month into the tour and the band are here at Saratoga Springs for what is, without doubt, one of the best recordings available from this tour. There is some doubt as to the source of this recording, but what is not in question is the superior sound quality that it has throughout, which leads me to suspect that it is taken from the mixing desk.

As usual, the band open the proceedings with a storming rendition of 'Dance on a Volcano', in which Daryl, Mike, and Chester battle away as if their very lives depended on it. 'Behind the Lines' is another glorious anthem led by Tony and Mike's incredibly dirty bass and Daryl's soaring guitar, which is absolutely incredible here. 'Follow You Follow Me' is next, and Phil puts in a wonderful vocal performance here.

Still promoting the relatively "new" *Abacab* album, the trio of 'Dodo-Lurker' and 'Abacab' itself are next and Phil really stretches his vocal chords here. Musical honours are shared, however, between Tony, Mike, and Chester who really unleash some savage power chords throughout, while Chester, as usual, is the musical backbone of the ensemble.

The biggest surprise of the 1982 tour though was the resurrection of the classic 'Supper's Ready', which was being performed in its entirety for the first time in five years. Phil's lead up to this classic is hilarious. He teases the audience in much the same way as he used to do with the introduction to 'The Lady Lies' whilst leading the audience down the garden path of "Two virgins ... Romeo and Juliet," the audience, who sound as though they are in a neighbouring venue, are obviously having hysterics as Phil finally announces the real identity of the song, and the band begin this magnificent opus in fine style with some lovely acoustic playing from Mike and Daryl. The mixture of high drama and low farce that makes this song so special need no real explanations but every member of the band has their moment to shine here and this is a truly glorious performance.

Book-ending this with 'Misunderstanding' only goes to serve to emphasise the breadth of Genesis' compositional skills, and besides which, it was the band's first bona fide hit in the US so why not play it? 'Man on the Corner' and 'Who-Dunnit' are next, both of which are tracks that frankly leave me cold, although even I have to grudgingly admit that the tongue-in-cheek humour of the latter deserves a better press than it has had from critics and fans alike.

By the time we reach the 'In the Cage' medley, it is easy to see that this is a band really on the top of their game. Instrumentally, this is top notch stuff. No one puts a foot wrong and by the time 'Afterglow' makes its majestic entrance into the proceedings it is obvious that the entire band are having the time of their lives. Daryl's guitar augments Tony's magnificent keyboard playing and Phil puts in a truly stunning vocal performance, full of drama and angst.

Nor was the rest of the show to be an anti-climax either, with 'Turn it on Again' giving the audience – and band – no time for a breather. Mike and Daryl trade some meaty licks whilst Chester handles the unusual time signature with his own inimitable style, laying down a flawless back beat, over which Tony puts down his own inimitable chords. Phil is in his element here too, evidently hamming up to the crowd and generally having a blast.

The ubiquitous "five minutes of thunder", otherwise now known as the "drum thing", lead us nicely into a storming version of 'Los Endos', which at times threatens to create a minor earthquake and closes the show in a suitably dramatic fashion. Of course, encores are expected, and they aren't long in coming either, beginning with Phil asking the audience, "If you know this one, you will sing along, won't you?" As if they would need any invitation to join in on the mighty 'Lamb Lies Down on Broadway', on which Phil really delivers an impassioned vocal underpinned by some superb playing from Daryl and Tony. The segue into the instrumental section of 'Watcher of the Skies' may be a little forced, but there is no denying the power of the music, during which the entire band evidently give their respective musical instruments some serious abuse.

'I Know What I Like' closes the show and once again the month or so on the road shows here as the performance is flawless. Tony and Mike trade some wonderful effects and Phil torments his tambourine before putting in a truly tongue-in-cheek vocal aided by some excellent backing vocals from both Tony and Mike. This is a superb ending to a marvellous recording – one of the best available from this tour.

WILHELM KOCH STADION, HAMBURG, GERMANY, 10 SEPTEMBER 1982

Set List: Dance on a Volcano/Behind the Lines/Follow You Follow Me/Dodo-Lurker/Abacab/Supper's Ready/Misunderstanding/In the Cage-Cinema Show-Raven-Afterglow/Turn it on Again/Drum Duet/Los Endos/The Lamb Lies Down on Broadway/Watcher of the Skies//
Source: Audience Recording.

This was another memorable gig for yours truly, it being my first trip overseas to see the band in concert, after having missed the chance to see them being booed in Leiden the year before in favour of watching Mr Hackett on my home turf.

The biggest surprise at this gig was the announcement on the tickets that the band had "Special Guests". Who were they? None other than archetypal Prog Rockers, King Crimson. For once the weather gods were kind to both us and the band and the day of the gig was a wonderfully sunny one. King Crimson opened up with a forty-minute or so set promoting their new album, *Discipline*, and they warmed up the crowd nicely.

With no new album to promote, this tour was fundamentally a continuation of the previous year's promotional work for *Abacab*. As such, the set was not expected to be radically different than the one that had preceded it but this time round there were to be several surprises. Even the opening trio of tracks was different this time round, opening with a stunning version of 'Dance on a Volcano' and 'Behind the Lines' with 'Follow You Follow Me' bringing up the rear to get the crowd in the mood.

Even Phil's banter was definitely on par as he poked gentle fun out of the unfortunate name of the venue. Even acknowledging the presence of a sizeable English contingent and promising to play, "*Die altes stuckes und die neues* stuckes ... *stuckes* everywhere!" Before the band launched into a full-blooded version of 'Dodo-Lurker', which elicited a solitary playful boo from someone who obviously remembered the previous year's antics. If these tracks rocked out in 1981, then they were ever further out this time round, reiterating Genesis' credentials as a *rock* band; an opinion reinforced even further by a marvellous rendering of 'Abacab' itself, during which Mike's bass and Daryl's guitar traded off some fearsome licks.

The biggest surprise of the evening, however, was reserved for the announcement after this track that the band had "dusted off their twelve-string guitars" to play a song that was ten years old that very evening. Total bollocks of course, but the announcement of 'Supper's Ready' sent everyone into orbit. I had never had the opportunity of seeing this classic performed and relished every moment. Was I the only one seeing the angel in the sun at the end? I think not! This was one of those evenings where the band and audience merged into one entity and it was bizarre to look behind me during the 'Apocalypse in 9/8' section to see a field of white crosses as everyone held their posters up to repel the evil one – a memorable moment!

Nor was the rest of the evening an anti-climax either. Contrasting 'Supper's Ready' with 'Misunderstanding', which followed it in rapid order, was an inspired choice, reiterating the sheer variety in the band's catalogue. 'In the Cage' retained its place as the emotional heart of the band's show with a performance high on drama, humour, and impeccable musicianship by all concerned. Nor had the legendary five minutes of thunder that preceded 'Los Endos' lost any of its fire. The evening closed in classic style with a perfect matching of 'The Lamb Lies Down on Broadway' and 'Watcher of the Skies', which sent everyone home happy. The recording here is an above average audience one that manages to capture the drama and excitement of the show without being spoiled too much by excessive crowd noise and is well worth a listen.

LEISURE CENTRE, DEESIDE, WALES, 22 SEPTEMBER 1982

Set List: Dance on a Volcano/Behind the Lines/Follow You Follow Me/Dodo-Lurker/Abacab/Supper's Ready/Misunderstanding/Man on the Corner/Who-Dunnit?/In the Cage-Cinema Show-Raven-Afterglow/Turn it on Again/Drum Duet/Los Endos/The Lamb Lies Down on Broadway/Watcher of the Skies/I Know What I Like//
Source: Audience Recording.

Aaah yes, the gig Genesis did on an ice rink! An unusual place for a gig to say the least but at the time the Leisure Centre was a regular venue for gigs, but not the most comfortable one, I can tell you! Mind you, I suppose you could say it was a "cool" gig. This is an audience recording that thoroughly reflects not only the cavernous size of the venue but also the excitement of the capacity crowd itself. By the time the band reached the UK for the final leg of the tour they were at their peak and none more so than at this gig. The opening pairing of 'Dance on a Volcano' and 'Behind the Lines' are driven by Chester's quick fire percussion and Mike's rock solid rhythms, while Daryl and Tony battle away leaving Phil to deliver an impassioned vocal, augmented by the rent-a-chorus crowd.

'Follow You Follow Me' is greeted like an old friend here and the crowd are in every bit as good voice as Phil on this one. Audiophiles among you will probably loathe this recording but I *love* it, probably because, once again, it is a gig I actually attended but even so, the audience are part of the show and they played a blinder at this gig!

'Dodo-Lurker' and 'Abacab' next and I was relieved to hear that the fans had taken the newer material to their hearts and there were no repeats of the now infamous booing incident that had marred several of the gigs on the 1981 tour. Phil's introduction is as corny as ever, setting up the rivalries between Manchester and Liverpool as well as exhorting the crowd not to push forward because the people at the front were having their nipples crushed! Anyone who thinks that Genesis don't do rock should listen to this recording, where once again Mike, Daryl, and Chester lay down as solid a rhythm as you could wish for and Tony's keyboards grind away like a glacier gnawing away at bedrock.

The announcement, after an extended intro by Phil, of the classic 'Supper's Ready' is greeted with hysteria by the crowd in exactly the same way as it had been a few weeks before when I saw the band in Hamburg. The performance here is equally as dramatic, finely wrought and simply magical.

The rest of the show is far from anti-climactic though. In fact, by the time the band reach the real climax of the show with the now ubiquitous 'In the Cage' medley, the audience were certainly ready for a change of pace. We didn't get it though, as the band tore through even more of their finest moments, including a sublime 'The Lamb Lies Down on Broadway' and a raucous 'I Know What I Like'. Certainly what this recording lacks in terms of sound quality it more than makes up for in terms of atmosphere and excitement, capturing Genesis at the peak of their game.

MARQUEE CLUB, LONDON, ENGLAND, 27 SEPTEMBER 1982
Set List: Dance on a Volcano/Behind the Lines/Follow You Follow Me/Dodo-Lurker/Abacab/Supper's Ready/Man on the Corner/No Reply at All/In the Cage-Cinema Show-Raven-Afterglow/Turn it on Again/Drum Duet/Los Endos/The Lamb Lies Down on Broadway/I Know What I Like//
Source: Audience Recording.

Earlier in the year, advertisements for a gig at the Marquee by "The Garden Wall" didn't fool Genesis fans and the mere few hundred tickets for this gig at the home of so many of their earliest triumphs were soon snapped up.

You can tell immediately that you are in a small room as compared to the resounding echo in some of the venues the band were now accustomed to playing. 'Dance on a Volcano' sounds suitably fiery and gets everyone in the mood. Straight from that to a particularly feisty 'Behind the Lines', in which Daryl and Chester really take the bit between their teeth. The rest of the band sound superbly confident as they should be after almost two months on the road. Phil sounds superb here, none of the hoarseness that you can hear in other recordings from this and subsequent tours. Mike plugs along with an almost reggae rhythm that certainly gives the song a far looser feel and the crowd evidently love it. A funky 'Follow You Follow Me' comes next. Daryl and Tony trade licks quite happily whilst the audience gives Phil a helping hand (or voice) with the singing.

Phil acknowledges the band's debt to the venue in his introduction to the next songs before being interrupted by a fan asking him to take his jacket off for some bizarre reason. I know the Marquee is in the midst of the Soho strip club area but even so! Anyway, on with the show. A hard hitting rendering of 'Dodo-Lurker' and 'Abacab', where once again the rhythm section of Mike and Chester really impresses. Chester doesn't miss a beat and Mike's bass must have given everyone in the venue a free foot massage – it's *loud*! 'Abacab' itself has by now become a firm favourite in the set and tonight it shows why it has acquired that position. Daryl and Mike prove they are no slouches in the hard rockin' department, while Tony lays down some typically enigmatic chords, and once again Chester holds the whole thing together with some really solid yet fluid playing.

Before the advent of the Internet, word of mouth was how fans found out about things like set lists. The gasp of surprise here when Phil announces a song celebrating yet another tenth anniversary tonight (must be like the Queen with a multitude of birthdays, eh?) is almost tangible. 'Supper's Ready' was born in places like the Marquee and so tonight's performance is a little bit special. Crowd and band are united in paying homage to this classic slice of Genesis and Phil needs no crib sheet tonight. He just has to read the lips of the fans at the front who are in fine voice throughout. The assembled acoustic guitars of Daryl, Mike, and Tony are gradually replaced as the song builds to its inevitable climax and by the time we reach it I am sure the entire audience can see the angel standing in the sun – Genesis seldom sound better than this.

From the sublime to ... well not quite the ridiculous but 'Man on the Corner' can't really be effectively compared to what has preceded it, although it is a fine slice of the slimmed-down Genesis that was rapidly emerging in the 1980s. 'Misunderstanding' also pales by comparison but the crowd seem to like it, and there is some boisterous singing throughout, which Phil seems to play up to.

Back to the classics for the evergreen 'In the Cage', which sounds infinitely better here in a smaller room. The claustrophobic atmosphere that the song generates is magnified by the confines of the club. Two months on the road has definitely paid off and the entire band are at the top of their game tonight. Tony's keyboards sound like a man climbing the walls whilst Chester and Mike are trying to batter their way out of the Marquee with their instruments. The instrumental (or should that be mental?) medley that leads us to the glorious climacteric 'Afterglow' certainly show the band at their peak and the finale itself is well ... nuff said!

The rest of the evening is far from an anti-climax though. A no-nonsense run through of 'Turn it on Again' keeps the momentum up. Thankfully, the taper just manages to turn the tape over in time to capture the start of the drum duet that Phil and Chester have made such an integral part of the show. Tonight they rattle along in perfect unison like a runaway train heading towards the inevitable

'Los Endos', which grows in stature with each performance. Tonight's is stunning and benefits enormously from being performed in a more intimate setting although at times it seems that the gig was going to become an open air one as the band seem intent on ripping the Marquee roof off!

A short break follows before the band return for the obligatory encores. A rattling percussive intro from Chester heralds 'The Lamb Lies Down on Broadway' and cue the audience going bananas. It's party time at the Marquee and everyone is taking part, although unfortunately a couple of nasty tape fades mean that we don't get to enjoy the complete performance. Was the taper spotted by security? Did their batteries let them down? We shall never know but thankfully, whatever the problem was, it was resolved in time to capture the encore: a blistering performance of 'I Know What I like', proving so hot in fact that even Phil says, "It's too hot for all that shit." Not too hot for the band to treat the lucky faithful here tonight to an uptempo celebratory conclusion to what was evidently a very special night.

HAMMERSMITH ODEON, LONDON, ENGLAND, 28 SEPTEMBER 1982 (Afternoon)
Set List: Back in NYC/Dancing with the Moonlit Knight/Carpet Crawlers/Firth of Fifth/Musical Box/The Lamb Lies Down on Broadway/Fly on a Windshield/In the Cage/Supper's Ready/The Knife/Solsbury Hill (Takes 1-3)//
Source: Soundboard Recording.

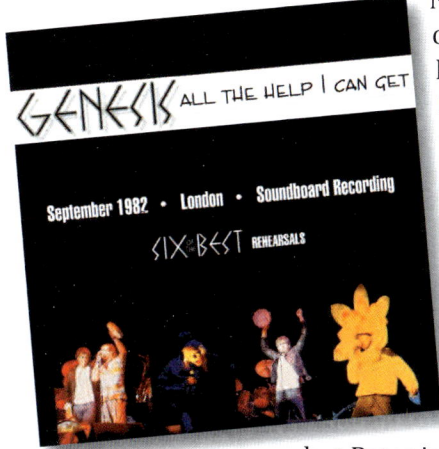

No, your eyes are not deceiving you. In the final run up to the imminent "Six of the Best" reunion gig, the band spent their afternoons at each of their three Hammersmith shows rehearsing the set for that gig with Peter Gabriel. Fortunately (for us if not the band) one of these rehearsals has recently surfaced and what fascinating listening it makes!

From the outset you can clearly hear how uncomfortable Peter sounds trying to sing some of these classics. 'Back in NYC' at least sounds good, although the contrast between Peter's unease and the confidence of the rest of the band, and Tony in particular is quite surprising. 'Dancing with the Moonlit Knight' sounds extremely strained. Peter is evidently struggling not only with the key the song is in but also to remember the words, which, I suppose isn't really surprising!

'Carpet Crawlers' works much better with some fine playing from Tony but Peter is still having vocal problems. Daryl and Tony, however, are right on the money with their playing. 'Firth of Fifth' sounds rather flat here. I suppose that may have something to do with the lack of the ambience generated by an audience. Once again Peter struggles to remember the lyrics but his musical accompaniment is workmanlike, helped no doubt by the presence of the song in the previous year's live set. Daryl here really stands out with some fine playing.

It is weird hearing 'Musical Box' without its accompanying story and once again Peter is having real trouble here. You can clearly hear Phil's backing vocals at times and the contrast between the two is quite surprising. Once again Daryl, who is always the guy the band look to, to tell them how songs go, is obviously leading them on this one. 'The Lamb Lies Down on Broadway' obviously has benefited from its inclusion in the current live set and musically this is every bit as good as it had been at any of the shows on this year's tour. Peter sounds much more comfortable with this one, although he is still tripping over lyrics at times. Phil and Chester put in a delightful percussive backing here.

'Fly on a Windshield' is a real surprise. The band put in a remarkable performance here, especially when you bear in mind that this song hasn't been performed as part of a live show for seven years. Tony and Daryl are truly awesome here. Daryl's guitar sounds like an aggravated wasp and Mike lets rip with some thunderous bass playing and this is obviously a track that the band are enjoying playing again. This is in turn followed by 'In the Cage' with Peter trying out some of his intro patter, while Tony, Mike, and Chester get the song started in typically dramatic fashion, although Peter is late with his cue – again and there are missed lyrics galore too – amusing for us, the unexpected listeners, but not something that he would want to be reminded of, I suspect – sorry, Peter!

'Supper's Ready' is a joy to hear even in this stripped down version. Musically, once again, the band lead the way and here Peter redeems himself with a sensitive reading of the part, which gets better as the song progresses towards its ultimate climax. With no audience present, however, this is a somewhat soulless presentation but fascinating to hear in its raw form nonetheless.

'The Knife' sounds surprisingly good too having only made an occasional appearance over the last few years. Peter still manages to conjure up the passion here and even though he changes pace halfway through it doesn't alter the fact that it still sounds great to hear him belting this one out. Daryl does a grand job taking on Mr Phillips' mantle here and Tony holds everyone on the firm and narrow throughout.

Three takes of the only non-Genesis song to be played at the reunion gig are next and with 'Solsbury Hill' it is the band who sound out of place for once. This is a deceptively easy song until you have to play it. Peter is assured and confident but the band sound surprisingly tentative here, which is a nice change! It is recordings such as this that fans love to hear and all too seldom have the chance. It isn't really surprising though. Careers can be made or broken by stuff like this but Genesis needn't worry, their reputation for live excellence is assured, and this is merely a fascinating warts and all glimpse behind the scenes.

CONCERT BOWL, MILTON KEYNES, ENGLAND, 2 OCTOBER 1982

Set List: Back in NYC/Dancing with the Moonlit Knight/Carpet Crawlers/Firth of Fifth/Musical Box/Solsbury Hill/Turn it on Again/The Lamb Lies Down on Broadway/ Fly on a Windshield/Broadway Melody of '74/In the Cage/Supper's Ready/I Know What I Like/The Knife//
Source: Audience Recording.

This was the event that Genesis fans had dreamed of since 1975! Gabriel reunited for one night only with his former cohorts. This was a charitable event to help rescue Gabriel from the financial problems accruing from the first WOMAD Festival a few months earlier. The event had been an artistic success but a financial disaster and this gig was the result of the band's desire to help their former band mate.

Personally, I doubt if the fans could have cared less about the reasons behind the gig but the only thing that mattered was, "Do you have your ticket for Milton Keynes?!" Fortunately I was one of the lucky ones who did have one and who braved the atrocious weather on the day. Sadly, no soundboard recording of this gig has appeared, although it does reside within the band's own sound archive along with the film of the gig too – yes, despite rumours to the contrary the gig *was* filmed!

Anyway, what we do have is an above average audience recording that certainly manages to give a very good impression of the atmosphere on that soggy night! The band won't mind me saying that this gig was not their finest hour – far from it and Peter's performance was shambolic at best, but when the magic happened, everything else could be forgotten – and forgiven! No one who was at the gig will ever forget Peter's emergence from the white coffin clad as Rael to lead us through 'One More Night' of nostalgia. Certain tracks worked really well. 'Carpet Crawlers' and 'Musical Box' were as electrifying as always. The token nods to both Gabriel's solo career and that of the band's post-Gabriel period – 'Solsbury Hill' and 'Turn it On Again' – were a nice gesture, though they seemed somewhat out of place here, and Peter merely proved once again how poor a drummer he was when he traded places with Phil during the latter!

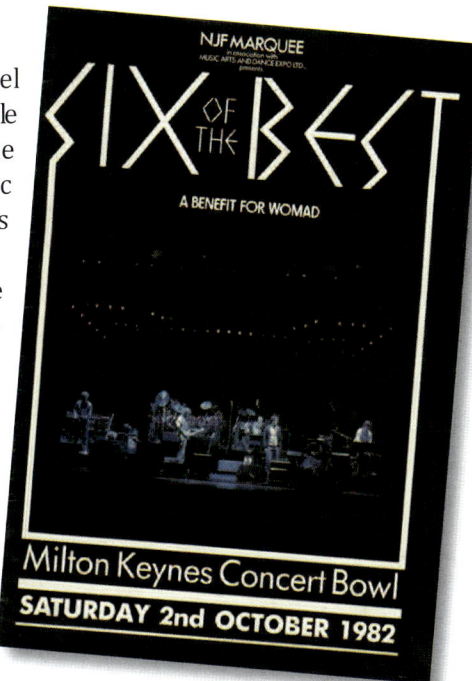

Seeing 'Supper's Ready' performed by Gabriel was astonishing. I still think that Phil sings it better than Peter ever can but there is no denying the raw passion that Peter brings to this track. I am sure that I wasn't the only one who nearly died of shock when Steve Hackett was announced on stage for the encores and no matter how ramshackle the performances of 'I Know What I Like' and 'The Knife' were in purely artistic terms, the sheer dynamism coming off the stage made up for it. This is another essential addition to any collection, and in lieu of the soundboard, the best available recording is that released by the FADE project some years ago.

A Selection Of Shows: Genesis & Solo Live Guide 1976-2014

PART ONE: GENESIS

A Selection Of Shows: Genesis & Solo Live Guide 1976-2014

Genesis

PART ONE: GENESIS

CHAPTER SEVEN
"I CAN SEE YOU MAMA"
THE MAMA TOUR 1983-84

By 1983 the band were undoubtedly one of the major forces in rock. Their progress over the preceding half a dozen years had been astonishing. Phil's arrival on the solo artist stage also must have made many question the potential longevity of the group itself. No such problems in 1983, however, when the band returned to record their first studio album since *Abacab*. A problematic affair it proved to be too. The first evidence of the new look Genesis appeared in the shape of 'Mama', a six-minute drum machine-led song about a man's obsession with a prostitute – hardly your typical Genesis fare now, eh?

The album itself, titled simply *Genesis*, swiftly followed and continued the trend that had been begun with *Abacab*. This is an album where you can easily see that the band struggled to find suitable material. The first four tracks are without doubt the best. 'Mama' and 'Home by the Sea/Second Home by the Sea' are among the most dramatic and musically satisfying on any Genesis album. Even 'That's All' provides some light comic relief. The rest of the album, however, is a mix of the mediocre and in the case of 'Illegal Alien', the downright offensive. It certainly made one wonder what the new stage show was going to be like.

Fortunately, no such problems were apparent in the selection of material for the new show. Once again, the emphasis was firmly on the new, with six tracks from the new album featuring in the live set and the remainder drawn from the preceding two albums. What older material was included was restricted to two extended medleys, although the second based around 'In the Cage' had already developed something of a history itself. Many fans were dissatisfied with this increasing restriction of the band's back catalogue. However, with a collection of material such as theirs something will always have to give way, and after all, tours are all about promoting *new* albums, aren't they?

The new stage show revolved entirely around the use of the Vari Lite that Genesis had invested so much time and effort in creating. The result was an astonishing visual display that has never been equalled. The use of these lights and the configurations they were able to achieve had to be seen to be believed and showed that the band still had an eye for the dramatic and a flair for the visual that augmented but never overpowered the music.

Once again, this was almost an exclusively US and Canadian tour with over seventy shows played on the North American continent between November 1983 and February 1984 before the band finally returned home for a series of five gigs at the National Exhibition Centre in Birmingham, which were filmed for the subsequent video release, the *Mama Tour*.

HORTON FIELDHOUSE, NORMAL, ILLINOIS, USA, 7 NOVEMBER 1983

Set List: Dodo-Lurker/Carpet Crawlers/That's All/Mama/Illegal Alien/Eleventh Earl of Mar-Ripples-Squonk-Firth of Fifth/Man on the Corner/Who-Dunnit?/Home by the Sea/Second Home by the Sea/ Keep it Dark/It's Gonna Get Better/Follow You Follow Me/In the Cage-Cinema Show-Raven-Afterglow/Abacab/Drum Duet/Los Endos/ Misunderstanding/Turn it on Again (Inc: Sixties Medley)// Source: Audience Recording.

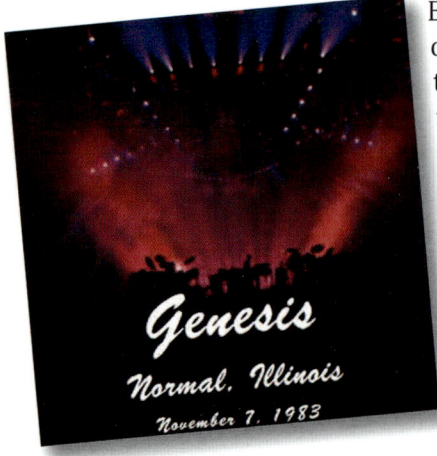

By 1983 Genesis were a bona fide super group and the predominant feature of the 1983/84 tour was the sheer size of the venues that they were now able to play and fill. In the US only the biggest indoor arenas were played and on this, the opening night of the tour, you get a very good idea of exactly how big these places are!

An audience recording again documents this show in lieu of any radio/soundboard recording and right from the start you can hear the echoey acoustics of what must be a massive hall. The set tonight is fundamentally different to what would become the standard set for the first leg of the tour and as such we are treated to a few rarities.

The opening salvo of 'Dodo-Lurker' is greeted by thunderous applause by the crowd and at times it is difficult to hear the band above the noise made by the audience! One thing is not in any doubt, however, and that is the band are determined to have a good time and it shows throughout the performance. 'Carpet Crawlers' and 'That's All' nicely bookend the old and new faces of Genesis before the drama is heightened by the drumbeat intro to 'Mama', at which point cue the audience going bananas. Even on an audience recording such as this there is no denying the sheer scale and atmosphere that this track generates.

Another interesting facet of this recording is the unusual selection of tracks for the first medley. By the time the band reached the UK in February of the following year, this had become a somewhat standardised affair, but the opening night sees the band still unsure of exactly what tracks to bring together. So here we have the unlikely combination of 'Eleventh Earl of Mar', in which we get not only the intro but almost the entire song, which is always a delight to hear, and this in turn gives way to a wonderful segue into 'Ripples', in which joint honours are shared by Tony and Daryl – when you can hear them over the audience hysterics, that is! 'Squonk' picks up the pace a bit next and Phil delivers it in fine style before the instrumental honours are once again shared by Tony and Daryl for an impeccable 'Firth of Fifth'.

'Man on the Corner' and 'Who-Dunnit?' are something of an anti-climax after the previous stuff but the audience greet them with wild applause and the band seem to be having a great time playing them. 'Keep it Dark' was, perhaps for me, the biggest surprise of this tour, it being one of the few tracks on the *Abacab* album that I liked. This one was a delight to hear for the first time, replete with Phil's corny story about the "other world", and it certainly didn't get any better as the tour progressed! Sadly, for some reason, the recording I have cuts out halfway through this track and into 'It's Gonna Get Better', which for me has to be one of the most disappointing tracks that Genesis have ever penned!

The rest of the show is fundamentally the same as it would remain for the rest of the tour with the exception of 'Abacab', which got the show finale off to a suitably explosive start before 'Los Endos' rounded off the show proper. 'Misunderstanding' and 'Turn it on Again' now accompanied by a hilarious medley of sixties hits rounded out a suitably impressive opening night, one which, from the evidence here, both the band and the audience thoroughly enjoyed.

TACOMA DOME, SEATTLE, WASHINGTON DC, USA, 10 JANUARY 1984

Set List: Dodo-Lurker/Abacab/That's All/Mama/Eleventh Earl of Mar-Squonk-Firth of Fifth/Illegal Alien/Man on the Corner/Who-Dunnit?/Home by the Sea/Second Home by the Sea/Keep it Dark/It's Gonna Get Better/Follow You Follow Me/In the Cage-Cinema Show-In That Quiet Earth-Afterglow/Drum Duet/Los Endos/Misunderstanding/Turn it on Again //
Source: Audience Recording.

The band were back on the road in the US again after their Christmas break and this recording is from the third gig on the second leg of the tour. Once again, an audience recording stands in for any soundboard/radio recording, and once again the sound betrays the sheer size of the venue played.

The openers 'Dodo-Lurker' and 'Abacab' fill the hall that reverberates to the massive sound that the band generate. The recording is somewhat lacking in bass but in some respects that is no bad thing because it would probably blow you speakers – not to mention seriously piss off your neighbours! The crowd are certainly on the band's side tonight and their presence is felt throughout the recording.

After the hard rock opening we are given a moment or two to regain our breath with the band's own cod country & western number, 'That's All', in which Phil's introduction doesn't get any less corny as he winds up the audience. The band certainly seem to be enjoying themselves but you would struggle to hear them above the audience who are in hysterics by this point. Tony's intro to 'Mama' is given an additional eerie touch by the echoey acoustics of the hall and Phil's vocal has just the right combination of angst and bathos.

The sop to the older fans is introduced by yet another corny performance by Phil who seems to be relishing his role as MC tonight. By this time in the tour, the medley had settled down to comprise segments of 'Eleventh Earl of Mar', 'Squonk', and 'Firth of Fifth', all of which are greeted with wild applause here. Daryl's guitar playing, augmented by Tony's keyboards on the former, is simply superb, while Mike and Chester's impeccable rhythm playing drive 'Squonk' along at a fine pace, and once again Daryl and Tony share the honours equally on a racy version of 'Firth of Fifth'. Daryl's guitar cuts through the crowd noise like a knife (pardon the pun!).

'Illegal Alien' was one of those handful of songs that Genesis have written that seems to have courted controversy but the audience tonight don't seem to care about that and the band put in a workmanlike performance. 'Man on the Corner' puts in another appearance here. Strange that it was soon to disappear from the set in time for the band's final UK shows. The remainder of this show consists of the by now standard set and here is little deviation from what has become a familiar set by a band road savvy if not perhaps a little road weary after some three months of touring. Either way, this recording once again manages to capture something of the magic of show, although its quality won't appeal to everyone.

LLOYD NOBEL CENTER, NORMAN, ILLINOIS, USA, 19 JANUARY 1984

Set List: Dodo-Lurker/Abacab/That's All/Mama/Eleventh Earl of Mar-Behind the Lines-Firth of Fifth-Musical Box/Illegal Alien/Man on the Corner/Who-Dunnit?/Home by the Sea/Second Home by the Sea/Keep it Dark/It's Gonna Get Better/Follow You Follow Me/In the Cage-Cinema Show-Raven-Afterglow/Drum Duet/Los Endos/ Misunderstanding/Turn it on Again (Inc: Sixties Medley)//
Source: Audience Recording.

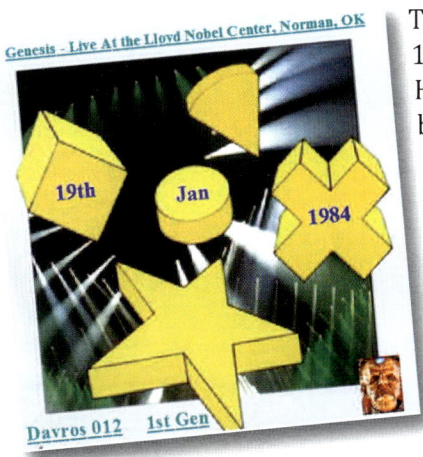

The massive tour of the USA and Canada took the band into the New Year of 1984 and usually the set had by now coalesced into a standardised one. However, even at this stage of their career, Genesis had the ability to take us by surprise occasionally, as this recording demonstrates.

Sadly, what we have here is a very mediocre audience recording, which is a shame, because from the outset it is obvious that the band have an enthusiastic crowd cheering them on every step of the way. As usual, the opening salvo of tracks is from the *Abacab* album and from what can he heard here, the band are in fine form. Tony and Daryl in particular grab the audience by the balls with some impressive playing. 'That's All' and 'Mama', which are prefaced by Phil's usual corny introduction, are fine in themselves but it is difficult to really gauge their effect from the recording.

After experimenting with the opening medley of the show earlier in the tour, it had settled into a recognised pattern. Until tonight, that is! 'Eleventh Earl of Mar' opens the medley in suitably dramatic fashion although sound quality really lets the recording down. It is what follows that makes this recording of interest though, as instead of segueing into the usual 'Squonk', tonight the band surprise us with 'Behind the Lines,' which then returns to the more usual 'Firth of Fifth' and 'Musical Box'. Interesting stuff and it is only a shame that the recording available is such a poor one.

The remainder of the show retains the same set list as had been performed throughout the previous shows that was to remain the same for the rest of them. As such, the real merit of this recording is only in the altered first medley and is of interest to collectors for that reason.

NATIONAL EXHIBITION CENTRE, BIRMINGHAM, ENGLAND, 25 FEBRUARY 1984

Set List: Dodo-Lurker/Abacab/That's All/Mama/Eleventh Earl of Mar-The Lamb Lies Down on Broadway-Firth of Fifth-Musical Box/Illegal Alien/Home by the Sea/Second Home by the Sea/Keep it Dark/It's Gonna Get Better/Follow You Follow Me/In the Cage-Cinema Show-Raven-Afterglow/Drum Duet/Los Endos/Misunderstanding/Turn it on Again (Inc. Medley)//
Source: Audience Recording.

The National Exhibition Centre in Birmingham was to be the sole venue for the band's new look performance on home ground. As such, anticipation was high for these gigs and the band did not let the capacity crowd down. If opening night nerves were present then they certainly didn't show as the band took the stage and took the audience by the scruff of the neck with the hard rockin' pairing of 'Dodo-Lurker' and 'Abacab', both of which had improved dramatically since their debut some three years earlier. The entire band give their all here. Mike and Daryl trade off some impressive licks whilst Tony's stabbing keyboard phrasings battle away in fierce competition with the rhythm section of Chester and Phil who threaten to bring the roof down with their percussive antics.

Calming things down, Phil's antics winding the audience up threatening to play some *Really* old songs," gets a rise out of the crowd before he introduces a song which "All you guys can take off your pants and all you gals can hitch up your dresses." Genesis playing country & western? Well ... in their own inimitable way, yes. 'That's All' is as much a send-up of the genre as 'Illegal Alien' was a wry look at America's immigrant problem and just as enjoyable in its own way. This is followed by 'Mama', one of those unpredictable Genesis tracks that insinuates its way into your senses before taking over. From the opening drumbeat and keyboard arpeggio, this is a stunning performance augmented by the echoey acoustics of the cavernous NEC building creating just the right dramatic vibe. Phil delivers a spine tingling vocal performance whilst the rest of the band conjure up the drama that makes 'Mama' one of the finest tracks in the Genesis catalogue.

The first of the increasingly regular medleys follows but at least this time the selection actually *works* rather well. Phil's introduction is hilarious, poking gentle fun at both the band and the fans with some good-natured banter emanating from the crowd as well. During the US tour the band had experimented with
several different versions of this medley to varying degrees of success before finally settling on this one. Opening with 'Eleventh Earl of Mar' was always going to be a vote winner as far as I am concerned and the segue from that classic into 'The Lamb Lies Down on Broadway' is a masterpiece of timing and musicianship. Following this with tantalising extracts from 'Firth of Fifth' and 'Musical Box' rounds of an unusually satisfying pocket history of the band's back catalogue as well as giving several individuals another chance to shine, none more so than Daryl, who once again took Steve's glorious guitar solo in 'Firth of Fifth' and made it his own.

A light-hearted moment follows with the aforementioned 'Illegal Alien', which once again gives Phil a chance to ham it up to the crowd and make full use of the "band radio" to check if the police are catching up with them – the "fugitives from justice". Not a classic Genesis song by any stretch of the imagination but the humour serves as a useful escape valve before the high drama of 'Home by the Sea/Second Home by the Sea'. Already a bona fide classic by the time it was recorded, here in the live context this became one of the most memorable latter-day Genesis tracks both musically and visually. Tonight's performance was nothing short of spectacular.

I was both surprised and delighted when I heard that 'Keep it Dark' was to feature in the new set and it was great to hear it at last. However, combining it with the weakest track from the new album – 'It's Gonna Get Better' – only served to dampen its effect somewhat, but at least it was there and I for one loved it! 'Follow You Follow Me' perked the crowd up again and led us nicely into the now traditional medley of 'In the Cage-Cinema Show-Raven-Afterglow', which continues to improve with age and once again gave the entire band a chance to show their mettle.

The climax of 'Afterglow' simply can't be surpassed as far as I am concerned but the band didn't take their feet off the pedals, oh no! The familiar 'Drum Duet' between Phil and Chester that has become such a welcome part of the show followed before a truly glorious rendering of 'Los Endos' brought the show proper to an end and left the crowd cheering for more. The band returned to give us the final pairing of 'Misunderstanding' and 'Turn it on Again' (complete with hilarious medley), which rounded off another superb night of Genesis music.

NATIONAL EXHIBITION CENTRE, BIRMINGHAM, ENGLAND, 29 FEBRUARY 1984

Dodo-Lurker/Abacab/That's All/Mama/Eleventh Earl of Mar-The Lamb Lies Down on Broadway-Firth of Fifth-Musical Box/Illegal Alien/Home by the Sea/Second Home by the Sea/Carpet Crawlers/Keep it Dark/It's Gonna Get Better/Follow You Follow Me/In the Cage-Cinema Show-In That Quiet Earth-Afterglow/Drum Duet/Los Endos/Turn it on Again (Inc. Medley)//
Source: Audience Recording.

This was the final night of the band's residency at the NEC and the final night of the tour as well. Fundamentally, this was the same show as the four preceding nights and even the presence of TRHs the Prince and Princess of Wales (or Charlie and Di to the rest of us) couldn't persuade the band to pull something different out of the hat to round off the tour. Mind you, the fact that they were filming all of these gigs for the forthcoming concert film, released some time later as the *Mama Tour*, may also have had something to do with that.

What we have here then is an average sounding audience recording. The NEC is notorious for its poor acoustics and you can certainly hear why that is so on this recording. I am not sure where exactly the taper was located but my guess would be somewhere at the back in the South Stand because at times the sound seems delayed as the acoustics relay the music behind the actual performance.

Performance wise, the band are as well rehearsed and fluent as they should be after four months on the road and the show contains all the usual mix of humour and drama that this tour brought to the fans that saw the shows.

A Selection Of Shows: Genesis & Solo Live Guide 1976-2014

Genesis

CHAPTER EIGHT
"INVISIBLE STRINGS"
THE INVISIBLE TOUCH TOUR 1986/87

With Phil's solo career going into overdrive and the burgeoning success of Mike's solo outfit – Mike & the Mechanics – the gaps between Genesis albums were becoming larger. Three years separate *Genesis* from its successor *Invisible Touch* and in terms of development those three years are akin to a lifetime. The intervening years had seen all three of the protagonists expand and develop their skills through solo projects, and so when they reconvened in the spring of 1986 to begin work on the new Genesis album, it was with a fresh sense of vitality and adventure. The resulting album was to be the band's biggest commercial success to date selling almost six million copies and spawning no less than five hit singles worldwide. The Genesis of 1986 would be completely unrecognisable to a fan from 1972 and indeed the band were to lose a great many of their older fans with this album. What they couldn't stomach was the sheer dynamism and catchiness of the material. If *Foxtrot* was pure "Prog" then *Invisible Touch* was pure "Pop" and this was what many of the diehard fans found hard to take. For every older fan that fell by the wayside, however, the band seemed to pick up two more new ones eager to investigate this "new" and "happening" band.

As usual, however, things are never quite that simple with Genesis, are they? Sure, songs such as 'Invisible Touch' and 'Throwing it all Away' are great examples of the popular songwriter's art. However, alongside them are more traditional Genesis tracks such as 'Domino' and even that rarity for a Genesis album, the instrumental 'The Brazilian', both of which demonstrated quite ably that the band had not lost any of its flair for long-form material and both of these tracks were to become highlights of the 1986/87 tours. The success of the album and its string of singles ensured that once again demand to see the band in concert was enormous both in the UK and worldwide.

To satisfy that demand, the band were soon to undertake their biggest tour since 1974's the *Lamb Lies Down On Broadway* tour, with one crucial difference: there were no cancellations owing to poor ticket sales this time round! in fact, the opposite was true and additional gigs had to be added to many venues to cope with the demand for tickets. Even in the UK, where two gigs at Wembley Stadium became three and finally a record-breaking four nights at this 72,000-seater stadium. This was truly a worldwide tour with gigs in Australia and New Zealand for the first time and Japan for only the second time ever, and in all over 112 gigs were played from the first at the Joe Louis Arena in Detroit, Michigan, USA on 17 September 1986, and the final night at Wembley Stadium, London, England on 4 July 1987.

Continuing to expand upon the Vari Lite technology that they had helped to create, the stage show once again placed the emphasis on lighting, essential in the size of venues that the band were now playing. The new Mk II *Vari Lites* were an infinite improvement over their predecessors and the resulting light show was an experience to behold. Musically, the emphasis was once again on the new material, although the 'In the Cage' medley of oldies was given a couple of different twists, depending on which territory you were lucky enough to catch it in. The tour saw Genesis break box office receipts records all over the world outselling fellow artists U2, who themselves were enjoying enormous success with their *Joshua Tree* album and tour by the rate of 2:1 in some territories. Not bad for a bunch of old Progressive farts, eh?

THE FORUM, LOS ANGELES CALIFORNIA, USA, 17 OCTOBER 1986

Set List: Mama/Abacab/Land of Confusion/In too Deep/Domino/Follow You Follow Me/That's All/Tonight, Tonight, Tonight/Throwing it all Away/In the Cage-In That Quiet Earth-Apocalypse in 9/8/Invisible Touch/Turn it on Again//
Source: FM Radio Broadcast/Transcription Disc.

Back on the road after a two and a half year hiatus, Genesis reached their apogee in terms of popularity with the *Invisible Touch* album, which spawned no less than five hit singles in the USA and elsewhere. A truly massive ten-month tour saw the band visit several territories that they had never (or seldom) visited before. They are in familiar territory here tonight though. An FM radio broadcast transcription disc captures the band's show at the Forum in Los Angeles, scene of several of their earlier triumphs.

Continuing the tradition of opening the show with a track from the album that preceded it, 'Mama' opens the show tonight and it is obvious that even at this early stage of the tour Phil's voice is already showing signs of strain as he reaches for the notes at several points during this song. 'Abacab' drives things along at a fine pace, featuring Daryl and Mike letting rip with some fine riffs, backed by Chester's usual rock solid rhythms.

The first offering from the new album is a fine version of 'Land of Confusion', which continues the hard rocking opening to the show before the pace is slowed down a little by 'In too Deep' most likely to give poor old Phil a chance to rest his voice, but even so, he still sounds hoarse at times here. Fans bemoaning the lack of the band's longer format songs must surely have had no complaints about the presence of 'Domino', as dramatic a slice of Genesis as anything that had preceded it and tonight, the performance is excellent. Tasteful and authoritative percussion from Chester underpins the rest of the band whilst Tony in particular overlays the rhythm section with some incredible playing. Phil also gives it his best and with his voice struggling at times. This only adds to the drama, although the sound is a little flat at times – equalised too much for radio, perhaps?

'Follow You Follow Me' and 'That's All' give the audience a chance to take the strain as Phil's voice begins to show more signs of strain, as evidenced by the lack of between songs chatter, not all of which has been edited out by the radio broadcasters. Daryl's country picking on the latter track is excellent too.

'Tonight, Tonight, Tonight' opens the second disc and immediately you can hear the strain that Phil is putting his voice through as he struggles to reach some of the notes. Musically, Mike takes the honours here, as his guitar rips through the air like a soul in torment. Once again, pacing themselves, 'Throwing it all Away' gives the audience another chance to do the work before we reach the highlight of the show: the in *the Cage* medley. By now this has become a well-established favourite but the band decided to give it a twist on the first leg of this tour by ending it with the 'Apocalypse in 9/8' section from *Supper's Ready*. Sadly, this was not destined to survive beyond the band's inaugural trip to New Zealand and Australia, which makes this recording even more vital for fans. Phil delivers a suitably impassioned vocal, raw and hoarse, while the rest of the band manage to depict an aural nightmare landscape to fill out the picture. Daryl's awesome playing battles away with Tony's immense chords like two giants in combat leading to the orgasmic climax of a truly apocalyptic finale, which is simply stunning.

After that even more recent classics, such as 'Invisible Touch' and 'Turn it on Again', which close this recording, simply fail to match the grandeur of what has gone before, leaving the crowd and us – the listener – exhilarated.

NATIONAL TENNIS CENTRE, MELBOURNE, AUSTRALIA, 10 DECEMBER 1986

Set List: Mama/Abacab/Domino/Your Own Special Way/In too Deep/The Brazilian/That's All/Home by the Sea/Second Home by the Sea/Throwing it all Away/In the Cage-In That Quiet Earth-Afterglow/Invisible Touch/Drum Duet/Los Endos/Turn it on Again//
Source: Audience Recording.

The band eventually got to Australia and New Zealand a mere seven years after it had first been discussed and for those fans lucky enough to see them at any of these shows they were in for an all too rare treat. Because of Musician's Union rules in those territories, the band had to be accompanied by local musicians for at least part of the show. Genesis, therefore, took the unprecedented step of using a four-piece string section to accompany them on a couple of songs during the show.

The rest of the set for the gigs on this tour was fundamentally the same as it had been at the start of the tour, although the band reverted to the more typical 'In the Cage' medley after their only gig in New Zealand, and so fans both in Australia, Japan, and Europe were deprived of the chance to hear the 'Apocalypse in 9/8' version of the medley.

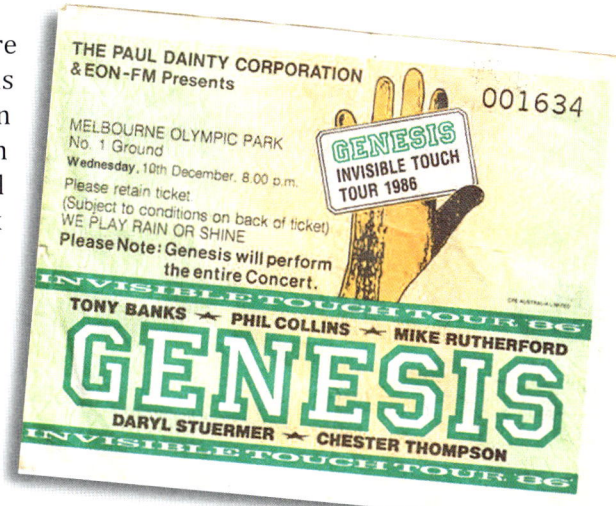

That apart, the shows were equally as entertaining as this recording taken from the band's first night in Melbourne shows. The opening salvo of 'Mama', 'Abacab', and 'Domino' gets the party off to a flying start. Sadly the quality of the available recording leaves something to be desired, although it does give an indication of the reception that the band were given on this their only visit to Oz.

The fans are then treated to the spectacle of the band accompanied by the above mentioned string section for a truly delightful version of 'Your Own Special Way' celebrating its tenth anniversary here. Phil gives the song a sensitive treatment and the strings, when you can hear them, are a delightful accompaniment to the rest of the band. This is followed by another string-driven performance, this time of 'In too Deep', which once again benefits from the additional musicians.

The rest of this gig is typical fare for the tour and can be heard in much better quality on other recordings that have been mentioned elsewhere. The intrinsic value of this one is the appearance of the string section and this is one of only a handful of recordings from this leg of the tour, with Auckland, New Zealand, and the following night to this one in Melbourne being the others.

PALAIS OMNISPORTS DE BERCY, PARIS, FRANCE, 2 JUNE 1987

Set List: Mama/Abacab/Domino/That's All/The Brazilian/In the Cage-In That Quiet Earth-Afterglow/Land of Confusion/Tonight, Tonight, Tonight/Throwing it all Away/Home by the Sea/Second Home by the Sea/Invisible Touch/Drum Duet/Los Endos/Turn it on Again//
Source: Audience Recording.

A rarity on this leg of the tour: an indoor show and even better, *no* Paul Young as opening act! That irritation dispensed with, the emphasis tonight was on entertainment pure and simple and that was something that Genesis gave out in spades!

Once again we have an audience recording here documenting the band and it is amazing how much more atmosphere these have over their sanitised radio counterparts. As usual, the industrial grind of 'Mama' opens the show, and in the cavernous spaces of the hall it echoes around nicely with Phil sounding in top form. Of course, the crowd are in equally good form, which will drive the audiophiles nuts if they ever bother to listen to this one!

Coupling this with both 'Abacab' and 'Domino' at the very start of the show would be to risk Phil's voice giving out completely but no such worries here. 'Abacab' gets off to a suitably rocky start with some excellent guitar work from both Mike and Daryl. Chester seems to be determined to have a good time too and his licks threaten to dismantle his drum kit at times. Phil's French has improved immensely as he manages to explain the "Domino Principle" without any problems. As for the song itself, well, it is a superb example of Genesis at their dramatic best. Layer upon layer of music appears with Tony, Chester, and Daryl shining throughout. In the latter part of the song Daryl and Chester threaten to take the roof off the hall with their playing!

'That's All' manages to calm everyone down for a few minutes but the pace is soon picked up again by both 'The Brazilian' and 'In the Cage', which simply beggars belief. Okay, so there is no 'Apocalypse in 9/8' tonight, but the performance is suitably apocalyptic without it. Segueing perfectly into 'In That Quiet Earth' and eventual to the orgasmic 'Afterglow', the entire band are simply stunning here and this is a triumph – what you can hear of it over an ecstatic crowd, that is!

Even 'Land of Confusion' rattles along in great style, but then again, the crowd tonight are in party mode and the show is a celebration. Phil continues his introductions in surprisingly good French as he introduces Daryl and Chester and then ... 'Tonight, Tonight, Tonight', which proves beyond doubt that Genesis can still write epic long form songs. I really do feel sorry for Phil, though, as this one takes it out of anyone's voice but he pulls it off like the trooper he is! Once again the rest of the band create a marvellous dramatic soundscape with Tony's chords cutting through the air like a knife.

'Throwing it all Away' continues the party atmosphere before Phil makes the audience earn their salt with an extended audience participation section leading us into the nightmare world of 'Home by the Sea'. Mike's guitar shreds the air and Tony's keyboards rampage through the cavernous spaces of the hall, augmented by some thunderous percussion from Chester and latterly Phil as well. It is on tracks such as this that a good quality audience recording beats any soundboard or radio broadcast as far as I am concerned. The excitement and sheer enjoyment of the crowd are almost tangible on this recording.

The party atmosphere continues with a thoroughly enjoyable 'Invisible Touch' before we get down to some serious air drumming for the now famous "five minutes of thunder" leading into 'Los Endos' and the end of the show proper. Phil and Chester have honed this into a work of art and I have seldom – if ever – heard it played better than here. Where they got their energy from is anyone's guess but they leave the audience exhilarated and baying for more. The rest of the band share in the overwhelming sense of triumph that oozes from everyone involved. It seldom gets better than this!

Only room for one encore, although the band could have played all night and the crowd would have still asked for more. What they get is a rampaging version of 'Turn it on Again', without which no Genesis show is complete. All in all, a bloody marvellous recording that captures the magic, the majesty, and the mayhem of a Genesis gig to perfection.

WEMBLEY STADIUM, LONDON, ENGLAND, 4 JULY 1987

Set List: Mama/Abacab/Domino/That's All/The Brazilian/In the Cage-In That Quiet Earth-Afterglow/Land of Confusion / Tonight, Tonight, Tonight/Throwing it all Away/Home by the Sea/Second Home by the Sea/Invisible Touch/Drum Duet/ Los Endos/Turn it on Again//
Source: FM Radio Broadcast.

By the time the band reached the UK for their final shows they had honed the performance down to a fine art. Initially set to play two shows at Wembley, demand dictated that it was extended to three and eventually to a record-breaking fourth night at the venue. Thankfully the BBC were on hand to record the final gig, which is the recording we have here.

With a standard set for every territory they played in, the UK shows were the same as they had been throughout the band's extensive European leg. No 'Apocalypse in 9/8' or string section for us then! Nevertheless, the band's performance here was astonishing. Opening with 'Mama', perhaps one of the most vocally demanding songs in the entire Genesis catalogue, there is no sign of strain on Phil's chords here as he rampages through a dramatic performance, one in which he is ably assisted by the marvellous playing of the rest of the band. Chester and Mike give a rock-solid rhythm section, while Daryl and Tony flesh out the song with some wonderful playing.

This is in turn followed by the high octane power of 'Abacab', and you can hear how well the crowd receive this rocking classic. Once again this really puts Phil's vocals to the test and he sails through it. Mike and Daryl also really shine here as they trade licks off each other, while Tony's keyboard phrasings pierce through and Chester's percussive dynamo threatens to bring the roof down. A brief respite for the crowd as Phil leads us through an increasingly corny and unnecessary (the crowd know the story off by heart by now) explanation of the "Domino Principle" leading nicely into – what else? – but 'Domino', yet another long form Genesis classic. Once again the entire band really get their teeth into the performance and the playing by one and all is simply magnificent.

'That's All' and 'The Brazilian' follow and both demonstrate the enigma that is Genesis. The former, a simple toe-tapper, works surprisingly well in the live context whilst the latter really gives the band a chance for an instrumental workout, as well as giving Phil's voice a well-deserved rest for a few minutes!

Time for our "trip down Memory Lane" next as the band give us oldies a treat. Taking 'In the Cage' out of the context of the *Lamb* was an inspired decision, and ever since its first appearance in the set back in 1978, the ensuing medley has grown and matured into a thing of beauty and grandeur. Tonight is no exception either. From the opening pulsating drumbeat to the final diminishing chords of 'Afterglow', the performance here is one designed to grab the audience by the throat and not let go.

The dynamics of this set give neither the band or the audience much time to recuperate. 'Land of Confusion' is a sop to the Genesis newbies in the crowd and probably gave some of the older fans their excuse to take a "pee break", not to detract from the song, which certainly has its merits for many fans, I suppose. 'Tonight, Tonight, Tonight' and 'Home by the Sea' back to back really pushes the limits of endurance, but here the band soar majestically above the crowd with masterful performances from each and every player.

Into the home straight next and the band drag out the big guns to deliver the final salvo. 'Invisible Touch', a bona fide crowd pleaser sets up the audience for the classic finale beginning with the now standard "five minutes of thunder" 'Drum Duet' between Phil and Chester leading into 'Los Endos' – the perfect way to close any Genesis gig really and played flawlessly here tonight. Show over, but everyone knows that the band will return for an encore and they are not long in returning to the stage to the throbbing chords of Daryl's guitar heralding 'Turn it on Again', which challenges everyone to dance to its irregular time signature, but by this time the capacity crowd don't care about that and the show, and indeed the tour, ends on a suitably high note.

A Selection Of Shows: Genesis & Solo Live Guide 1976-2014

Genesis

82

CHAPTER NINE
"FAR FROM 'FADING LIGHTS'"
THE WE CAN'T DANCE TOUR 1992

By 1991 it had been an agonising five year wait for a new Genesis album. The intervening years had seen every member of the band achieve greater or lesser solo success. The plethora of solo projects began to make fans think that the band were over. Nothing could be further from the truth, however, as they proved when in late October the first signs of their new collaboration emerged in the shape of the darkly dramatic single, 'No Son of Mine'. Once again, not your typical pop song. This one tells the story of a young boy fleeing an abusive family relationship and its aftermath. A brilliantly observed story accompanied by an equally dramatic and evocative monochrome video.

The new album, *We Can't Dance*, was to be the band's first double studio album since 1974's the *Lamb Lies Down On Broadway* and the band took full advantage of the longer playing time on the then relatively new Compact Disc format to expand the number of tracks to a massive thirteen. Anyone bemoaning the Genesis of old could not be disappointed by this album. Sure, there were pop singles aplenty – 'I Can't Dance', 'Jesus He Knows Me', etc. – but there were also welcome lengthy epics including 'Driving the Last Spike' and the truly awe-inspiring 'Fading Lights'. There was no shortage of material as the abundance of B-sides to the several singles from the album demonstrated, here was a band in full command of its faculties and enjoying itself again at the composition stage.

Demand for tickets for the new tour was every bit as high as it had been on previous outings but this time the band opted to scale down touring commitments to a mere sixty shows during the summer of 1992. These shows were in the biggest venues possible, however, and because of this the band once again expanded the stage production envelope by using the production prototypes for the Sony "Jumbotron" video screens, which were an enormous leap over previous visual efforts being able to combine into a single unit for certain songs or separate into three separate elements for others. Either way, the result was that even if you were one of the "little people" at the back of a venue, you still had a decent view of the on stage proceedings. Musically, the show placed the emphasis firmly on the new album and its predecessor with a meagre twenty minutes being devoted to material that preceded that album. Older fans may have mourned the passing of even the evergreen 'In the Cage', but, in the words of the song "All things must pass". What you had here was a slick, modern, and efficient show that certainly ticked all the right boxes with the capacity crowds that attended the shows.

Taking everyone by surprise again, the band returned to the UK in the autumn of 1992 for a series of shows at Earls Court Arena in London, preceded by an even more surprising visit to some of the smaller Provincial theatres which they hadn't played since the heady days of 1980. The stage show was obviously of a smaller nature for these more intimate gigs. Nor did the set change sadly either, but for fans who had never had the chance to see the band in such an intimate atmosphere, these gigs were not to be missed. And for those who did miss either tour, the band captured it in all its glory by filming the six nights at Earls Court and at least two gigs from the summer US tour for posterity. The Earls Court performances were released under the title, the *Way We Walk in Concert* in 1993 on VHS and subsequently on DVD. This was the band's first concert film release that documented an entire show and as such is hard to beat.

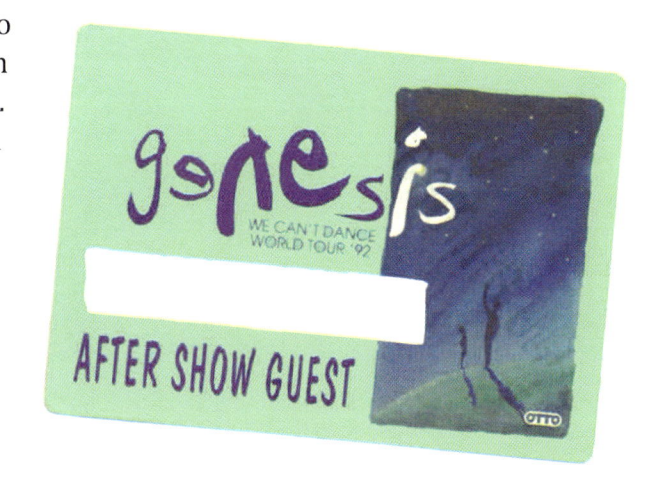

GOODYEAR BLIMP HANGAR, DALLAS, TEXAS, USA, (REHEARSALS), MAY 1992
Set List: Hold on my Heart/Way of the World/Domino/Throwing it all Away/Interview/I Can't Dance/Tonight, Tonight, Tonight/Turn it on Again/Follow You Follow Me//
Source: Audience Recording.

This is an unusual one with it being a behind the scenes look at the band in rehearsal in the final couple of days before the US tour was due to commence. Several of the tracks here have different arrangements to those which would eventually be used during the gigs, none more so than 'Turn it on Again' and 'Follow You Follow Me', both of which have a far funkier feel to them. The former in particular has some very meaty bass lines from Mike, while the latter has some country style picking from Daryl. Of most interest to collectors though is the performance of 'Way of the World', a track which was not destined to make it through to the actual concerts themselves. There are reputed to be several lengthier recordings of the rehearsals for this tour in the hands of private collectors and there are many more in the band's own archive, but what we have here is the only material in general circulation to fans.

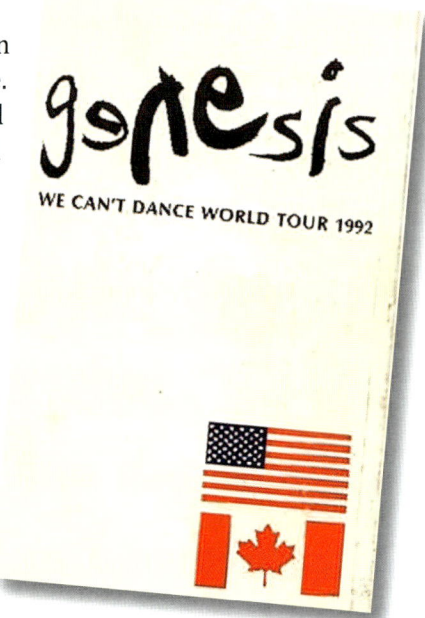

OLYMPIASTADION, MUNICH, GERMANY, 5 JULY 1992
Set List: No Son of Mine/Driving the Last Spike/Throwing it all Away/Dance on a Volcano-The Lamb Lies Down on Broadway-Musical Box-Firth of Fifth-I Know What I Like/Hold on My Heart/Jesus He Knows Me/Fading Lights/I Can't Dance/Tonight, Tonight, Tonight (Shortened Version)/Invisible Touch/Turn it on Again//
Source: Edited FM Radio Broadcast.

With the US tour over, the band took up residency in Europe and fortunately we have several radio broadcasts that document this year's visit, including this excellent one from the band's show in Munich. Sadly though, like most of these things, this one has been judiciously pruned to fit in with broadcast schedules.

As such, the show opener – 'Land of Confusion' – is missing, and the broadcast starts with a workmanlike version of 'No Son of Mine'. Phil's voice, which has long since lost the angelic quality for which it was renowned, sounds quite strained here. Musically though the band put in an adequate performance with Daryl getting in some excellent guitar licks. Phil makes reference to the fact that a strike by French truck drivers had affected the tour schedule and once again the "*alte stucke*" of years gone by makes a reappearance as he introduces 'Driving the Last Spike'. Daryl and Mike trade off some meaty licks here, over which Tony puts in some suitably orchestral playing. Once again, the performance is adequate but somehow falls a bit flat to my ears.

Strangely, the running order of the show – or what there is of it – has been altered, as next up we have one of those songs I love to hate – 'Throwing it all Away' – which, as usual, has Phil leading the rent-a-chorus crowd through the proceedings. Once again his voice sounds quite strained here but the musical accompaniment is fine. The sop to the older fans comes next in the shape of the longest medley that the band ever put together. With lengthy segments from such classics as 'Dance on a Volcano' and 'The Lamb' to contend with, the band put in a much better performance here, especially on "The Lamb", where Tony takes the honours with some superb playing, in combat with some fine rhythm playing from Daryl and meaty bass from Mike. Phil's voice continues to show signs of strain but, to be honest, that adds to the atmosphere, especially during a fine rendering of the latter part of 'Musical Box'.

Whoever edited this show for broadcast, took perverse delight in leaving out many of the highlights (no 'Home by the Sea', for example) but thankfully, 'Fading Lights' is here in all its glory. This is Tony Banks at his magnificent best. The sheer majesty of this song defies description, really, and Phil puts in a superb performance, with the evident strain in his voice adding to the sheer emotion of the piece. Chester, whose percussion is never less than impeccable, plays a blinder here too, underpinning the entire piece. Daryl and Mike also shine, especially on the extended instrumental section, which is very much a worthy successor to the *Apocalypse* section of the great *Supper's Ready*!

Fundamentally the rest of the show is left intact and we have an enjoyable romp through 'I Can't Dance',

A Selection Of Shows: Genesis & Solo Live Guide 1976-2014

PART ONE: GENESIS

the truncated version of 'Tonight, Tonight, Tonight', 'Invisible Touch', and finally 'Turn it on Again', all of which are delivered in fine style. This is an interesting if at times irritating recording, but one which collectors will definitely enjoy.

KNEBWORTH PARK, STEVENAGE, ENGLAND, 2 AUGUST 1992
Set List: Land of Confusion/No Son of Mine/Driving the Last Spike/Dance on a Volcano-The Lamb Lies Down on Broadway-Musical Box-Firth of Fifth-I Know What I Like/Throwing it all Away/Fading Lights/Jesus He Knows Me/Home by the Sea/Second Home by the Sea/Hold on My Heart/Domino/Drum Duet/I Can't Dance/Tonight, Tonight, Tonight (Shortened Version)/Invisible Touch/Turn it on Again//
Source: FM Radio Broadcast.

Here is another chance to reacquaint myself with why I hate this venue so much! You would think that after all the years of gigs that have happened at this venue, that they would have learned a lesson or two about stewarding and night time post-gig lighting! Not a bit of it. Thankfully, at least the weather was on our side for this one and the day remained fine and dry throughout, which certainly made a welcome change! With only two gigs in the UK for the 1992 summer tour, this was an extremely popular gig and the crowd was at capacity for it.

Also being the last night of the summer tour, the band themselves were in fine form with much humour in evidence throughout the course of the gig. Opening the show with 'Land of Confusion' it was evident from the outset that the band were determined to entertain the capacity crowd. Following this with 'No Son of Mine', once again demonstrated the two sides of Genesis: humour and drama. Indeed, the band's new album that was to feature largely in the set had amply demonstrated that Genesis had more than one string to their bow. Fans bemoaning the loss of the band's lengthier epics surely had nothing to complain about on the new album. 'Driving the Last Spike', which was the next song in the set, showed that the band still had the ability to write long form and the performance here is a thing of great beauty. Phil's vocals, already stretched during 'No Son of Mine', still manage to bring the right degree of pathos to this tale of the early English railways, while Mike and Tony in particular deliver an impeccable performance throughout this latter-day classic.

Our trip down "Memory Lane" is next and this time the band took the brave step of replacing the now standard 'In the Cage' medley with a brand new one! Anyone who was at any of the 1992 gigs will no doubt tell you how effective it was augmented as it was by the band's new light show. Combining elements of several classics the new look medley gave the entire band a chance to shine. 'Dance on a Volcano' allows Daryl, Mike, and Chester to let rip in the rhythm department, while 'The Lamb' is Tony's moment to shine before the final trio of 'Musical Box', 'Firth of Fifth', and 'I Know What I Like' bring everyone together, including the audience during the sing-along finale – marvellous stuff!

PLAYHOUSE THEATRE, EDINBURGH, SCOTLAND, 29 OCTOBER 1992
Set List: Land of Confusion/No Son of Mine/Old Medley/Fading Lights/Jesus He Knows Me/Dreaming While You Sleep/Home by the Sea/ Second Home by the Sea/Hold on My Heart/Domino/Drum Duet/I Can't Dance/Tonight, Tonight, Tonight (edited version)/Invisible Touch/Turn it on Again//
Source: Audience Recording.

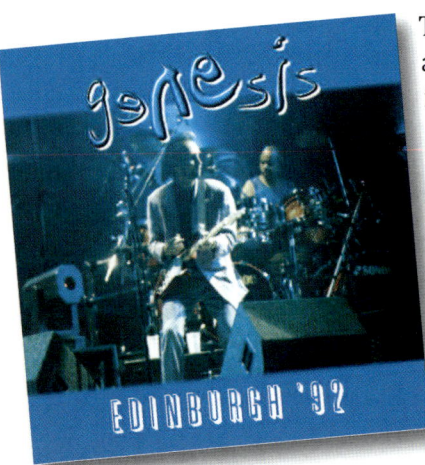

The announcement of the provincial theatre dates ahead of the six night stint a London's Earls Court Arena took fans completely by surprise and demand for tickets for these gigs – the band's first in theatres in the UK since 1980 – was incredible with single tickets changing hands on the black market for as much as £400 each for a £22 ticket!

Scotland has always been a stronghold for the band and so with only this gig in Edinburgh to satisfy the Scottish fans, the band were playing to a capacity crowd eager with anticipation. Just as they had done during the summer shows, the band opened with 'Land of Confusion' and immediately, apart from the audience who make their presence felt from the outset, so too does Phil's ongoing vocal problem. He sounds terrible here.

'No Son of Mine' is greeted by a cheer and immediately you sense that the band are pulling out all the stops here. Mike's bass fills the hall and Tony is at his most sepulchral. However, the problem of Phil's voice just won't go away. At best he sounds hoarse here, at worst completely out of tune. Fortunately for him, the audience are more than prepared to sing the parts for him. The old medley put together for this tour goes down well even if Phil's introduction sounds lacklustre to say the least. Sound wise, the recording is rather flat, probably owing to the acoustics of the hall and the taper's location (somewhere in the circle, I suspect). The audience are in fine voice again and know all the right places to cheer or applaud and there is plenty to get their teeth into here. 'The Lamb' was designed for performance in halls such as this and the crowd really get behind the band on this one and throughout the rest of the medley.

'Fading Lights' sounds infinitely superior in an intimate setting such as this. Tony has seldom sounded better, with his majestic keyboards creating just the right feeling of sentimentality without descending into mawkishness. Phil's voice has managed to regain some of its gravitas here and he gives an authoritative performance. Daryl and Mike also give their all to what many fans regard as the last great classic Genesis song – great stuff!

'Jesus He Knows Me' and 'Dreaming While You Sleep' contrast the comic and serious sides of the band superbly well. Daryl's almost country-style picking on the former augmented by a rock steady beat from Chester lifts the song into a bona fide party in which the Edinburgh crowd take their part with collective glee. The latter features some haunting playing from Tony and some impressive guitar work from Mike and Daryl, which makes me wonder why this song wasn't played more often during this tour.

Phil's intro to 'Home by the Sea' certainly hasn't improved with age but it is an essential part of the song and both he and the audience are obviously enjoying their respective roles – especially his "victims" in the front row! Thankfully the song itself has grown in stature and the opening guitar and keyboard work prove beyond doubt that Genesis can rock out but only in their own "special" way, of course! Here, for once, Phil's ragged vocal actually helps the song. The atmosphere is lifted by his performance and you can almost suspend your disbelief for a few minutes. The extended instrumental part of the song gives everyone a chance to indulge themselves. Tony certainly seems to be going for it here and I am sure there was plenty of air keyboarding and air guitaring among the audience here too.

'Hold on My Heart' gives everyone a chance to catch their breath but it is here that Tony and Mike really come into their own. The simplicity of the playing belies the beauty of what is created and with Phil's voice giving the song an even greater feeling of sentimentality, this is a rare performance of the song, which I can actually say I enjoy! 'Domino', introduced in its usual fashion by Phil, is greeted with enthusiasm by the crowd. Dramatic and dynamic, the song definitely sounds more highly charged within the confines of a smaller hall. Phil's voice once again is given an added edge by the fact that he is obviously straining to reach the notes at times; a real drama within the imagined one of the song. Chester is the hero this time, with some stunning percussion that underpins everything, which at times threatens to go nuclear.

The now famous 'Drum Duet' also works infinitely better within a smaller room. Here every note is heard perfectly. If only other rock drummers could learn from this entertaining yet concise performance – something I certainly can't say for other drum solos I have heard over the years! Sadly, on this tour it doesn't lead to the glorious 'Los Endos' but instead 'I Can't Dance'. You can almost feel the disappointment, but hey, Genesis have never pandered to their audience, have they? Daryl and Mike redeem themselves though with some fine playing and Phil certainly seems to be in his element hamming up for the crowd, who are soon giving him a typically Scottish rent-a-crowd accompaniment.

With Phil's obvious vocal problems I am surprised that 'Tonight, Tonight, Tonight', even in its truncated form, wasn't dropped but it works remarkable well. Tony and Mike create the right atmosphere, with their chords echoing around the hall. Once again, Chester is impeccable in the percussion department and God bless him, Phil gives it his all and I am sure there was a supply of cough linctus ready for him after the show. No rest for the wicked though, as the drum pattern heralding 'Invisible Touch' arrives and the audience, already in party mood really get into the swing of it and a driving version ends the evening in fine style leaving everyone happy.

ROYAL ALBERT HALL, LONDON, ENGLAND, 16 NOVEMBER 1992

Set List: Land of Confusion/No Son of Mine/Driving the Last Spike/Old Medley/Fading Lights/Jesus He Knows Me/Home by the Sea/Second Home by the Sea/Hold on My Heart/Domino/Drum Duet/I Can't Dance/Tonight, Tonight, Tonight/ Invisible Touch/Turn it on Again//
Source: FM Radio Broadcast.

Phil's recurring vocal problems led to the rescheduling of some of the band's first provincial theatre gigs in the UK and the last gig of the tour was eventually to end up being at the Civic Hall in Wolverhampton. Sadly though no live recording of that gig is in general circulation, and so instead we have this truly remarkable recording from the band's first ever gig at the prestigious Royal Albert Hall in London from the day before. With a live album already in the cans from this tour (*The Way We Walk in Concert –Volume 1 the Shorts*, had actually been released on the day of this concert and its sequel – the *Longs* – was to be released on 9 January 1993), it is surprising that the band were captured for posterity on the radio again, but as usual they did us proud with this excellent recording.

Opening, as usual, with a funky, rhythm-driven 'Land of Confusion' tonight, Mike and Chester take the honours with a superbly catchy rhythm section. Even the crowd are audible in the mix here, although perhaps because of the surroundings, they are a mite restrained in their participation. Phil's vocal problems, which had led to the reorganisation of these final UK shows, are obviously in evidence here and he sounds strained from the start. Cries for 'Supper's Ready' are ignored as the band continue with 'No Son of Mine', which is given a rather flat performance tonight. Phil's voice doesn't help matters but there is little real excitement in the song as it is here.

'Driving the Last Spike' gives Mike another chance to shine as he lead the proceedings with some fine licks, over which Tony lays down a typically understated keyboard part. The song rolls on very much evoking the motion of a train but thankfully there are no train wrecks tonight, only a wonderfully evocative and emotional performance of another underrated song from the new album. Irritatingly, the Capitol Radio adverts regularly interrupt the proceedings but fortunately we have Phil's torrid tale of sexual desire between Romeo and an inflatable Juliet, leading to the eventual deflation – literally of said Juliet. However, instead of 'Cinema Show', we have the extended medley of old material explosively led by Mike's introduction to 'Dance on a Volcano' and musically this is as flawless as you would expect. 'The Lamb Lies Down on Broadway' is impeccable too, but somehow the sound quality is decidedly flat on this recording. Perhaps it has been compressed to death or maybe the infamous poor acoustics of the Royal Albert Hall are getting the better of things. One thing is for sure, it does Phil's vocals no favours at all. He sounds ragged throughout this and what remains of the medley.

The crowd are evidently enjoying themselves and why not? 'Fading Lights' ushers in what is undoubtedly the last classic long form epic that the band were ever to write with Phil in the band, and of course, subsequent events have made it even more poignant. Tony is lord of his domain here but more than ably assisted by the rest of the band. Chester's percussion is tastefully underplayed and Phil manages to pull off a suitably eloquent vocal delivery, rich in emotion and drama.

'Jesus He Knows Me', preceded by Phil's increasingly acerbic observations about the role of TV evangelists, gives the crowd a moment of light relief. No such luck for Phil, as his voice is beginning to sound increasingly strained by this point, but the song is saved by an impeccable performance from the rest of the band. 'Home by the Sea' is preceded by Phil's attempt to whip up audience participation, although no one believes him when he says that the band have never done this before ... Another long form classic that has simply got better with age and there is nothing to find fault with in this performance, in which every member of the band never puts a foot wrong. Mike and Chester drive the performance along with a menacing rhythm section and Tony glissades over them like a disembodied spirit, which is quite appropriate really.

'Hold on My Heart' has never been a song that incites any degree of enthusiasm or excitement for me and tonight is no exception really. It is followed by 'Domino' and some more audience participation, which is quite amusing. The song itself is once again strangely flat and it would appear that the mix for radio hasn't been done properly here, making the result rather unsatisfactory to my ears, but the crowd seem to have enjoyed themselves, so what do I know? The 'Drum Duet' is much better and a particularly fine demonstration of Phil and Chester's combined percussive talents leading irritatingly enough though into 'I Can't Dance' instead of the expected 'Los Endos'. I can't say that I have any great enthusiasm for this song either but there is no doubting that it is a bona fide crowd pleaser as you can hear from the reaction on this recording.

'Tonight, Tonight, Tonight', preceded by another irritating commercial break, is much more to my taste, it being a marvellous example of Genesis at their dramatic best. It simply echoes around the hall, whose acoustics add measurably to the sense of drama. Tony is at his symphonic best here whilst Mike and Daryl's guitars are like souls in torment – wonderful stuff and even Phil's strained vocals add to the effect. Poor Phil, no rest for his tortured tonsils though, as this leads into the familiar drum pattern intro to 'Invisible Touch', which really taxes Phil's powers of performance. He acquits himself admirably though, but he does have the backing of the capacity crowd

With the tour being sponsored by Volkswagen, the band did the necessary publicity in return.

who are obviously fully in the swing of things by now.

Mike's power chords herald the intro to 'Turn it on Again', the only encore tonight, and both the band and audience give it their best shot. This is a celebration and a triumph in which everyone has their part to play. Phil is evidently in his element as cheerleader for the night and the rest of the band are equally enthusiastic as indeed are the crowd who don't need no incitement to join in the celebrations and this closes the evening in suitably ebullient fashion.

THE CHRONICLE (WOLVERHAMPTON), FRIDAY, NOVEMBER 20, 1992   Page 3

World class performance from a world class group

● Phil Collins on stage at the Civic Hall.

Review by JUSTINE FLAVELL

SUPERGROUP Genesis chose a Wolverhampton venue for the last date of their 1992 World Tour.

The concert was originally set for October 26, but was cancelled due to lead singer Phil Collins's viral infection.

Phil's: "I bet you thought we weren't coming," was greeted with a cacophony of sound from the Civic Hall audience on Tuesday.

Before the concert keyboard player Tony Banks said they preferred to play newer material. But Phil found the audience wanted to hear blasts from the past.

"We're going to be playing some old songs," brought cheers. "And some very, very, very old songs," produced an even bigger noise from the sardine-packed fans.

They kicked off with uptempo Land of Confusion, showing Mr Collins's voice hadn't suffered unduly after his illness.

On stage with Phil, Tony and Mike Rutherford were their regular sidesmen Chester Thompson on drums and Daryl Stuermer on guitar.

We knew we were in for a treat when Phil announced: "We've slung some pieces of our past together." This medley included: Lamb Lies Down on Broadway; I Know What I Like in Your Wardrobe; That's All and Follow You Follow Me.

Their "newer" material was, however, equally well received, with songs such as Jesus He Knows Me, No Son of Mine and The Way We Walk standing out.

"Now the part you've all been waiting for," said Phil. "Audience participation time." This didn't bother the masses, they'd been participating in every song so far. But Phil obviously wanted us to suffer, so we had to shout, wave our hands in the air — the usual stuff.

They'd "done this show 80-odd times" since May, this, however, wasn't apparent. It all seemed fresh and exciting, not tired and hurried as you'd expect after such repetition.

The small venue didn't have a detrimental effect on the sound, it all came over excellently.

After two hours of world class entertainment from a world class group, the audience still wanted more. So Genesis obliged. They performed Tonight, Tonight, Tonight, Invisible Touch, Abacab and Turn It On, as encores.

For those fans who were unable to get tickets for this sell-out concert, there is some good news. When asked if they'd tour again, Tony Banks said: "I would think so."

But will we ever see them at such an intimate, accessible venue? I think not.

Phil... 'other things in life'

Rocker Collins to quit Genesis

EXCLUSIVE
by ANDY COULSON

SUPERSTAR Phil Collins is quitting legendary group Genesis — the band that made him famous — after 28 years.

Phil, 44, said yesterday: "If Genesis are going to record an album or go on tour it will be with someone else — not me."

The singer, who last year dumped wife Jill, 38, for 22-year-old Swiss beauty Orianne Cevey, said recording and touring with Genesis had become a "treadmill."

He added: "There are other things to life."

Genesis have had a string of hits since 1967 including Mama, Follow You, Follow Me and Turn It On Again. Phil will concentrate on his solo career — and acting.

An insider said Phil may return to the group for a farewell tour.

CHAPTER TEN
"NOT ABOUT US"
THE CALLING ALL STATIONS TOUR 1998

Fans old and new alike were astonished by the announcement on 29 March 1996 that Phil Collins had left the band. The eulogies started immediately, and like those written previously when Peter had left, proved to be just as misjudged. It was to be a further three months before the band with a nice sense of irony announced Phil's replacement on 6 June 1996 (the anniversary of the D-Day landings in World War II). It was certainly D-Day for the band. Most fans had never heard of the guy who replaced Phil – Ray Wilson – and those who had were not impressed by his previous credentials as frontman for Grunge band one-hit wonders, Stiltskin.

The wait was soon over and the new look band released their new album, *Calling all Stations*, on 2 September 1997, preceded by the first single, the quirky 'Congo' a week before. The album had a mixed reception. In the UK it made the Number 2 spot for one week before rapidly sliding down the chart, while in Germany it was top of the charts for several weeks. The situation in the USA, however, was far more serious. With no real promotion in the USA (Atlantic Records appear to have got cold feet over the nature of the album and pulled most of its promotional budget), the album managed a disappointing Number 53 in the Billboard chart before disappearing altogether.

An initial tour of the major arenas in the USA was downsized to theatres and eventually scrapped altogether as fans in the US voted with their feet and abandoned the band. For a while it looked as though a similar fate would befall the dates announced for Europe and the UK. Thankfully, this was not to be the case and the *Calling all Stations* tour of Europe began in Budapest, Hungary, on 29 January 1998. But Genesis had not only lost Collins but also long-standing tour musicians Chester Thompson and Daryl Steurmer. Drumming duties were performed by Nir Zidkyahu, an Israeli session drummer, who had played with Hidden Persuaders. Anthony Drennan, who had previously worked with Paul Brady and The Corrs was brought in on guitar.

This tour was musically far more satisfying than either of its two immediate predecessors. The emphasis was on the band's back catalogue and those increasingly irritating medleys were dropped. Several older classic tracks were reinstated, including 'The Lamb Lies Down on Broadway' and 'Carpet Crawlers', although for many the highlight of the entire show was the unexpected acoustic medley incorporating 'Follow You Follow Me', 'Lover's Leap', and the band's current single, 'Not About Us'.

Visually, the show combined the "Jumbotron" screens again, although irritatingly enough they were static and separated from each other, which diminished the effect of the visuals, especially during songs such as 'Calling all Stations' and 'Home by the Sea'. The screens were not present at every gig, however, owing to weight restrictions on many venue roofs. This in itself did not detract from the shows and in fact gave a different atmosphere to each gig. The tour lasted until the beginning of April before winding up at the Hartwall Arena in Helsinki, Finland, on 5 April 1998. That was not quite the end of the matter, however, as the band were invited to headline two of the biggest open air festivals in Germany, namely "Rock Im Ring" and "Rock Am Park" in Hockenheim and Nuremburg respectively, ahead of such alumni as Bob Dylan.

Reaction to the new look band and album had been satisfactory in Europe and the UK but the disappointing downturn of sales in the USA dented the band's ego. Sadly, Ray Wilson has been blamed for the band's demise, as they effectively put up the shutters as a recording/touring unit at the end of 1998. However, nothing could be further from the truth. No one in their right mind could have expected Ray to fill the shoes left vacant by both Peter and Phil. Sales of over two million units of the *Calling all Stations* album worldwide are nothing to be sneezed at and many bands would kill for sales figures of that magnitude. The emphasis in the new album had been on harder, darker material and the subsequent shows marked out Genesis as a bona fide Rock band, which is what they had always been. Had Mike and Tony had the intestinal fortitude to persevere with Ray, the disappointing way in which the band's recording history ended might have been entirely different. As it stands, 1998 marked the end of Genesis as a recording entity, but one with a back catalogue of albums and live performances that is the envy of many, as I hope, this book proves.

RTL TV STUDIOS, PARIS, FRANCE, 17 SEPTEMBER 1997
Set List: No Son of Mine/Congo/Land of Confusion/Small Talk/Mama/Not About Us/Dancing with the Moonlit Knight/Follow You Follow Me/Calling all Stations/ Invisible Touch/Shipwrecked/Alien Afternoon/Turn it on Again//
Source: TV/Radio Broadcast.

This was the first real test of the new look band in front of an audience. This was a radio/TV show concert in front of an invited audience. The broadcast is interesting for the inclusion of several numbers that were to be dropped from the live set. 'Small Talk', for instance, never made the final shortlist for the set and it is obvious why that is the case from this broadcast. Its reliance on effects makes it singularly unsuited to performance in some of the cavernous halls that the band were scheduled to play. It is a great run through for Ray's vocals and Mike's guitar playing, however. The band are obviously still finding their feet with the new material, however, and this is a far from confident performance. In places the band sound very hesitant, although on tracks such as 'Mama' they really catch fire and Ray's impassioned vocal delivery gives this one a dimension that even Phil at his best could not deliver. With tracks such as 'Small Talk' and 'Shipwrecked' not making it through to many live concert performances, this is an essential document for collectors. Ironically a five track sampler from this show was given to the winners of the VH1 competition to see the band at the only open full dress rehearsal for the tour at Bray Film Studios in late January 1998.

MED ET 2, COPENHAGEN, DENMARK, 15 NOVEMBER 1997
Set List: No Son of Mine/Congo/Land of Confusion/Calling all Stations/Turn it on Again/Alien Afternoon/Invisible Touch/ Shipwrecked/
Source: TV/Radio broadcast.

Here is another promotional broadcast, this time from Danish radio. Once again, the band are still finding their feet, as you can hear from the fluffed lyrics in 'No Son of Mine' at the outset. Mike's guitar work here is particularly impressive and Nir's percussion is tasty and tight. 'Congo' follows, with an unusually extended introduction. Once again there is some nifty guitar playing from Mike, while Tony lays down a particularly dramatic chord sequence and some unusual effects are obvious throughout making this a unique version of the song.

'Land of Confusion' follows, although irritatingly the between songs conversation with the presenter has been edited out of this recording, which always makes me suspicious of the origins of a recording. The song itself is pretty much a standard version of the track, although there are some interesting keyboard effects used by Tony here, and once again Mike's guitar playing is a lot brasher than the usual performance version. Ray's vocals sound a little bit hoarse here and he does struggle to deliver the song and there is a rather curious edit just before the end of the song. 'Calling all Stations' has a radically different opening to it and the performance here is absolutely marvellous making this one of my favourite performances of this song. My suspicions about the origins of the recording are allayed somewhat by a smattering of the presenter's voice before the track, although he sounds more Dutch than Danish to me!

'Turn it on Again' and 'Alien Afternoon' nicely contrast the old and new faces of Genesis. 'Turn it on Again' is certainly a heavier version here than elsewhere. The bass pedals and fuzz guitar are dominant giving the song a punchier feel. Ray sounds much more comfortable here, although he fluffs the lyrics occasionally, but delivers the track in fine form, ably assisted by the rest of the band. 'Alien Afternoon' is a studio perfect rendition of this moody classic. Tony's keyboards are a delight here and the only weak link appears to be Nir's percussion, which is all over the place!

Closing the short set with 'Invisible Touch' and another rare performance of 'Shipwrecked', this is another useful addition for collectors and does include several unique versions of some of the tracks.

BRAY FILM STUDIOS, WINDSOR, ENGLAND, 23 JANUARY 1998

Set List: No Son of Mine/Land of Confusion/The Lamb Lies Down on Broadway/Calling all Stations/Hold on My Heart/That's All/There Must Be Some Other Way/Domino/Carpet Crawlers/Firth of Fifth (Instrumental)/Congo/Home by the Sea/Second Home by the Sea/Dancing with the Moonlit Knight/Follow You Follow Me/Lover's Leap/Mama/The Dividing Line/Invisible Touch/Turn it on Again/Throwing it all Away/I Can't Dance//
Source: Audience Recording.

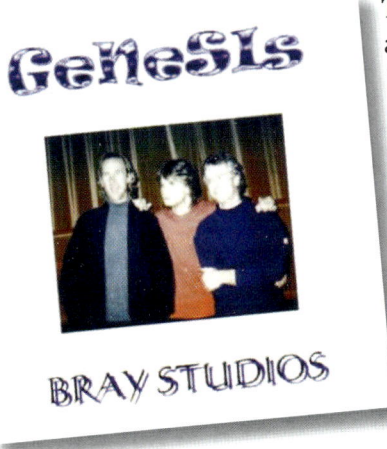

This was the first fully staged gig featuring the entire new stage show and was a final dress rehearsal for the band before they set off for Europe. Performed in front of an invited audience of a mere 200 lucky fans, this was the first chance that anyone got to see the new look band's new show properly.

The band opened the show with 'No Son of Mine' continuing the tradition of opening a new live set with a track from the preceding album and immediately you are taken with just how strong a voice Ray Wilson actually has. He manages to give the song every bit as much passion as Phil. The other new boys – Nir Zidkyahu and Anthony Drennan – are also conspicuous, with Nir's drumming in particular being very effective here, while Tony and Mike deliver the goods as always.

'Land of Confusion' follows and it doesn't really suit Ray's vocal style but he certainly seemed to be enjoying himself performing it. 'The Lamb Lies Down on Broadway' was a surprise choice but an inspired one, giving Ray a far better chance to shine, although Tony's nerves do get the better of him at the start. Mike grabs the song by the scruff of the neck with some meaty bass playing whilst Nir hammers hell out of his kit.

Our first glimpse of the new material is next with the title track to the new album, 'Calling all Stations', which was already a firm favourite of mine before the tour and it grows even more in stature in the live context. This is a bona fide Genesis classic in which everyone plays their hearts out. Mike's bass playing is phenomenal and Ray delivers an incredibly anguished vocal performance. Nir's percussion is rock solid whilst Tony and Anthony augment this fine performance with some impeccable playing.

'Hold on My Heart' and 'That's All' were next at this gig, but whether it was a combination of lack of audience response or perhaps the fact that Ray was patently uncomfortable singing them, I am not sure, but either way, this gig was to be the only one where they were played in front of an audience, making this recording an essential one for collectors.

'There Must Be Some Other Way' also gave us a further example of Ray's fine vocal range, while 'Domino' really tested it to the limits, with the rest of the ensemble delivering another fine performance. Another classic followed with 'Carpet Crawlers', which, along with the subsequent acoustic set, was to prove to be one of the highlights of the show. Without doubt, Ray delivers the goods here with a jazzy vocal of which his predecessors

Rehearsing the acoustic set at Bray Film Studios in Windsor.

would be proud. Tony has a couple of senior moments with the intro but the rest of the band are faultless, kudos especially to Anthony Drennan, who puts down a superb guitar part.

Another surprise came next with the instrumental end section of 'Firth of Fifth' being used to segue into 'Congo', perhaps the quirkiest track from the new album. Old and new merge surprisingly well here, although many purists complained at Anthony Drennan's treatment of Steve's solo – personally I thought it was great!

'Home by the Sea' gives everyone another chance to stretch their legs before the bona fide highlight of this and every subsequent show, an acoustic set comprising the intro to 'Dancing with the Moonlit Knight', followed by 'Follow You Follow Me', and a brilliant rendering of 'Lover's Leap'. Simply having the opportunity to watch the band in acoustic mode was an unforgettable delight and it is evident from this recording that the audience thoroughly enjoyed it as much as the band did.

Always a band of contrasts, they followed this with 'Mama', without doubt the most physically demanding song for Ray's voice to cope with, but he handles it like a trooper here and delivers a stunning performance, while the rest of the band back him to the hilt.

Then we are into the home straight and a run through a selection of some of the band's latter-day hits, but not before we have another long form track from the new album. 'The Dividing Line' is another of those songs that fans either like or loathe. Whatever your shade of opinion, no one could doubt the energy being generated by the band here.

The final salvo of tracks opened with 'Invisible Touch', a song which places incredible strain on any singers' voice, and Ray does struggle with it but he redeems himself with an excellent performance on 'Turn it on Again', which also gives Mike and Tony another chance to shine.

The encores were disappointing and the subject of much discussion among the fan base both during the tour and subsequently. Personally I felt that neither 'Throwing it all Away' or 'I Can't Dance' were songs that did either the band or Ray any justice. Indeed, he looked very uncomfortable singing both of them, but I suppose the band decided to play it safe with the set list this time round. As first nights go, the band played a blinder, although they must have known they were in safe hands with an audience of their most devoted fans to cheer them on. Recording wise, the result is clear if a little flat, mainly owing to the acoustics of the room itself but enjoyable nonetheless.

PETOFI SPORTSHAL, BUDAPEST, HUNGARY (REHEARSALS), 28 JANUARY 1998

Set List: No Son of Mine/Land of Confusion/The Lamb Lies Down on Broadway/Calling all Stations/Hold on My Heart/Alien Afternoon/There Must Be Some Other Way/Domino/Carpet Crawlers/Firth of Fifth/Congo/Home by the Sea/Second Home by the Sea/Dancing with the Moonlit Knight/Follow You Follow Me/Lover's Leap/Mama/The Dividing Line/Invisible Touch/Turn it on Again/Throwing it all Away/I Can't Dance//
Source: Audience Recording.

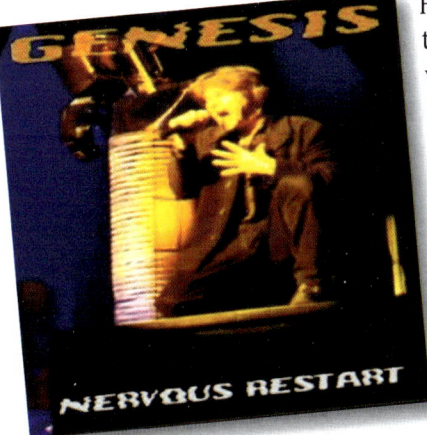

Here is the last day of rehearsal for the tour, with the opening night being at the same venue the following night. This recording (and its accompanying video) make for a fascinating behind the scenes look at the last run through before the punters get their chance. The video is especially interesting and amusing because it shows how relaxed the band are despite how many nerves they must have been experiencing on the day.

Set wise, the band had already made several changes from the performance the week before at Bray with 'That's All' biting the bullet. 'Shipwrecked' took its place, probably owing to its recent release in Europe as the follow-up single to 'Congo'. What we have here is a complete run through of the live set for the benefit of both band and sound/lighting technicians, and so the band allow themselves the luxury of the odd screw-up here and there.

Right from the start, the band sound and look incredibly relaxed, indeed, it is weird watching the DVD of this performance with no audience in front of the band. Ray sounds in good voice throughout the opening pairing of 'No Son of Mine' and 'Land of Confusion'. Being a rehearsal, there are few if any introductions to the songs and so it is left to Tony's keyboards to introduce the mighty 'Lamb Lies Down on Broadway' and it is here that the band's choice of Ray as singer really proves to be an inspired one. He doesn't sound like a Collins/Gabriel clone but with a voice more akin to Peter's he gives this classic a suitably respectful interpretation. New boys Nir Z. and Antony Drennan too, have slotted in without any trouble.

Calling all Stations as an album certainly deserved a better reception than it was given at the time and the title track certainly proves that Genesis can do heavier material. Mike's dirty bass lines and Nir's rock solid percussion give this one a suitably dramatic edge, while Ray delivers a marvellous emotional vocal. 'Hold on My

Heart' survived the Bray rehearsal, but this is to be its last performance, and I for one was glad when it was dropped. This kind of material really doesn't suite Ray's voice and he sounds (and looks) uncomfortable singing it.

Another slice of Genesis drama next, with the haunting tale of alien abduction that is 'Alien Afternoon'; another classic slice of long form Genesis. Tony and Mike share some reggae-tinged chords whilst Ray's lilting vocals gradually give way to a more impassioned one as the tale unfolds.

'There Must Be Some Other Way' is another good example of how good a rock voice Ray really has. It is a deceptively simple song, underpinned by some fine playing from Tony, Anthony, and Nir. 'Domino' also suits Ray's vocals perfectly and musically, the rest of the band give this a fine accompaniment with kudos going to Nir for a fine percussive delivery. Perhaps the most surprising thing about this tour was the return to the set of several tracks that fans had long since thought forgotten. None was more surprising than 'Carpet Crawlers', which makes a welcome return here. Once again, Ray's vocal has echoes of his predecessor without sounding derivative. Anthony also gives the guitar part a sensitive treatment and once more Nir is the glue that holds it all together.

To my mind the only disappointment with the new set is the separation of the instrumental section of 'Firth of Fifth' from the song. It sounds disjointed and somehow out of place. Mind you, Anthony nails Steve's solo here in fine style, so it's not all bad! Segueing surprisingly easily into this, 'Congo' actually improves in the live context. I have always felt that this was too quirky a song to be single material but like 'Abacab' before it, it definitely grows in performance.

'Home by the Sea' is another classic that Ray was to eventually take to new heights at several shows later in the tour. Tonight though, the song sounds slightly flat, perhaps because there isn't a proper audience to give it the edge that it deserves. Musically too it is a workmanlike performance, not surprising, given the fact that this is a rehearsal rather than a gig. Without doubt the highlight of the new show was to be the acoustic medley that comprised 'Dancing with the Moonlit Knight', 'Follow You Follow Me', and 'Lover's Leap' from *Supper's Ready*, all of which were to be swallowed with a whole heap of relish by fans at the shows on the tour. Tonight we get to hear the band sans audience and they sound (and look) relaxed and comfortable and the choice of material was inspired with everyone enjoying a lighter moment in the evening.

Back to the drama next with 'Mama', a song which at times really taxed Phil's vocals, but one which Ray is totally at home with. In fact, his darker voice actually adds to the atmosphere of the song. Mike and Tony demonstrate that they haven't lost the ability to conjure something special from the simplest of materials. 'The Dividing Line' is another underrated song from the new album too. Here there is some fine hard rock playing from Mike and Antony, while once again Nir provides an impressive rhythmic background.

The finale of the set brings us back to Genesis the hit-making machine with the quartet of 'Invisible Touch', 'Turn it on Again', which close the show proper. Ray sounds perfectly at home here and if you watch the film of this gig he is smiling throughout and obviously having a great time. 'Turn it on Again' certainly sounds more akin to Ray's own style of music and the band are obviously enjoying another chance to rock out – even the handful of people in the audience are having a good time too.

The encores are the only time where I personally think that Ray is perhaps a bit less than comfortable. However, here he encourages the select "audience" to join in during 'Throwing it all Away', which has never been a favourite of mine, but there you go. The show closes with the hilarious 'I Can't Dance' and it is evident that this has been chosen purely to please the newer fans. Hilariously on the video, you can see the lucky fans who were witnessing this performance doing the "walk" routine, which even brings a smile from Tony Banks – a rarity in itself!

SPORTOVINHALA, PRAGUE, CZECH REPUBLIC, 2 FEBRUARY 1998

Set List: Mama/Calling all Stations/There Must Be Some Other Way/The Lamb Lies Down on Broadway/Alien Afternoon/Congo/Domino/Home by the Sea/Second Home by the Sea/Turn it on Again/No Son of Mine/Land of Confusion/Shipwrecked/ Invisible Touch//
Source: FM Radio Broadcast.

When the overall attitude of fans towards the final recording line up of Genesis is taken into account, we are nonetheless lucky that the *Calling all Stations* tour of 1998 has been better served by radio and TV broadcasts than many that preceded it.

This show was the third one on the tour, and another that took in a territory that had previously been ignored by the band. Broadcast on both TV and radio, it is interesting to note that both the TV and radio broadcast contain tracks that were seldom (if ever) played after this gig. Running order has gone to pot on the radio broadcast, however, which opens with the grind of 'Mama', in which Ray's voice does an admirable job of emphasising the drama of the track, while Mike and new boy Anthony Drennan do a great job in the guitar department.

Like Phil, Ray does an adequate job of introducing some of the songs in a phonetic version of the language, but we go back in time here, as 'Calling all Stations' is next to be broadcast. Here Mike is the lord of all he surveys as his bass dominates all around it and Nir and Tony augment it with some fine playing. Ray's performance perfectly captures the fundamental drama of the song, echoing both Peter and Phil at times, to my ears. Another new song is next – 'There Must Be Some Other Way' – another fine slice of melodic rock from Genesis and a damn fine vocal here from Ray. Musically, it is Nir and Mike who keep this train rolling with some fine rhythm playing overlaid by the usual impeccable chords from Tony, although he still sounds a little unsure at times.

'The Lamb Lies Down on Broadway' has no such problems. Ray is pitch perfect here and Tony lays down a superb background, over which Mike and Anthony put in a fine performance, and Nir rattles the traps with gusto. This show has obviously been edited for broadcast purposes, and so sadly we are missing most of the between songs rapport between Ray and the crowd. 'Alien Afternoon', a song destined to be in and out of the set list over the coming shows, appears here in a very workmanlike version, in which Ray's voice and Tony's eerie keyboard phrasings bring shivers to the spine.

'Domino' also gains somewhat from Ray's altogether more ballsy vocals, which add enormously to the edginess of the song. Tony's keyboards stab like a maniac's knife underpinned by the rock solid rhythm section of Mike and Nir. 'Home by the Sea' is another beneficiary of Ray's vocal style, and if he had any nerves they certainly don't show in this assured and confident performance.

Of the remaining tracks on the broadcast, perhaps the most interesting to collectors is the all too rare appearance of 'Shipwrecked'. Not the greatest track by the band but certainly one that in the live context works so much better than it does on record. The broadcast ends with 'Invisible Touch', a song which puts enormous strain on a singer's vocal chords and it is no surprise that, even with a lowered key, Ray at times sounds slightly strained here, but nonetheless this ends another enjoyable performance and one that once again will be of interest to collectors.

HALLE TONY GARNIER, LYON, FRANCE, 20 FEBRUARY 1998

Set List: No Son of Mine/Land of Confusion/The Lamb Lies Down on Broadway/Calling all Stations/Carpet Crawlers/There Must Be Some Other Way/Domino/Firth of Fifth/Congo/Home by the Sea/Second Home by the Sea/Dancing with the Moonlit Knight/Follow You Follow Me/Lover's Leap/Mama/The Dividing Line/Invisible Touch/Turn it on Again/Throwing it all Away/I Can't Dance//
Source: Audience Recording.

This show was mid-way through the tour and one that the author has very good memories of! I suppose a Genesis gig on your birthday is the ideal birthday present for any Genesis fan, and so this gig was the best gift I received in 1998 – and courtesy of the band's management as well! Having already seen the band's rehearsal show at Bray a few weeks before, I had a good idea what to expect but even so, excitement was high as I entered the cavernous hall for tonight's spectacle.

As usual, the opening salvoes of the show placed the emphasis on the latter-day Collins material with a dramatic 'No Son of Mine' opening the proceedings, and one which gave Ray a chance to really shine with his darker vocals giving the song a harder edge. Mike's stabbing guitar phrasings cut the air like a knife too, adding even more tension to the performance. 'Land of Confusion' also sets the tempo for the rest of the gig, with Mike and new drummer Nir Z. providing a rock solid rhythm section, while Ray delivered yet another suitably impassioned vocal performance.

'The Lamb Lies Down on Broadway' was next without fanfare or introduction (not that it needs one!). Tony's arpeggio was sufficient introduction to send the audience into paroxysms of delight. Once again, Ray really came into his own here with his vocals giving the track some eerie echoes of his predecessor. Tony really shines here too. His playing is tasteful and understated throughout. Ray has his chance to indulge in a bit of "Franglais" as he introduces the first of the new tracks in tonight's show; the title track to the new album, 'Calling all Stations', which was already a favourite of mine from the moment I heard the studio version. Tonight's performance was simply superb. Mike, Anthony, and Nir conjured up just the right amount of drama and pathos between them, over which Tony's impeccable chords soared like a spirit. Ray's anguished vocals brought this track stunningly to life too.

Another helping of 'Lamb' next with a beautifully understated performance of 'Carpet Crawlers', in which Ray once again delivered with great gusto and verve. 'There Must Be Some Other Way' also showed the power of Ray's voice, while Mike and Tony provided a suitably dramatic but subtle accompaniment, and Nir overlaid everything with some impeccable percussion. 'Domino' has already become a favourite in Genesis' live show and tonight's performance was equally high on drama as usual. Sadly, the visuals let the side down here because of the separation of the three "Jumbotron" screens that completely spoiled the visual effects. Musically, however, this was another masterful performance with Tony and Nir sharing the musical honours and Ray grabbing the audience by the scruff of the neck and giving 110 per cent as usual.

Segueing the instrumental section of 'Firth of Fifth' into 'Congo' was never going to please some of the older fans but, I for one, thought that Anthony Drennan brought a new slant to this instrumental classic and 'Congo' itself was a nice, if typically quirky, slice of Genesis – a successor to the likes of 'Happy the Man' in some respects and just as enjoyable. Without doubt though, the highlight of this show, as at the others which I was lucky enough to see on this tour, was the acoustic medley comprising wonderful versions of 'Dancing with the Moonlit Knight', 'Follow You Follow Me', and 'Lover's Leap', which really was a delight to see and hear – especially seeing Tony on guitar again!

The rest of the gig mixed and matched old and new stuff although the emphasis on this final section was definitely on the hits. Some of them worked better than others. 'Turn it on Again', for example, suited Ray's rock credentials but I am sure I was not the only one sharing Ray's obvious discomfort at having to sing 'Throwing it all Away' and 'I Can't Dance', neither of which really suitable for ending what had otherwise been another excellent night's entertainment from the band.

INTERNATIONAL ARENA, CARDIFF, WALES, 5 MARCH 1998

Set List: No Son of Mine/Land of Confusion/The Lamb Lies Down on Broadway/Calling all Stations/Carpet Crawlers/Alien Afternoon/Domino/Firth of Fifth/Congo/Home by the Sea/Second Home by the Sea/Dancing with the Moonlit Knight/Follow You Follow Me/Lover's Leap/Not About Us/Mama/The Dividing Line/Invisible Touch/Turn it on Again/Throwing it all Away/I Can't Dance//
Source: Audience Recording.

The European tour must have been satisfying for the band with audience reaction to the new line up and new album being very favourable and attendances were good. The real test, however, must have been to try and convince the fans at home in the UK of the calibre of the new line up. It is strange to think that merely a few days before, I had been present at the worst Genesis performance I have ever seen at Earls Court, and here in Cardiff I was about to witness the best performance I had ever seen them give!

Don't ask me why this was the case, but opinion among the fans who were at the band's second night at the International Arena is agreed that this was another magical night's performance by the band. Maybe it was the fact that the band hadn't been seen in Wales since 1980 and the fans were up for it? Whatever the reason, from the moment that the band took the stage, something special was happening. The opening trio of 'No Son of Mine', 'Land of Confusion', and 'The Lamb Lies Down on Broadway' were all delivered flawlessly. Ray's vocal on the latter was impeccable.

Ray's banter about the previous incumbents of the vocalist's position was warmly received and if there was any doubt about the reception of the newer material. 'Calling all Stations' itself was received by a hearty cheer from the crowd and deservedly so. If Genesis' credentials as a *rock* band were in doubt, then this song alone restored them! Mike in particular grabbed the track by the scruff of the neck and let rip with some awesome riffs. 'Carpet Crawlers' was an inspired choice, as not only is Ray's voice ideally suited to it, but it also gave the rest of the band a chance to quietly shine. Anthony Drennan gave a smart rendering of Steve's part.

'Alien Afternoon' also made a welcome return here after a couple of days out of the set. Another dark and atmospheric track, this was yet another golden opportunity for everyone to shine. Mike and Tony's almost reggae shuffle contrasted nicely with Ray's smoky vocals and Nir Z. was the glue that held everyone together. Ray's plea for sympathy over not getting the women and Tony's erectile problems gets a modicum of audience appreciation, although I am sure that Tony was none too happy! Happily 'Home by the Sea' was another glorious slice of Genesis delivered piping hot and still imbued with all the excitement that only such a Genesis "long" can generate!

The unexpected highlight of this new look show followed with an acoustic trio of classics, including 'Follow You Follow Me', 'Lover's Leap', and the current single, 'Not About Us', really worked and tonight the band nailed the performance to perfection. The rest of the show was the by now typical mix of hits that sent everyone home happy, which must have done the same for the band itself, and they certainly deserved it. This performance was a belter by anyone's standards!

HARTWALL ARENA, HELSINKI, FINLAND, 5 APRIL 1998

Set List: No Son of Mine/Land of Confusion/The Lamb Lies Down on Broadway/Calling all Stations/Carpet Crawlers/Alien Afternoon/Domino/Firth of Fifth/Congo/Home by the Sea/Second Home by the Sea/Dancing with the Moonlit Knight/Follow You Follow Me/Lover's Leap/Not About Us/Mama/The Dividing Line/Invisible Touch/Turn it on Again/Throwing it all Away/I Can't Dance//
Source: Audience Recording.

This was the last show of the European tour proper and one that I was privileged to attend myself, even enjoying a pre-show snowball fight outside the arena prior to Showtime. Well, the bars in Helsinki are incredibly expensive, so I had to do something to keep warm, folks! The band had been firing on all cylinders during the shows that I had seen and I was certainly expecting nothing less than the same here. I was a bit concerned after hearing that the shows immediately preceding this one in Bielefeld and Stockholm had been cancelled owing to Ray experiencing vocal problems. However, I was assured prior to flight time that the gig was going ahead, so off I went.

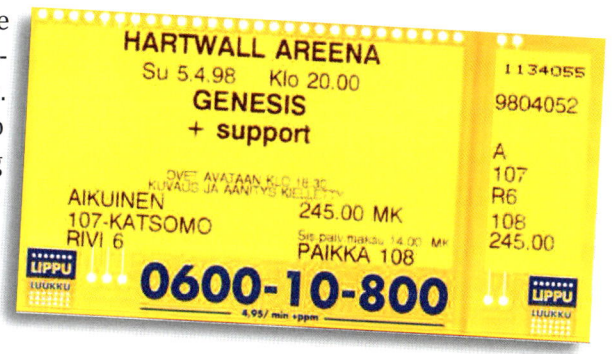

The Hartwall Arena was a brand new ice hockey arena and massive. However, the band had no problems filling it with an enthusiastic and surprisingly young audience. I assume that many of the spectators were from neighbouring territories that had no other chance of seeing the band. Either way, they can be heard giving the band an enthusiastic and vocal reception as they emerge on stage. The quality of this audience recording is above average and the taper had obviously found himself a good position from which to record the gig. Sound is balanced and clean throughout and not marred by too much audience chatter. Ray's introductions to the first batch of songs in Finnish are hilarious, although his efforts are appreciated by the audience. Even after all this time, Tony still managed to play a few bum notes in the intro to 'The Lamb'. Musically, however, the rest of the gig is as near perfect as you would expect. Anthony Drennan really plays his heart out on 'Firth of Fifth', stamping his own interpretation on to the track, while on such percussion-driven tracks as 'Second Home by the Sea' and 'Congo', Nir Zidkyahu hammers the shit out of his kit and gives both tracks the kind of harder edge they need.

The corny introductions, however, were another matter and even the blushes of Tony Banks were not spared by Ray's humorous comments that preceded 'Home by the Sea'. Being the last gig of the tour, there was a certain amount of schoolboy humour going on, especially during 'I Can't Dance', where if you are wondering why the audience are laughing, it is because unlike previous gigs, the "girl" that Ray selected from the audience is none other than Giles; a member of the band's road crew, suitably attired, of course. And as for the moose warning sign... well, less said the better, really! All in all, a nice recording of a great final show.

A Selection Of Shows: Genesis & Solo Live Guide 1976-2014

Genesis

PART ONE: GENESIS

CHAPTER ELEVEN
"A SELECTION OF SHOWS"
THE TURN IT ON AGAIN TOUR 2007

I, like just about every other Genesis fan, was taken completely by surprise by the announcement on 6 November 2006 that Genesis were reforming with Phil Collins, Chester Thompson, and Daryl Stuermer for "a selection of shows" as Phil so euphemistically put it during the conference itself. The reasons for this decision are patently obvious to anyone. The band had their enormous back catalogue of albums freshly transferred to the new digital 5.1 format to promote. This was a major investment by EMI, the band's record company. So far no other artist of Genesis' calibre has committed their entire catalogue to this format and it represented a potentially enormous loss if it didn't prove popular with us; the punters. Fortunately, no such worries were necessary. The albums are a magnificent testament to the musicianship and creativity of all the musicians involved and to their producer, Nick Davis.

Ostensibly, therefore, with no "new" product to promote, what exactly were we to expect at these gigs? Well, this was a great chance for the band to revisit their entire back catalogue and polish off some oldies for the fans. Thankfully, this is exactly what we got. A great deal of thought had evidently gone into the music and the visual presentation, which, even by Genesis' standards, was amazing. Old and new fans must have gone away happy from these gigs where just about every album from *Foxtrot* onwards was represented by at least one track. Even the medleys were given a new slant and opening the show with a slimmed-down version of the *Duke* suite was inspired. Old and not so old material sat happily side by side here and as a resume of the band's career these shows were hard to beat. The band had finally taken a leaf out of both Peter Gabriel and Steve Hackett's books by making *every* recording of every gig on both the European and subsequent US tours available to us as soundboard recordings, thereby effectively beating the bootleggers and generating even more revenue from the tour.

Phil's on-going health problems which led to the announcement of his retirement from musical activity back in 2011 seem to have resolved themselves and recent reports have led to speculation that he might return to live performances at some point although nothing is planned at the moment. Peter's continuing disinterest in re-joining his old band mates took a slight deviation when the classic five posed earlier this year for a photo shoot in conjunction with a full career documentary for both a BBC broadcast and commercial DVD release. And despite the rumours of another on stage Genesis reunion, the prospects of that in the near future look unlikely especially when you bear in mind the current round of touring activities by Peter, Mike and Steve which are to continue well into 2015 the likelihood of any similar activity by any Genesis line up is slim at best but never say never! Thankfully though, their rich legacy of music is secure for future generations to enjoy.

Turn it on Again press conference, The May Fair Hotel, London, 6 November 2006

HALL 5 FLANDERS EXPO, BRUSSELS, BELGIUM, (REHEARSALS), 4 JUNE 2007
Set List: Behind the Lines-Duke's End-Turn it on Again/No Son of Mine/Land of Confusion/In the Cage-Cinema Show-Duke's Travels-Afterglow/Hold on My Heart/ Home by the Sea/Second Home by the Sea/Follow You Follow Me/Firth of Fifth-I Know What I Like/ Mama/Ripples/Throwing it all Away/Domino/Drum Duet/Los Endos/Tonight, Tonight, Tonight (Shortened Version)/Invisible Touch/I Can't Dance/Carpet Crawlers//
Source: Audience Recording/DVD.

This was the final chance for the band to iron out any potential wrinkles in the production and also the first opportunity to gauge the reaction of an invited audience, with members of the official fan club and selected others (myself included) invited to attend. Seeing the stage set up for the first time you could not fail but to be impressed by its sheer scale. Genesis have always been a band that staged remarkably visual shows and this one was to be no exception. Having avoided any potential spoilers on the Internet, the performance was to take me completely by surprise. Yes, there were some predictable moments, not least the performance of several of the "hits", but the show itself was a glorious résumé of the band's magnificent back catalogue.

With new visuals for such classics as 'In the Cage' and 'I Know What I Like', it was evident that a lot of thought (as well as money) had gone into this production. The band themselves were relaxed and comfortable and Phil was in good form even admitting that the story that preceded 'Home by the Sea' would be scary when he had finished writing it! Musically the band were tight and on form throughout and the show gave everyone a chance to shine. Daryl's solo on 'Firth of Fifth' was razor sharp, while Tony's impeccable playing augmented many classics, while Mike drove the band along with some mean bass licks. An unexpected highlight was the brand new introduction to 'Los Endos', which featured Phil, Chester, and a stool! Yes, they paid homage to the origins of their now famous 'Drum Duet' by performing it on a stool before launching into 'Los Endos' itself. Another surprise was the sedate finale of 'Carpet Crawlers', which was absolutely awesome. With a show like this to perform, the fans were certainly being spoiled by the band this time round – even the medleys were good this time round!

PART ONE: GENESIS

ARENA, AMSTERDAM, NETHERLANDS, 1 JULY 2007

Set List: 'Behind the Lines'/Duke's End/Turn it on Again/No Son of Mine/Land of Confusion/In the Cage-Cinema Show-Duke's Travels-Afterglow/Hold on My Heart/Home by the Sea/Second Home by the Sea/Follow You Follow Me/Firth of Fifth-I Know What I Like/Mama/Ripples/Throwing it all Away/Domino/Drum Thing/Los Endos/Tonight, Tonight, Tonight/Invisible Touch/I Can't Dance/Carpet Crawlers//
Source: Encore Series Soundboard Recording.

Wow! What an amazing recording this one is! With the set being the same every night it is sometimes difficult to appreciate exactly how *different* each night's performance can actually be.

Tonight, the band are evidently on top form. The opening trio of 'Behind the Lines', 'Duke's End', and 'Turn it on Again' roar out of the traps like a cannonball. The entire band sound as if they are playing as if their lives depended on it. Even the echoey acoustics of the arena augment the drama of the proceedings. 'No Son of Mine' sounds incredibly dramatic here with Phil's voice echoing ghostlike around the hall, while the rest of the band put in an incredible performance taking this classic track to new heights.

The high octane performance continues with a storming version of 'Land of Confusion', in which the rhythm section of Mike, Chester, and Daryl really go to town on things. While the old farts among the audience are given a treat next with the evergreen 'In the Cage' medley. Not as straightforward as usual this time, though. The inclusion of 'Duke's Travels' before the climactic 'Afterglow' proves once again to be an inspired choice adding even more drama to an already electrifying performance. Phil's voice does show signs of strain at times but that only serves to add to the claustrophobic atmosphere generated by the band – difficult to do in a setting such as this! Once again, Mike and Tony battle away in glorious fashion, while Chester holds the entire performance together with some sterling drumming.

'Hold on My Heart' gives everyone a chance, no doubt, to collect their breath but the respite doesn't last long. Phil's introduction to 'Home by the Sea' definitely hasn't improved with age. Never mind, the song itself has grown enormously since 1983 and tonight's performance is another blinder. Tony's keyboards echo around the arena like the demented spirit that is the subject of the song. Mike, Daryl, and Chester don't put a foot wrong either, especially during the instrumental 'Second Home by the Sea', where Chester and Phil's percussion threaten to tear the walls of the arena down. Yet more treats follow for the older fans, with Daryl's guitar heralding the evergreen 'Follow You Follow Me', which is another track that simply gets better with age. Speaking of age, the band once again decided to truncate 'Firth of Fifth' to the instrumental section, most likely to give Phil's poor old chords a rest. No rest for the band though, as they rampage through another wonderful rendering of this classic. Daryl has certainly made this one his own and his soloing here is absolutely stunning. The 'Cosmic Lawnmower' makes another welcome appearance here as the band treat us to 'I Know What I Like'. Cue audience going wild. "We love you, Phil!" can clearly be heard at one point. Musically, this is another excellent performance from everyone, and indeed, the band seem to be feeding of the evidently enthusiastic crowd who can also be heard singing along, definitely making this a more "live" effort than other recordings.

The remainder of the recording is of similar high quality. 'Mama' has seldom sounded so highly charged, and 'Ripples' comes across superbly well too, augmented by some audience participation. 'Domino' also roars along at a frantic pace and just when you think that Phil's chords might give out, they give him a break (?) with the 'Drum Duet', leading into yet another marvellous performance of 'Los Endos'.

No rest for the wicked, though. 'Tonight, Tonight, Tonight' and 'Invisible Touch' really test Phil's vocal powers (and those of the audience) and, as usual, the show ends with the quiet resolution of a magnificent performance of 'Carpet Crawlers'. Without doubt, this is one of the best of the crop of "official bootleg" recordings from this tour and one that no fan should be without.

OLYMPIASTADION, BERLIN, GERMANY, 3 JULY 2007

Set List: Behind the Lines-Duke's End-Turn it on Again/No Son of Mine/Land of Confusion/In the Cage-Cinema Show-Duke's Travels-Afterglow/Hold on My Heart/Home by the Sea/Second Home by the Sea/Follow You Follow Me/Firth of Fifth-I Know What I Like/Mama/Ripples/Throwing it all Away/Domino/Drum Duet/Los Endos/Tonight, Tonight, Tonight (Shortened Version)/Invisible Touch/I Can't Dance/Carpet Crawlers//
Source: Encore Series Soundboard Recording.

Berlin is a city that holds a lot of memories for me and I was delighted to finally have the chance to see Genesis there on this tour. The Olympiastadion still retains the shell of the building which infamously hosted the 1936 Olympics, and as I entered, black and white images of those games kept flitting through my mind. Not for long though, as Genesis emerged on stage to a tumultuous roar from the crowd and my attention was drawn very much to the here and now.

As usual, the opener comprised a marvellous medley from *Duke*, which got the crowd in the mood to party. Phil's comments about the weather (it was pouring down at the time) got a laugh from the crowd, most of whom were getting drenched, but they didn't mind cos Genesis were here and they weren't going to let a little rain spoil the party! 'No Son of Mine' somehow managed to fill the cavernous stadium and was suitably dramatic. Phil's slightly hoarse vocal gave an added edge to the song, while Mike and Tony really conjured up a suitably dark and atmospheric feeling to it, helped no doubt by the surroundings.

There was no messing around tonight, as the band launched straight into 'Land of Confusion', which had a mighty sound in this prestigious stadium. Mike, Chester, and Daryl battled away with each other as if their lives depended on it. One criticism of these shows that I know was shared by many fans was the positioning of 'In the Cage' and its new medley so early in the set, as it followed next. "*Alte stucke*," as Phil explained, but honestly I think the crowd knew what was coming and the anticipation was almost tangible as the throbbing chords of the intro heralded the arrival of this classic slice of Genesis. Augmented by brand new and impressive visuals, this was a treat for the ears and the eyes with each and every member of the band putting 110 per cent into their performance. Choosing to augment the extracts from 'Cinema Show' with 'Duke's Travels' proved to be an inspired choice and throughout it was Tony who stole the show. He says he isn't a natural performer. Well by God he certainly was tonight! The music soared majestically towards its ultimate climax and by the time we reached 'Afterglow', the crowd were ecstatic. Daryl's soloing during 'Travels' brought a lump to the throat and I am sure by the time 'Afterglow's' final chords faded away, there wasn't a dry eye in the stadium – and that's nothing to do with the weather, either!

Fearing that the band might have peaked to early, a lull in the proceedings followed with 'Hold on My Heart', which I am sure gave Phil as much as the audience a much needed breather. No rest for the wicked though as Phil's "ghost story" led us into the supernatural world of 'Home by the Sea'. Sound-wise, this recording manages to capture the atmosphere in the stadium to perfection. From Mike's stabbing chords at the start, augmented by Tony's almost orchestral keyboards, the song builds to a suitably dramatic climax with the extended 'Second Home by the Sea', an excuse for the band to stretch their musical legs and they take it with a heap of collective glee. Phil's voice, now definitely showing signs of strain, gives the song just the right amount of angst.

'Follow You Follow Me' calms things down for a few minutes. It is great to hear Daryl's almost banjo-like guitar playing contrasted so well with Tony's lush chords. Chester delivers another impeccable percussive backing and Phil sings his heart out. The instrumental section of 'Firth of Fifth' sounds disjointed with no song to back it up, but musically it is still a superb piece, in which Tony and Daryl really take the honours. Daryl's soloing in particular threatens to tear the roof off the stadium – hold on ... what roof?!

A definite trip down Memory Lane next though, as once again the 'Cosmic Lawnmower' revs up for this evergreen (pun intended) classic. Already impressive visuals take on a new meaning here as images of the band past and present flash across the screens. And if you were in the front row you might even have caught sight of yourself at times too! You can ever hear Mike and Tony on the chorus and everyone is obviously having a great time living in the past for once. Phil's tarantella has also lost none of its power to amuse and entertain, although I bet he had some bruises afterwards!

The band really chose to give the fans what they wanted on this tour and the remainder of tonight's show drew upon their magnificent back catalogue with no low points – apart form 'Throwing it all Away' – which is a song I have always detested, and despite the rain, Genesis shone through and gave Berlin and those *"auslanders"* such as myself something to remember and cherish from tonight's show, and this recording captures that magic perfectly.

OLD TRAFFORD STADIUM, MANCHESTER, ENGLAND, 7 JULY 2007

Set List: Behind the Lines-Duke's Travels-Turn it on Again/No Son of Mine/Land of Confusion/In the Cage-Cinema Show-Duke's Travels-Afterglow/Hold on My Heart/Home by the Sea/Second Home by the Sea/Follow You Follow Me/Firth of Fifth-I Know What I Like/Mama/Ripples/Throwing it all Away/Domino/Drum Duet/Los Endos/Tonight, Tonight, Tonight (Shortened Version)/Invisible Touch/I Can't Dance/Carpet Crawlers//
Source: Encore Series Soundboard Recording.

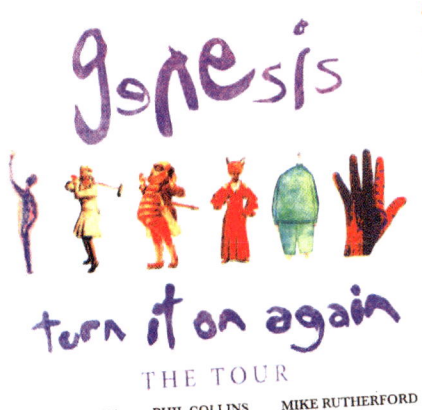

Without doubt, this was the best performance that I saw of this tour. This gig had it all: power, majesty, humour, and a fantastic setting. This stadium is not called "the theatre of dreams" for nothing! And that is coming from a proud Scouser! Tonight, Genesis were intent on making a dream come true for their British fans.

The opening salvo of 'Behind the Lines-Duke's End-Turn it on Again' was greeted by thunderous applause by the crowd. Here was a band determined not to take any prisoners. Phil prowled the stage like am angry tiger

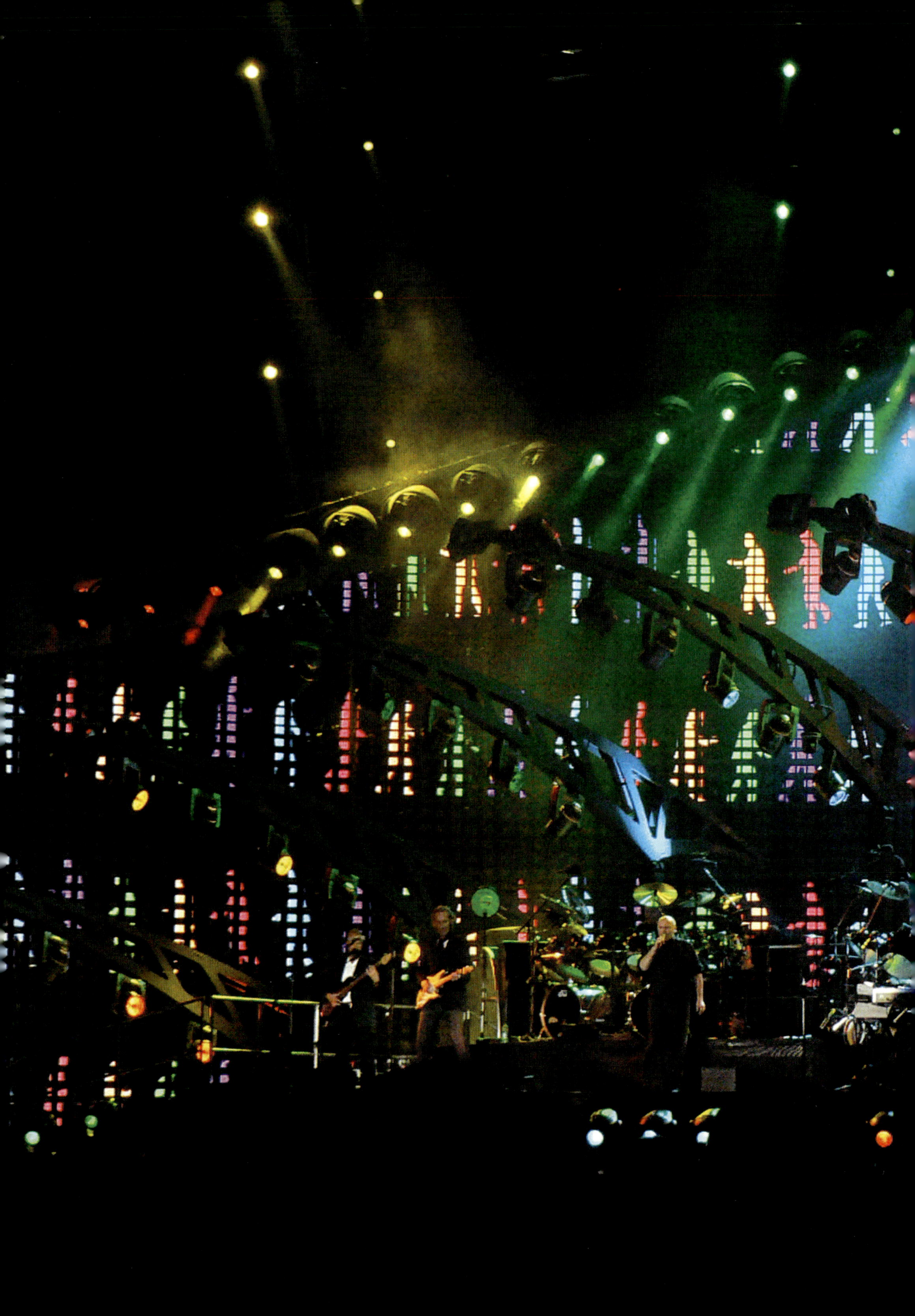

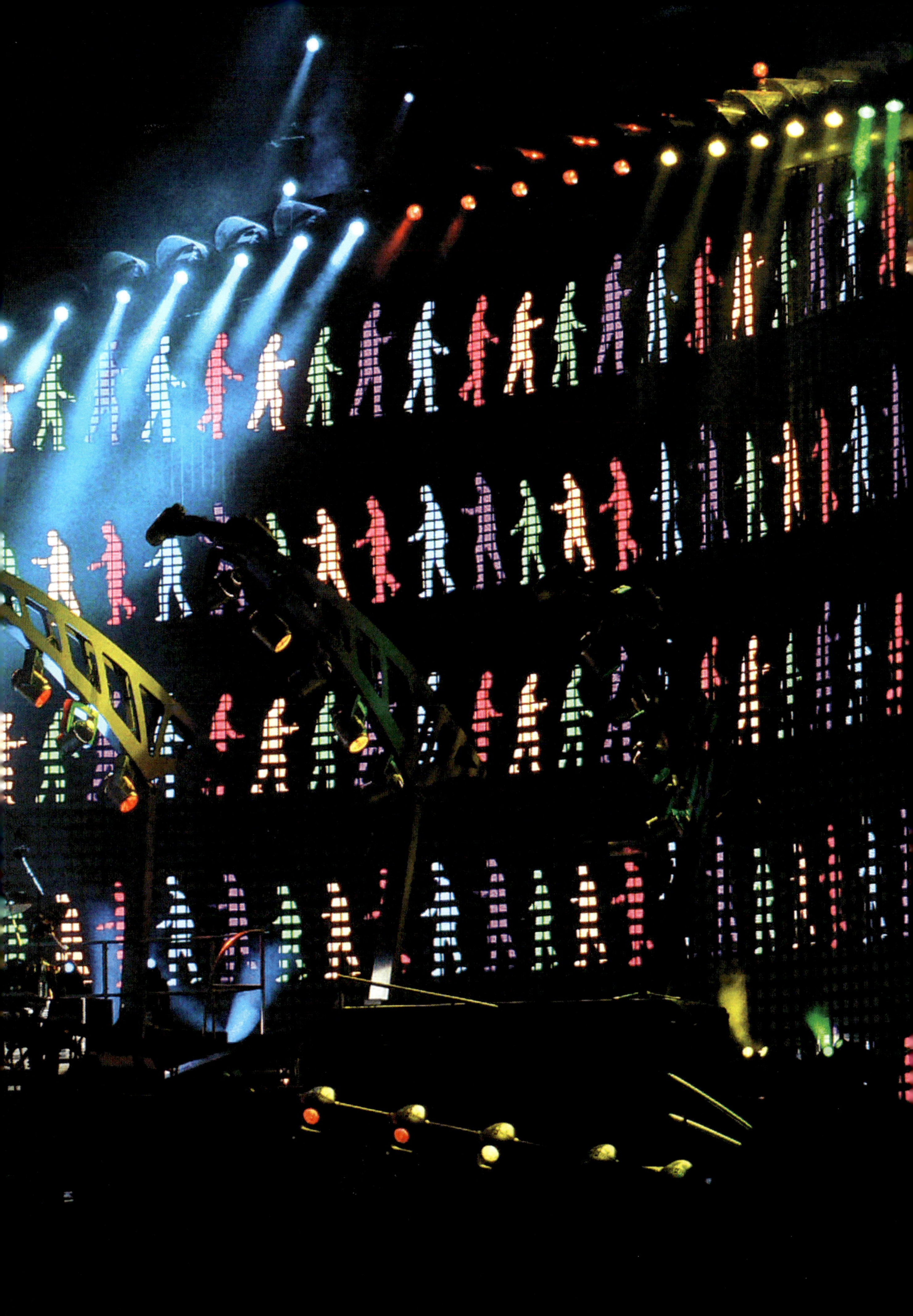

throughout the performance whilst the rest of the band provided an equally ferocious musical accompaniment.

'No Son of Mine' was obviously slightly more familiar to certain elements of the crowd and it was delivered in fine style here. Phil managed to give the vocal delivery just the right amount of drama, while Tony and Mike's combined instrumental work was underpinned by a rock solid rhythm section in Daryl and Chester. The crowd lapped up 'Land of Confusion' too, before the band gave us older fans a marvellous treat with the wonderful 'In the Cage' medley, which this time included 'Duke's Travels', before launching into the majestic 'Afterglow'. Visually and musically, this was a stunning performance, although I still think that this particular part of the show should have been reserved until darkness had settled in properly. Kudos here in particular to Daryl and Tony who played as if their very lives depended on it.

'Hold on My Heart' seemed somewhat out of place next to the preceding bevy of classics, but once again, the contrast served to illustrate just how varied Genesis' music had become over the years. Phil's "ghost story" certainly hasn't improved with age, but who cares? 'Home by the Sea/Second Home by the Sea' improves on each and every tour and it was truly awesome here, aided in no small part by the incredible visuals that accompanied it. A real chance for the band to flex their musical muscles, to which they all seemed to relish enormously.

'Follow You Follow Me' brought a lump to my throat and so memories flashed through my mind as I watched the band perform it. Daryl's guitar playing here was superb and once again the accompanying visuals were both clever and entertaining but not overpowering. 'Firth of Fifth' and 'I Know What I Like' were greeted like old friends, which indeed they are. Once again, Daryl and Mike put in some superb playing, while Tony's keyboards augmented the performance seamlessly, and Phil belted out the vocals whilst hamming up for the crowd once again – just like old times!

Another contrasting pair next. The industrial grind and melodrama of 'Mama' worked against the acoustically-driven 'Ripples' and both worked superbly. Phil's voice sounded strained during the former but that was not at all surprising given the demands that had been placed on his voice all day. He also took great delight in winding up the Scouse contingent in the audience by praising the stadium. Not that he seemed bothered at all and he was obviously enjoying himself.

'Throwing it all Away' provided yours truly with a welcome pee-break but I was back in time for an incredibly powerful performance of 'Domino' complete with Phil's explanation of the "Domino Principle" to a crowd that was only too aware of it! Always a masterpiece, tonight's performance was no exception, with the entire band grabbing the audience by the scruff of the neck as the drama unfolded before our eyes and ears.

The wonderfully tongue-in-cheek drum stool duet followed leading into what else? 'Los Endos', of course. This evergreen simply cannot be beaten as a show closer and tonight Phil and Chester gave it their all to awesome effect whilst the rest of the band heightened the drama by their impeccable playing. Surprisingly on this tour though, this was followed by the shortened version of 'Tonight, Tonight, Tonight' and 'Invisible Touch', which really tested Phil's vocals and the stamina of the rest of the band – and of course, also the audience participation of the crowd, but the pace never slackened for a moment, bringing the show proper to a suitably explosive conclusion.

I must admit that I could live without 'I Can't Dance', but there is no denying that it is a bona fide crowd pleaser and tonight was no exception. From the opening guitar chords, the crowd lapped it up and band and audience were magically united in celebration, and the show was closed with the sublime majesty of 'Carpet Crawlers', which brought the evening to a suitably emotional close.

TWICKENHAM STADIUM, LONDON, ENGLAND, 8 JULY 2007

Set List: Behind the Lines-Duke's End-Turn it on Again/No Son of Mine/Land of Confusion/In the Cage-Cinema Show-Duke's Travels-Afterglow/Hold on My Heart/ Home by the Sea/Second Home by the Sea/Follow You Follow Me/Firth of Fifth-I Know What I Like/Mama/Ripples/Throwing it all Away/Domino/Drum Duet/Los Endos/Tonight, Tonight, Tonight (Shortened Version)/Invisible Touch/I Can't Dance/Carpet Crawlers//
Source: Encore Series Soundboard Recording/FM Radio Broadcast.

Returning to their home turf for their second and final UK gig of the tour, the band had a lot to live up to after the spectacle that was Manchester, regarded by many fans and some members of the crew as the best gig of the tour. Thankfully, the gig was exactly that – a spectacle. In the setting of one of England's finest sporting stadia, they didn't put a foot wrong – well apart from Phil swearing when it started to rain and ironically mentioning that the BBC would probably edit his comment out of their broadcast (which they did!).

The problem with such a standard set as this one is really how to differentiate between each gig. After all, the set is the same each night. Fortunately, the performances themselves were widely different, although mainly notable for how few technical cock-ups or fluffed lines took place. Twickenham itself was a marvellous performance, with the band comfortable in the knowledge that they were in front of their home crowd, relaxed and up for some fun, which they duly did as you can clearly hear on this excellent recording. Strangely enough, for once, the radio broadcast actually sounds significantly *better* than the soundboard recording. Well to my ears it does anyway!

BMO FIELD, TORONTO ONTARIO, CANADA, 7 SEPTEMBER 2007

Set List: Behind the Lines-Duke's End-Turn it on Again/No Son of Mine/Land of Confusion/In the Cage-Cinema Show-Duke's Travels-Afterglow/Hold on My Heart/Home by the Sea/Second Home by the Sea/Follow You Follow Me/Firth of Fifth-I Know What I Like/Mama/Ripples/Throwing it all Away/Domino/Drum Duet/Los Endos/Tonight, Tonight, Tonight (Shortened Version)/Invisible Touch/I Can't Dance/Carpet Crawlers//
Source: Encore Series Soundboard Recording.

The band finally returned to the USA and Canada for the final leg of this "selection of shows" as Phil so euphemistically called the tour. As was the case in Europe, only the largest stadia were to be graced by the band and here we have the recording from their second show in Toronto, which has long been a stronghold for Genesis. Unusually, two different stadia were used.

Right from the start, you are aware that this is a capacity crowd who are in full voice. The opening trio of songs are accompanied by an enthusiastic crowd, although Phil's voice sounds quite hoarse at times. Not surprising really! The band are in fine form and Phil is giving his usual bullshit introductions, which are lapped up by the crowd. With the set remaining the same as it had been for the European shows it is amazing that the band do not sound bored by this time, but there's no sign of that in either 'No Son of Mine' or 'Land of Confusion', which are delivered flawlessly. In fact, Phil's raspy vocal manages to increase the drama of the former. Tony's keyboards are augmented by some fine ensemble playing by Mike and Chester and for once you can even hear Mike singing on the chorus!

'In the Cage' – by now the longest serving song in the Genesis set – sounds simply superb here tonight. Tony leads the chase with some impeccable playing, augmented brilliantly by Mike and Chester. The performance really is something special, and once again, Phil's hoarse vocals add greatly to the dramatic effect. Once again, the alteration in the medley works extremely well and here Daryl takes his cue to shine putting in some damn fine licks, and by the time we reach the climatic 'Afterglow', the band are definitely in overdrive.

By the time we reach 'Mama' it is obvious that Phil is having real problems and he sounds worn out. Not that he gives anything less than 100 per cent though. Once again Tony and Mike really go to town on this song and hearing this performance really does send shivers down the spine. Even a song like 'Ripples', which is deceptively unassuming takes it out of the voice and Phil's impassioned vocal delivery here really does show the strain. Daryl, Mike, and Tony deliver a truly beautiful performance, which once again makes me wonder why this song was not performed more often over the years. With the rest of the set aimed fairly and squarely at the "hits" element of the band's catalogue it remains for the classic 'Drum Duet' and 'Los Endos' to give the old farts in the audience something to cheer about and they certainly do as you can hear on this recording! The real surprise of the show, however, remains the final encore: 'Carpet Crawlers', which simply gets better each and every time – a wonderful way to end another magical night.

****

PART ONE: GENESIS

A Selection Of Shows: Genesis & Solo Live Guide 1976-2014

PART TWO: PETER GABRIEL

Peter Gabriel

CHAPTER TWELVE
"EXPECTING THE UNEXPECTED" 1977

In the autumn of 1975, Peter left the Genesis "machinery" uncertain of what he might do next in his career. It was not long, however, before he was back in the studio recording demos for what was, in February 1977, to become his first solo album. Graced with what was soon to become the usual mix of catchy rhythms and eclectic soundscapes, it wasn't long before he undertook his first tour as a solo artist beginning with a string of shows in the USA followed by more in Europe and the UK.

His decision to return to the music business was justified by the qualified success of both the album and the single, 'Solsbury Hill', both of which achieved what must have been gratifying success both at home and abroad. With only one album's worth of material to draw from, it was obvious that Peter was going to have to make some reference to his previous work and indeed he did so with performances of both *Back in NYC* and the *Lamb Lies Down on Broadway*, which alternatively featured as encores during the various legs of the tour.

Perhaps what took the fans more by surprise than this was the inclusion of Marvin Gaye's. 'Ain't That Peculiar' and The Kinks' 'All Day And All Of The Night', featuring regularly in the show to the bemusement of fans and critics alike. Even more unusual for the time was the decision to "road test" material that Peter was still working on, and tracks such as 'Indigo' and 'White Shadow' appeared under various guises at shows.

Fortunately from the outset, Peter's live solo performances have been well documented by recordings and this tour is no exception.

MUSIC HALL, CLEVELAND, OHIO, USA, 15 MARCH 1977

Set List: Here Comes the Flood/On the Air/Moribund the Burgermeister/Waiting for the Big One/A Song Without Words (Indigo)/Excuse Me/Solsbury Hill/Ain't That Peculiar/Why Don't We/Humdrum/Slowburn/All Day and all of the Night/Here Comes the Flood (Reprise)/Modern Love/Down the Dolce Vita/Back in NYC//
Source: Mix Desk Recording.

Thankfully, right from the start of his solo career, recordings of gigs have been plentiful and this one is an excellent example of one of the first shows Peter performed in the USA. Opening with a solo vocal/piano rendition of 'Here Comes the Flood', this is Peter at his most emotional and the quality of this recording is superb. The tempo picks up a pace with the as yet unrecorded 'On the Air'. This was to become a feature of Gabriel's shows, which has lasted until very recently, that he would road test new material to gauge audience reaction to it and this one races out of the traps at a frantic pace.

Thunderous drums herald the arrival onstage of the urban paranoia of 'Moribund the Burgermeister', Peter still hasn't mastered the art of using a microphone properly, though as on occasions the vocals are quite muffled but the rest of the band more than make up for it with a surprisingly funky version. This is followed by Peter's interpretation of a late night jazz club for 'Waiting for the Big One', which works incredibly well. Another new song next and one without words at the time of recording, exaggerated by some vocal effects (helium possibly?) we will later come to know this one as 'Indigo', but here we have a prime example of Gabrielese. This is followed by the delightfully camp barber shop-driven 'Excuse Me', which if this recording is anything to go by was one that the entire band had a blast performing. What the audience thought is anyone's guess!

Time for the hit single next, as the band launch into 'Solsbury Hill'; always a classic and is performed simply but effectively here. Peter's love of Motown is put on display next with a marvellous rendering of 'Ain't That Peculiar'. Peter's band swallow this one with glee and deliver a marvellous interpretation, although Peter does struggle with the vocal delivery at times. 'Why Don't We' is another new and still unrecorded song, which is a great shame, because it generates a fantastic atmosphere on this recording.

'Humdrum' opens deceptively quietly with Peter's vocal and piano, but as we have come to expect from him, the calm is soon shattered as the rest of the band join in with some marvellous playing, especially Larry Fast's synthesisers. A tango rhythm permeates the song but I doubt if the audience were dancing during this one! Story time next and this is probably the closest we get to Peter's Genesis stories, with a bizarre lead into 'Slowburn', which manages to generate a superb atmosphere, especially with its symphonic introduction that bursts into flames with some impressive playing from the rest of Peter's band. His vocal has seldom sounded better than it does here.

'All Day And All Of The Night', The Kinks classic, gets the suitable rock 'n' roll treatment here with thunderous drums, hard rocking guitar, and a suitably harsh vocal from Peter – I love this performance! From the ridiculous to the sublime next as the atmosphere calms down for a superbly atmospheric performance of 'Here Comes the Flood', reprised and even better second time round. You can hear a pin drop as the audience are rapt by the performance. Party time arrives with 'Modern Love' and a look at man's obsession with consumer goods delivered in Peter's own unique way! The band get right behind him on this one and the result is one of the best recorded versions of this classic that you will ever hear. Band intros next leading into a nice riposte as some wag in the audience asks "Who are you?" to which Peter replies, "I'm Down the Dolce Vita." No prizes for guessing what closes the show then, eh? A fantastic rocking version.

'Back in NYC' heralds a rapturous cheer from the crowd as Peter delivers the only reference to his previous band mates. A suitably raucous and rocky version delivered with a particularly fiery vocal from the man himself bringing this superb recording to a dramatic close.

APOLLO THEATRE, MANCHESTER, ENGLAND, 7 SEPTEMBER 1977

Set List: Here Comes the Flood/Slowburn/Moribund the Burgermeister/Modern Love/Indigo/Humdrum/White Shadow/Heard it Thru the Grapevine/Excuse Me/Waiting for the Big One/Solsbury Hill/Down the Dolce Vita/On the Air/All Day and all of the Night/Here Comes the Flood/The Lamb Lies Down on Broadway//
Source: Audience Recording.

The tour to promote the new album was to last until the autumn of 1977 and by the time Peter arrived back in the UK there had been several changes to the set. Thankfully we have once again a good representative selection of recordings that document them and this one from Manchester is undoubtedly one of the best.

Opening again with an impassioned version of 'Here Comes the Flood', there is none of the hesitancy that had been evident at some of the earlier gigs, and this in turn leads to a magnificent performance of 'Slowburn' with some superb guitar playing and percussion adding to Peter's superb vocals. A delicious segue leads nicely into the urban paranoia of 'Moribund the Burgermeister', in which Peter hams things up nicely, and the rest of the band sound in superb form.

'Modern Love' has been bumped up the set list and roars out of the traps here in a magnificently fiery version, augmented by the echoey acoustics of the theatre. Peter sounds completely confident here and the band coaxes a stunning performance out of him here. 'Indigo' has by now been worked out pretty much as it would eventually appear on Peter's next album. This is a vast improvement on the earlier versions and the recording here is simply amazing. No messing about here. 'Humdrum' starts in an understated fashion with piano and vocals before opening up.

Peter was still road testing new material even at this late stage of the tour, so what we have next is an improvised version of what would become 'White Shadow' on the next album. It is fascinating to hear this classic in its embryonic stage, although even here the essential drama is plain to hear. 'Heard it Thru the Grapevine' also has benefited from some time on the road. An extended rippling synth and flute interpleads into a delightful version of this Motown classic.

Peter gently takes the piss out of the audience exhorting them to be quiet during the "difficult" task of concentrating on 'Excuse Me', and there is some good-natured banter going on throughout this wonderfully camp version. 'Waiting for the Big One' has improved enormously too and gets a deserved reaction from the crowd.

After the band intros it is hit single time. Cue audience going nuts as 'Solsbury Hill' gets everyone in celebratory mood. A superbly emotional performance is captured in excellent quality here. 'Down the Dolce Vita' no longer concludes the show proper but is nonetheless delivered piping hot before the audience is treated to yet another new song, namely 'On the Air', which is greeted with silence as the audience is unfamiliar with it. For an as yet unrecorded song, this version is simply stunning and captures Peter and the band on the top of their game.

'All Day and all of the Night' closes the show proper with another rocking version replete with audience participation. Peter gives us his best Jagger impression and hams it up for the crowd and even the band gets in on the act – excellent stuff.

'Here Comes the Flood' calms things down for an incredibly atmospheric performance, which the crowd treat with the respect it deserves, reserving their applause until the end – simply magnificent. The show closes with Peter's only reference to his time with Genesis, but by this part of the tour the audience are treated to 'The Lamb Lies Down on Broadway' itself, and there is no restraining the crowd who go ballistic for this one. You can almost feel them. Band and audience are unified in celebration here and this performance brings another excellent recording to an end. Sadly, the track fades out before the end. I assume this is because the taper ran out of tape. A shame, but nevertheless, this is an excellent record of another magnificent gig.

PART TWO: PETER GABRIEL

CHAPTER THIRTEEN
"CASTING A WHITE SHADOW" 1978-79

1977 must have been a highly satisfying year for Peter. Not only had he returned to the music business but he had done it in style with a hit album and a hit single to boot!

Not one to rest on his laurels, however, Peter was soon back in the studio at work on what is so often that problematic second album. Engaging the services of Robert Fripp no less as producer, the results were soon available for all to see when the second album was released on 3 June 1978.

Darker in feel and concept, this one was much more challenging for the fans than its predecessor had been. The new wave had hit the British music scene in the intervening months, and surprisingly enough Peter embraced this fully, appearing at several festivals in the company of the likes of the Tubes and the Sex Pistols. What they made of his parody of 'A Whiter Shade of Pale' is anyone's guess! Several songs from the new album had been road tested in front of the fans during the 1977 tours and the new set drew heavily on both albums. Peter's acknowledgement of his previous work with Genesis was relegated to the performance of 'The Lamb' as an encore. Thankfully, this tour is once again documented by a healthy selection of recordings.

BATTERSEA PARK, LONDON, ENGLAND, 16 SEPTEMBER 1978

Set List: On the Air/Moribund the Burgermeister/Perspective/Flotsam & Jetsam/White Shadow/Waiting for the Big One/A Whiter Shade of Pale/Slowburn/I Don't Remember/Solsbury Hill/Modern Love//
Source: Audience Recording.

Peter Gabriel at a punk music festival? Surely not? Oh yes, folks. Peter was to try out his own particular brand of music at several new wave festivals during the summer of 1978, of which this was one of the best.

Clad in orange hi vis jacket and white suit he and his band of merry men took the stage with a rampant performance of 'On the Air', which is certainly in keeping with the fast and furious ethos of the new wave movement. Peter rasps out the vocals like a man possessed. Speaking of possession, 'Moribund the Burgermeister' makes his paranoid entrance to the proceedings and it sounds like Peter was having a ball hamming things up for this one.

'Perspective' gets things back into the thrash groove (if there is such a thing), and Peter's percussion section are the driving force here delivering a tasty and tight back beat, over which Peter and sax player Timmy Capello battle away. 'Flotsam & Jetsam' is introduced by Peter asking the audience to show their approval or disapproval before proceeding to fuck the intro up – just another night eh, Peter? This one sounds strangely out of place in a festival setting.

'White Shadow' and its synth intro and almost jazzy rhythms also sounds misplaced here but the crowd seem to give it their attention nonetheless. 'Waiting for the Big One' gets some cheers as it starts and Peter once again soon gets in character with his best drunk impression. This is fun and taken in the right spirit by the crowd.

'A Whiter Shade of Pale' gets the Gabriel treatment, heaven alone knows what Bach and Procul Harum thought of it, but personally I think this is a monstrous parody that even for a new wave festival is poor at best. Peter sounds desperate to get the crowd on side here and it deservedly falls flat on its face – sorry, Peter!

'Slowburn' works considerably better as Peter returns to his own medium here. The rest of the show combines equally classic Gabriel tracks, including a remarkable early version of 'I Don't Remember', with some superb bass playing from Tony Levin. Not the greatest recording but an interesting document of one of the more bizarre Gabriel gigs.

STONEY BROOK UNIVERSITY, NEW YORK, USA, 24 OCTOBER 1978
Set List: Me & My Teddy Bear/On the Air/Moribund the Burgermeister/ Perspective/Humdrum/New Song/White Shadow/D I Y/ Waiting for the Big One/Flotsam & Jetsam/Exposure/Slowburn/I Don't Remember/Solsbury Hill/Modern Love//
Source: FM Radio Broadcast.

Rightly acknowledged as one of the best recordings in Peter's archive, this one is a delight from start to finish. 'Me & My Teddy Bear' gets things off to a suitably bizarre start before the band emerges on stage to the synth intro of 'On the Air', which is simply awesome here. Peter's vocal is full of angst and impassioned and raw with the months of touring whilst his new band delivers a magnificent backing soundtrack. 'Moribund the Burgermeister', although somewhat more sedate in pace, is nonetheless equally manic in terms of performance.

Peter's homage, if you can call it that, to the new wave movement is next, with a racy and brash 'Perspective', with some tasty percussion and sax playing give this an edginess lacking in earlier performances. 'Humdrum' is altogether more restrained, but nevertheless, a sterling performance is turned in here by Peter and the band. Another example of Peter's testing new material next, with a strange little ditty without real lyrics, just Gabrielese, almost like a live studio rehearsal and not something you see many artists attempt on stage. As it progresses though, those among you with keen ears will recognise the germ of the idea that eventually became 'Not One of Us', on Peter's as yet unrecorded third album two years later.

'White Shadow' is impeccably performed with some superb Frippertronics from Mr Robert Fripp and 'D I Y', the putative hit single, comes across with plenty of vim and vigour here with Peter in particularly fine form as he delivers the lyrics with a healthy mixture of angst and humour. 'Waiting for the Big One' is much more at home in its surroundings tonight than it had been on the previous recording. Once again, this is a performance with Peter definitely acting up to the crowd.

'Flotsam & Jetsam' follows the band introductions and we even get an excellent version of 'Exposure', the collaborative effort between Fripp and Gabriel, which is suitably atmospheric here. The rest of the show highlights old and new Gabriel material closing with a racy version of 'The Lamb Lies Down on Broadway' with a natty extended keyboard intro. Peter doesn't really need to sing here; just lead the choir, as the crowd go nuts. A suitable reaction to a remarkable performance captured here in excellent quality.

READING ROCK '79, READING, ENGLAND, 26 AUGUST 1979

Set List: Biko/On the Air/D I Y/Humdrum/No Self Control/White Shadow/Mother of Violence/Animal Magic/I Don't Remember/Modern Love/Moribund the Burgermeister/Perspective/Solsbury Hill/Here Comes the Flood/The Lamb Lies Down on Broadway//
Source: Audience Recording.

With work still progressing on what would become his third album, Peter once again opted to road test some of his new material at a handful of shows that he performed at festivals throughout the summer of 1979. Here we have an above average audience recording of his performance from the Reading Festival, which was something of a rarity, being the only time that two members of Genesis performed there the same year (Steve Hackett performed there on the 28th).

Opening with an extended and largely improvised version of 'Biko', even in this raw unfinished form, the song still has the power to move and Peter is giving it his all here. 'On the Air' gets a cheer of recognition from the crowd as it races out of the traps. Sadly, as is so often the case with Peter, his microphone technique (or lack of it) ensures that the vocals are somewhat muddy, but what the heck? The crowd know all the words anyway! 'D I Y' also gets an enthusiastic reception from the crowd and here it is the rhythm guitar of Jo Partridge and bass of John Giblin that lay down a funky and upbeat tempo.

Peter then acknowledges his last appearance at Reading with Genesis back in 1973 before calming things down slightly with 'Humdrum', which sounds somewhat disjointed, probably because this is not Peter's usual band and many of the musicians are evidently not as familiar with the nuances of the song as they should be. 'I Don't Know How to Stop' (soon to be known as 'No Self Control') opens with an extended keyboard/bass jam, over which Gabriel improvises lyrics as if this was a day in the studio – fascinating stuff. The performance is radically different from the one we know now but even here the germ of the song is clear to see.

'White Shadow' soars above the crowd like an eagle in stately majesty, much to the delight of the crowd. Giblin's bass playing here is particularly tight and the percussion by Preston Hayman is excellent. Sadly, Peter lets the side down here by fluffing the lyrics – typical Gabriel really! 'Mother of Violence' is greeted by another enthusiastic cheer, although the intro is once again radically different from last year's tour, but once the acoustic guitar and keyboards kick in we are back on familiar and enjoyable territory. Surprisingly, Peter sounds somewhat nervous here. I don't know why, as the crowd are evidently lapping this one up.

Band introductions next, including one for "A skeleton from my past," as Peter refers to Mr Phil Collins to an enormous cheer, and then into a "tampered with" version of 'Animal Magic', which once again is given a complete revamp leading up to the chorus where band and audience join in. Another fascinating reworking of something fans are familiar with. 'I Don't Remember' now sounds much more like the classic it was to become on the next album. Giblin and Phil Collins lay down a superb rhythm section here and Peter's vocal is as raw and savage as a caged tiger.

'Modern Love' gets the crowd in the mood with an incredibly funky and frenetic performance, which the band are evidently enjoying, and the crowd gladly take their part as you can hear. 'Moribund the Burgermeister' slows things down with its tale of urban paranoia. Driven along by a simple keyboard refrain and some neat percussion and sax this one still has the magic.

A rip roaring guitar intro gives us all some 'Perspective', as once again Peter has wisely chosen his songs wisely aiming straight for the festival crowd. This one proves if it needed proving, that Gabriel can do rock and roll and this one is a fantastic balls to the wall performance. A drum intro and hand claps from the audience lead nicely into a loose and funky 'Solsbury Hill', which has the Reading Festival Choir augmenting it.

'Here Comes the Flood' elicits what is probably the biggest cheer thus far. Stripped back to piano and voice, and fuck ups this one even gets the majority of the crowd to listen – a rare feat at festivals! Having acknowledged his past with performances of 'Back in NYC' and 'The Lamb Lies Down on Broadway' on the previous tour, Peter does it again with 'The Lamb', and cue the audience going stratospheric, a suitably emphatic ending to what was a superb show.

CHAPTER FOURTEEN
"TOURING WITHOUT FRONTIERS" 1980

By the end of 1978, Peter had been on the tour/album/tour treadmill for over two years and it was to be a further two years before a new album by him was to see the light of day. He did give fans a taster of what to expect during his festival performances during the summer of 1979 where he was joined at several of them by a certain Mr Philip Collins no less.

Expect the unexpected had always been the watchword with Peter and his third album was to be no exception. How many other artists could write songs about assassins and South African civil rights leaders and at the same time pay a playful homage to the knockabout UK TV series "It's A Knockout" at the same time? The album contained a whole series of thought provoking songs dealing with subjects far and away removed from the usual chart fodder. So provoking was it in fact that Peter's US record company labelled the album "commercial suicide". A catchy little ditty titled 'Games without Frontiers' proved them wrong, however, and reached the upper echelons of the UK charts, even though the video was banned by the BBC (not for the lyrics that contain the words, "we piss on the goons in the jungle," but for the use of children's dolls in the video no less!).

Unusually, the tour to promote the album began *before* the album was available to the fans. This meant that the shows were definitely a mixture of the expected and the unexpected, as Peter and his band presented a healthy dose of the newer material, which sat alongside the established stage favourites extremely well. Once again, the extensive tour was well documented by live recordings, from which I have selected a few to give a flavour of what the shows were like.

SOPHIA GARDENS, CARDIFF, WALES, 7 MARCH 1980
Set List: Intruder/The Start/I Don't Remember/Solsbury Hill/Family Snapshot/ Milgrams' 37/Modern Love/Not One of Us/Lead a Normal Life/Moribund the Burgermeister/Mother of Violence/Humdrum/Games without Frontiers/And Through the Wire/I Go Swimming/Biko/On the Air/Here Comes the Flood//
Source: Soundboard recording.

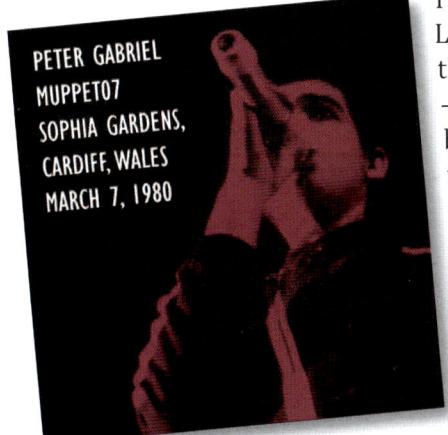

This one was not called *Technical Fuck Up* on the vinyl LP release for nothing. Let's just say that Peter and the band were definitely at home to "Mr Cock-Up" this evening in Cardiff. Not that you would know it from the paranoid opener – 'Intruder' – which features some incredible jagged guitar playing from new boy David Rhodes. Peter's vocal here is definitely akin to Norman Bates and the threatening atmosphere that the band generate is almost tangible at times.

Solo saxophone heralds 'The Start', which segues nicely into an upbeat and funky 'I Don't Remember', in which Tony Levin's bass threatens to bring the roof down – it will even shake your hi fi speakers if you have a copy! Once again, David Rhodes overlays everything with a spiky guitar refrain. A little trip back in time next for a ragged version of 'Solsbury Hill', in which Peter's vocal gives a little indication of the problems he was to experience later in the gig owing to influenza.

'Family Snapshot' takes us to an altogether darker place – the mind of an assassin. Solo piano and voice generate just the right atmosphere of bathos, as we have some sympathy with our subject, as he (and the band) gradually reach a peak of frenzy and anticipation brought vividly to life through the music and a suitably emotional vocal from Peter.

'Milgrams' 37' is next; an unusual track re-telling the tale of the social experiments conducted by Dr Stanley Milgram in the 1960s. The hypnotic refrain of "we do what we're told" is accompanied by a metronomic drumbeat from Jerry Marotta and a suitably paranoid guitar refrain from David Rhodes. 'Modern Love' lightens things up a bit as Peter delivers his tongue-in-cheek view of modern society's fascination with consumerism in typically Gabrielesque fashion.

'Not One of Us' brings us back to the darker side of life again. Peter's screaming vocal and the incessant rhythm driven by Levin and Marotta are augmented by an incredibly funky sound as the song progresses. 'Lead a Normal Life' is once again a wonderful observation of life from an outsider's perspective, this time an inmate of an asylum. A deceptively quiet intro soon gives way to an anguished vocal from Peter and this rates as an astonishing performance all round.

The theme of paranoia continues with 'Moribund the Burgomeister' – a control freak's nightmare brought vividly to life here. Guitar, keyboards, and voice all bring the lyrical imagery of the song to life. 'Mother of Violence' is also delivered in an almost claustrophobic atmosphere. Guitar and keyboard being played ever so slightly out of tune emphasise that all is not well in the world that the song depicts.

'Humdrum' in comparison is played relatively straight here with an impressive vocal from Peter and some delightful keyboard playing from Larry Fast – oh, and once again there is an incredibly meaty bass from Mr Levin! The current hit single is next. 'Games without Frontiers' is delivered in a suitably camp fashion by Peter and the band, with Rhode's guitar once again incredibly spiky – so sharp in fact I am surprised he didn't cut himself playing it!

'And Through the Wire' picks up the pace a bit with a racy keyboard and percussion-led romp, and although the band's attempts at harmony vocals fall humorously flat, the result is somehow all the more impressive for it. Peter, always the experimenter, had begun the trend of road testing as yet unrecorded material in front of his audiences right from the start, and he we have another experiment, which as yet has to be officially "released" from the laboratory. 'I Go Swimming' features yet another example of Gabrielese, as it is obvious that the lyrics are far from finished. Musically and vocally raucous, rough and ready, and a real delight.

A synth drone, David Rhode's banshee-like guitar and some rock steady percussion from Jerry Marotta, announces the arrival of 'Biko'; already a classic and one in which Peter invites the audience to join in on. The atmosphere generated by this song cannot be easily described but suffice to say, it must have been electric in the hall if this recording is anything to go by.

Show over and all that remains are the encores, which aren't long in coming, with 'On the Air' lightening the mood somewhat with a jaunty guitar and percussion-led performance, which I am sure had the audience bopping in the aisles. 'Here Comes the Flood' ends the show in a suitably stately manner befitting a truly remarkable evening, which has thankfully been captured in this incredible recording.

Gabba-Gabba Gabriel

Peter Gabriel
OXFORD NEW THEATRE

The crowd are getting impatient. The support band — Interview — has been and gone. The *Close Encounters* trailer is finished, and — apart from bawling out the inevitable "Wallyee" — all that's left to do is gawp at the safety curtain.

Slow handclaps give way to the strains of neo-symphonic moog music. At last the curtain rises, and the audience stares at an unpeopled stage. An enormous step-ladder stands stage centre, flanked by another to its right.

The ceiling gantry is strewn with plain white utility lamps that hang at assorted lengths. There are perhaps four TV screens scattered around the stage. They're turned on, but instead of projecting an image they buzz soundlessly with white light.

There is no band. Most of all, there is no sign of Peter Gabriel.

Eventually he and the rest of the band, each of them wearing what resemble (they might even be) fluorescent red road-workman's vests, stumble onto the stage. They appear from the intimate auditorium not, as is customary, from backstage.

You don't notice Gabriel straight away. He positions himself so that his body is flat against the highest part of the ladder. The band blasts into (an apt) "On The Air", opening cut from the last Gabriel album, and he somehow manages to leap down without blowing his cool. *(That could've been painful.—Ed.)*

The sound's appalling as Gabriel's vocals struggle against the confused might of his band. But then this *is* Gabriel's first show in over a year, the first of three 'secret gigs' prior to a Euro-tour and what, on paper, looks like a very hot Knebworth. With his burly build and hair beginning to show on his recently shorn skull, he looks like a skin-head. His bassist (Tony Levin) and guitarist (Sidney McGinnis) are also members of the Bald Is Beautiful Club.

Despite his appearance, Gabriel's movements onstage remain for the most part anything but macho. Only when after spitting out a Ramones-like quick-fire "1234" to introduce a rapido arrangement of "Whiter Shade Of Pale", and during a leather jacket clad encore of "The Lamb", does Gabriel actually utilise his potentially menacing looks.

For the Procol Harum classic, introduced by a slightly sardonic Gabriel as "a BOF anthem", he demently hurtles amongst the audience, actually concluding this master-stroke with a fully-fledged gob: a punk version of "Whiter Shade Of Pale"? Think about it.

While Gabriel didn't seem as self-assured as he was last year, he doesn't waste an opportunity to give his all to a performance. His presentation ideas — disappearing into the audience for all of a (it must be said) rather sloppy rendition of "Solsbury Hill" — continually delight and bewilder his rapturous audience.

As his recent album showed, Peter Gabriel's star is in the ascendant. Like his music, his 1978 stage work is as inventive and original as ever.

If you want to talk in terms of New Wave, then look no further than Peter Gabriel.

Steve Clarke

JO CHESTER for GAILFORCE
presents
PETER GABRIEL
plus support
SOPHIA GARDENS
CARDIFF
FRIDAY, 7th MARCH, 7.30 p.m.
Ticket £3   No 0222

VREDENBURG, UTRECHT, NETHERLANDS, 6 SEPTEMBER 1980

Tracks; Intruder/The Start/I Don't Remember/Solsbury Hill/Family Snapshot/Milgrams' 37/Modern Love/Not One of Us/Lead a Normal Life/Moribund the Burgermeister/Mother of Violence/Humdrum/Bully for You/Games without Frontiers/And Through the Wire/I Go Swimming/Biko/On the Air/D I Y//
Source: Audience Recording.

Several months separate this recording from the previous one mentioned and even in that time, as we have come to expect from Peter, things had been worked upon and changed.

An incessant drumbeat heralds the band onstage accompanied by a suitably enthusiastic reaction from the crowd before the nightmare that is 'Intruder' gets under way proper. The echoey acoustics of the hall make David Rhode's guitar and Larry Fast's keyboards even more eerie than normal and Peter's vocal is verging on the demoniac. Once again, the sax and keyboards of 'The Start' segue beautifully into an uptempo rendition of 'I Don't Remember', which lives up to its name, as Peter is obviously having problems remembering the words at times!

David Rhodes leads the parade as the band belt out a jaunty version of 'Solsbury Hill' replete with audience participation – just as it should be!

'Family Snapshot' elicits a cheer from a crowd obviously well familiar with the new album. The drama and pathos of the subject are played out in equal measures here by a band evidently at the peak of their powers and the result is a marvellous version of this classic Gabriel track.

'Milgrams' 37' is preceded by the extended story of the experiments that had been the subject of the song. This is an odd song but one that only a master of performance such as Peter could get away with. Here it is both dramatic and hypnotic. From drama to humour in one bound, as Peter once again brings us his own unique take on consumerism with some amazingly pithy lyrics and a delightfully over the top musical performance from the band.

'Not One of Us' gives us yet another outsider's perspective and this is continued with a deceptively simple marimba and keyboard intro to perhaps one of the most powerful songs by Peter up to this point – 'Lead A Normal Life' – which is a deeply disturbing examination of an inmate of an asylum. Madness of a different sort next as 'Moribund the Burgermeister's' obsession with order and conformity are delivered in a marvellously camp version. Peter is evidently having a blast hamming it up here for the crowd.

'Humdrum' is delivered again in a relatively straight performance, which makes it stand out all the more amidst all the mayhem and madness that has preceded it. Time for another new track – 'Bully for You' – which is one of a handful of collaborations Peter had done with Tom Robinson. Here we have an all too rare performance of it by Peter.

Back to more familiar territory next with the hit single, 'Games without Frontiers', which contrasts nicely with its predecessor, showing further evidence, if any were needed, of how much Peter is a master of balancing light and shade within his shows.

'And Through the Wire' and 'Biko' both deliver important messages and seldom if ever has there been such an effective protest song as the latter and the audience response here is typical of its growing stature in Peter's set.

Sadly that is all that we have of this above average audience recording. There appear to have been several edits made to the tape, as 'On the Air' and 'D I Y', which were played at this show, are missing from the recording in my possession. Maybe the taper ran out of tape? Either way, he/she is to be commended for bringing us this above average audience recording of another excellent show by Peter and his band.

CHAPTER FIFTEEN
"THE RHYTHM OF THE HEAT" 1982-83

Peter disappeared off the radar again after the conclusion of the 1980 tour. He was far from idle, however. Always the eternal experimenter, Peter was already ahead of the field in regard to embracing the various new technologies that were coming into use at this time.

None intrigued Peter more than the Fairlight; a synthesiser which, like its predecessor the Mellotron, could utilise sounds and give musicians a broader palette from which to work. The Fairlight was much more advanced than the Mellotron, however, and Peter explored it fully on his next album. Exploration was definitely the word for this album, as Peter travelled the World in search of new and interesting sounds and rhythms to incorporate into his expanding range of musical ideas. Taking his time, the end results justified his (and our) patience, and the end result was finally released to an expectant fan base on 10 September 1982. Fans had, had the opportunity to experience Peter's new show at the inaugural World of Music, Arts and Dance – later abbreviated to WOMAD – Festival, which had taken place in St Austell over the weekend of 16-18 July 1982. The show was a mesmerising mix of rhythms and showmanship that garnered plaudits from fans and critics alike.

The tour proper began in the USA in the autumn and was to be Peter's most extensive to date. Split between two tours of the USA a further two tours of Europe and sandwiched in between these a tour of some of the provincial theatres here in the UK. Peter brought his explosive new show to an expanding audience and they loved it as the selected recordings mentioned here show.

SHOWERING PAVILION, SHEPTON MALLET, ENGLAND, 16 & 18 JULY 1982
Set List (16th): San Jacinto/The Family & the Fishing Net/I Have the Touch/Lay Your Hands on Me/Shock the Monkey/I Go Swimming/The Rhythm of the Heat/Shosholosa/Kiss of Life/Biko//
Source: Audience Recording.
Set List (18th): A Ritual Mask/Dog One, Dog Two, Dog Three/Indian Melody/ Across the River/Across the River Reprise//
Source: Audience Recording.

These were probably two of the most significant concerts thus far in Peter's career. Both were part of the highly adventurous inaugural World of Music Arts and Dance Festival, which we now know as the WOMAD festival. Taking the opportunity to promote music from his fourth and as yet unreleased album, anyone who was at these gigs will tell you just how remarkable they were.

Opening the first gig with 'San Jacinto' and 'The Family and the Fishing Net', it is evident that Peter is quite nervous and he forgets lyrics throughout both of them, and the audience can't help him because they haven't heard them before! That doesn't detract from what are amazing performances here. Aided by the Burundian drummers of Ekome, Peter takes us into the dark heart of the human psyche here and thankfully the drama is captured to perfection on this excellent recording.

Another new track next, and the incessant rhythm of the percussion takes us into 'I Have the Touch', which still sounds like a work in progress here, featuring an extended intro, probably because Peter missed his cue. This performance is somewhat stilted when compared to subsequent ones but that is to be expected, I suppose, of any first public performance.

'Lay Your Hands on Me' is next and once again you really had to be there to fully understand the sheer drama generated by this one. Still being worked on lyrically and musically, the rhythms build up to what to this day remains one of the most impressive "risks" taken by any artist, as Peter allowed himself to fall into the audience for the first time. Sorry, but even the best of sound recordings can't really capture the magic and drama of that, but this one does its best!

'Shock the Monkey' is another new one, and once again the band are still somewhat tentative with their delivery here, but once everything gets going the end result is another excellent performance, which is followed in turn by a funkified version of 'I Go Swimming'. This was still an unrecorded song, although one with a few years' pedigree in terms of live performance. This is an altogether more confident performance from Peter and the added percussive element from Ekome takes this one to heights it seldom reaches elsewhere.

'The Rhythm of the Heat' is without doubt the masterpiece of the show tonight. A hypnotic rhythm is set up by Jerry Marotta and the drummers of Ekome whilst Peter gradually works himself up into a frenzy with stunning results at the song's climax. I have never seen or heard a more emphatic performance from Peter than this. Even the rhythmic fuck-up seems to add to the end result.

'Shosholosa' gets a rare outing tonight and with the added presence of Ekome it definitely benefits. This is a magnificent example of just how far Peter was prepared to go to explore and bring music from other parts of the world to Western audiences years before Paul Simon got the credit for doing so. The emphasis on rhythm and percussion continues with the glorious celebratory free for all that is 'Kiss of Life', a raucous and at times wonderfully over the top performance, which everyone seems to be enjoying. Peter certainly sounds in fine form with his nerves gone at last, as the realisation that the end result of his hard work have paid off – artistically if not financially.

There is no mistaking what comes next as the synth drone heralds the arrival of the magnificent 'Biko' – cue audience going ape shit here, with the rhythm section augmented by the claps of the crowd. Always an emotional song, this takes on a special resonance tonight, and the end result is an astonishing version. The crowd here give every indication of being highly satisfied with Peter's new material, which must have been gratifying

Peter returned to the stage at the Showering Pavilion on 18 July for a somewhat shorter but just as surprising set, including some special guests: Peter Hammill and Shankar no less. The set opens with Hammill delivering an incredible performance of 'A Ritual Mask', which is somewhat discordant but effective nonetheless.

A trio of what are really improvised jams comes next under the titles of 'Dog 1-3'. Gabriel is improvising throughout and some of this material eventually surfaced as the single B-side, 'Soft Dog'. Strange but somehow appropriate it is Shankar whose violin stands out here. This is followed by 'Indian Melody', which is another extemporised musical work out, in which Peter and Shankar duel with each other.

A more formalised track next with 'Across the River', although the vocal performance was still open to some improvisation, musically this and its reprise, which concludes this excellent quality recording, are really an excuse for the band to rock out and improvise their hearts out.

MAPLE LEAF GARDENS, TORONTO, ONTARIO, CANADA, 8 NOVEMBER 1982

Set List: the Rhythm of the Heat/I Have the Touch/I Go Swimming/Family Snapshot/The Family and the Fishing Net/Shock the Monkey/ Not One of Us/Lay Your Hands on Me/Intruder/Solsbury Hill/John Has a Headache/Kiss of Life/San Jacinto/On the Air/Biko// Source: Audience Recording.

After unleashing the unexpected at the Shepton Mallet gigs in July, Peter began what was to be his most extensive tour to date in the USA in the autumn of 1982, including this recording from the cavernous Maple Leaf Gardens auditorium in Toronto. Right from the start you get an idea of the sheer size of the venue by the echoey nature of the recording as the hypnotic drum rhythm of 'The Rhythm of the Heat' sets up an air of expectancy as Peter toys with the crowd. In fact, from my viewpoint, the acoustics of the venue help generate an even deeper feeling of claustrophobia on this one and it is stunning.

Not letting up on the pace, the frantic rhythms of 'I Have the Touch' come next with Peter and the band laying down an incredibly display of rhythm with kudos going to Tony Levin and Jerry Marotta. The display of athleticism continues with 'I Go Swimming'; an older track which has still not been committed to an album. It is always one of those tracks that is sometimes possible to be somewhat blasé about. You can't but help but get drawn in by the rhythm and once again it is Peter's rhythm section that drive this one along barely pausing to draw breath.

'Family Snapshot' is introduced without any ado and is another slice of classic Gabriel. Even in this setting Peter's impassioned vocal generates just the right amount of tension and suspense as the brilliantly observed story of the assassin and his "target" is played out in dramatic fashion. This is followed by 'The Family and the Fishing Net', and once again, the atmosphere is as tight as a funeral drum throughout as Peter and the band keep their hands on the throats of their instruments as paranoia stalks through the auditorium.

The atmosphere lightens a bit as Peter shocks his monkey (!). Percussively driven, this one gets the crowd going, while Peter sounds as if he is having a great time playing up to the crowd. The outsider gets his/her moment in the sun next with 'Not One of Us', which is already a classic. With the added element of an enthusiastic crowd and vibey auditorium, it takes on added resonance and is extremely enjoyable.

Always prepared to take his audience on an adventure, Peter himself took a risk with the next track – 'Lay Your Hands on Me' – as in the middle of it he would invariably "dive" into the crowd as a demonstration of trust. This could have backfired with potentially lethal consequences had the audience not played their part but no worries here. Without doubt one of Peter's most dramatic and emotional songs, this recording manages to capture all of that in spades.

'Intruder' and 'Solsbury Hill' bookend the drama and humour of Peter's shows nicely. The former is replete with suppressed anger and rage, while the latter is a veritable celebration of life, one which the band and crowd evidently grab with both hands tonight if the evidence here is anything to go by!

Another rarity, as 'John Has a Headache' comes next. Even by Gabriel's standards this is one of the strangest songs he has ever performed, although from internal evidence, it would be completely in keeping with today's financial scandals, featuring as it does, a businessman coming to terms with the demise of his lifestyle. This one didn't feature in many performances, so we are lucky to have this one.

'Kiss of Life' also didn't feature too regularly in the show, which is a pity, because it is upbeat, up-mood, and rude, but here we have it with the entire band evidently in their element as they turn the somewhat sombre proceedings into a party, to which the audience obviously don't need an invitation! 'San Jacinto' takes us back to the more serious side of Peter's music with its extended take on the two sides of life in the Midwest of America. It doesn't matter how often I hear this one, it always sends the shivers up and down my spine, and tonight's recording is no exception.

The show is rounded off by another magnificently contradictory pairing. The upbeat and catchy 'On the Air' gets the crowd off their duffs and in full participation mode whilst 'Biko' with its incredibly emotional and relevant message never fails to get a reaction. Stately, at times mannered, but always full of raw emotion. The band and the crowd get right behind Peter here and close the show on a high.

APOLLO THEATRE, GLASGOW, SCOTLAND, 12 SEPTEMBER 1983

Set List: Rhythm of the Heat/I Have the Touch/Not One of Us/The Family and the Fishing Net/Shock the Monkey/Family Snapshot/Intruder/Games without Frontiers/Humdrum/D I Y/Lay Your Hands on Me/Solsbury Hill/I Don't Remember/San Jacinto/On the Air/Biko/Here Comes the Flood/Kiss of Life//
Source: Audience Recording.

Peter's first UK tour in over three years brought him to Glasgow towards the end of the tour for what was to prove to be an exceptional performance as this excellent audience recording shows.

'Rhythm of the Heat', full of suppressed anger and tension, opens the show. You can practically hear a pin drop as the audience hang on every word from Peter as he delivers a stunning version of this classic track. 'I Have the Touch's' syncopated rhythms give the band and the audience a chance to loosen up a bit. Tony Levin's bass stutters like a machine gun whilst the audience evidently know every word.

'Not One of Us' rattles along at a furious pace. The echoey acoustics of the theatre give it an added sense of drama. Peter certainly sounds full of confidence as he puts in a superb performance. Once again, Levin and new boy David Rhodes provide a tasteful accompaniment. The ritual of the wedding is examined next as only Peter can, with the claustrophobic 'Family and the Fishing Net'. The keyboards and an insistent drum rhythm build up an atmosphere of tension and that is even before Peter starts singing! When he does, this new song takes on the mantle of an instant classic – if there were an Oscar for vocal performances then Peter would have won it for this performance.

Light relief à la Gabriel next, with 'Shock the Monkey', and cue full audience participation throughout. Peter even leaves the opening lines to the audience who are fully conversant with it. Unusually though, the audience actually *add* to the atmosphere, of which rates as one of the best Gabriel recordings in circulation. Who else but Peter could write a song about the musings of an assassin and make it work? 'Family Snapshot' remains a vivid and thought-provoking look into the mind of its subject and Peter takes on the character here almost appearing possessed by it in fact – marvellous stuff. Paranoia continues to reign as the band let rip with 'Intruder'. Jerry Marotta and Larry Fast generate the atmosphere with a haunting drum patter and some suitably spooky keyboard chords whilst Peter's vocal will send up your spine as you listen to it.

'Games without Frontiers' is given an extended and quite different introduction to many others on the tour. Rhodes and Fast lay down some excellent rhythms before Gabriel joins in. Maybe Peter forgot his cue? Either way this is a familiar song with a new twist. 'Humdrum' gets us back to where it all began for Peter and once again the crowd hang on every word. The hall acoustics once again work in favour of the song and it is certainly more full of atmosphere than on many other recordings you may hear.

'D I Y' is greeted like an old friend, which I suppose by now it is! Peter spits out the lyrics with real venom and the rest of his band are taken along by the sheer passion of the performance. However, that is nothing compared to the sheer passion and atmosphere of 'Lay Your Hands on Me', with a fantastic atmosphere generated by keyboards and drums, and the song builds to the stunning climax where Peter literally puts himself into the hands of the audience and the result is bedlam! Party time continues with an incredibly vibrant 'Solsbury Hill' and the band are obviously feeding off the vibe from this incredible crowd who are in fine voice themselves as you can hear.

'I Don't Remember' gets the Levin treatment as he gets down and dirty with some incredible bass lines, while Peter and the rest of the band are joined by the audience for the chorus in another remarkable performance. Peter's story leading up to 'San Jacinto' is listened to in rapt silence by the crowd, but once he mentions the title, the crowd are fully behind him. This is a masterpiece of a performance, even the version on the subsequent *Plays Live* album pales into insignificance when compared to this, and I envy the lucky people who saw this.

Larry Fast lets rip with some synth lines before Peter roars 'On the Air', and the crowd go wild yet again, but this is one in which the band and the audience are supposed to work together on and you will seldom hear a better combination than this. 'Biko' needs no introduction really and so Peter keeps it short, but the performance rates as one, which even listening to it for the purposes of this book still sends shivers up and down my spine.

This gig should have come with a warning for those of a delicate disposition. The drama of 'Biko' is followed by the raw emotion of 'Here Comes the Flood', giving no respite from the flood of raw emotions, which is evidently filling the Apollo tonight. Peter goes and spoils it of course by fucking it up halfway through, much to the audience's amusement. He starts it again and gets the audience to help him along, which they are only too willing to do, resulting in a true partnership between performer and audience.

Peter returns to the stage to introduce the band and then launch into a ramshackle 'Kiss of Life', which I am sure some of the audience might have needed by now after this incredibly energetic performance. Without doubt, one of the best Gabriel performances captured on this superb recording.

A Selection Of Shows: Genesis & Solo Live Guide 1976-2014

Peter Gabriel

PART TWO: PETER GABRIEL

CHAPTER SIXTEEN
"A CONSPIRACY OF HOPE ON MERCY STREET"
1986-87

It must have been an exhausted but contented Peter who finished the 1982/83 tour. Fan reaction to the new album had been positive even if it had garnered mixed reviews from the critics.

Once again the gaps between albums were becoming longer as Peter explored more and more differing avenues of musical endeavour. In addition to this, his involvement with several charitable projects occupied him fully in the interim. Fans were beginning to wonder what had become of their hero when the only thing to appear since the fourth album was the soundtrack to Alan Parker's acclaimed film, *Birdy*, in 1985.

Late April 1986 saw the first fruits of Peter's endeavours as the 'Sledgehammer' single and award-winning video hit the music stores and our TV screens. What a complete change for the fans! Here was a song that was upbeat, catchy, and accompanied by a fantastic video ensuring its success in the charts, this being something Peter's fans had not been used to in the past. The album *So* was released on 19 May and went to the top of the charts both at home and elsewhere.

With such a successful album under his belt a tour was expected, but as usual with Peter, things were not to be quite as we expected. His involvement with the human rights charity Amnesty International had begun several years earlier, so when a campaign to bring its work to the wider attention of the public in the USA was suggested, Peter was eager to be involved. The resulting tour, *A Conspiracy of Hope*, opened on 4 June 1986 taking in several major US cities before culminating with a televised show at the Giants Stadium in East Rutherford, New Jersey, on 15 June.

At these gigs, Peter premiered a couple of new numbers alongside established classics and the shows were extremely well received. Then it was down to the serious business of promoting the new album, which began in earnest on 7 November with a tour, which drew upon the best of Peter's existing catalogue alongside a healthy dose of the new album. The tour was to extend well into 1987 taking in shows in the USA, Europe, and the UK to rave reviews. With the growing advent of recording technology, this tour is well represented by audio and video recordings from which I have selected a few choice morsels here.

GIANTS' STADIUM, MEADOWLANDS, NEW JERSEY, USA, 15 JUNE 1986
Set List: Red Rain/Shock the Monkey/Family Snapshot/Sledgehammer/San Jacinto/Biko//
Source: FM Radio/TV broadcast.

With the much delayed new album now in the cans, Peter opted to showcase some of it at the series of shows he had been invited to take part in during the summer of 1986 in aid of the Amnesty International charity, bringing the message of human rights to audiences in the USA.

The Conspiracy of Hope tour, as it came to be known, took in several major US cities in June 1986, and thankfully we have this marvellous radio broadcast of the final gig from the Giants Stadium in New Jersey. 'Red Rain' opens the show and even though this is a brand new track, its impact is immediate here, even in the echoey expanses of the massive stadium. 'Shock the Monkey' gets a cheer of recognition from the crowd and we are even more fortunate that the show was also broadcast on TV, and the footage combined with this recording gives an excellent idea of just how powerful Peter's performance was on the night.

Peter then takes a little trip back for 'Family Snapshot', which the crowd give an enthusiastic reception. Just how big the stadium is can be heard by the echoey acoustics but they only serve to add even more effect to Peter's impassioned performance. Back to the new stuff next, with an outrageously upbeat 'Sledgehammer'. This is definitely one of the sexiest songs that Peter has ever written and here it is delivered in a masterful way. The entire band give this a truly remarkable performance, which the crowd evidently love.

The human rights message is delivered forcefully but without any element of preaching by the final two songs in Peter's performance. 'San Jacinto' puts the emphasis on human rights within the USA itself with its marvellous story of the Apache Brave's initiation into the tribe – simply marvellous. Of course, the best is kept till last, as Peter delivers one of the most impressive versions of 'Biko' that you will ever hear driving the message home as only he can.

UNITED NATIONS BUILDING, NEW YORK, USA, 16 SEPTEMBER 1986
Set List: Red Rain/In Your Eyes/Biko/(I Ain't Gonna Play) Sun City//
Source: Audience Recording.

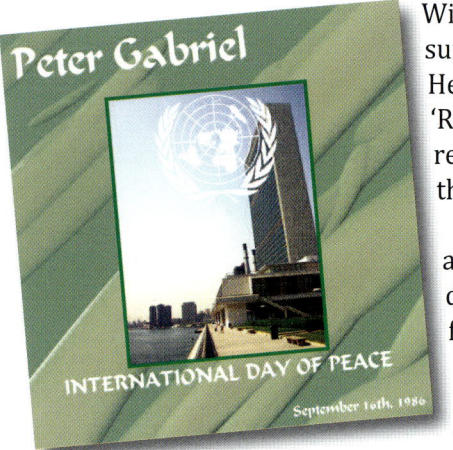

With Peter's credentials as a campaigner for human rights it was not surprising that he was present at this fundraiser for the University of Peace. He is in fiery form, as his preamble to the show indicates, and the first song, 'Red Rain', is equally fiery. With a scratch band on stage with him, the end result is somewhat ramshackle but the passion of the performance more than makes up for that here.

'In Your Eyes' had by now become another classic in Peter's repertoire and here it has a passion and fire that belies the somewhat under rehearsed delivery. Here we get to hear the magnificent vocals of Youssou N'Dour live for the first time and he lifts the performance to something above average.

'Biko' really needs no introduction and so the band deliver it without one. For once they sound as if they have put in the hours learning this one and the performance is definitely better than those which have preceded it.

The finale is introduced by Little Stephen and the *Sun City* album's anti-Apartheid anthem '(I Ain't Gonna Play) Sun City' rocks out the UN Building. This is a funky and upbeat version, which features both Little Stephen and Peter in a gloriously upbeat performance, which still manages to get its message across here.

NATIONAL EXHIBITION CENTRE, BIRMINGHAM, ENGLAND, 1 JULY 1987
Set List: Floating Dogs Intro/San Jacinto/Red Rain/Games without Frontiers/Family Snapshot/Intruder/Shock the Monkey/No Self Control/Mercy Street/This Is the Picture/Big Time/Don't Give Up/Solsbury Hill/Lay Your Hands on Me/Sledgehammer/Here Comes the Flood/In Your Eyes/Biko//
Source: Audience Recording.

Birmingham's NEC has seen more than its fair share of triumphs by Genesis, Phil Collins, and Peter Gabriel, but seldom has it hosted a more impressive series of gigs than those which Peter performed there in the summer of 1987.

This recording is taken from the second night of the three-night stint at the venue, and as the intro music of 'Floating Dogs' is replaced by the introduction to 'San Jacinto', you can almost feel the anticipation. As Peter emerges on stage he is accompanied by a rumbling bass line from Tony Levin that threatens to shake the building's foundations. Drama builds throughout the song and is continued with the next performance, namely an impassioned 'Red Rain', which simply defies description.

'Games without Frontiers' is upbeat, uptempo, and rude, with Gabriel spitting out the lyrics with unaccustomed venom whilst the rest of the band deliver a tasty and tight musical accompaniment. 'Family Snapshot' echoes around the massive arena and the echoes give it an even more dramatic effect than usual. Gabriel's voice is astonishing here, and the sense of unease it generates is continued with a fantastic performance of 'Intruder', which generates a superbly unpleasant atmosphere. If you were at home you would be definitely looking under the bed during this one!

A bit of light relief comes next with a funky 'Shock the Monkey', which sees Gabriel prowling round the stage like an animal in a cage. Rhythmically it is Manu Katche who is the driving force behind this one with some rock solid percussion. 'No Self Control' was destined to be one of the highlights of these gigs, with the incredibly simple but highly effective use of the lighting gantries, which augmented a superbly emotional vocal performance from Gabriel himself, which is captured extremely well in this recording.

'Mercy Street' also benefited from tasteful lighting but it is the wonderful vocal and musical performance from Peter and the band that is spellbinding to hear. Without doubt, this is one of Peter's finest songs and one of the best performances of it I have ever heard. 'Audition Night' is next, or 'This is the Picture', which is a strange little song, but one which serves as an ideal opportunity for Peter to introduce all of the band for our delectation.

A swift tape change leads us into 'Big Time', which is already a favourite with fans and here it is served up fast, furious, and funky, with the rhythm section of Katche and Levin in particular laying down some serious grooves. Another song with a serious message comes next with 'Don't Give Up'. Here we have an impeccable performance, stately and restrained but cram packed full of emotion, even though he has no female counterpart to duet with tonight.

'Solsbury Hill' is greeted like an old friend and the audience take their cue to join in with some typically out of time percussion of their own, but what the hell? It's our show too, isn't it? Peter sounds relaxed and confident, basking in the enthusiasm that is washing back from the crowd. Then comes the undoubted highlight of the evening; 'Lay Your Hands on Me', and I have to say that from my vantage point in the South Stand, this was to be one of the most memorable performances I have ever seen. A lengthy keyboard intro is built upon by rumbling bass and drums before Peter starts the vocal performance, which in itself is a masterpiece in building tension and suspense. Of course we all know it is leading up to that moment when Peter "dives" into the crowd, but even so, the sheer drama of the performance is captured to perfection here even without the benefit of visuals!

'Sledgehammer' brings the mood up with its infectious and catchy rhythms. Peter is evidently buoyed by the audience and the performance here is brim full of confidence. A solo piano can only mean one thing: 'Here Comes the Flood'. Once again the echoey acoustics of the hall seem to generate an atmosphere of their own and once Peter starts to sing, the audience are transported back to the heady days of 1977 for a magnificent performance.

'In Your Eyes' has rapidly established itself as a stage favourite and tonight we have the added bonus of the magnificent vocals of Youssou N'Dour, whose band, Les Super Etoiles De Dakar had supported Peter, which gives the song even more power and authority than normal and is a cue for the audience to start to party, which they do with evident relish.

The synth drone heralds the arrival of another classic that the audience know instinctively before Peter even opens his mouth. It is of course 'Biko' and the raw emotion that this song generates needs no explanations from me – magnificent – nuff said!

CHAPTER SEVENTEEN
"HUMAN RIGHTS IN THE SECRET WORLD"
1988-94

Peter had barely drawn breath after the end of the 1986/87 tour when he became involved in an even more adventurous project to bring Amnesty International's message to a much wider audience.

The Human Rights Now! tour was an extremely ambitious project resulting in a series of high profile concerts at venues on almost every continent spreading the message of the Universal Declaration of Human Rights to as many people as possible. Peter was joined on this tour by fellow Conspiracy of Hope stalwart, Sting along with up and coming star Tracy Chapman, and rock alumnus Bruce Springsteen, and Peter's guest at several of his 1987 shows, Youssou N'Dour. Along the way they were joined by many local artists eager to participate.

The tour was a great success and once again Peter took the opportunity to premiere some as yet unreleased music in the shape of 'Of These Hope' from the soundtrack to Martin Scorsese's controversial film, the *Last Temptation of Christ*, which Peter opened his performances with. Alongside this were several old and new favourites which managed to entertain and inform in equal measures.

The tour concluded in Buenos Aires on 15 October, after which Peter indulged in further charitable efforts over the next few years, appearing regularly at events as part of the now flourishing WOMAD Festival, as well as continuing work on his follow up to *So*, an album which was to be even longer in its gestation period.

The album, entitled *Us*, was eventually released on 28 September 1992, preceded by yet another high profile single, 'Digging in the Dirt', accompanied by an equally high profile video. The tour for the album began in earnest after a few warm up shows in Stockholm on 13 April 1993, before proceeding to take in concerts in the USA, Europe, Australia, and further afield, concluding with an appearance at the twenty-fifth anniversary celebration of the Woodstock Festival.

CARLTON BAY, ST AUSTELL, ENGLAND, 28 AUGUST 1988
Set List: Across the River/Red Rain/Don't Give Up/No Self Control/Islamic Offbeat (Off These Hope)/Sledgehammer/In Your Eyes/Biko//
Source: Audience Recording.

By the time of this recording, the WOMAD Festival had become a well-established and highly successful worldwide event, at which Peter on occasions turned up as a "guest". Such was the case at this performance.

Sharing the stage with Youssou N'Dour and Shankar again, the result was a mixture of familiar and unfamiliar opening with a superbly atmospheric rendition of 'Across the River', which builds from a slow and understated beginning to something frantic and almost demented.

Back to more familiar territory next for 'Red Rain' and 'Don't Give Up'. The former loses none of its impact in the open air setting of the show and the band serve it up hot and tasty here. 'Don't Give Up' also still has a stately majesty, which makes it one of Peter's best songs whatever the setting.

'No Self Control' opens with the usual funky rhythms of drums and guitar, although sadly either the sound engineer has Peter too low in the mix or the taper was in one of those awkward spots where sound just disappears. Either way, Peter's vocal performance is mainly lost in the ether here.

'Islamic Offbeat' shows that Peter is still prepared to road test new stuff and this incredibly atmospheric improvisation will later morph into 'Of These Hope', from Peter's superb soundtrack to the controversial Martin Scorsese film, the *Last Temptation of Christ*. Here it is already an astonishingly emotional piece of music, which the band deliver in magnificent fashion. The remainder of the show draws upon some of Peter's most notable songs, including extremely enjoyable performances of 'Sledgehammer' and 'In Your Eyes', where the presence of Youssou N'Dour lifts the song to truly amazing heights. The show closes with – what else? – but 'Biko', still sadly as relevant in 1988 as it had been when written back in 1979.

WEMBLEY STADIUM, LONDON, ENGLAND, 2 SEPTEMBER 1988
Set List: of These Hope/Games without Frontiers/Family Snapshot/Shock the Monkey/Don't Give Up/Sledgehammer/In Your Eyes/Biko//
Source: Audience Recording.

Less than a week separates this recording from the preceding one but what a difference a week makes! Peter had already made his support for Amnesty International plain with his involvement in 1986's *Conspiracy of Hope* tour and here he was again involved in the much more ambitious global messenger that was the *Human Rights Now!* Tour, which over the next couple of months was to take Amnesty's message around the world.

Kicking the tour off at home in Wembley, Peter's set took place in the middle of the day and hence lost much of its visual impact, especially owing to technical problems with the video screens, but that didn't really matter. The music is the message and here we have it in spades.

Opening with 'Of These Hope', which sadly fell victim to the old Wembley Stadium's appalling acoustics and an irritatingly inattentive crowd, but it nonetheless served as another marvellous example of Peter's skill with soundscapes. The rest of the set was evidently drawn with the intent of getting the message of man's inhumanity across, so we have the marvellously acerbic send up of the futility of warfare that is 'Games without Frontiers' replete with Peter goose-stepping around the stage really hammering home the message.

'Family Snapshot', always a favourite, even manages to do something unexpected here. It actually gets the crowd's attention whilst 'Shock the Monkey' gives the populists among the crowd something to get their teeth (and vocal chords) into. 'Don't Give Up' gives us another superbly emotional performance from Peter, on which he is helped by Tracy Chapman, who puts in a magnificent delivery.

'Sledgehammer' and 'In Your Eyes' effectively warm the crowd up for the real heart of Peter's performance, 'Biko'. It is only a pity that the quality of this recording is so mediocre because, as someone who attended the show, I can vouch for the fact that the performance of it here rates as one of the best I have ever seen from Peter.

HALLAM FM ARENA, SHEFFIELD, ENGLAND, 24 MAY 1993
Set List: Come Talk to Me/Quiet Steam/Games without Frontiers/Across the River/Slow Marimbas/Shaking the Tree/Blood of Eden/San Jacinto/Lovetown/Shock the Monkey/Washing of the Water/Solsbury Hill/Digging in the Dirt/Sledgehammer/Secret World/In Your Eyes/Biko/Here Comes the Flood//
Source: Audience CD/DVD.

This was another show that I was lucky enough to attend. The Hallam FM Arena is another of those incredibly massive places that have sprung up all over the UK in recent years. Massive but not overpowering as you can hear on this enjoyable audience recording, which gets under way with a particularly fiery 'Come Talk to Me'. As I recall Peter was definitely in his element tonight, feeding off the enthusiasm. The band were too and in particular Manu Katche aren't far behind him.

An extended introduction leads us into the sultry and somewhat sleazy world of 'Steam', replete with innuendo and some downright funky bass lines from Tony Levin. The crowd know what's coming and keep their ammo dry until the right moment but then all hell breaks loose. 'Games without Frontiers' is given a jazzy makeover tonight, thanks most likely to

David Sancious' leanings. It makes no difference, as the crowd still lap it up.

'Across the River' is prefaced by a ramble about the establishment of the WOMAD Festival. With Shankar accompanying him, Gabriel manages to bring this hauntingly brittle track vividly to life here and the acoustics of the hall for once work in favour of the performance, which is simply stunning. 'Slow Marimbas' conjures up another sound picture, leading nicely into the funky 'Shakin' the Tree' and the crowd get down to some serious moves, emulating those of Peter and the band on stage, who are obviously really enjoying themselves playing this one.

'Blood of Eden' is a laid back and almost stark performance this evening. Peter's vocal sends shivers up and down the spine as the raw emotion it manages to convey isn't lost even on a less than perfect recording such as this one. The marimba-like keyboard and bass intro to 'San Jacinto' build an atmosphere that is hard to describe unless you have seen it in the flesh, so to speak. Like sunrise on a mountain top, which is quite an apt analogy, given the subject. Without doubt, this is one of the most evocative and passionate songs that Peter has ever recorded and in concert it never fails to move the listener, and tonight is no exception.

A work out for Messrs Levin and Katche next with the extended introduction to 'Love Town', a track which rather leaves me cold I'm afraid, but there is no denying its efficacy tonight as the crowd love it. The infectious rhythm of 'Shock the Monkey', driven along by some sparkling riffs from David Rhodes, gets the crowd in the party mood again. Peter roams the stage thrusting his pelvis out in an outrageously suggestive manner.

'Washing of the Water gets an almost sermon-like keyboard intro and we are expecting the Reverend Gabriel to deliver a sermon here. Instead, we get another deeply moving and atmospheric performance that is magnificently restrained and evocative. The mood is lightened by the completely un-danceable 'Solsbury Hill', but Peter and the band are augmented by a crowd that wants to party, so they give it their best shot.

The funkiness continues with 'Digging in the Dirt', featuring a marvellous Hammond organ-styled intro and rattling bass lines and percussion that drive this one along in a meaty and tight version, with Peter in complete control throughout as he teases the crowd. Same can be said of 'Sledgehammer', complete with extended bass intro leading into an explosion as the song takes off and the crowd go ballistic.

'Secret World', by now well established as the evening's set closer, is executed impeccably here tonight with fine performances from the entire band, but special kudos to David Rhodes and Manu Katche, who really deliver the goods here. Of course, encores aren't long in coming and the celebrations are led by a truly joyous 'In Your Eyes', in which Joy Askew gives a remarkable performance of Youssou N'Dour's vocal part.

The synth drone and drum beat need no introduction as 'Biko' bursts into the arena. This is a song with an important message to impart and Peter does it without descending to preaching to his audience. You can almost feel the raw emotion that is generated by both the band and the audience here in a truly electrifying performance of this classic. And that is it so you would think, but no, Peter had a further surprise in store for the audience tonight as he returns to the stage to acknowledge all the people who helped put the show on and then send the audience home in raptures as he sits at the piano to deliver a mesmerising 'Here Comes the Flood', which really defies description. You had to be there, I suppose.

ENTERTAINMENT CENTRE, SYDNEY, AUSTRALIA, 1 MARCH 1994

Set List: Come Talk to Me/Steam/Games without Frontiers/Shock the Monkey/Across the River/Shaking the Tree/Blood of Eden/San Jacinto/Family Snapshot/Kiss That Frog/Solsbury Hill/Digging in the Dirt/Sledgehammer/Secret World/In Your Eyes/Biko//
Source: Audience Recording.

The Secret World tour was Peter's most extensive to date and was one that literally took him to virtually every continent, including Australia for the first time (apart from Peter's Womadelaide performances the year before, that is), and here we have one of those inaugural Australian gigs

As usual 'Come Talk to Me' opens the set and it is sadly through a somewhat weedy-sounding recording that we get the first indications of how Mr Gabriel took on Oz. Even here, though, the sheer excitement and tension of the performance isn't hard to appreciate. 'Steam', with its almost locomotive rhythms replete with innuendo comes next and the extended intro leads into a feisty performance of the song itself, which the entire band seem to be having a blast playing. Sadly the recording quality remains tinny throughout, so it isn't really possible to appreciate the sheer dynamism generated by Tony Levin, David Rhodes, and Manu Katche here. Sadly the quality of this recording lets the performance down and it is a great shame because this is a show chock full of classics, including another haunting performance of 'Across the River', 'San Jacinto', and many others.

PART TWO: PETER GABRIEL

CHAPTER EIGHTEEN
"GROWING UP" 1998-2009

The gaps between Peter's albums had become wider but even by his standards the gap between *So* and its successor may have seemed inordinately long but Peter has never been one to rush his craft and of course, his altruistic involvement in many charitable projects also ate into his time and he continued to nurture his baby, the now fully established WOMAD Festival, with regular guest appearances at events both in the UK and elsewhere.

The first indications of the direction Peter would be taking on his next album appeared at a concert that he took part in Paris on 10 December 1998 as part of the fortieth anniversary celebrations for the signing of the Universal Declaration of Human Rights by the United Nations. This was followed by a further airing of new material at a WOMAD event in Seattle in 2001 before the album itself, entitled *Up*, was released on 23 September 2002, preceded by the highly entertaining 'Barry Williams Show' single and video. Always one to embrace new technology, Peter's new look stage show for the subsequent tour took in everything from video screens to zorb balls. I'm sure the kitchen sink was lurking in their too somewhere! The tour got under way in September 2002, with an extensive US tour before visiting Europe and the USA as well as further afield, which also saw Peter revisit some of his older material to the delight of his fans. His touring activities since 1998 have become surprisingly frequent and are still ongoing.

In an attempt to beat the bootleggers, Peter also began to release official live recordings of the gigs making the subsequent tours the best documented of any member of Genesis.

PALAIS OMNISPORTS DE BERCY, PARIS, FRANCE, 10 DECEMBER 1998
Set List: Red Rain/Signal to Noise/In Your Eyes//
Source: Audience Recording.

Once again, Peter became involved in the promotion of the fortieth anniversary of the signing of the Universal Declaration of Human Rights by the United Nations in 1948.

This was the first time audience had seen Peter in concert since the end of the massive *Secret World Tour* in 1994 and here he sounds understandably under rehearsed. His short set opens with 'Red Rain', an upbeat and passionate performance and this recording does manage to capture some of that atmosphere here. With a new album now under way Peter also treated the audience to a sneak peek at one of the tracks, entitled 'Signal to Noise'. This is still very much a work in progress and the introduction on piano is somewhat different to what would be the finished version some three years later. No doubting the effect of the song though, as this is an incredibly raw and emotional performance, aided to great effect by another stunning vocal show from Youssou N'Dour. 'In Your Eyes' brings this surprisingly short recording to a celebratory close, with no 'Biko' tonight. Perhaps it had served its purpose with the end of Apartheid, which had fallen in the intervening years, and so 'In Your Eyes' serves to celebrate success rather than anything and the enthusiastic Parisian crowd soon get involved bringing another enjoyable recording to a close.

MARYMOOR PARK, REDMOND, SEATTLE, USA, 29 JULY 2001
Set List: Here Comes the Flood/Red Rain/Digging in the Dirt/Family Snapshot/Come Talk to Me/Mercy Street/Solsbury Hill/Signal to Noise/In Your Eyes/Father, Son/When You're Falling//
Source: Audience Recording.

Back to WOMAD again here with a raucous audience recording, which despite the obvious shortcomings in terms of quality, does manage to bring something of the atmosphere through.

Opening with the solo piano and voice of 'Here Comes the Flood', it is evident from the start that Peter still has the power to command an audience, although he does sound hesitant at times as if he is struggling to remember the words. 'Red Rain' sounds somewhat flat tonight but that might be down to less than normal rehearsal time.

A funky 'Digging in the Dirt', driven along by bass and percussion sounds somewhat uncertain at times. But once it gets going it certainly gets a grip of the crowd. 'Family Snapshot' gets an instant reaction from the crowd and here Peter at last seems to have found his mojo, as the performance is confident and inspired. It's a pity the crowd don't shut up and listen to it!

'Come Talk to Me' heralds the first public appearance on stage of Peter's daughter Melanie and here we get an altogether different introduction, which is rhythmic, upbeat, and sexy. The entire performance is radically different from what had gone before or indeed what was to follow making this an interesting recording for collectors.

'Mercy Street' is stripped back to percussion, piano, and voice, and is incredibly effective in that setting. Much more familiar is the upbeat 'Solsbury Hill', which is the cue for the audience to join in, although for once they don't spoil the effect and the result is a raucous but celebratory acknowledgement of Peter's return to performance.

'Signal to Noise', first heard back in 1998, has evidently had much more work done to it and sounds altogether more confident than it did then. Peter's soulful vocal commands the audience's attention from the start turning into the undoubted highlight of the evening.

'In Your Eyes' seems somewhat out of place after what has preceded it but with the added presence of the members of Afro Celt Sound System, it soon turns into another delightful upbeat version. Another treat for the audience is next with 'Father, Son', an emotional homage to Peter's father, which calms the audience down and sends them home happy.

RADIO FRANCE, PARIS, FRANCE, 24 OCTOBER 2002

Set List: Darkness/Red Rain/Growing Up/Mercy Street/My Head Sounds Like That/The Barry Williams Show/More than This/Sledgehammer/In Your Eyes//
Source: TV/FM Radio Broadcast.

With the new *Up* album not long released, Peter began his promotional duties for it with a series of TV/radio appearances, of which this is one of the best. The emphasis is most definitely on the new material here with a suitably dramatic 'Darkness' opening the proceedings. Having struggled with the studio album, live the new material comes into its own and grabs you by the scruff of the neck.

Even 'Red Rain' sounds somewhat lacking following on from this, although it is still an impressive rendition, and Peter's vocals still manage to capture the right combination of angst and anguish throughout. 'Growing Up', replete with staccato, tattoo-like rhythms, and another impeccable vocal delivery shows how much better the album sounds in the live context.

'Mercy Street' opens with an a cappella vocal that gives the song an entirely new feel. Always a delight to hear it is nothing else than that here and the studio crowd welcome it like an old friend. 'My Head Sounds Like That' opens with a tick-tock rhythm, a clock ticking away the remnants of a life perhaps? A much more sedate and restrained performance here, which like so much of Peter's music, leads to a dramatic crescendo. 'The Barry Williams Show' – a delightfully tongue-in-cheek look at TV chat shows –saunters out of the traps here in a wonderful funky performance. Humour is replaced by the malevolent industrial grind of 'More Than This', which is given a blistering treatment by Peter and his new band before we return to slightly more familiar territory for the two closing numbers, 'Sledgehammer' and 'In Your Eyes', both of which give the crowd something to get up and dance to, ending a marvellous recording in a suitably celebratory mood.

AUDITORIO NACIONAL, MEXICO CITY, MEXICO, 4 NOVEMBER 2002

Set List: Father, Son/Darkness/Red Rain/The Barry Williams Show/My Head Sounds Like That/Technical F**k Up/Downside Up/More than This/Second Technical F**k Up/Come Talk to Me/Mercy Street/Digging in the Dirt/Growing Up/Animal Nation/Solsbury Hill/Sledgehammer/In Your Eyes/Family Snapshot//
Source: Audience Recording.

An unusual opener tonight – 'Father, Son' – gets things off to a low-key start. With Peter's new record focussing on the vagaries of life, this one is a particularly poignant tribute to Peter's own father, and as usual he packs more emotion into a deceptively simple song than many of his peers could.

Darkness takes us to a much more dramatic place, with a heart rending and emotional exploration of neuroses and their outcomes. Musically this is as dark and angry as a storm at sea whilst Peter's vocal hovers between agony and ecstasy – a remarkable effort. 'Red Rain' gets an enthusiastic cheer from the crowd as Peter introduces it in Spanish. Here the band put in a sterling performance with guitar, drums, and bass all etching out a sonic landscape, over which Peter embroiders a vocal performance chock full of emotion.

I admit I struggled with the new record but at least one track struck a chord with me straight away: 'The Barry Williams Show', Peter's very own tongue-in-cheek look at our fascination with reality TV shows. Funky, upbeat, and rude, this is a real delight and light relief from the unremitting drama of the preceding tracks. 'My Head Sounds Like That', also introduced in Spanish, takes us back to a repressive vibe. This is Peter at his most thought provoking and challenging

'Downside Up' is accompanied by a technical fuck up that gets a cheer from the crowd. It seems that even after all these years Peter can still get a rise out of a crowd with that one! Once the song gets going, however, it is a truly lovely version with a haunting vocal from Peter's daughter Melanie, making her first concert stage appearances with her dad on this tour. 'More Than This' gets under way with some spiky industrial guitar noise before the rest of the band find their groove and the song builds to a enthralling climax generating an altogether more optimistic vibe.

Yet another technical fuck up follows, which Peter announces as "Secundo fuck up". He is evidently having some banter with the audience here and sounds as if he is laughing as he introduces 'Come talk to Me', which is always a highlight of any Gabriel show. Driven along by an impressive keyboard intro, Peter is joined by the Mexican choir as he starts singing and the song, and then gets the lead out with some seriously heavy percussion from Ged Lynch. 'Mercy Street' is always a high point of any Gabriel show and tonight is no exception. Peter manages to wring every ounce of emotion out of his voice, and when that is combined with the wonderful vocals of his daughter Melanie, this song soars to new heights, which is exactly what it does here tonight.

'Digging in the Dirt' gets down and dirty with some marvellous organ sounds making it almost sound like some sleazy underground jazz club. Peter's vocal, soulful and emotional, fits the mood and the crowd add their own six penn'th to the proceedings in another ensemble performance. 'Growing Up' has the feel of a latter-day 'Intruder'. Both rhythmically and vocally this is a magnificently emotional performance. The incessant rhythms and almost spoken word vocal generate a raw and claustrophobic atmosphere that the acoustics of the hall simply add to.

'Animal Nation' is another of those songs that Peter has yet to commit to record. This one sounds like a throwback to the late '70s in feel and mood and I can hear echoes of several of his older songs. For some reason Mott the Hoople's 'All the Young Dudes' enters my head whenever I hear this one. Speaking of oldies, 'Solsbury Hill' gets the biggest cheer of the evening, and the crowd go nuts here. Peter sounds relaxed and confident whilst the band seems to be having a fine time too, which is as it should be.

'Sledgehammer' kicks straight in tonight, with no teasing intro, just a straightforward shit-kicking version with the crowd in fine voice. 'In Your Eyes' is upbeat too and accompanied by the crowd. Always a crowd pleaser, there is no doubting the pleasure of the crowd here. A marvellous vocal duet between Peter and Melanie accompanied by some excellent percussion from Ged again gives this one the necessary impetus that is carried along by an extremely vocal crowd. 'Family Snapshot' is a strange choice for a final encore but it works remarkably well and brings another enjoyable recording to a fine dramatic end.

CONFERENCE CENTRE, BRIGHTON, ENGLAND, 24 NOVEMBER 2003

Set List: Burn You Up, Burn You Down/Red Rain/More than This/Secret World/Games without Frontiers/Downside Up/Mercy Street/Darkness/Digging in the Dirt/Signal to Noise/Growing Up/San Jacinto/Shock the Monkey/Solsbury Hill/Sledgehammer/I Grieve/In Your Eyes/Biko//
Source: Soundboard Recording.

Something of an oddity this one, it being a standalone fund raising performance and Peter's first full band gig in the UK for several years. With a new album to promote the band get right on with it with a marvellous funky version of 'Burn You Up', which gets things off to a good start. Peter sounds as if he is enjoying himself and his new band delivers the goods with a tasty and tight performance.

'Red Rain' gets an enthusiastic cheer and deservedly so. This classic dramatic slice of Gabriel thunders out of the traps with some superb playing in both the bass and drums departments whilst David

Rhodes' rhythm guitar is the glue holding it all together. Peter jokes about the cost of going to South Africa the day after this gig and asks the audience for their contribution (who says rock stars don't have a sense of humour, eh?). Nothing humorous about 'More than This', however, which is packed with raw emotion and sounding infinitely superior to the recorded version.

'Secret World' doesn't really need any introduction and the audience are right behind Peter and the band during this one, which is followed by a wonderfully upbeat 'Games without Frontiers', a song with a serious message that still manages to be completely entertaining. This is no mean feat but Peter and the band do it with ease here. More audience banter next before 'Downside Up', an altogether more stark performance in which Peter and Melanie really wring every ounce of emotion out of their voices with a truly stunning version.

Peter sounds incredibly relaxed as he gets the band in the centre of the stage for story time. The story being that of Anne Sexton and is, of course, 'Mercy Street'. An a cappella introduction gives this an entirely different feel to its usual delivery. Different but every bit as effective, this is a truly magnificent performance of a beautiful song. From the light back to the dark side next, featuring a paranoid version of 'Darkness'. This is one of the most atmospheric performances of the evening. Peter puts in a particularly frightening vocal delivery replete with menace and suppressed anger.

An archaeological song next, or 'Digging in the Dirt'. This is a right down and dirty funky version too with some marvellous keyboard playing and an infectious rhythm generated by Levin and Rhodes. And there is no rest for the wicked as the band continue the groove with a storming version of 'Signal to Noise' and another slightly eerie delivery of 'Growing Up', both of which are markedly superior to their recorded counterparts.

More cobweb removal next as Peter and the band dust off the evergreen 'San Jacinto', which still manages to send shivers up and down the spine every time I hear it. Peter evidently has the audience in the palm of his hand by this part of the show and his performance is a master class in restraint and control. No need for restraint with 'Shock the Monkey', as it is an outright upbeat crowd pleaser, complete with a superbly infectious rhythm section. Speaking of infectious, I defy anyone not to tap their toes at the very least when they hear 'Solsbury Hill', and by the sound of it the crowd tonight were doing a damn sight more than tapping their toes as the band give a wonderful performance with Peter sounding in his element leading the choir.

'Sledgehammer' practically introduces itself and Rhodes and Levin get the crowd going with a truly funky intro accompanied by claps and singing from the crowd 'Waiting for the Big One' (pun intended). It isn't long in coming and this one grabs the crowd and shakes them till the pips drop – marvellous stuff!

Peter's shows are always ones of contrast and they don't get much wider than that between 'Sledgehammer's' raucous fun-filled innuendo and the angst of 'I Grieve', a spine tingling performance augmented by the use of a backing tape of the vocal from the late great Nusrat Fateh Ali Khan. Peter's soulful voice compliments Khan's shrill and anguished one like two souls in torment. The show is closed by a pairing of two classic Gabriel tracks. 'In Your Eyes' gives the audience one last chance to party and both they and the band grab it with evident glee here in a remarkable performance, even by Peter's standards, before the synthesiser drone heralds the arrival of 'Biko'. Peter acknowledges that they haven't played it for a while and in a week's time they will be getting to play it in South Africa for the first time. It must have been an incredibly emotional feeling for Peter and it certainly comes across in this recording, which is raw and chock full of feeling.

KING'S DOCK, LIVERPOOL, ENGLAND, 30 JUNE 2004

Set List: 'Here Comes the Flood'/Red Rain/Secret World/White Ashes/Games without Frontiers/Downside Up/Burn You Up, Burn You Down/The Tower That Ate People/San Jacinto/Digging in the Dirt/Solsbury Hill/Signal to Noise/Sledgehammer/In Your Eyes/Biko// Source: Soundboard Recording.

Aaah, the memories! Yes, this was one gig I wasn't going to miss! Twenty-one years since my home town had had the pleasure of a gig by Peter and tonight was going to be special.

Thankfully, the proceedings were recorded by another of the series of official bootlegs, which Peter had inaugurated back in 2003, so what we have here is a superb quality recording of what was a great night. Peter emerges on stage for a piano-driven version of 'Here Comes the Flood', at the end of which the crowd go suitably ballistic and Peter cheekily says, "I should quit while I am ahead." No chance of that with a Scouse crowd, Peter!

With the show being held inside the King's Dock "Summer Pops" festival tent, the usual visual part of the show was missing and the emphasis was purely on the music, which suited me down to the ground, and this was amply demonstrated by tracks such as 'Red Rain' and 'White Ashes', which were delivered flawlessly by an evidently well-rehearsed band. 'The Tower That Ate People' was another surprise. I had heard Peter perform this track before but this time the atmosphere and delivery were stunning and *loud*! 'Burn You Up, Burn You Down' simply gets better and better and tonight's performance is a belter.

The highlight of the show for me (and for many others in the crowd if the reaction was anything to go by) was 'San Jacinto'. Simply lit by white lights and performed exactly as it had been back in1987, even if you can't see the visuals on the recording, just close your eyes and you are back there – stunning stuff! 'Games without Frontiers' and the 'Segways' … well I suppose you had to be there to appreciate the joke but the performance doesn't need translation, as the sheer good humour of band and audience are plain to hear.

'Signal to Noise' was one of the few tracks from the new album that I liked instantly and it has certainly grown in performance, aided by Peter's reference to the current situation in Iraq, and the crowd really get behind the band here.

Once again, Peter manages to save the best until last with a particularly upbeat 'In Your Eyes', although many in the audience evidently thought the show was over and started vacating the building before the synth drone of 'Biko' brought everyone back for a truly awesome performance, chock full of raw emotion, which is captured to perfection on this stunning recording.

PIAZZA GRANDE, AREZZO, ITALY, 5 JULY 2007

Set List: The Rhythm of the Heat/On the Air/Intruder/D I Y/Washing of the Water/Steam/Blood of Eden/Love Town/No Self Control/Solsbury Hill/Mother of Violence/Family Snapshot/Lay Your Hands on Me/Big Time/Signal to Noise/Secret World/Sledgehammer/In Your Eyes/Biko//
Source: Soundboard Recording.

This is another official bootleg and a magnificent soundboard recording from the intriguingly titled *Warm Up* tour. Warm up for what is still anyone's guess but who cares?! 'Rhythm of the Heat' opens this one and it is a truly claustrophobic performance driven along by some fine percussion and a truly awesome vocal from Peter. 'On the Air' makes a welcome reappearance in Peter's set after an absence of over twenty years and it still sounds fresh as the day it was first performed.

Even in an open air setting such as this, 'Intruder' still makes you feel incredibly claustrophobic, and with a band as tight as this, the atmosphere is almost tangible. Peter is obviously in his element acting out the character's twisted fantasies in a magnificent performance. 'D I Y' lightens the mood somewhat with Peter's exhortation to take your life into your own hands and it is still a delightfully tongue-in-cheek romp.

Moving slightly forward in time next for 'Washing of the Water', which is a much more restrained and sedate performance, and still features an incredibly emotional vocal from Gabriel before the mood gets seriously funky with a down and dirty performance of 'Steam', featuring some seriously meaty percussion and another confident performance from Gabriel himself who is evidently winding the crowd up. 'Blood of Eden' takes the pace down again as Gabriel balances the show like a juggler. Once again some fine percussion is augmented by equally tasteful guitar playing from David Rhodes and Gabriel himself is supreme in another emotive performance accompanied by his daughter Melanie.

'Love Town' is one of those songs which you either love or hate. I'm not at all convinced by it and tonight's performance does nothing for me, I'm afraid, but the crowd seem to like it. Peter redeems himself with an incredible performance of 'No Self Control' driven along by Richard Evans' marimba and by the rest of the band. The pace is upped a bit for 'Solsbury Hill', which takes on the mantle of a celebration tonight and it is obvious that everyone is having a good time here.

'Mother of Violence' calms things down again. Melanie Gabriel takes the lead here and it is strange to hear this one without Peter, but a female perspective (pun intended) gives this one an added poignancy. David Rhodes' guitar rattles around like a wasp in a jam jar, while the rest of the performance is given in a truly understated but deeply effective manner. 'Family Snapshot', introduced in Italian, generates another incredibly dramatic atmosphere, with a vivid examination of the subject's thought processes and the possible outcome of his/her mission.

There is no let-up in the drama as 'Lay Your Hands on Me' begins. Peter is a bit too stately for the "dive" into the audience these days but nonetheless, this performance doesn't really need it to be effective. This is masterpiece of building suspense and tension that only a performer of Gabriel's calibre can deliver.

'Big Time' defuses the tension at a stroke as the band get down and funky for an extremely enjoyable performance, which everyone is evidently enjoying, while 'Signal to Noise' manages to convey a real sense of despair and anger, aided and abetted by the truly awesome vocals of the late great Nusrat Fateh Ali Khan.

'Secret World' closes the show in a suitably upbeat fashion. A confident and relaxed Gabriel leads the band through a marvellous performance before they take their bows in front of an evidently ecstatic crowd.

Of course, encores are expected and they aren't long in coming either, opening with the outrageously funky extended intro to 'Sledgehammer', accompanied by the crowd who then go stratospheric as the band give a meaty, beaty, tight, and tasty version of this classic slice of Gabriel. 'In Your Eyes' is also driven along by some tasteful percussion and keyboards. The only downside is Melanie's vocals, which sound rather weedy when compared to those of Youssou N'Dour, but she does her best and the crowd don't seem to mind. Sadly, 'Biko' still has its message to impart, although Apartheid has long since bitten the dust. There are other tragedies still being played out in the world and this song has as much resonance today as it did back in 1977. A magnificent ending to what has obviously been another superb concert by a reinvigorated Gabriel and his band.

EXPLANADA DEL MONUMENTAL, LIMA, PERU, 20 MARCH 2009

Set List: The Rhythm of the Heat/On the Air/Intruder/Steam/Blood of Eden/Games without Frontiers/No Self Control/Mother of Violence/Darkness/The Tower That Ate People/San Jacinto/Down to Earth/Secret World/Solsbury Hill/Sledgehammer/Signal to Noise/In Your Eyes/Red Rain/Father, Son/Biko//
Source: Soundboard Recording.

The so-called *Warm Up* tour continued at sporadic intervals throughout 2007 and 2009, culminating with a short series of shows in South America, of which this recording taken from the official bootleg is a fine example.

The haunting instrumental 'Zaar' opens the proceedings, as Peter and the band take the stage to start the evening proper with 'The Rhythm of the Heat'. This is another magnificent performance, although Peter's vocal is a little off kilter to start with. But he soon hits his stride with a confident and increasingly dramatic delivery. Restrained percussion and keyboards build to a completely hypnotic rhythm until the spell is broken and the drama explodes in a brilliant conclusion.

'On the Air' takes us back to the days when punk ruled the airwaves. Probably the closest Peter gets to a punk sound, this pungent little ditty rattles along at a ferocious rate, driven by the sterling percussive work of Ged Lynch and stabbing guitar phrases of David Rhodes. 'Intruder', replete with psycho accompaniment from David Rhodes, and Ged Lynch really gets going when Keyboardist Richard Evans lets loose with some truly remarkable keyboard sounds. Peter is having a blast as he assumes the mantle of the character of the song with relish making this another memorable version.

'Steam', upbeat, funky, and rude, is driven along by Tony Levin's incredible bass lines. A truly enjoyable rendition is given here and I would imagine that the crowd were up and boogieing during it! 'Blood of Eden' calms things down again with a stately and refined performance, in which Peter puts in a truly remarkable vocal augmented by those of his daughter Melanie and Angie Pollock, both of whom are sublime here.

'Games without Frontiers' gets under way with a wonderful spiky guitar and keyboard intro, feeling almost like musical barbed wire. Peter manages to screw up the intro, which makes for an amusing moment but he doesn't miss a beat and the band carry on regardless, with Tony Levin in particular putting down a truly excellent bass rhythm. A marimba-led 'No Self Control', which is a delightfully paranoid version here tonight, featuring incessant rhythms and some searing guitar from David Rhodes, simply elevate this to a master class in atmosphere and mood.

'Mother of Violence' is also all repressed atmosphere, despite the acoustic beauty of the music. Here Melanie really delivers the goods on the vocal, while David Rhodes' guitar buzzes around like a wasp in a bottle, which adds an unsettling edginess to the performance. 'Darkness' generates a superbly emotive atmosphere too. The contrast between Peter's superbly emotional vocal and a quite simple musical accompaniment make for a remarkably effective effort.

'The Tower That Ate People' grabs the audience by the scruff of the neck with some scorching guitar work from Rhodes and superb percussion from Ged Lynch. Peter's rasping vocal sounds like he is delivering the words through a megaphone. It's superbly effective whatever he is doing!

'San Jacinto' doesn't really need any more superlatives thrown at it but here's one more – brilliant! I personally think that Peter reached his creative peak with 'PG 4' and this track is always a masterpiece and tonight is no exception. A new track next, namely 'Down to Earth'. This is an altogether more upbeat song, sounding almost jazzy, with a swinging rhythm section and is eminently enjoyable.

'Secret World' is as magnificently majestic as ever. Ged's rock solid percussion drive the song along accompanied by some wonderfully understated guitar and keyboard work. The upbeat mood continues with a celebratory 'Solsbury Hill', and from the sound of it, the crowd were up and dancing by now. They are certainly in good voice, which is as it should be, of course!

'Sledgehammer' keeps the mood upbeat and funky, especially the rhythm section, which puts down an incredibly bouncy sound, over which Peter puts in a superbly soulful vocal. The mood takes a more serious turn next with the remarkable 'Signal to Noise', which builds from simple beginnings to a frighteningly anguished performance, in which the taped vocal by the late Nustrat Fateh Ali Khan simply provides the icing on a magnificently atmospheric offering.

It's not all doom and gloom, however, as 'In Your Eyes' gets the encores under way in a typically upbeat fashion. Peter and Melanie are joined by a chorus of voices from a crowd, who are obviously thoroughly enjoying tonight's performance, and who can blame them? The crowd want 'Biko' but Peter is going to make them wait, as 'Red Rain' thunders into life, thanks to some fantastic playing from Messrs Rhodes, Lynch, and Evans. Their Herculean efforts are contrasted nicely with 'Father, Son', which is a magnificently observed homage to a father from his son, with Peter accompanied on piano – simple but brilliantly effective. Peter finally rewards the audience's patience with the synth drone and drums heralding the arrival of 'Biko'. This is always an emotional moment in the show and one that sadly has just as much of a message to impart today as it did when it was written all those years ago. The show draws to a close on what was, I am sure, a wave of shared emotions.

CHAPTER NINETEEN
"AN INFUSION OF NEW BLOOD" 2010-2012

Almost eight years were to elapse before Peter emerged with a new album for the fans. He cannot be accused of being idle though with an intensive series of tours taking up a considerable slice of the time.

However, by 2010 fans were becoming impatient for a new offering from Peter and as usual he opted to take us by surprise with the *Scratch My Back* project. Ostensibly a two- part effort whereby other artists would "cover" tracks by Peter and he would reciprocate by covering theirs. The first part, Peter's interpretations of other artists' music, was released under the title *Scratch My Back* in April 2010. Well received critically, the fan base was of mixed opinions on this one, and the other half of the project has yet to see the light of day.

Prior to the release of the album, Peter had undertaken a short series of concerts in which both material from this album and tracks from his own back catalogue were performed by an orchestra, no less! This project continued with the subsequent release of an album of the orchestral variations of Peter's songs on 10 October 2010 under the title, *New Blood*. Subsequent shows with the orchestra have taken place in Europe, the USA, and South America with the final batch due to take place in May 2012. A DVD of the shows at London's Hammersmith Odeon has been released under the title *New Blood Live in London* and several of the shows have been sound recorded and a selection of which are included here.

PALAIS OMNISPORTS DE BERCY, PARIS, FRANCE, 22 MARCH 2010
Set List: 'Sledgehammer' (False Start)/Heroes/The Boy in the Bubble/Mirrorball/Flume/Listening Wind/The Power of the Heart/My Body is a Cage/The Book of Love/I Think it's Going to Rain Today/Apres Moi/Philadelphia/Street Spirit (Fade Out)/San Jacinto/Downside Up/Digging in the Dirt (F**k Up)/Digging in the Dirt/Wallflower/Signal to Noise/Washing of the Water/Blood of Eden/The Rhythm of the Heat/Darkness/Solsbury Hill/In Your Eyes/Don't Give Up/Low Light//
Source: Audience Recording.

Paris, Bercy! A venue I know very well and a magnificent setting for a show such as this. It is a massive venue and its acoustics take their toll of the opening number as Peter and the orchestra fuck up 'Sledgehammer'. This is evidently a deliberate ploy to break the ice, as Peter then goes on to explain that the first half of the show will be comprised of the tracks form the *Scratch My Back* album. As such, Bowie's 'Heroes' opens the set proper and is a restrained version building to an impressive climax. Peter sounds understandably nervous as he gets thing sunder way, but he doesn't have to worry, as he evidently has the audience in the palm of his hand.

'The Boy in the Bubble' and 'Mirrorball' come and go with barely a ripple. It is understandable that with a project such as this, some interpretations work better than others, and to my ears Peter doesn't really find his feet until we get to 'The Power of the Heart', which is a truly remarkable performance, aided enormously by the acoustics of the venue, which give it an added emotional impact. This is retained as Peter and the orchestra give us 'My Body is a Cage', proving to be a much more satisfying and convincing rendition in the live context.

With the second half of the show drawing on Peter's own material, to these ears, this half of the show is a) much more interesting and b) much more convincing. A rippling keyboard introduction leads us into 'San Jacinto', always one of Peter's most impressive songs, and here the brittleness of the orchestral treatment is contrasted by an impassioned vocal from Peter, which is quite stunning. Even newer material such as 'Downside Up' gains an interesting new slant under the orchestral treatment.

One real delight here is an all too rare performance of 'Wallflower', which is every bit as emotion packed as 'Biko'. A stark solo piano introduction moves like raindrops on a prison cell before Peter delivers an equally stark and impassioned vocal, which is a thrilling performance. 'Signal to Noise' works equally well here too. The strings sound a discordant note, a stark warning and the song moves at a ponderous rate, weighed down by sheer emotion. The rest of tonight's show mixes old and new classics in equal measure, including stirring performances of 'The Rhythm of the Heat', 'In Your Eyes', on which Peter is accompanied by the legendary Youssou N'Dour, and a magnificent 'Don't Give Up' brings the evening to a celebratory close.

BBC STUDIOS, LONDON, ENGLAND, 19 NOVEMBER 2011

Set List: Heroes/Wallflower/Intruder/Signal to Noise/San Jacinto/Downside Up/Mercy Street/Father, Son/Rhythm of the Heat/Solsbury Hill/Red Rain/Don't Give Up//
Source: FM Radio Broadcast.

Peter still seems to get regular coverage for his projects on the BEEB and this one was no exception. Having already aired some of the material from the *New Blood* project on shows such as *Later... with Jools Holland*, here is a fuller showcase for the new album.

Bowie's 'Heroes' opens the show with a sustained string refrain and a sedate, restrained performance, which lacks nothing in terms of atmosphere. 'Wallflower' gets a rare outing here. Always viewed as the poor relation to 'Biko', when stripped down to piano and strings it is anything but a poor relation. A cloying, claustrophobic atmosphere is generated throughout and Peter's voice delivers just the right emotion without going overboard.

A 'Psycho' styled string introduction leads us into the equally paranoid world of the 'Intruder'. This is definitely one that will raise the hairs on the back of your neck. Peter sounds in his element delivering this creepy performance – a classic reinterpretation!

'Signal to Noise' and its observations of the futility of war and its aftermath takes on a new resonance here with a slow, sedate string performance and superbly emotional vocal delivery from Peter and Anne Brun. 'San Jacinto' is given a new lick of paint too, yet still the drama and passion of the original is retained here in a truly brilliant performance.

'Downside Up's' new string arrangement sounds a little bit too *Wallis & Gromit* for me but the performance is still a pungently brittle gem. 'Mercy Street' also shines a little bit more brightly in this new arrangement with Peter sounding in incredible form. His smoky vocals contrast with the shimmering percussion and strings.

'Father, Son' is something of a rarity in Peter's oeuvre. This is a deeply personal and sentimental song dedicated to his father, which works surprisingly well in this setting. 'Rhythm of the Heat' still manages to capture something of that sense of claustrophobic panic that the original did. In fact, the strings give an extra edginess to the result worthy of a film soundtrack.

'Solsbury Hill' is always a delight to hear and after all the drama and tension, it is evident that both Peter and the audience are ready for a bit of light relief, which this classic easily provides. 'Red Rain' shimmers like rain on glass with another inspired arrangement, giving a fresh look at a familiar subject, while 'Don't Give Up' is every bit as relevant in these recession hit times as it was back in 1986 and it brings this marvellous recording to a suitably emotional close.

CHAPTER TWENTY
"GETTING THINGS BACK TO FRONT" 2012-14

Peter's increased touring activity took an even more surprising turn when, in the autumn of 2012 he announced what he humorously called his *Back to Front* tour. Ostensibly a celebration of what was the high water mark in terms of his commercial (if not artistic) career with the release of the *So* album in 1986, this series of gigs still managed to pull off a few surprises as the resulting recordings reveal.

It had been quite some time since Peter had road-tested material that had not actually been completely worked up in the studio, but here he was opening the shows with an incomplete "work in progress" before dividing the rest of the show into several segments, culminating with the performance of the *So* album in its entirety.

A US-only tour in 2012 was soon augmented by further shows in Europe and the UK in 2013. More gigs are planned for 2014 in which, no doubt, Peter will continue to surprise and entertain his audiences in equal measure.

As usual, all of the shows from the tours have been released as official bootlegs.

WELLS FARGO CENTRE, PHILADELPHIA, PENNSYLVANIA, USA, 21 SEPTEMBER 2012

Set List: Oh But/Come Talk to Me/Shock the Monkey/Family Snapshot/Digging in the Dirt/Secret World/The Family & the Fishing Net/Solsbury Hill/No Self Control/Washing of the Water/Red Rain/Sledgehammer/Don't Give Up/That Voice Again/Big Time/Mercy Street/Milgrams' 37/This is the Picture/In Your Eyes/The Tower That Ate People/Biko//
Source: Soundboard Recording.

Peter's decision to revisit the *So* album on the occasion of its twenty-fifth anniversary has resulted in yet another fascinating tour, thus far of the USA and Canada, but with further dates in Europe and the UK planned for later this year, fans are in for a treat. Once again, Peter has opted to make all of the recordings available as official bootlegs and this is one of the early shows.

Opening with Peter explaining the rationale behind the show, we are treated to a "song-in-progress". This takes us right back to the start of Peter's career where he would often road test unfinished material in front of his audiences. Performed on piano accompanied by Tony Levin, this one has a somewhat sentimental tinge to it and obviously needs a lot more work before it enters the Gabriel canon, but it is nonetheless another fascinating behind the scenes look at Peter's compositional processes.

Band intros are followed by a performance of 'Come Talk to Me' stripped down to the bare bones of guitar, piano, and accordion of all things! Not that that prevents it from being an inspired performance. Peter sounds suitably emotional throughout and for once the crowd are well behaved and don't go overboard with their enthusiasm! A new acoustic arrangement of 'Shock the Monkey' takes the audience by surprise but they soon get into the groove. Surprisingly, this new arrangement doesn't pack the same punch as the full scale version but it is interesting to hear nonetheless.

'Family Snapshot' doesn't really need any introduction. Always a highlight of any show by Peter, this version is no exception, even in a more basic stripped down format. Peter still has the audience in the palm of his hand as he acts out the story of the frustrated assassin. Augmented by two new female backing singers, the end result is astonishing. Drama is piled on top of drama as a raunchy groove is laid down by the rhythm section of Manu Katche and Tony Levin for a sensational performance of 'Digging in the Dirt', which is funky, upbeat, and downright rude!

'Secret World' opens with some superb keyboard work from David Sancious and impeccable rhythm guitar from David Rhodes, while Peter's vocal performance is once again augmented by the presence of his backing singers, which lift this version to new heights in terms of pure emotion. 'The Family & the Fishing Net' gets off the ground with some eerie synth noises and Rhodes' guitar sounds like an angry wasp before Peter's piano leads us into the claustrophobic world which the song portrays. It really doesn't get any better than this.

Time for some light relief next as 'Solsbury Hill' gives the audience something to get their teeth into. Always a joy to hear and tonight it was evidently no exception, as the crowd are in active participation throughout what sounds like a particularly fine version of this classic. The light is replaced by the darkness once again as Peter simply says, "No Self Control." Nuff said, really. The entire band delivers this masterpiece of emotion flawlessly.

'Washing of the Water' sounds strangely out of place in this set. I don't really know why, as it is every bit as emotional as ever, but it doesn't convince this listener this time round. 'Red Rain', however, is another matter entirely! it races out of the traps and takes the audience and the listener along with it in a tidal wave of emotions. Rhodes' guitar work and Katche's percussion give this a marvellous edgy feel making it an impressive version.

Tony Levin's bass heralds the arrival of 'Sledgehammer' and cue audience going nuts as this classic slice of Gabriel signals the arrival of party central here in Philadelphia! The band sound relaxed and Peter is evidently having a real blast as he gives this performance 110 per cent – superb stuff. 'Don't Give Up' gives everyone time for reflection, especially in these recession hit times, and as usual, Peter and the band deliver it with a superb mix of raw emotion and pathos.

'That Voice Again' gets under way with one of Peter's famous technical fuck-ups before the song starts. I can now understand why this one was only performed at a handful of gigs back on the 1986/87 tour, as it sounds disjointed at times and lacks the essential conviction of performance that marks out Peter's finer works. Nonetheless, it is great to have the chance to hear it again in the live context. 'Big Time' gets the band and the audience back in the party groove once again with an uptempo, funky performance, which everyone is evidently enjoying enormously, especially Mr Levin, whose bass threatens to bring the roof down.

'Mercy Street' delivered a cappella at the start never fails to send shivers up and down the spine and here is no exception. For raw emotion and feeling, this one is hard to beat, and tonight's performance was evidently a classic one. 'Milgrams' 37', although only released on the *So* album, has a much longer pedigree but sounds out of place here to my ears, as does 'This is the Picture', but the crowd seem to like them both, so what do I know?

'In Your Eyes' brings the presentation of the *So* album to a close in fine style with a truly remarkable performance. The band intros are followed by the agonised introduction to 'The Tower That Ate People'. This is without doubt one of Peter's angriest tracks and one that takes no prisoners here. Speaking of prisoners, the finale is reserved for what is without doubt the most emotional song in Peter's entire catalogue. 'Biko' is sadly as relevant today as it was when it was written back in 1977. Words really can't describe the raw passion and emotion that this song generates and here it brings what was obviously a fantastic evening to a truly electrifying close.

O2 ARENA, LONDON, ENGLAND, 21 OCTOBER 2013

Set List: Oh But/Come Talk to Me/Shock the Monkey/Family Snapshot/Digging in the Dirt/Secret World/The Family & the Fishing Net/No Self Control/Solsbury Hill/Why Don't You Show Yourself?/Red Rain/Sledgehammer/Don't Give Up/That Voice Again/Mercy Street/Big Time/Milgrams' 37/This is the Picture/In Your Eyes/The Tower That Ate People/Biko//
Source: Soundboard Recording.

Peter's increasingly rare appearances in the UK have become more London-centric and tonight's opening show of a mere four in his own country is no exception. The O2 Arena is the location for this gig and as you can soon hear it is a cavernous space.

Peter's decision to open these gigs with a "work-in-progress" is a brave one, but 'O But' (as we think this one is to be called) falls somewhat flat here. Thankfully, as Peter himself acknowledges, "the cavalry" soon arrive as the rest of the band take the stage and an acoustically driven 'Come Talk to Me' gees the proceedings up nicely. I had my reservations about hearing some of these songs performed in what is essentially an "unplugged" setting but this one works extremely well.

'Shock the Monkey', also stripped down to guitar and voice, works extremely well. Peter's voice doesn't quite carry the same power that it used to but it is still an incredibly effective instrument in its own right. This slightly funky version gets the crowd participating nicely, although in a suitably restrained manner – this is London after all! 'Family Snapshot' gets a cheer of recognition and this is one of those songs that never fails to send shivers up and down the spine. Here the combination of an acoustic presentation and the sheer power of Peter's vocals drives this one along superbly well.

The real meat of the show begins with an awesome version of 'Digging in the Dirt', which is propelled along by the superlative rhythmic bass of Tony Levin and some funky keyboard phrasings from David Sancious. Always a favourite, this one works a treat to my ears. This is followed by an equally emotional 'Secret World' and a superbly eerie "The Family & the Fishing Net' where David Rhodes' guitar wail manages to bring just the right element of paranoid angst to proceedings. This one has seldom sounded better than it does here and Peter delivers the vocal to perfection.

'No Self Control' has also definitely improved with age and it is hard to describe the sheer emotion and drama that this song evokes. Let's just say tonight's performance is top notch! The audience who, up until now have, been remarkably respectful, get their moment to shine next with 'Solsbury Hill', which is obviously too much for one member of the audience who screams in delight. And why not, I ask? This is after all one of Peter's most accessible songs and the crowd lap it up and it sounds as if the band do too.

Another new song makes its entrance next: 'Why Don't You Show Yourself'. A slow bluesy guitar riff gets this one under way and Peter is accompanied on vocals by Ann Brun and Jennie Abrahamson, which would be a superb combination, but whether it is down to the acoustics of the venue or the sound man getting it wrong, the resulting vocal is muffled at best, which is a shame.

Next up the reason for tonight's performance: the *So* album in its entirety. It gets underway with a superb 'Red Rain', which is funky and dramatic at the same time. This is Peter Gabriel proving that you *can* be successful *and* artistic at the same time. Okay, his pipes don't quite carry the same range as they did in 1986, but so what? (Pun intended.) the end result is still an astonishing performance, followed by an equally emphatic 'Sledgehammer'. The audience know what's coming and the clapping and shouting precedes the arrival of the song by a good while as Mr Levin's phenomenal bass teases the crowd. But once the song finally arrives the band are unleashed and put in superb performances all round.

'Don't Give Up' was a song with special resonance in the 1980s and it still resonates in today's straitened environment. A classic, pure and simple. 'That Voice Again' – one of only two tracks from the album not to get a regular outing during the *So* tour – makes its appearance next, and I have to say, it sounds somewhat contrived and forced when compared to what has preceded it, but you can't have everything, can you?

Another emotional classic next, as an a cappella introduction ushers us on to 'Mercy Street', and once again here is proof, if it were needed, that you can have a song with a message that still sounds bloody good when treated as a song. Peter's soulful vocal has lost none of its power here – marvellous stuff! From the sublime to the slightly ridiculous next, as Peter sends himself up with 'Big Time' and another cue for the audience to go nuts. It is the impeccable percussion of Manu Katche and Tony Levin, augmented by some damn fine rhythm guitar from David Rhodes, which drives this one along superbly well.

'Milgrams' 37' sticks out like a sore thumb here, as indeed it did on the album in 1986. A refugee from an earlier album, this one doesn't really make the kind of impact that it used to do when it was included in Peter's performances. The same can be said for 'This is the Picture', which falls slightly flat tonight.

Things are redeemed, however, with an outstanding performance of 'In Your Eyes'. A heart and soul lifting experience on record, live it takes on an entirely new character and tonight was evidently no exception, as band and audience are united in celebration, after which the band take their deserved bows and leave the stage.

Of course the audience know that encores are due and they aren't kept waiting long for them either. I have to admit that the entire *Ovo* project left me cold at the time, so 'The Tower That Ate People' isn't something that I am going to get excited about – sorry, folks! 'Biko' of course, is entirely different matter of course! This is one of only a handful of songs that can raise shivers up and down my spine and reduce me to tears of raw emotion whether I am listening to the album version or live. In the live context this song is impossible to beat and it brings what was evidently an extremely enjoyable evening's music to a suitably evocative close.

****

A Selection Of Shows: Genesis & Solo Live Guide 1976-2014

PART THREE: STEVE HACKETT

Steve Hackett

150

CHAPTER TWENTY-ONE
"THE ACOLYTE STEPS OUT OF THE SHADOW OF THE HIEROPHANT" 1978

Steve's first solo foray had been released during the hiatus following Peter's decision to leave the band in 1974 and the subsequent album, *Voyage of the Acolyte*, achieved considerable success both here in the UK and elsewhere when it was released in the summer of 1975. Steve himself admitted that once he had that experience under his belt, going back to the band was something that he found increasingly difficult to manage but he did so for a further two years, resulting in the glorious swansong albums that are *A Trick of the Tail* (1976) and *Wind & Wuthering* (1976), before finally opting to leave the band in the autumn of 1977.

Going solo was never going to be an easy task, as responsibility for everything from album artwork to tea-making now firmly fell firmly on Steve's shoulders. However, Steve is nothing if not resourceful and he set to work with a vengeance, opting to broaden his musical palette by including musicians from the USA who were (at the time at least) relatively unknown in the UK as guests on the album. The result was *Please Don't Touch*, Steve's second solo outing, which was released in April 1978. This was an album that expanded Steve's reputation for inventive musicianship and lyrical excellence. The album was well received by fans and critics and it was not long before Steve started to miss the roar of the greasepaint and the smell of the crowd (as he put it) and set about putting together a new band in order to perform his material live.

Fans had their first opportunity to see Steve's new look in the autumn of 1978 with his first solo gig being at the confusingly named Chateau Neuf in Oslo, Norway, on 4 October 1978. Steve's shows have been a musical adventure from the outset and these early shows were no exception.

APOLLO THEATRE, MANCHESTER, ENGLAND, 24 OCTOBER 1978

Set List: Land of a Thousand Autumns/Please Don't Touch/Racing in A/Ace of Wands/Carry on up the Vicarage/Ace of Wands/Hands of the Priestess/Icarus Ascending/Narnia/(Acoustic Set: Black Light-Blood on the Rooftops-Horizons)/Kim/The Optigon/A Tower Struck Down/Spectral Mornings/Star of Sirius/Shadow of the Hierophant/Clocks/I Know What I Like//
Source: Audience Recording.

For a tour with only a handful of gigs, this one is well represented by recordings, but of these, without doubt, the best one for my money is that taken from Steve's show at the Apollo Theatre Manchester. Maybe my opinion is a little bit biased because this was the first time I ever saw Steve in concert. Opening the concert with 'Land of a Thousand Autumns' and 'Please Don't Touch' got the show off to a fast and frantic pace, which was not slowed down any way by 'Racing in A', on which we get to hear Mr Hicks' dulcet tones for the first time. The entire band "race" (pardon the pun) through this one in fine form and I am sure that any doubts that Steve may have had about solo live performance must have been blown away by the audience reaction to him and his new band.

Steve's sense of humour is on display in the next number with the hilarious "police message" (red and yellow psychopath indeed!) intro. 'Carry on up the Vicarage' fuses the elements of Vaudeville and the *Carry On* films in a gloriously camp tribute to Ms Christie and her creations. It really does sound as if the entire band are having a real hoot playing this one. A couple of relative "oldies" next when Steve introduces them as tracks from an album that was "very well received by the taxman!" 'Ace of Wands' and 'Hands of the Priestess' cement their positions as stage favourites from the get go. Both songs are presented in faultless versions here, with the latter coming across particularly well, no doubt owing to John's impeccable flute playing and Nick Magnus' scintillating Mellotron playing.

Steve Hackett

With a new album to promote, we receive a healthy infusion from it at these shows, continuing with the tale of 'Icarus Ascending', which is a suitably dramatic performance. Peter Hicks' vocal manages to bring a suitably angst edge to the song, while the rest of the band, and the rhythm section of Dik Cadbury and John Shearer in particular, underpin everything with some very tasteful playing. Unfortunately a change of tape means that the beginning of 'Narnia' is missed from this recording, but what there is of the song gives a suitably impressive rendering of it.

As we know now, no Steve Hackett show is complete without some form of acoustic performance. As usual, the audience indulge in some jovial banter for their favourite tracks before Steve treats us to a medley comprising extracts from 'Black Light' (still a long way from seeing the light of day on *Bay of Kings*), along with 'Blood on the Rooftops' and a ubiquitous 'Horizons'. 'Kim' follows this up and it is greeted with a cheer from the crowd. This is marvellous track and one that is delivered in fine style by Steve and John.

Steve's explorations of "New Technology" takes us off on a slightly bizarre ramble next as he introduces 'The Optigon' with its almost *Keystone Cops* feel, which leads us nicely to the aural nightmare that is 'A Tower Struck Down', where the band really take the audience by the scruff of the neck and shake them. Steve has always road tested new material in front of his audience before committing to record and here we have the first example of that with the guitar synth introduction to what we now know as 'Spectral Mornings'. A glorious version is captured here, replete with stunning performances from every band member. Kudos to John Shearer and Nick Magnus who augment Steve's playing and take the performance to magical heights, as you will hear if you listen to this recording. 'Spectral' is a live favourite from the very start!

Back to where it all began next with Star of Sirius which is surprisingly good although it is a track that doesn't really suit Peter's vocals, the backing harmonies are exquisite though and the rest of the band deliver another enjoyable performance which is followed by an equally emotional and enigmatic rendition of Shadow of the Hierophant. The show is rounded off with another as yet unrecorded number: Clocks which blows away any remaining cobwebs from the band and audience alike before the finale of the evening, a ramshackle and very much tongue-in-cheek homage to Steve's former bandmates in the form of I Know What I Like which elicits an enormous cheer from this partisan crowd. All in all, an extremely enjoyable recording and with no extant "Live Archive" release from this tour, this one fills the gap quite nicely.

CHAPTER TWENTY-TWO
"GREETING THE SPECTRAL MORNING" 1979

Barely twelve months had elapsed before Steve was back on the road again with another album to promote. Several tracks from it had been road tested on the 1978 tour to acclaim from the fans.

The new album, 'Spectral Mornings' cemented Steve's reputation as one of the UK's finest musicians, and the title track has gone on to become the most revered in Steve's entire catalogue and deservedly so! With the new album under his belt and a new band determined to help Steve realise his musical vision, he set off on the first of two tours that were to occupy the greater part of 1979.

The first was a European and UK tour, which featured most of the new album alongside favourites from its predecessors. The second was a UK-only affair in the autumn with a slightly different set, including the only performances of an underrated Hackett classic, 'The Virgin & the Gypsy'. Once again, material that Steve was working on appeared in the shows with 'The Steppes' being the most frequently performed under its working title of 'Eric'. Thankfully, there are several recordings available from both these tours and they are also covered by the discs from the *Live Archive '70s, '80s, '90s* series.

EMPIRE THEATRE, LIVERPOOL, ENGLAND, 24 JUNE 1979
Set List: Land of a Thousand Autumns/Please Don't Touch/Tigermoth/Every Day/Narnia/The Red Flower of Taichi Blooms Everywhere/Ace of Wands/Carry on up the Vicarage/(Acoustic Set - Black Light-Blood on the Rooftops-Horizons)/Kim/The Optigon/A Tower Struck Down/Spectral Mornings/Star of Sirius/Shadow of the Hierophant/Clocks/I Know What I Like/Racing in A/Ace of Wands/Racing in A (acoustic section reprise)//
Source: Audience Recording.

The album/tour/album treadmill had firmly taken hold of Steve by the beginning of 1979. Capitalising on the success of the previous year's shows with a brand new album to promote (some of which had been "road tested" in front of audience during that tour), Steve undertook no less than two tours of the UK and Europe in 1979. The first of these was a UK-only affair and is well documented by live recordings, including Steve's first appearance at the Reading Festival.

This tour is covered by the first of the discs in the *Live Archive '70s, '80s, '90s* box set, but for those of you who were fortunate to attend any of these gigs there are several other recordings that document it as well. From these I have once again selected one that has personal significance to me. The spring tour brought Steve to Liverpool for the first time as a solo artist and his first gig here was ironically enough on the first anniversary of my first Genesis gig (Knebworth Park, in case you were wondering). What a way to celebrate an anniversary with a gig by the maestro himself!

Taken from a master recording made by a fan at the gig, what we have here is an extremely enjoyable performance. Capitalising on the success of the 1978 shows, Steve continued to expand the musical envelope, as both he and the band explored the music they were creating and the audience's reaction to it. Once again opening the show with 'Land of a Thousand Autumns/Please Don't Touch', the band made their statement of intent crystal clear: here was a band intending to *rock*. Interestingly enough, Steve is still referring to 'Tigermoth' by its working title of 'Lay Down Your Arms (Surrender to Mine)'. No matter, it is a stunningly dramatic performance that still sends shivers up and down my spine whenever I hear it. Steve's guitar wails like a frustrated banshee throughout whilst the rest of the band provide an equally frantic accompaniment.

Nick Magnus's sepulchral introduction to 'Every Day' makes one expect a sermon from the Reverend Hackett and in a way that is what we get with this staunchly anti-drug song's message to the fore. Peter Hicks' vocals deliver the song with just the right amount of angst and verve. This is followed by 'The Red Flower of Taichi Blooms Everywhere', which is a marvellous instrumental that grows in magnificence every time, and John's flute playing is spot on the money here.

A little story about Steve's horoscope and tarot card readings leads us nicely into 'Ace of Wands', which is another piece which has survived the test of time and still appears regularly in Steve's live shows. Here it is a joy to behold and the band serve this classic up piping hot and delicious as ever. Mayhem and madness à la Hackett

A Selection Of Shows: Genesis & Solo Live Guide 1976-2014

Steve Hackett

next with the outrageously camp and tongue-in-cheek homage to Agatha Christie that is 'Carry on up the Vicarage', and what a carry on it is, too!

As we have come to expect, no Hackett show is complete without its acoustic moment, and once again Steve delivers some as yet unrecorded music in the shape of 'Black Light', which had been performed on the 1978 tour and was still some four years away from appearing on album. A tantalising snippet of 'Blood on the Rooftops' comes next followed by truly wonderful performances of 'Horizons' and 'Kim'. The typically brash Liverpudlian audience mar this somewhat with some unnecessary shouting but otherwise the performance is excellent throughout.

From h-fi to lo-fi next with yet another outing for Steve's "sunny friend", 'The Optigon'. This is a truly eccentric device put to good use with a superb segue into 'A Tower Struck Down', which elicits a well-deserved cheer from the crowd. Once again the "Mighty Mellotron" of Nick Magnus is to the fore here, along with the rhythm section of John Shearer and Dik Cadbury, who are no slouches either and the track ends with a suitably explosive climax, out of which 'Spectral Mornings' emerges like a phoenix from the ashes. Cue the audience going wild here as Steve launches into what is probably his most famous anthem – stunning stuff, then and now!

Classic follows classic as the band take us back a little bit with a wonderful performance of 'Star of Sirius' and the portentous 'Shadow of the Hierophant' before the metronomic beat of the introduction to 'Clocks' sets the pace for the show closer. Returning after a short break, the 'Cosmic Lawnmower' is back again with a rather camp but very welcome performance of 'I Know What I Like'. The show is brought to its conclusion with a zesty performance of 'Racing in A' and an acoustic reprise that seems to send everyone home happy.

APOLLO THEATRE, GLASGOW, SCOTLAND, 23 OCTOBER 1979

Set List: Please Don't Touch/Tigermoth/Every Day/Ace of Wands/The Virgin and the Gypsy/The Steppes/Narnia/Sentimental Institution/The Red Flower of Taichi Blooms Everywhere/Star of Sirius/Spectral Mornings/A Tower Struck Down/Clocks/(Acoustic Set: Blood on the Rooftops-Horizons)/Kim/The Ballad of the Decomposing Man/Hercules Unchained//
Source: Audience Recording.

Surprisingly enough, Steve returned to concert stages in the UK for a second tour in the autumn of 1979, consolidating the success of both the new album and the earlier shows with a slightly revised set list, which we get to hear in this recording from Glasgow.

Sound-wise it is not perfect, so audiophiles among you probably won't give this one a second glance. That is a shame though, because what it lacks in audio quality it more than makes up for in atmosphere, right from the frantic opener of 'Please Don't Touch/Tigermoth'. Steve and the band are in great form. So are the crowd, which is typical of Glasgow audiences, as I can verify!

'Every Day' thunders along at a rapid pace. John Shearer's drums thunder out a wall shaking rhythm and the rest of the band are carried along on his impetus. There is no rest for the wicked, as 'Ace of Wands' is greeted by cheers from the crowd before the frenzied, almost paranoid performance, grabs the audience by the scruff of the neck.

An all too rare performance of another Hackett classic comes next. 'The Virgin & the Gypsy' is a truly glorious workout for the band, especially for the harmony vocals of Hicks, Cadbury, and Steve himself. I have always wondered why this one hasn't been reinstated in the set but at least we have it here in all its glory. John's flute playing leads us into the as yet unrecorded but soon to be stage favourite, 'The Steppes', which obviously takes the audience by surprise, as they don't recognise it. This is yet another case of Steve road testing new material and it goes down a storm here.

'Narnia' – Steve's left of centre tribute to the world of C. S. Lewis – is next and once again the band put in a sterling performance, especially Mr Hicks, whose vocal performance here is stunning. Another new one comes next, as Steve recreates the era of Artie Shaw and the big band sound of the Forties with 'Sentimental Institution'. Delightfully tongue-in-cheek, this works surprisingly well, and even the crowd take to it.

'The Red Flower of Taichi' is always a treat to hear and should be reinstated in Steve's live set, in my opinion. Here it is augmented by the acoustics of the Apollo itself, which give John's flute an added atmospheric edge – spine-tinglingly good! 'Star of Sirius' is another underrated classic too. I am sure that Steve's new band will give this one a go sometime soon but here we have it in all its original glory.

The BBC2 theme tune as Steve introduces it is next, 'Spectral Mornings' here with the marvellous synth intro, which has been omitted of late. Always destined to be a classic, there isn't really anything else I need to say about this one, is there? From the sublime to the outrageous next, as 'A Tower Struck Down' rampages around the room like some demented dervish. There is no respite as John Shearer's metronomic intro gets the already partisan crowd up and at 'em for 'Clocks', which threatens to bring the house down (literally!)

The band take their bows but the audience are in no mood to let them get away without encores. Steve soon returns, running through an acoustic guitar exercise, which leads nicely into the paraphrase of 'Blood on the

Rooftops' and 'Horizons', which you can barely hear over the audience reaction. 'Kim' is greeted with rapturous applause too before the audience settle down and pay rapt attention to this marvellous instrumental.

The band return to the stage for the truly bizarre, with 'The Ballad of the Decomposing Man'. Calypso rhythms and Steve on helium (nothing stronger I trust!) going absolutely nuts is the best way to describe this one. 'Hercules Unchained' closes the evening with Steve's attempt at a camp impression of Judas Priest, which is the cue for the band to really let their hair down, and Satan's stomp boxes are definitely to the fore here, bringing this extremely enjoyable recording to a suitably raucous close.

PART THREE: STEVE HACKETT

CHAPTER TWENTY-THREE
"WELCOMING THE DEFECTOR" 1980

The new decade began with several crises including Russia's involvement in Afghanistan (some things never change it seems). Britain had its first female premier in Margaret Thatcher and all in all the world had suddenly become a much less secure place.

Sensitive to these changes, Steve returned to the now de rigueur format of a concept album, and his next release, *Defector*, told the story of a defector ostensibly from the Eastern Bloc, although the lyrics could be interpreted either way. Musically intense and lyrically vivid, the album brought the story to life as only Steve's writing could, and he and the band were soon off on the road again for what was to be their most extensive tour to date, including shows in the USA and Canada for the first time. The shows brought Steve's new album to its audience in fine style and classics such as 'The Steppes' and 'Jacuzzi' became instant favourites in the live show and have remained there to this day.

CITY HALL, SHEFFIELD, ENGLAND, 17 JUNE 1980
Set List: Slogans/Every Day/The Red Flower of Taichi Blooms Everywhere/Tigermoth/Kim/Time to Get Out/The Steppes/The Toast/Narnia/Acoustic Set/Sentimental Institution/Jacuzzi/Spectral Mornings/A Tower Struck Down/Clocks/Please Don't Touch/The Show-It's Now or Never/Hercules Unchained//
Source: FM Radio Broadcast.

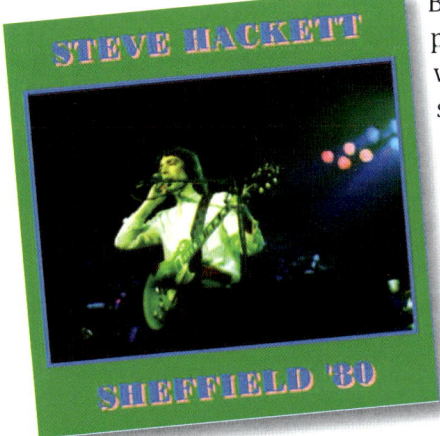

Back in the days when Genesis and its various solo members still got radio play here in the UK it wasn't unusual to find one of them gracing the airwaves with a live concert performance, and Sheffield's Hallam Radio broadcast several gems, including this 1980 performance from Sheffield's City Hall.

'Slogans' gets things off to a suitably frantic start, which is a new number, giving Steve and the band a chance to collectively ladder their tights with some fast and furious playing, in which Nick Magnus, Steve, and John Hackett are augmented by a percussive master class from John Shearer. 'Every Day' sounds like an anthem of triumph and I suppose it was tonight, as Steve later announces that new album *Defector* has entered the UK charts.

'The Red Flower of Taichi Blooms Everywhere' still remains the kind of title you would dread getting in a game of charades but musically it still sends shivers up the spine. John's flute casts a spell over the listener, as Steve and Nick weave an enchanted soundscape of monumental proportions here, which segues quite nicely into 'Tigermoth'. This is not quite the petite butterfly but a monstrous aural nightmare of a beast in which the entire band provide a manic accompaniment to Steve's banshee-like guitar riffs.

'Kim' is an oasis of acoustic calm giving everyone a chance to get their breath before it is 'Time to Get Out'; another frantic number from the new album, featuring some sepulchral keyboards from Mr Magnus and another ethereal flute from Mr Hackett Jnr. This leads nicely into 'The Steppes'; one of Steve's most dramatic and magnificent sound pictures, which is bleak and windswept in reality, and just as bleak is the picture executed so well here by Steve and the band.

A slightly drunken 'The Toast' rambles along in a warm and fuzzy manner with some slightly off-key vocals from Peter Hicks, Dik Cadbury, and Steve himself, although I am assured that no substances were harmed in the making of this performance! Nick Magnus executes a stately waltz on the mellotron, accompanied by the haunting flute of John Hackett – beautiful stuff.

From one frozen landscape to another as Steve takes us to 'Narnia' next for a delightfully camp homage to the C. S. Lewis classic. Peter Hicks' vocals are suitably over the top and Dik Cadbury puts in some nifty bass lines here too. Back to the small orchestra next as Steve gives us the obligatory acoustic set, which tonight includes snippets from 'Blood on the Rooftops' and 'The Barren Land', before 'Horizons' gets a cheer from the crowd.

It's back to the days of Artie Shaw and Satchmo next for 'Sentimental Institution' and the chance for Steve's 'Optigon' to make its mark on the proceedings. Always a treat and sadly no longer in Steve's live shows, this song is a peach of a performance. Always a master of light and shade, 'Jacuzzi' takes us to the bright lights of LA, with a suitably jaunty performance in marked contrast to what has gone before it.

'Spectral Mornings' gets an enthusiastic cheer from the crowd and deservedly so, as it soars from the stage like a soul released. I think there is no need for me to use any more superlatives with this one, are there?

'A Tower Struck Down' and its assembly of noises and effects is like something out of a Hammer Horror film laced with a particularly dark vein of humour. This one leads us nicely into the evening's finale of 'Clocks', which tonight is preceded by another number being road tested, as Steve breaks in what was to become 'Cradle of Swans' on the *Cured* album barely a year later. Hauntingly driven by guitar synth and drums, it segues nicely into the now familiar intro to 'Clocks' and John Shearer's moment to try and tear down the City Hall singlehandedly. Mind you, Dik Cadbury's bass pedals take no prisoners here either!

A bizarre guitar synth intro leads into the truly amazing 'Please Don't Touch', which really isn't ideal listening for the faint hearted. Building from a small beginning this grows to a truly awesome finale with some particularly tasty bass and drum licks from Cadbury and Shearer. It is Shearer and Cadbury who lead the parade at the start of 'The Show' and this plea for the rights of music is a delight, and one which I for one still miss in Steve's shows, but it is a glorious performance here tonight.

'O Sole Mio' ('It's Now or Never' to most of you or the Cornetto Ice Cream advert music to people of a certain age) is next and indeed Nick Magnus's vocoder gives the game away in a marvellously camp delivery of a song that was to get the band into a certain amount of trouble in Italy later in the tour. The evening is rounded off by another tongue-in-cheek number as Steve emulates the new wave of British Heavy Metal with his very own balls to the wall number, with the suitably over the top 'Hercules Unchained', which closes this excellent recording.

GRAND CASINO, MONTREUX, SWITZERLAND, 13 JULY 1980

Set List: Slogans/Every Day/Spectral Mornings/Time to Get Out/The Steppes/Narnia/Acoustic Set/Jacuzzi/A Tower Struck Down/Clocks//
Source: FM Radio/TV Broadcast.

Barely a month separates this recording from the Sheffield one above but this time round we have the advantage of being able to bring this one to you in both sound *and* vision, as it was broadcast on both radio and TV.

Being part of the world famous Festival, this is a shorter performance than its predecessor but that takes nothing away from the excitement of the show, which once again opens with a frantically garish 'Slogans' leading into another anthemic performance of 'Every Day', in which Steve and Peter Hicks' vocal harmonies are incredibly good.

With no time to waste, the band press on regardless with an impressive 'Spectral Mornings'. This one is a rock symphony in miniature, with Steve's guitar playing rising to even greater heights – I think you get the idea, if not watch the DVD! 'Time to Get Out' shimmers like sunshine on water, especially Magnus's exquisite keyboard introduction.

From the bright lights of the west to the frozen landscape of 'The Steppes' next. A magnificent introduction on flute by John Hackett is joined by equally impressive performances from the rest of the band, especially Dik Cadbury and John Shearer who combine power with good taste in their playing. Once again another frozen landscape is brought vividly to life with Steve's homage to the land of 'Narnia' and C. S. Lewis' creations.

The acoustic set is a well-established part of Steve's shows and tonight we get pretty much the same material as we had on the Sheffield recording. The added bonus is that if you manage to track down the DVD, you can watch in awe as Steve gives a virtuoso performance of several favourites.

From brittle acoustic gems to the hot tubs and golf clubs of L A next with 'Jacuzzi'. This is a simmering performance that races along on the coat tails of John Hackett's flute and Nick Magnus's keyboards. Bright lights lead to darker nightmares as 'A Tower Struck Down' takes us back to where it started for Steve. His guitar stabs the air and wails like a soul in torment throughout this furious performance, which once again segues into the as yet unrecorded intro to 'Cradle of Swans' and a truly rampaging 'Clocks', which is sadly cut short on both audio and video versions – don't you just love it when TV timeslots do that?! Anyway, what there is of this superb performance makes this another essential addition to any Hackett fan's collection.

PART THREE: STEVE HACKETT

CHAPTER TWENTY-FOUR
"TAKING THE CURE" 1981

With so much change going on in the outside world, it was obvious that Steve could not remain inured to it but even by the standards of the day what he did next took his fan base completely by surprise.

Once again, tracks from an as yet unrecorded follow up album to *Defector* had been road tested during that tour, with 'Cradle of Swans' being included as part of the acoustic set and snippets of 'Overnight Sleeper' appearing elsewhere. These gave no indication of the seismic shift that Steve was to take in producing this album.

Cured was released on 21 August 1981 and fans were surprised if not shocked to see that Steve had dispensed with the services of most of his now regular band, taking on the vocal duties himself, and retaining Nick Magnus on keyboards and drum programming – yes, *Cured* features one of the early drum machines! Stripped back and made leaner, the resulting album may well be compared with Genesis' *Abacab* album from the same year. Simpler and more accessible songs made this a much more acceptable proposition for some especially in the USA where Steve gained much more radio air play for this one.

Touring began in the UK in late August, including Steve's second appearance at the Reading Festival. The new look show served up both the new album and helpings from its predecessors in equal measure, with none of the negativity that attended some of Genesis' gigs as they took their album out on the road at roughly the same time.

READING ROCK '81, READING, ENGLAND, 28 AUGUST 1981
Set List: The Air-Conditioned Nightmare/Every Day/Ace of Wands/Funny Feeling/The Steppes/Overnight Sleeper/Slogans/A Tower Struck Down/Spectral Mornings/The Show/Clocks//
Source: FM Radio Broadcast.

Aah, the memories! Yes yet another rainy day at Reading. This was Steve's second performance at this legendary festival, his first time being in 1979. With a new album and new band in tow Steve opted to debut the new album in front of the festival crowd (yours truly included), and thanks to the BBC's Friday Rock Show we have the results here for our perusal. Strange to think that they didn't record Peter Gabriel's set two days earlier though.

With a festival crowd to please, and only a relatively short time slot, Steve galloped out of the traps with 'The Air-Conditioned Nightmare'; a bona fide rocker if ever there was one! New drummer, Ian Mosley, gives this one just the added edge to sharpen Steve's attack and this is an instant crowd pleaser. 'Every Day' is announced as a "cross between 'Mantovani' and 'Weather Report', but the crowd cheer it like an old friend. Here it is Nick Magnus' magnificent keyboards that lift this one to new heights. 'Ace of Wands' also keeps up the frantic pace, with Steve riffing away as if his very life depended on it, ably assisted by some impeccable percussion from Mr Mosley and meaty bass rhythms from new boy Chas Cronk. John Hackett's flute soars over the fray like a dove of peace. 'Funny Feeling', with its staccato rhythms, feels somewhat out of place here and this is the first time we get to hear Steve's dulcet tones on vocals.

'The Steppes' opens with some truly awesome flute playing from John before the rest of the band join in on this marvellous visual depiction of the Siberian landscape – still marvellous even after all these years! 'Overnight Sleeper' opens with some frantic acoustic playing before Nick Magnus and Chas Cronk's battling keyboards and bass take it away to an entirely different level. 'Slogans' is also fast and furious giving neither the band or the audience time to get their breath, which is the way bands have to be at festivals even these days, I'm afraid. Not that it seems to matter here tonight, as the entire band seem to be relishing the chance to flex their collective muscles on this one.

Back to where it all began for Steve next with 'A Tower Struck Down', replete with special effects and as paranoid as ever in a truly demented performance, out of which 'Spectral Mornings' arises like the proverbial phoenix from the ashes, eliciting a massive and deserved cheer from the crowd. 'The Show' closes the performance appropriately enough with its plea for musical respect in what was to be the last time it was to appear as part of a Hackett live set, which is a shame really because it is a belting song. Encore? of course there was! And what else could it be but 'Clocks'? This version is fast, frantic and threatens to blow the PA system sky high. No quarter asked or given on this one, which brings this excellent recording to a shattering conclusion.

COMMODORE BALLROOM, VANCOUVER, CANADA, 7 DECEMBER 1981

Set List: The Air-Conditioned Nightmare/Jacuzzi/Funny Feeling/Ace of Wands/Picture Postcard/The Steppes/Every Day/The Red Flower of Taichi Blooms Everywhere/Tigermoth/Acoustic Set/Kim/Overnight Sleeper/Hope I Don't Wake/Slogans/A Tower Struck Down/ Spectral Mornings/Land of a Thousand Autumns/Please Don't Touch/The Show//
Source: Radio/Audience Recording.

Steve's tour in support of the *Cured* album was an extensive one that took him back to the USA and Canada for the second time in less than a year. Here we have an extremely enjoyable audience recording from one of those shows that gets underway with a fast and furious 'The Air-Conditioned Nightmare', in which Steve and new bass player Chas Cronk battle away with some ferocious riffs. 'Jacuzzi' keeps the pace up nicely and Steve is obviously on the helium again. Despite the evident coldness of the evening, the 'Jacuzzi' is warm and vibrant, with another rippling flute solo from John Hackett and some equally colourful keyboards from Nick Magnus.

The staccato rhythms of Ian Mosley lead us nicely into 'Funny Feeling'. This is a rare example of Mr Hackett trying for radio play. This nifty little song gives Steve and Chas a chance to share harmonies, although it is obvious that Steve is still trying to find his "voice", so to speak. Interesting to reflect that whilst Steve was giving his band and sound a complete revamp and getting away with it, his former band mates in Genesis had a tough time at some shows with their own revamped sound on their concurrent tour promoting the *Abacab* album. Maybe Steve's fans are that little bit more indulgent, who knows? But their patience is rewarded next with a jaunty 'Ace of Wands', which still sounds as vibrant as ever, despite its vintage status.

'Picture Postcard' brings the new album into sharp focus again with a somewhat jazzy performance especially from Steve, Chas, and Nick. Cocktails on the beach, sir? A laidback and confident Hackett can he heard here. From the beach to 'The Steppes' next, and once again it is John Hackett's flute that sets up the atmosphere here, with a brittle and frosty solo before the rest of the band join in to create an icy musical landscape.

'Every Day' gives both the band and the audience a chance to warm up a bit with a version driven along by the bass of Chas Cronk and the syncopated rhythms of Ian Mosley. Steve's vocal delivery here sounds surprisingly like Peter Hicks' and he is joined in the vocal department once more by Cronk whilst Nick Magnus lays down an impeccable keyboard backdrop. 'The Red Flower of Taichi Blooms Everywhere', originally intended as a protest about the treatment of Vietnamese refugees, now belongs firmly in the realm of Steve's finest travelogue moments. Here his oriental styled guitar is accompanied by a shimmering flute which weaves about like a silk pennant at a Chinese New Year celebration and some equally oriental styled percussion and is a delight to the ears.

'Tigermoth' emerges out of the latter like a hatchling from a chrysalis. This is no delicate butterfly though, but instead a percussion-driven nightmare in which Steve's guitar wails like a soul in torment and makes this one a suitable candidate for a Hammer Horror soundtrack.

"Some steam guitar" comes next, or acoustic guitar to those of you unfamiliar with Steve's parlance. The usual medley has the audience in raptures here as 'Horizons' threads its magical way through the room. This is followed by a serene and beautiful 'Kim', in which Steve teases the audience with a snippet from 'Blood on the Rooftops'. Here he and his brother John execute a stately ballet between the acoustic guitar and flute, which is a joy to behold. The acoustic guitar is ramped up for the introduction to 'Overnight Sleeper' where, sad to say, Steve sounds as if he is shouting rather than singing. He gets it more or less right on the next one, 'Hope I Don't Wake', which has a slightly country & western tinge to the vocal delivery but it works well enough, even if Steve's voice does sound a mite strained at times.

'Slogans' follows some guitar tuning and Steve's acknowledgement of the radio recording of tonight's show and here the entire band rampage like a herd of buffalo through this aural nightmare of a track. Each and every member uses the entire arsenal of effects and instruments at their disposal and it wouldn't surprise me if someone was playing the kitchen sink on stage during this one! The nightmare continues after the well-deserved band introductions with 'A Tower Struck Down', which threatens to tear the Commodore's roof off.

'Spectral Mornings' arises phoenix-like out of the rubble of the tower and Steve's guitar delivers some astonishing riffs, by turns laughing and crying but always an uplifting anthem that raises the spirits. Steve's guitar synthesiser gets an outing next as we enter the 'Land of a Thousand Autumns'; another of those wonderfully evocative instrumentals of his that you wish would last longer. Mind you, this does segue into 'Please Don't Touch', which is more than enough of an instrumental mouthful for anybody, methinks!

Tonight's performance is rounded off by a meaty version of 'The Show'; another one of those delightful anthemia songs that Steve sadly doesn't write anymore. Here it's a balls to the wall performance with Steve getting so carried away he even fluffs the lyrics, but his guitar does his talking for him here in another enjoyable effort rounding off a superior quality recording.

CHAPTER TWENTY-FIVE
"HIGHLY STRUNG" 1982-83

By the beginning of 1982 Steve was at work on several projects, although problems within the Charisma organisation which would lead to its absorption by Virgin Records within the year meant that he lost his fight with A & R over both a live album and an acoustic project that he had been working on for a few years.

Despite these problems, Steve persevered and by the end of the year he was able to showcase some of his material at a one off gig in London before taking to the road again in the UK, only this time it was in April 1983. *Highly Strung* was released on 23 April 1983, preceded a week before by the single 'Cell 151', which gave Steve his highest chart entry for ages.

For touring purposes, Steve retained the services of Nick Magnus, along with Chas Cronk on bass and Ian Mosley on drums. By now fans had grown accustomed to Steve's singing and his vocal range had improved greatly since his tentative beginnings on *Cured*. The result was another highly satisfying tour that has been well documented by live recordings.

THE VENUE, LONDON, ENGLAND, 13 DECEMBER 1982
Set List: The Steppes/Funny Feeling/Hackett to Pieces/A Tower Struck Down/Spectral Mornings/Acoustic Set/Horizons/Kim/Overnight Sleeper/Slogans/Tigermoth/The Show/Clocks/The Air-Conditioned Nightmare/Hackett's Boogie//
Source: Audience Recording.

Another charitable gig and a late night one, as Steve apologises for it and the fact that people might miss their trains, chariots, or whatever you go home in. Sadly the tape on this one runs slightly fast, which is a shame because otherwise the quality of the recording is very good.

The evening opens with 'The Steppes'. An ethereal flute from John Hackett and keyboards from Nick Magnus give a majestic opening to the show. 'Funny Feeling' is as catchy as ever and with the benefit of *real* drums it always comes across infinitely superior to its drum machine-led recorded counterpart. Steve is still trying to find his vocal range and sounds as if he is straining at times here.

A bit of tuning up comes before the only new offering of the evening, namely 'Hackett to Pieces'. A samba rhythm leads nicely into a frantic instrumental workout for the entire band who seem to be enjoying themselves. A fast and frantic 'Tower Struck Down' is next, before which Steve acknowledges the rather wet reunion with his old band mates that had taken place at Milton Keynes barely two months earlier, and then a delightful segue into 'Spectral Mornings', which sounds odd here, owing to the tape running slightly fast, but a good performance nonetheless.

Steve switches to the small orchestra of acoustic guitar next for a run through some of his finest compositions, ignoring the cries for 'Supper's Ready' and 'Racing in A'. Instead we get the evergreen 'Horizons' and 'Kim', both of which are greeted with applause by the crowd. From the sublime to the ridiculous next as 'Overnight Sleeper' wakes the crowd up from their reveries with an altogether more confident vocal performance from Steve and the new band are driven along by the effortless percussion of Ian Mosley.

No peace for the wicked or "Sing, you bastard!" as one wag from the audience cries out before the garish nightmare that is 'Slogans' rips through the venue before Steve's guitar synth soars above the audience, and the 'Tigermoth' takes flight in a truly magnificent version – one of the best you will ever hear. 'The Show' and 'Clocks' bring the end of the gig proper in fine barnstorming style. Of course there has to be an encore, although this time the audience are in for a surprise, as instead of 'I Know What I Like', they are treated to 'The Air-Conditioned Nightmare' and the only other new offering tonight, which is a souped-up 'Hackett's Boogie', bringing what was evidently another enjoyable evening to a close.

EMPIRE THEATRE, LIVERPOOL, ENGLAND, 26 APRIL 1983

Set List: The Steppes/Camino Royale/Funny Feeling/Can't Let Go/Weightless/Always Somewhere Else/Hackett to Pieces/Slogans/Give it Away/Spectral Mornings/Acoustic Set/Kim/Overnight Sleeper/Cell 151/Please Don't Touch/Every Day/Waling Through Walls/The Show/Clocks/Hackett's Bogi //
Source: Audience Recording.

Yes, another trip down Memory Lane for yours truly. I managed to take in this gig from my front row seat and what a marvellous gig it was too. It's only a shame that it is captured here on a very mediocre recording.

'The Steppes' opens proceedings, and the echoey acoustics of the theatre give it an added atmosphere, most of which is sadly lost in the muddy quality of this recording, which sounds as if it was recorded from the back of the balcony! Things improve a little bit as the band dive straight into a jazzy 'Camino Royale', with the entire band putting in a top notch performance.

A staccato drum pattern heralds 'Funny Feeling'. This is a somewhat unusual attempt by Steve to "go commercial". A catchy hook and infectious rhythm drive it along at a fair old lick as it segues into 'Can't Let Go' before returning to 'Funny Feeling' again and loosening up band and audience nicely.

The emphasis is on the new album as you would expect, and 'Weightless' glides along on the back of some tasty percussion from Ian Mosley who proves to be the engine powering the performances throughout the evening. 'Always Somewhere Else' is also a fine ensemble performance showcasing every member of the band. Steve lays down some fine licks around which the rhythm section of Ian Mosley and Chas Cronk do battle in fine style before a samba rhythm leads into 'Hackett to Pieces'. This is another freeform instrumental workout that keeps the rate of revs suitably high. Sadly the recording is marred quite badly here by some severe bass distortion, although it does give an indication of how *loud* the band were on the night.

'Slogans' suffers from some distortion too, although it is an improvement on the preceding track and once again the rhythm section of Cronk and Mosley are the real impetus here, although once Steve gets going his rate of knots is incredible! 'Give it Away' is another of the new tracks that fits superbly well in the context of the live set and it is surprising to reflect on how little of this album was to survive into Steve's next live rock shows.

'Spectral Mornings' soars into the room next. This is always a treat to hear but here it is once again marred by distortion that ruins what was otherwise a superb performance. The acoustic set fares a little bit better with no distortion here, just a rather distant sound, although there is no denying the enthusiasm of the crowd who greet both 'Horizons' and 'Kim' with evident relish.

'Overnight Sleeper' builds from a frantic acoustic rhythm into the supercharged beast that we all know. Chas Cronk's bass rattles the room whilst Ian Mosley also threatens to tear the roof off with some incredible percussion. 'Cell 151', complete with dedication and cello intro, is much better. Nick Magnus dominates here with some inspired playing and at last Steve finally delivers a convincing vocal in what has to be the most unlikely "hit" record of 1983!

The Mellotron and guitar synthesiser announce 'Please Don't Touch' before Steve's guitar howls like a banshee in what was, as I recall, a mind-blowing performance but sadly one that this recording doesn't really capture all that well. Once again the problems of distortion ruin 'Every Day' for the listener but through it you can just about pick out the germ of what was a great performance.

'Walking Through Walls' and 'The Show' close the evening's proceedings and it is a nice contrast between the old and the new that worked well on the night. And for once the distortion is minimal, but the recording remains rather flat, which is a pity.

'Clocks' brings the band back on stage for the encores and that and 'Hackett's Boogie' (or was it Bogie?) give everyone something to get up and cheer for. For what I still remember as a marvellous night, it is only a pity that it isn't served by a better quality recording, which just goes to prove that even the best bootleggers can't get it right every night!

CHAPTER TWENTY-SIX
"YOU CAN'T BEAT A PAIR OF NYLONS" 1983

As mentioned before, Steve had been working on an acoustic project for several years but was unable to persuade Charisma of its merits, so after their demise and the cancellation of his contract with Virgin Records who absorbed Charisma in 1983, Steve had to look elsewhere for an outlet for the acoustic album.

This came in the shape of START Records, who were to release the acoustic album, *Bay of Kings* and Steve's next album, 1984's *Till We Have Faces*. *Bay of Kings* was yet another surprise for Steve's fans, although not quite as big a one as his taking on the vocal duties. After all, there had always been acoustic moments in his shows before. An album's worth of acoustic music proved too much for some of his fans though, and indeed, owing to poor advertising, several gigs on the subsequent tour of university halls in the UK were subject to less than appreciative behaviour from a crowd expecting a rock gig.

Fortunately, the recordings that do survive from this tour serve to show a side of Steve's music that has become increasingly important to him in the years that have elapsed since.

MOUNTFORD HALL, LIVERPOOL UNIVERSITY, LIVERPOOL, ENGLAND, 27 OCTOBER 1983

Set List: Horizons/Time-Lapse at Milton Keynes/Bay of Kings/Calmaria/Hands of the Priestess/Jacuzzi/Overnight Sleeper/The Barren Land/Blood on the Rooftops/Guitar Exercise/Tales from the Riverbank/Second Chance/Chinese Improvisation/Petropolis/Kim/Water Wheel/Butterfly/The Journey/Ace of Wands/Cradle of Swans/Untitled Piece/Horizons (Reprise)//
Source: Audience Recording.

Known to this writer as "the one that got away". Yes, in the balmy days before the advent of the Internet it was far harder to find out about gigs than it is now, hence the fact that Steve's *Bay of Kings* tour in the autumn of 1983 remains the only UK tour by Steve that I never saw. Not that I am bitter about that at all – grr!

Anyway, Steve had been working on acoustic material for quite some time but had failed to persuade his record company of the validity of such a project. Bear in mind this was still several years before MTV and the Unplugged phenomenon. Thus Steve and his brother recorded this album themselves and decided bravely to tour it as an acoustic duo at university halls up and down the UK in the autumn of 1983. Thanks to incredibly poor advertising, several shows were cancelled and at others Steve and John received a less than warm welcome from students expecting a full rock band!

No such problems here at Liverpool University's Mountford Hall though, where Steve and John were greeted with enthusiasm and warmth as this excellent audience recording shows. Just what the crowd thought as Steve emerged on stage clad in coat tails and white gloves is anyone's guess, but as soon as the music starts with 'Horizons', the crowd are evidently right behind Steve and deservedly so, as this concert is a master class. 'Time Lapse at Milton Keynes' gets a cheer. Steve starts somewhat hesitantly here before the rhythm takes control and he gets the small orchestra under way to slyly include a snippet of 'Blood on the Rooftops'. The audience are evidently listening in rapt attention throughout. 'Bay of Kings', the new album's title track, is next and it is a delight; a stately and serene performance that is still quite something to hear. The audience seem to like it too.

'Calmaria' is stately in performance too, with a magnificent soundscape all painted by one man and his acoustic guitar, which is incredible, really! 'Hands of the Priestess', 'Jacuzzi', and 'Overnight Sleeper' are all performed by Steve and his brother John and in their new acoustic setting. They shimmer like polished diamonds. The former in particular is probably the closest we shall ever get to hearing it as Steve and John originally conceived it all those many years ago.

'The Barren Land' is next, although incorporating some very familiar bits and pieces this one has remained a staple in Steve's live set right up to the present day and deservedly so. An acoustic guitar exercise next that once again includes several familiar references, not least 'In That Quiet Earth', which gets a ripple of applause, and yet more as Steve glides effortlessly into 'Tales From the Riverbank', bringing back childhood memories for some in the audience, no doubt.

'Second Chance', the TV theme, sees Steve joined on stage by his brother once more and it is a delight to hear the two musicians as they perform an almost visual waltz as flute and guitar combine to weave another mesmerising performance. 'The Chinese Jam' has some familiar references in it if you listen carefully, before we are given another one of Steve's place pictures in the shape of 'Petropolis', which is a city in Brazil. Vibrant and colourful, this one is a travelogue in miniature. Staying on the Brazilian theme, Steve pays homage to his then wife Kim in another delightful performance.

A new piece next, which would subsequently become 'Concert for Munich' on his second acoustic album, is here in its original form with some superb flute from John. The rest of the show is comprised mainly of new material that Steve is evidently road testing, as is his wont, but they merge seamlessly between classic performances of 'The Journey', 'Ace of Wands', and 'Cradle of Swans' to round out an extremely enjoyable performance and a well-recorded one at that!

VANBRUGH DINING HALL, YORK UNIVERSITY, YORK, ENGLAND, 14 NOVEMBER 1983

Set List: Horizons/Blood on the Rooftops-Time Lapse at Milton Keynes/Bay of Kings/Calmaria/Hands of the Priestess/Jacuzzi-Overnight Sleeper/Hairless Heart/The Barren Land/Hammer in the Sand-Tales of the Riverbank/Second Chance/Chinese Improvisation/Petropolis/Kim/Butterfly/Concert for Munich/The Journey/Ace of Wands/Cradle of Swans/Jazz on a Summer's Night/Horizons (Reprise)/Kim (Reprise)//
Source: Audience Recording.

Barely two weeks separate this and the previous recording but even in that short time Steve and John had refined their performance even further.

Still opening with the cheery wistfulness of 'Horizons', this is another masterful performance chock full of classics and new classics in the making. Despite the cancellation of several shows and poor reception at others, for audiences such as this one that were prepared to actually *listen* to the new material, there were to be several treats in store throughout the performance.

Once again, Steve was ably accompanied by his brother on several of the tracks, including another delightful rendering of 'Hands of the Priestess', which is all serenity and calm before jaunty performances of 'Jacuzzi' and 'Overnight Sleeper', both of which work superbly well in their new acoustic setting.

Other highlights include lovely versions of 'Tales of the Riverbank and 'Kim', alongside several as yet unrecorded tracks, including ones we now know as 'Concert for Munich' and 'Jazz on a Summer's Night' and a couple that remain unrecorded to this day, making this another essential recording for Hackett collectors.

PART THREE: STEVE HACKETT

CHAPTER TWENTY-SEVEN
"TUNING THE GTR" 1986

No tour was undertaken to promote 1984's *Till We Have Faces*, and Steve effectively disappeared off the radar for over a year before rumours began to circulate that he had joined forces with ex-Yes man, Steve Howe, for a new project.

These rumours were confirmed when the first fruits of that project appeared as the single 'When the Heart Rules the Mind' appeared. Upbeat and catchy, this was quite a surprise for Steve's fans and seeing him on the *Chart Show* no less was quite satisfying, I am sure! The album, entitled *GTR*, was released on 28 April 1986 and pierced the Top Ten in the UK. The USA was where this album really took off though, with high Billboard chart placings for both the album and the single.

With success assured in the USA, an extensive tour was organised for the summer months with a handful of shows in the UK tagged on almost as an afterthought. Thankfully several excellent recordings survive from this tour, which is also captured on the excellent King Biscuit series radio recording.

TOWER THEATRE, UPPER DARBY, PENNSYLVANIA, USA, 28 JUNE 1986
Set List: Cuckoo Cocoon/Black Light/Calmaria/Cavalcanti/Horizons/Mood for a Day/Ram/Second Initial/Untitled Pieces/Clap/A Place Where Time Runs Slow/Jekyll and Hyde/Here I Wait/Prize Fighters/Imagining/Hackett to Bits/Spectral Mornings/In That Quiet Earth/I Know What I Like/Toe the Line/Sketches in the Sun/Pennants/Roundabout/The Hunter/Reach Out (Never Say No)/You Can Still Get Through/When the Heart Rules the Mind/Jekyll and Hyde (Reprise)//
Source: Audience Recording.

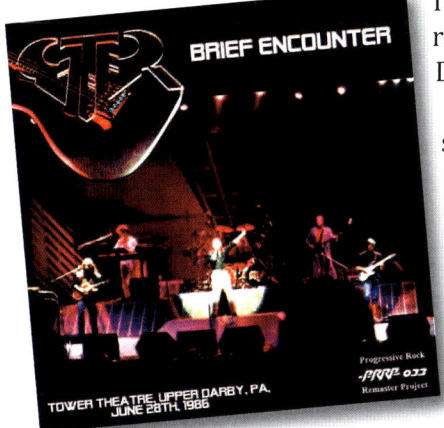

The *GTR* tour was almost exclusively a US affair and from it a handful of recordings are in circulation, including this audience recording from Upper Darby; scene of several triumphs by both Genesis and Yes in their heyday.

Sadly, as usual with US audiences, they seem to be more intent on screaming and shouting than actually *listening* to the musicians they have paid top dollar to come and see, which is a shame because this sounds like it was a good night to see the *GTR* super group. Mr Hackett opens the proceedings with a selection of acoustic numbers, including at least one which we now know as 'Cavalcanti' from his as yet unrecorded second acoustic album, *Momentum*. Performance-wise, Steve sounds confident and happy throughout his set before Mr Howe takes his bows and performs an equally entertaining selection of his best known acoustic moments – not that you can hear much of the performance over the audience noise!

They are joined onstage by keyboards man, Matt Clifford for another unreleased track, 'From a Place Where Time Runs Slow', which is a nifty little number, before the rest of the *GTR* combo emerges for the main event.

It is interesting to hear how mediocre the *GTR* material sounds when compared to both the acoustic stuff that has preceded it and the selection of Genesis/Yes/Hackett classics, which are also thrown into the pot. How can anything on the *GTR* album be compared in the same breath as 'Spectral Mornings' or 'Roundabout'? Only the debut single, 'When the Heart Rules the Mind', comes anywhere near the kind of quality displayed by the aforementioned tracks.

Not that it seems to bother the crowd who cheer each and every song, probably without even really knowing what they are listening to. I guess it all depends on whether you are a fan of supergroup combinations, really. Some fans will love this performance, others such as myself are only glad that I gave the whole *GTR* "experience" a miss.

CHAPTER TWENTY-EIGHT
"GAINING MOMENTUM" 1988-90

Unfortunately the *GTR* project was not destined to be a long lived one and it resulted in acrimony and legal disputes that tied Steve's hands for quite a while. In the meantime, he returned to the realm of the "small orchestra" for a follow-up to 1983's *Bay of Kings* album.

Momentum took that format and expanded it with much more technical playing from Steve and some truly wonderful performances throughout. The album gained widespread critical acclaim, although not all the fans were convinced again, but the crowds that went to see Steve and his brother John on the subsequent tour of the UK and Europe were enthusiastic in their responses to Steve's unplugged approach.

With the situation within the UK record industry becoming increasingly difficult for artists such as Steve, the period after the conclusion of the *Momentum* tour was to be a difficult one. Record deals became harder to find and negotiate and Steve was eventually to decide to establish his own record label – Camino – in order to enable his music to be heard. The creation of this label and Steve's own recording studio occupied much of the intervening period by putting all of this together. Fans not used to lengthy periods of inactivity from Steve were relieved when he made an all too rare TV appearance for the short-lived Bedrock series of live concert broadcasts but it was to be a further two years before fans got to hear the results of his labours.

OPERA HOUSE, MANCHESTER, ENGLAND, 1 MAY 1988

Set List: the Journey/Horizons/Bay of Kings/A Bed, a Chair, and a Guitar/Time-Lapse at Milton Keynes/Tales of the Riverbank/Ace of Wands/Hands of the Priestess/Jacuzzi/Overnight Sleeper/Cavalcanti/Second Chance/Portrait of a Brazilian Lady/Still Life/Jazz on a Summer's Night/Concert for Munich/Notre Dame Des Fleurs/Momentum/Electric Guitar Improvisation/Silver/The Carrot That Killed My Sister//
Source: Audience Recording.

I missed Steve's first acoustic tour back in 1983 (but we won't talk about that, will we?!), so I was delighted to be able to catch up with his "small orchestra" at this show at Manchester's Opera House.

I have vivid memories of this one having organised the first of many interviews with Steve prior to this show. Steve and his brother John emerge onstage to applause and launch into 'The Journey' and 'Horizons' getting things off to a nice start. Steve sounds relaxed as he introduces 'A Bed, a Chair, and a Guitar' as a remark his father had made, and a homage once again to the concrete cows of Milton Keynes for a delightful version of 'Time Lapse at Milton Keynes'.

Steve is sufficiently relaxed to deal with a request for 'Supper's Ready' from one of the more enthusiastic members of the crowd with a witty retort: "That was before the war," which gets a laugh from the crowd. This recording manages to capture both the atmosphere and the humour of the evening, as well as demonstrating once again exactly how far Steve's acoustic playing had come since *Bay of Kings*. Tracks such as 'Portrait of a Brazilian Lady' and 'Notre Dame Des Fleurs' are sedate, almost severe in form, but there are also some moments of great humour, none more so than the show's closer, the bizarrely titled, 'The Carrot That Killed My Sister'!

ROYAL CONCERT HALL, NOTTINGHAM, ENGLAND, 14 MAY 1988

Set List: Acoustic Medley/Horizons/Bay of Kings/A Bed, a Chair, and a Guitar/Time Lapse at Milton Keynes/Tales of the Riverbank/Ace of Wands/Hands of the Priestess/Jacuzzi/Cavalcanti/Second Chance/Portrait of a Brazilian Lady/Still Life/Jazz on a Summer's Night/Concert for Munich/Notre Dame Des Fleurs/Momentum/Guitar Synth Improvisation/Kim/Silver/The Carrot That Killed My Sister//
Source: Audience Recording//

This is an incredibly bright recording and one of the best that I have heard from this tour. As usual, Steve opens the show with an acoustic ramble, including a snippet from 'Blood on the Rooftops' to tease the crowd before giving us the evergreen 'Horizons'.

'Bay of Kings' is as stately and serene as ever, and the quality of this recording really beggars belief. Every note is crystal clear and sharp as Steve lulls the audience into a state of semi-somnolence with his magnificent playing. The jaunty 'A Bed, a Chair, and a Guitar' picks the pace up slightly but this isn't a rock and roll show and there is no need for flash and pretension here, as the music speaks in volumes!

'Time Lapse at Milton Keynes' acknowledges once more that rather wet evening back in 1982 when Steve was all too briefly reunited with his former band mates before Steve dedicates the next number to, "My hamster ... I had two of them. Both of them worked." 'Tales of the Riverbank' once again brings a few happy memories to any member of the audience of a certain age (yours truly included) and is another delightful performance.

Steve then introduces his brother John on to the stage for another delightful run through 'Ace of Wands', which even in this setting still manages to bring a shiver to the spine. Speaking of shivers, 'Hands of the Priestess' is simply amazing here. This is an austere, almost severe piece, which shines like sunshine through stained glass as both musicians weave their magic for their attentive audience. 'Jacuzzi' gallops along at a fair old pace as the two protagonists battle it out in a civilised manner, of course!

'Cavalcanti' is next, and is probably the closest that Steve gets to a Baroque performance in the real sense of the word. Refined, measured, vibrant and incredibly moving, this is a stunning version. 'Second Chance' is another lovely moment in which both musicians deliver a shimmering performance full of sunlight. 'Portrait of a Brazilian Lady' is a vivid evocation of its subject, refined and yet hinting at the fire within.

'Still Life' is an altogether more severe, almost austere, jazz-tinged piece, which to me has echoes of the nursery rhyme Baa, Baa, Black Sheep' running through it for some obscure reason! Thankfully the taper has managed a quick tape change so not even a note of the performance is missed, which is just as well, because to have missed any of 'Jazz on a Summer's Night', which is the next track, would have been criminal. Here Steve and John execute a musical ballet, replete with some truly remarkable passages, which lead in turn to the equally stunning 'Concert for Munich', which is where the phrase "small orchestra" really comes into its own. This is a performance worthy of any concert hall in the country and is breathtaking in its beauty.

Another as yet unrecorded track comes next, namely 'Notre Dame Des Fleurs', which was to wait until 2000 before it finally gained release on the 1986 *Feedback* album. Steve's homage to the French author Jean Genet is a suitably romantic piece with a wistful refrain and tune in which you could almost imagine echoing out of some bistro on the banks of the river Seine. The new album's title track, 'Momentum', follows another swift tape change. This is a nifty percussive little number that gallops along at a fair rate of knots and closes the show. A change of scene entirely next as Steve returns to the stage and switches from acoustic guitar to one of the new Stepp DGI guitar synthesisers for a few minute of improvisation, which sounds really quite out of place after what has gone before it but hey, this was advertised as the *guitar* concert, so we get both sides of the coin. Even the snippet of Katchachurian's 'Sabre Dance' doesn't really fit here – sorry, Steve!

Normal service is resumed as Steve is re-joined by John for a superb version of 'Kim', which is stately, serene, and beautiful like the lady herself. Another new and even now unrecorded piece is next. 'Silver' shimmers like the precious metal it describes before the show reaches new surreal depths with the bizarrely titled 'The Carrot That Killed My Sister' in which audience participation is encouraged and indulged in. A suitably rhythmic percussion is indulged in by Steve whilst John puts in some suitably jazzy chords on the flute in this delightfully colourful track that closes another excellent performance.

CENTRAL TV STUDIOS, NOTTINGHAM, ENGLAND, 30 SEPTEMBER 1990

Set List: Camino Royale/Please Don't Touch/Every Day/In That Quiet Earth/Depth Charge/Wonderpatch/In the Heart of the City/Black Light/Horizons/Jacuzzi/Theatre of Sleep/Jazz Jam/Spectral Mornings/Clocks//
Source: TV Broadcast.

A welcome return to rock here with Steve and a new look band performing as part of the short-lived Bedrock TV series. Yours truly was lucky enough to attend this one and it was great to see Steve with a band once again, I can tell you!

The show gets under way with a swaggering 'Camino Royale'. After his initial struggles to find his own vocal style, here Steve nails it at last with a deceptively laidback approach. Musically, the rest of his band get behind the beat with a remarkable performance in which Steve finally gets to put his trusty harmonica to good use! Back to the old days next as the band race into 'Please Don't Touch' and seldom have I heard as polished a performance of this classic as the one you get here. Steve's new keyboard player Julian Colbeck lays down a superbly symphonic backdrop, over which Steve and his new rhythm section of Dave Ball (bass) and Fudge Smith (drums) battle away in truly impressive style.

'Every Day' and 'In That Quiet Earth' get the biggest cheer thus far from the crowd. The harmonies on the former are to die for whilst the appearance of the latter marks the start of the gradual rehabilitation of material from his former "beat combo" into his live shows – all done in Steve's own inimitable fashion, of course! John Hackett shines here as he lays down a truly remarkable performance on the flute.

'Depth Charge', 'Wonderpatch', and 'In the Heart of the City' give us yet another example of Steve road testing new material, something he has always done and here we have three prime slices of Hackett. The first, since its appearance here, has been through so many changes it is difficult to keep up, but in instrumental form here this is Hackett at his very best. His playing here is awesome and once again he is augmented by some fine ensemble playing, especially from Fudge Smith who lays down some impeccable rhythms. 'Wonderpatch' is a strange little link, mainly on keyboards, which segues nicely into the aural nightmare that is 'In the Heart of the City'. This is a brilliant observation of the stresses and strains of modern day life. A regimented marching rhythm and some sound effects get this one under way before Steve's declamatory vocal gets under way – one of Steve's best lyrics to my mind.

No Hackett performance would be complete without a bit of "agnostic guitar" and tonight is no different, as Steve serves up a delightful helping from the small orchestra in the shape of 'Black Light' and the ubiquitous 'Horizons', which of course gets a cheer! An acoustic 'Jacuzzi' comes next with some superb flute playing from brother John.

It's back to the new stuff again with another pairing. 'Theatre of Sleep' is one of Steve's dreams brought vividly to musical life. This one owes something to the same idea as 'Please Don't Touch' but either way it is a delightful addition to the Hackett canon and with some superb harmony vocals this one should have become a live favourite but hasn't for some strange reason! 'Jazz Jam' does exactly what it says on the tin; this one is an extended instrumental jam giving the rest of the band the chance to flex their muscles, which they take here with evident glee.

Speaking of flexing muscles, the closing pairing of 'Spectral Mornings' and 'Clocks' give everyone the perfect send off. Sadly by now, the former has been deprived of its eerie synth intro but it doesn't really matter when you are confronted by one of the best instrumentals ever written – nuff said! As for 'Clocks' …. well, apparently it was written in imitation of something from a Hammer Horror film soundtrack, so that's what you get – a rampaging monster of an instrumental bringing this recording to a suitably spectacular close.

PART THREE: STEVE HACKETT

CHAPTER TWENTY-NINE
"TOUR NOIR" 1992-93

The years from 1988 onwards were to be difficult ones for Steve. The UK record industry had changed out of all recognition and established artists such as him were finding it increasingly difficult to gain a fair hearing with record executives obsessed with the "next big thing". With Steve's absence from the scene becoming protracted, fans began to wonder if they would ever have the pleasure of seeing their hero again. Steve himself has admitted that he even considered retiring at the time.

Thankfully, Steve opted to record his own music and lease it at first to record companies before finally establishing his own record company, Camino, in 1997. The first sign of this new approach was the *Guitar Noir* album, which was released on 21 May 1993, preceded by a US tour in the autumn of 1992, during which Steve gave the new material a thorough work out in front of appreciative crowds.

Shows in South America, Steve's first on that continent, followed before he returned home for his first rock tour in the UK in over ten years. The new show drew heavily on the new album with a selection of older classics bringing the show to a highly satisfying close. Once again, there are many decent recordings from this tour, including the show from the Clapham Grand Theatre, which features as part of the *Live Archive '70s, '80s, '90s* set and I have included a couple of the more interesting ones here.

THE STRAND, REDONDO BEACH, CALIFORNIA, USA, 8 SEPTEMBER 1992

Set List: Myopia Medley/Camino Royale/A Vampyre with a Healthy Appetite/Flight of the Condor (Sierra Quemada)/Take These Pearls/Always Somewhere Else/ in the Heart of the City/Walking Away From Rainbows/There Are Many Sides to the Night/In That Quiet Earth/Dark as the Grave/Etruscan Serenade (Omega Metallicus)/Depth Charge/Every Day/Acoustic Set/The Stumble//
Source: Audience Recording.

Steve had been off the radar for a few years by the time he re-emerged in the autumn of 1992 for the *Tour Noir* of the USA. As audiences were to find out, he had been far from idle in the interim and the results of his labours are to be heard on this extremely enjoyable recording.

With a new band, Steve takes to the stage and roars into life with a medley comprising snippets from several classics, all of which are greeted with cheers by the enthusiastic crowd. From the sound of it this was a small room, but the crowd more than make up for it with their accompaniment. 'Camino Royale' has seldom of ever sounded as vibrant as it does here. Julian Colbeck's keyboard phrases shimmer like the sun upon water whilst Steve is more than happy delivering some incredibly spiky riffs and a much more confident vocal than back on the *Highly Strung* tour of almost ten years before.

The first of the new stuff is next, featuring the eccentric 'A Vampyre with a Healthy Appetite', delivered through a megaphone no less! This proves worthy successor to the left of centre classics of yore (or should that be gore?!). Dave Ball and Hugo Degenhardt on bass and drums respectively drive this one along with some impressive licks of their own whilst Steve still proves that he is king of sustain with gorgeous guitar refrain. The sustained guitar work continues with 'Flight of the Condor' (subsequently re-titled 'Sierra Quemada'). With another amazing guitar performance and pan pipe-style keyboards, this one really manages to evoke its subject to perfection.

A natty almost Brazilian samba rhythm is set up by Dave and Hugo next as Steve takes us in search of the ocean's jewels in 'Take These Pearls'. Here it has to be said that his vocal delivery has finally achieved a level of competence which ensures that the emotional content of the song is conveyed to perfection. 'Always Somewhere Else' sounds somewhat out of place here but it does give the band a chance to flex their musical muscles and each and every member of the band does exactly that in this racy little version.

'In the Heart of the City' and its story of urban angst gets a marvellous, almost industrial delivery here. Harmonies delivered by Dave and Hugo take this one far above average, while Julian Colbeck's Thunderbirds-styled keyboards threaten to lift the roof. Steve sounds in particularly fiery form here and the vocal has an edge to it that is lacking from the recorded version. The atmosphere is calmed a bit next with some delightful acoustic guitar and keyboards from Steve and Julian during the awesome 'Walking Away From Rainbows', in which you can almost hear a pin drop as the crowd listen completely mesmerised.

'There Are Many Sides to the Night' and its tale of a prostitute's motivation for her trade shows how far Steve has come in terms of his song writing and he even manages to get his harmonica out of the closet too, with a darkly emotional song which he and the band deliver in a deliciously melancholy fashion.

With the emphasis being on the new stuff, Steve's announcement of 'In That Quiet Earth' gets a suitably enthusiastic cheer from the crowd before he and the band launch into a particularly feisty performance. Steve in particular sounds in his element riffing away like crazy whilst his rhythm section gets to grips with Genesis' time signatures as if born to them. 'Dark as the Grave' calms things down somewhat with this samba-driven elegy. Steve is still struggling with the vocal on this one but that only seems to add extra poignancy to the delivery tonight.

Etruscan Serenade is little more than an excuse for a marvellous workout between the bass of Dave Ball and the percussion of Hugo Degenhardt with the pair of them battling away to the evident appreciation of the crowd. Their powerhouse antics lead nicely into 'Depth Charge', the glorious anthem which Steve lifts to new heights tonight with some truly inspired playing.

A slightly thrash version of 'Every Day' sends the crowd into hysterics and who can blame them? This is always a delight to hear and this performance is definitely a memorable one. No Hackett show is complete without an acoustic moment, and tonight's is replete with snippets from several of Steve's classics, including at least one which had yet to see the light of day before culminating in the evergreen 'Horizons'. A rather sharp edit leads into the finale in which Steve gets his blues arpeggios out of the closet for a rampaging version of 'The Stumble', in which the entire band let loose and let their hair down in a marvellous stomping version, which is a delight to hear.

WULFRUN HALL, WOLVERHAMPTON, ENGLAND, 28 MAY 1993

Set List: Myopia Medley/Camino Royale/A Vampyre with a Healthy Appetite/Sierra Quemada/Take These Pearls/In the Heart of the City/ Walking Away From Rainbows/There Are Many Sides to the Night/Dark as the Grave/Depth Charge/In That Quiet Earth/Bass-Drum Duet/Always Somewhere Else/Lost in Your Eyes/Every Day/Blood on the Rooftops-Horizons/Cinema Paradiso/Spectral Mornings/Firth of Fifth/Clocks/Myopia Medley (Reprise)//
Source: Audience Recording.

Steve finally brought his new band to the UK for his first rock tour in ten years in the spring of 1993 and here we have one of the best of those performances captured in an excellent audience recording.

With a new album only released the week before, Steve opted to give the audience the biggest helping of new material in one go for many a year. Racing out of the starting gate with a medley comprising 'Myopia', 'Imagining', 'Please Don't Touch', and several other snippets, this was a newly re-energised Hackett, sleek and confident and full of high powered riffs.

'Camino Royale' is getting its last live performance on this tour as well and here we have a fine version with some tasty percussion from new drummer Hugo Degenhardt. Steve sounds in fine form here and he delivers a suitably tongue in cheek vocal. Steve keeps his tongue firmly in his cheek for the first offering from the new album; the weird and wacky 'A Vampyre with a Healthy Appetite', which is a worthy successor to the likes of 'Carry on up the Vicarage'. It certainly is a carry on tonight with the entire band evidently having a blast.

'Sierra Quemada' had been road tested in the US under the title of 'Flight of the Condor' but whatever title it goes under, this is another of those magnificent musical soundscapes that only Steve can create. Here he soars above the rest of the band like a veritable bird on the wing for a truly impressive performance. 'Take These Pearls' is also a dignified, almost stately, track followed by the tale of urban angst that is 'In the Heart of the City', complete with sound effects. Steve delivers the vocal in an almost scat style, while the rest of the band, in particular Julian Colbeck and Hugo Degenhardt, give a suitably convincing impression of a city scape.

'Walking Away From Rainbows' is a reflection on leaving a place, person, or even ... a band. This is a truly remarkable piece of music, in which Steve and Julian execute a miniature ballet of acoustic delight, which has the audience in raptures. 'There Are Many Sides to the Night' and 'Dark as the Grave' are equally dramatic, with Steve once again almost speaking the lyrics, and the musical accompaniment is understated but highly effective throughout.

'Depth Charge' had only previously appeared on the *Time Lapse* live album but of course we now know it under several guises. It is a widescreen epic of a track given the full treatment here tonight. Steve's guitar soars away over a tight percussive rhythm and then new guys Hugo Degenhardt and Dave Sinclair give the audience a master class in rhythm with a bass/drums duel replete with some seriously funky bass licks and tasty paradiddles.

'Always Somewhere Else' sounds strangely out of place here and Steve then digs out his harmonica for a little blues moment leading into the hard rocking 'Lost in Your Eyes', in which he and Dave Sinclair exchange some mean riffs.

'Every Day' gets the crowd's attention and here we have a slightly different arrangement to this evergreen classic. Every bit as enjoyable as ever though, with some fine harmonies and a great organ sound from Julian Colbeck. 'Spectral Mornings' also threatens to blast through the walls as Steve and the band deliver this, his undoubted signature tune, in a particularly vibrant performance, which in turn leads nicely into the blistering guitar solo from 'Firth of Fifth', which really doesn't need any more words from me now, does it?

'Clocks' signals the end of the show proper and cue audience participation time with clapping and cheering. Hugo and Dave give the audience a foot massage as their notes reverberate through the floor. Steve cuts loose with a truly demented guitar riff to bring the evening to a magnificent close.

Of course it isn't over and Steve returns armed with an acoustic guitar for the obligatory medley including snippets from 'Blood on the Rooftops', 'Black Light', leading into the simple elegance of 'Horizons'. Whilst on the subject of elegance, what else can describe the theme from 'Cinema Paradiso'? Superbly executed here by Steve and Julian in a breathtaking show of sheer musical excellence.

'In That Quiet Earth' is given the Hackett treatment tonight, and he sounds completely in his element cutting loose with some inspired riffs, while the rest of the band rage around him. Because the audience have been so good, they are even treated to an extra encore, namely a reprise of the opening medley bringing this superb quality recording to a close.

CHAPTER THIRTY
"NOT NECESSARILY ACOUSTIC" 1994-1998

Now that Steve was back in the groove so to speak, his touring and recording activity began to pick up pace. 1994 saw the release of two contrasting albums. *Blues with a Feeling*, as its title suggests, is a blues based album of originals and covers of blues standards. Sadly no shows were undertaken in support of it – not yet at any rate!

Returning to the acoustic format, Steve gave us another first with an acoustic live album. Still preceding the age of "unplugged", Steve got there first with *There Are Many Sides to the Night*, which was recorded during Steve's acoustic tour of Italy in 1994. Once again, during these shows, new material was given an airing and several old Hackett classics were given the acoustic treatment to great effect.

Never ceasing to surprise his fans, Steve's next project was one that definitely set tongues wagging. *Genesis Revisited* took an affectionate look at some of Steve's finest moments with his former band, along with a couple of new compositions and an uncompleted Genesis track dragged kicking and screaming out of the archives. Sadly only a handful of shows were performed in support of this album and they were in Japan but the results were soon available on the resulting *Tokyo Tapes* live album and DVD.

Keeping the fans guessing, his next project was definitely one that took his fans by surprise. Originating from two or three acoustic pieces that Steve had been working on, they were soon to be expanded into the magnificent orchestral interpretation of Shakespeare's classic *A Midsummer Night's Dream*. Released under the auspices of EMI's Classics division, the album reached the top of the classical charts and gained positive reviews. Sadly, no performance of it has been organised but I am sure that one day it will gain its deserved place in the orchestral repertoire.

TEATRO AURORA, COMO, ITALY, 26 NOVEMBER 1994
Set List: Beja Flor/Kim/Second Chance/Oh How I Love You/The Journey/Baroque/Walking Away From Rainbows/Concerto in D/A Blue Part of Town/There Are Many Sides to the Night/Ace of Wands/Cinema Paradiso/Blues Coda/Jazz on a Summer's Night//
Source: Audience Recording.

This is an interesting recording and one of only a handful from this series of acoustic shows. Sadly it opens halfway through the show but the quality of the recording makes up for the omissions. 'Beja Flor', which is the first track we hear, is still unreleased and is followed in rapid succession by the classics 'Kim' and 'Second Chance', where Steve is joined by Julian Colbeck and lovely versions they are too. It's definitely not "rock 'n' roll but we like it," as Steve says in his introductions.

'Oh How I Love You', appearing here acoustically many years before its final official release on the 1986 *Feedback* album in 2000, makes a fascinating look into the development of what would become one of Steve's finest songs. 'The Journey' takes us back to his first acoustic foray and the version performed here is magnificent.

A rambling 'Baroque', an improvised homage to Bach follows, with Julian Colbeck augmenting Steve's arpeggios in fine style. 'Walking Away From Rainbows', already established in the live set, fits perfectly within the acoustic setting of the evening's gig. Colbeck's playing here is sublime and we continue in that vein with Steve's tribute to Vivaldi with 'Concerto in D', which is breathtaking in its execution, proving Steve's mastery of the classical form.

An unexpected performance comes next as Steve breaks out his harmonica for a rambling acoustic treatment of 'A Blue Part of Town' from the recently released *Blues with a Feeling* album. If nothing else, this proves that he really should give some consideration to including material from that album in the live set, as this works particularly well here.

A heady mix of old and new finished the recording with the likes of 'Ace of Wands' nestling securely between more recent Hackett offerings before the show concludes with the wonderful 'Jazz on a Summer's Night'.

CHAPTER THIRTY-ONE
"DARKTOWN RIOTS" 2000-2002

As I mentioned before, Steve finally established his own record company, Camino, in 1997, and the first album to be released under that label was 1999's *Darktown*; a dark, menacing, and thought provoking album.

Steve returned to the world of rock with a handful of shows that showcased some of the material from it before setting off an extensive tour of South America in 2001, which was captured for posterity in the resulting *Somewhere in South America* live album and DVD.

In addition to this, Steve still managed to cram in some more acoustic shows this time in the company of his brother and new keyboard player Roger King, who had been working with Steve since the *Revisited* project, and has now become a mainstay of Steve's recording/touring band. Once again, fans can relish the show as the concert from Steve's gig in Hungary was recorded for the *Hungarian Horizon* CD/DVD package. Several recordings from those tours are also examined here.

STEVE HACKETT
DARKTOWN

RELEASE DATE: 26 APRIL 1999
CAMINO RECORDS   CAMCD17

One of rock's most uncompromising and complex individuals, the inventor of 'tapping', has moved on. More revealing than ever before and firmly autobiographical, DARKTOWN is as personal a Hackett album as you're likely to see. The guitar work is as alive and inspired as ever and the usual impossibly big and haunting sounds are occasionally twinned with Ian McDonald's searing, angst-ridden sax bellowing from places only glimpsed in a child's nightmare.

DARKTOWN is a series of miniature movies or short stories - but don't zoom in on one fragment - you need the whole picture which is detailed to say the least.

> "I didn't want to impress my personality on any of it ... just to go at it like a character actor, turning up in different guises to help the plot along."

Hackett hasn't flinched from exploring the limits of the term 'progressive', he drags that much maligned genre screaming and kicking into the 21st century. The album opens with "Omega Metallicus", a remarkable 'beats' driven guitar tour-de-force where everything you hear that isn't bass and drums is wrung from the electric guitar. In the Latin-tinged "Dreaming With Open Eyes" the entire percussion picture springs from Hackett's nylon guitar - slapped, plucked, sampled and looped. The ride through the dark continues - who could fail to be moved by the evident pain of "Jane Austen's Door"? - and when light finally emerges in the shape of tracks such as "Days of Long Ago", with Jim Diamond's soulful vocal, the sense of relief has been well earned. Finally there's a magnificent goodbye with "In Memoriam", a deceptively relaxed and world-weary but ultimately salient observation.

Steve Hackett has never lacked the nerve and imagination to take risks, try out new techniques and push forward the boundaries regardless of the consequences. He has always gone out on a limb, even courted unpopularity in his pursuit of fresh musical satisfaction.

This is a record from someone who has lived and needs to tell you what he's discovered - an exorcism, from the harshest moments to the most cherished memories.

A nightmare themepark of an album.

For further information, interviews, competitions
Please contact:
SHARON CHEVIN at THE PUBLICITY CONNECTION

CASTELLO MALATESTIANA, CESENA, ITALY, 11 JULY 2000
Set List: Mechanical Bride/Serpentine/Watcher of the Skies/Hairless Heart/Firth of Fifth/Riding the Colossus/The Steppes/Walking Away From Rainbows/Sierra Quemada/A Vampyre with a Healthy Appetite/Gnossienne #3/A Tower Struck Down/Darktown/Camino Royale/In Memoriam/Horizons//
Source: Audience Recording.

With Steve's last proper electric tour almost eight years in the past, fans were beginning to wonder what he had been up to. The short tour of Italy that took place in the summer of 2000 gave them their answer.

An avant-garde opener, some keyboard effects, and guitar leads us into 'Mechanical Bride', still some three years from seeing the light of day on to *Watch the Storms*. Here it is given a typically balls-to-the-wall performance, including an extended instrumental jam giving Steve's new band a chance to flex their collective muscles.

Another new one is next. 'Serpentine', or as it was to become known later as 'Serpentine Song', which is a delightful homage to Steve's father. Being an open air gig, sadly the sound often goes astray and indeed the performance is obviously one of a work still very much in progress giving us a nice insight into the evolution of a track.

No such insights necessary for the next trio of pieces, bona fide classics from Steve's time with the "beat combo" as he humorously refers to his band mates in Genesis. 'Watcher of the Skies' is preceded by a curious guitar riff before Roger King lets rip with those famous chords and cue the audience going wild. With a new band behind him, this is the first time we get to hear Gary O'Toole's phenomenal percussive and vocal talents and the result is astonishing. This is confirmed by the superb playing of 'Hairless Heart', which Steve brings vividly to life, reiterating as if it were necessary exactly what Genesis lost when he left all those years ago. Roger King also delivers a superb emulation of Mr Banks' finest chord progressions making this a fascinating listen. A short acoustic prelude heralds the arrival of the evergreen 'Firth of Fifth' in an extended instrumental version à la 'Revisited'. Not that that matters, as both Banks and Hackett's parts are brought to us steaming hot and equally delicious – this is a gourmet feast for Hackett and Genesis aficionados and the crowd make their pleasure known.

Ben Castle's saxophone makes a plaintive background to the echoey introduction to 'Riding the Colossus'; one of the bona fide new classics from the *Genesis Revisited* album. Already a favourite with this listener from that album and tour, here it is taken to new heights with a solo from Steve that is guaranteed to rip the hairs off your neck.

'The Steppes' takes us back to the heady days when Steve used to tour pretty much every year. Instead of John's flute, we have Ben's slightly oriental sax intro, which leads into a ponderous, evocation of the sweeping grandeur of the subject matter of the track. 'Walking Away From Rainbows' became a firm favourite with audiences back in 1993 and it has lost none of its simple grandeur here. Roger and Steve reflect off each other like sunlight on water – marvellous stuff!

Some percussion from Gary leads us into the soaring majesty of 'Sierra Quemada' – the scorched earth, an apposite title given the searing heat generated by Steve's solo here, which is every bit as magnificent as its recorded counterpart.

From the sublime to the slightly ridiculous next, featuring some freeform sax-blowing from Rob Townsend. This leads us eventually into the equally left of centre 'A Vampyre with a Healthy Appetite', which is definitely a worthy successor to the likes of 'The Ballad of the Decomposing Man', and is just as entertaining.

Steve and his brother had not long released their album of interpretations of the music of Erik Satie, so it is entirely in keeping for at least one track from that album to appear in concert form. So 'Gnossienne #3' does not sound at all out of place here with Ben Castle once again doing a splendid job in John's place.

Back to where it all began for Steve next with a remarkably rowdy version of 'A Tower Struck Down'. Steve's guitar howls like the proverbial banshee at times whilst the rest of the band once again rock out, with some fine ensemble playing kudos to Mr King again, whose keyboards and effects bring the widescreen version of the track to life here. As the tower falls and the bell tolls, we move to the much more recent past with 'Darktown'; one of Steve's darkest and angriest songs delivered with a magnificently menacing effects laden vocal and some equally fiery guitar playing – seldom has Steve sounded so feisty!

Another short instrumental passage leads us into a long established classic that we shall soon be saying goodbye to as 'Camino Royale' bows out of Steve's live set in a typically uptempo performance, driven equally by the sax and percussion of Castle and O'Toole.

Something of a rarity comes next with 'In Memoriam'; one of the stand out tracks from 1999's *Darktown* album. Delivered here at a stately and suitably elegiac pace, Steve and the band bring this one to life with a poignancy rare at rock gigs.

The mood lifts from one of remembrance to one of celebration as the show concludes with Steve's own acoustic masterpiece, 'Horizons', which brings this excellent recording to a suitably bright conclusion. Sadly the encore of 'Los Endos' is missing here but what we do have more than compensates for that omission.

BB KING'S CLUB, NEW YORK, USA, 28 JUNE 2002
Set List: the Floating Seventh/Mechanical Bride/Myopia Medley/Serpentine Song/Watcher of the Skies/Hairless Heart/Firth of Fifth/Riding the Colossus/Pollution B/The Steppes/In Memoriam/Slave Girls/A Vampyre with a Healthy Appetite/Spectral Mornings/Lucridus/Darktown/Camino Royale/Every Day/Los Endos//
Source: Audience Recording.

Steve set off on his first US tour in a long time in the autumn of 2002 and here we have an excellent recording from BB King's Club in New York.

Once again, Steve was road testing new material, so we get the left field 'Floating Seventh' and 'Mechanical Bride' to open the show. Steve is still working on this one and the vocal performance is radically different to what it would eventually become but musically the band are right on the money here.

The 'Myopia Medley' from 1993 has survived and makes its reappearance here tonight in an extended form, including snippets from 'Los Endos', 'Ace of Wands', and 'Please Don't Touch'. Steve is in great form here and the rest of the band, especially Roger King and new drummer Gary O'Toole, really go to town on this one.

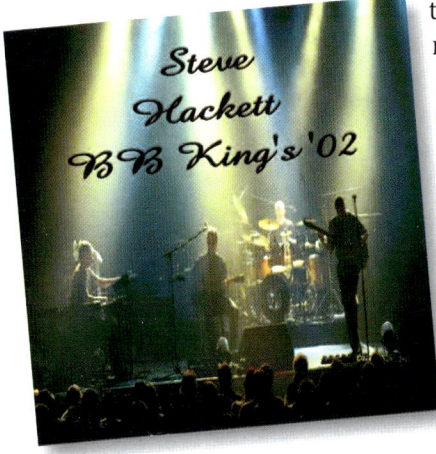

Another new number comes next, namely 'Serpentine Song', which is destined to become a classic live favourite. Here we get an early glimpse at it. Harmony vocals from Steve, Gary, and Rob make this a joy to hear and Roger King's keyboards take this one to another level of excellence. With Steve opting to "revisit" his Genesis past (pun intended) it is no surprise that 'Watcher of the Skies' gets a hysterical reaction from the crowd. Not surprising, really. Roger King in particular nails this one to perfection. 'Hairless Heart' features a stunning guitar/keyboard duet between Steve and Roger, which is guaranteed to send shivers up the spine of any fan. This and 'Firth of Fifth' get the crowd going again and no wonder, as Steve is simply on fire here.

Same goes for his performance on 'Riding the Colossus', which roars out of the traps after a deceptively calm sax solo from Rob Townsend. This one just gets better every time it is performed. 'Pollution B' – another one of Steve's bizarre experiments – gets out of the laboratory here, while Rob Townsend gets all oriental as he leads us into 'The Steppes', and a sudden chill descends over BB King's as the Siberian winter is brought vividly to life here by Steve and the band.

An emotional performance and a rare one at that of 'In Memoriam', dedicated to John "The Ox" Entwistle, who had died the day before tonight's gig. Obviously the song takes on special significance tonight and here we get to hear it sounding quite different to its recorded version still several months away.

'Slave Girls' is a monstrous guitar primal scream moment, leading into the equally left field 'A Vampyre with a Healthy Appetite', which has an unexpected swagger in its step tonight. Once again Steve is obviously having a good time and hams it up to perfection with his Hammer Horror style vocal. Next we have an unusual version of 'Spectral Mornings' with keyboard introduction restored and sax accompaniment from Rob Townsend before Steve lets rip with those familiar riffs glorious stuff as ever.

Another of Steve's test tube babies escapes from the laboratory next with 'Lucridus', leading us into the paranoid claustrophobia of 'Darktown'; without doubt one of the darkest and angriest songs Steve has ever committed to record, and tonight the band serve up a magically fiery version.

'Camino Royale' makes its last appearance in the set during this tour and here we have a delightfully uptempo performance driven along by some inspired percussion from Gary O'Toole and bass lines from Terry Gregory. Rob Townsend's sax delivers a sexy solo and Steve gets to grips with a particularly emphatic vocal performance.

'Every Day' is given a workmanlike outing here, with great work from the rhythm section again, and Steve is augmented in the vocal department by some fine harmonies from Gary and Rob making it a rather nifty version. The show is brought to a stunning climax by the extended instrumental workout otherwise known as 'Los Endos', although as usual from Steve, replete with some other extra bits and pieces turning it into a percussion-driven epic.

NAIMA CLUB, FORLI, ITALY, 1 NOVEMBER 2002

Set List: Horizons/Gnossienne #1/Bouree-Bacchus-Improvisation-Firth of Fifth/Bay of Kings/Syrinx-Imagining-Second Chance-Jacuzzi-Overnight Sleeper/The Barren Land/Kim/Cuckoo Cocoon-Dancing with the Moonlit Knight-Blood on the Rooftops/Time Lapse at Milton Keynes/Improvisation/Hairless Heart/Cinema Paradiso/Gymnopedie #1/Jazz on a Summer's Night/Cavalcanti/Walking Away From Rainbows/Tales of the Riverbank/Concert for Munich/The Journey/Skye Boat Song/By Paved Fountain/Hands of the Priestess/Ace of Wands/Idylle-Aubade-Meditation//
Source: Audience Recording.

Without doubt one of the finest audience recordings available and one that captures one of the early acoustic trio shows to perfection. An opening salvo – if you can call such gentle music that – of 'Horizons' and 'Satie's Gnossienne #1' is performed with style and grace by Steve and his brother John and keyboards man Roger King.

Steve is in fine form chatting away to the audience in a mixture of Italian and English before the trio launch into a delightful medley of pieces by Bach and Genesis. 'Bouree' will be no stranger to anyone who is a fan of Jethro Tull and it is odd to hear it in such an unfamiliar setting (John doesn't wear a cod piece for a start!). This morphs into 'Bacchus', which first appeared in Steve's set back in 1994 and it has gained enormously by trip performance.

John's flute battles away with the other protagonists before Steve and John proceed to blow the audience away with an acoustic rendering of the instrumental section of 'Firth of Fifth', which is performed to perfection, teasing the audience with the merest snippet, before returning to 'Bacchus' and rapturous applause.

'Bay of Kings' is preceded with an acoustic ramble, which fans will come to recognise as part of the *Metamorpheus* album, still some three years away. 'Bay of Kings' itself is stately, flowing like a galleon at anchor, and seldom have I heard it better than on this recording. John is given a solo spot next with a shimmering performance of 'Debussy's Syrinx', which segues into a tastefully slowed down acoustic section from GTR's 'Imagining', in which Steve and Roger King perform an instrumental ballet, leading us nicely to 'Second Chance'; that delightful B-side from the 1980s, which is always a joy to hear.

'Jacuzzi' and 'Overnight Sleeper' are given the acoustic treatment here too and this is almost like hearing a demo of the pieces stripped back to their bare essentials but it still works and the audience love it.

'The Barren Land' and 'Kim' are next, both being austere and serene in their beauty, proving beyond doubt Steve's mastery of the demands of classical form and style. These contrast nicely here with a surprisingly sprightly medley of some of Steve's finest Genesis moments, culminating in a magnificent instrumental performance of 'Blood on the Rooftops', which simply takes the breath away. Before we pay homage to the concrete cows of Milton Keynes as Steve pays homage to that wet nigh twenty years before when he and his Genesis pals were all too briefly reunited for the night – lovely stuff!

The Chinese improvisation that has been part of his set for many years is augmented tonight by some soaring flute playing by John and menacing keyboards from Roger. This is almost like something from a late night tales of mystery and suspense soundtrack and is quite unsettling at times. 'Hairless Heart' gets a good reaction from the crowd and deservedly so. Restrained and stately, this is a gem of a performance.

The rest of the recording is equally enjoyable, including several tracks which are still staples in Steve's show to this day. Watch out for the hilarious but gentle put down of an unfortunate member of the audience who has left his/her mobile phone on too. This recording is an essential part of any Hackett fan's collection and my congratulations to whoever recorded it. The result is a truly remarkable document of what was obviously a great night.

PART THREE: STEVE HACKETT

CHAPTER THIRTY-TWO
"WATCHING THE STORMS" 2003-2004

By now Steve was well and truly in his stride and with his own record label and recording studio in hand he was able to concentrate on producing music without having one eye on the studio clock.

Taking a leaf out of Peter Gabriel's book, the first of the *Live Archive* series of albums was released during this period. Documenting Steve's appearance at the 2002 NEARfest in the USA, this was an indication of what was to come. Writing and recording took up most of the year before Steve emerged with his first rock album since *Darktown*. to *Watch the Storms* was released on 25 May 2003 and if its predecessor was the darker side of Steve, then this was definitely sunshine after the rain. Full of light-hearted moments and brilliantly observed vignettes of people and places, this is one of Steve's most accessible albums.

Without doubt, the strangest Hackett tour also took place during 2003 with a short series of what can literally be described as "have acoustic guitar will travel" shows in Borders Bookstores in the USA, which saw Steve armed with a trusty acoustic guitar and some anecdotes.

He also brought the magic of the album to the UK with his first tour here since 1993 and the fans loved it. The shows were a heady mix of old and new and several older favourites were dusted off and brought back into the fold. The tour continued into 2004 and formed the basis of the next *Live Archive* album, although most of the gigs from this tour are also available in fan recordings.

BORDERS BOOKSTORES, PHILADELPHIA, & BRYN MAWR, PENNSYLVANIA, USA, 8 AUGUST 2003

Set List (Philadelphia): Mexico City-Classical Gas-Black Light/Brand New-Sapphires-Segovia-Horizons-Cuckoo Cocoon-In That Quiet Earth-Blood on the Rooftops-Tales of the Riverbank/Skye Boat Song/By Paved Fountain/Bay of Kings/The Pool of Memory, the Pool of Forgetfulness-Cavalcanti//
Source: Audience DVD Recording.
Set List (Bryn Mawr): A Bed, a Chair, and a Guitar/Cavalcanti/Tales of the Riverbank/Mexico City/Rebecca/Horizons/Cuckoo Cocoon-Blood on the Rooftops-After the Ordeal/The Journey/Bouree-Racing in A- Skye Boat Song/By Paved Fountain/Black Light/The Pool of Memory, the Pool of Forgetfulness-Bay of King //
Source: Audience DVD Recording.

Without doubt the most unusual setting for a show – a bookshop! Steve sarcastically comments on this fact as he gets started. Looking incredibly relaxed here he is at the first of two shows he performed on the same day within the bounds of Philadelphia. Hilariously opening with the riff to 'Smoke on the Water', he gets underway with 'Classical Gas', preceded by a medley of material form the as yet unrecorded *Metamorpheus* album, along with a few bum notes! Steve doesn't seem to mind and the audience are in rapt attention throughout. This set is shorter than its sequel, most likely owing to time constraints, but nevertheless Steve manages to cram a heck of a lot into his thirty or so minutes and the punters obviously cannot believe their luck!

The Bryn Mawr performance is an evening one that makes for a slightly longer performance. Steve is still relaxed, regaling the audience with some stories of his childhood musical experiments. The camera focuses on Steve's set lists and there is a slight edit before he quite appropriately opens proceedings with 'A Bed, a Chair & a Guitar'. It is odd to see him surrounded by piles of books and the resulting performance, although strange in terms of its setting, works remarkably well.

'Cavalcanti' is next, which is another almost austere piece and one that observes the truest classical form. The galloping figure sounds incredibly good in this setting and Steve has his audience enthralled throughout. 'Tales of the Riverbank' doesn't quite get the reaction it has in the UK, but then again, the Yanks probably haven't been lucky enough to see GP and Hammy in action! An edit takes us to the as yet unrecorded 'Mexico City', which is every bit as vibrant as the place it describes. Some percussive playing sees him tease the audience with a snippet from 'Rebecca' from to *Watch the Storms*, all of which pass unremarked by the crowd who are evidently mesmerised by the performance.

Of course, 'Horizons' does get a ripple of polite applause and it is another delightful version, as is the snippet from 'Cuckoo Cocoon', which comes next followed by 'Blood on the Rooftops', both of which seem to wake the crowd up from their reveries at last. Another surprise comes with a snippet from 'After the Ordeal' before this delightful medley culminates with 'The Journey'. This was an astonishing performance all round and we see a smiling and relaxed Steve evidently enjoying himself as much as his audience who give him some well-deserved applause.

'Bouree' is next, and J. S. Bach's classic, which may be familiar to Jethro Tull fans among you, is given the Hackett treatment here, leading into something that sounds like 'Pop Goes the Weasel' on acid. Another snippet from 'Racing in A' leads nicely into the magic of the 'Skye Boat Song', which is simply magical here. 'By Paved Fountain' from the magnificent *A Midsummer Night's Dream* album gets an outing tonight. This is an unabashedly romantic piece that works brilliantly even in such an unlikely setting!

Sadly there is a rather savage edit next, which leads us straight into another medley of familiar snippets, leading into 'Black Light'; another delightful track from Steve's first acoustic album, *Bay of Kings*, and another edit leads us to a brief chat in which Steve explains the background to his first solo acoustic album and his earliest musical endeavours, thence to a magnificent performance of 'Bay of Kings', which incorporates another snippet from *Metamorpheus*; 'The Pool of Memory, the Pool of Forgetfulness', bringing this fascinating recording to a suitably restrained close.

VILLA BERG, STUTTGART, GERMANY, 9 NOVEMBER 2003
Set List: Every Day/Watcher of the Skies/Pollution B/The Steppes/Please Don't Touch/Firth of Fifth/A Vampyre with a Healthy Appetite/Spectral Mornings/In Memoriam//
Source: FM Radio Broadcast.

Radio broadcasts are becoming rarer for Steve these days, so it is a delight to have this one from the European leg of the to *Watch the Storms* tour. As usual, a rambling introduction by the announcer, who even gives the set away, leads nicely into 'Every Day'; a classic which the band have dusted off again for this tour to the delight of fans. Roger King's almost symphonic keyboards are accompanied by some superlative percussion from Gary O'Toole whilst the main man is no slouch in the riffage department!

Steve had decided to revisit (pun intended) his Genesis past on this tour, so 'Watcher of the Skies', driven by Roger's awesome keyboards, is next. Frighteningly good it is too!
'Pollution B' and effects-laden segue leads perfectly into 'The Steppes', which is without doubt one of Steve's most impressive aural landscapes. Tonight is no exception as Rob Townsend's oriental tinged sax soars over the audience generating a frisson every bit as cold as the landscape itself. Roger and Gary augment the frigidity of the

performance too whilst Steve's guitar howls like a wolf in the Siberian night – brr!

'Please Don't Touch' races out of the traps at a frantic pace, driven by Gary's awesome percussion and Rob's superb sax playing. Mr H. himself is in superb form again, leading the troops over the top in a magnificent display of musicianship, which is continued as Steve segues into the spine-tingling guitar solo from 'Firth of Fifth', which threatens to tear the roof down.

From the sublime to the ridiculous next as we are taken to the backstreets of New Orleans for 'A Vampyre with a Healthy Appetite'; a raucous tongue-in-cheek excuse for Steve to cut loose with some of Satan's stomp boxes one more time.

Steve's signature tune is next, namely 'Spectral Mornings', and it doesn't matter how many times I hear it (and that's a fair few I can tell you, folks!), it still manages to send shivers up and down my spine. Here Steve and the band are in particularly fine form and Steve's guitar is simply on fire!

The recording closes with another rarity – 'In Memoriam' – which didn't get an outing on the UK leg of the 2003 tour for some reason. This is one of Steve's more reflective and thought provoking tracks, here we have a particularly poignant performance with the band in suitably restrained and Steve's vocal is delivered almost rapper-style, which makes for an interesting listen.

KING GEORGE'S HALL, BLACKBURN, ENGLAND, 7 MARCH 2004

Set List: Valley of the Kings/Mechanical Bride/Circus of Becoming/Frozen Statues/Slogans/Serpentine Song/Ace of Wands/Hammer in the Sand/Acoustic Set/Second Chance/Blood on the Roopftops/Fly on a Windshield/Please Don't Touch/Firth of Fifth/A Dark Night in Toytown/Darktown/Brand New/The Air-Conditioned Nightmare/Every Day/Clocks/Spectral Mornings/Myopia Medley-Los Endos//
Source: Audience Recording.

This was another venue Steve had never played before. As had become the norm by now, the show opened with the contrasting triptych of 'Valley of the Kings', 'Mechanical Bride', and 'Circus of Becoming', which managed to demonstrate both the lighter and darker sides of Hackett.

A frenzied 'Slogans' contrasts nicely with a deliciously sedate 'Serpentine Song', which simply gets better with every performance. 'Hammer in the Sand' is simply glorious too, with Steve and Roger King merging harmoniously, augmented by a lovely soprano sax solo by Rob Townsend. The acoustic set features a few new snippets, including a couple from the as yet unreleased orchestral album, *Metamorpheus*, along with Steve's homage to Mason Williams' hit 'Classical Gas', before returning to more familiar territory with 'Black Light' and of course 'Horizons', which no Hackett show would be complete without.

Steve then announces his brother John on stage to accompany him and Roger on a wonderfully understated performance of 'Second Chance' and a highlight of this and every other show on this year's tour, the first complete performance of 'Blood on the Rooftops', which I have to admit reduced yours truly to tears each and every time I saw it.

As if that wasn't enough, Steve went even further back next with a truly outstanding performance of 'Fly on a Windshield', which simply rips the hairs off the back of your neck as Steve and the band rampage through it. They don't give the audience any breathing space either, as they then launch into an equally ferocious version of 'Please Don't Touch', which certainly brought back some memories for the older Hackett fans among the audience. This trip down Memory Lane continues with the now familiar segue into the instrumental section of 'Firth of Fifth', which simply blows you away each and every time you hear it.

Back to the new stuff next, featuring 'A Dark Night in Toy Town', as yet unrecorded. It is another anti-drug song and one with a syncopated rhythm – truly a nightmare ride in a hellish fairground! This is in turn followed by Steve's examination of his own nightmares at the hands of school ground bullies – 'Darktown' – the only representative from the sadly underrated album of the same name. 'Brand New' is the final representative of Steve's new album and amusingly here it is that he chooses to forget the opening lines!

We are then given a final salvo of oldies beginning with 'The Air Conditioned Nightmare', which is as magnificent as ever. 'Every Day' continues our nostalgia trip and the harmony vocals here are excellent and musically this is one where the entire band are evidently having a blast playing. Speaking of blasts, 'Clocks' rounds off the show in a suitably frenetic fashion, leaving the audience gasping but cheering for more.

It isn't long in coming either, as Steve and the band retake the stage to cheers to deliver the coup de grâce of tonight's show. Despite some wags cheering for 'Harold the Barrel' and 'The Knife', Steve opts for the safer route and 'Spectral Mornings' threatens to lift the roof off its foundations. This one simply can't be beaten, I'm afraid, and Steve plays it as if his very life depended on it. An extended version of 'Myopia' leads us into Steve's revamped version of 'Los Endos', which brings the curtain down on yet another superb performance from Steve and his band of merry men.

CHAPTER THIRTY-THREE
"ACOUSTIC METAMORPHOSES" 2005-2007

If 1997's *A Midsummer Night's Dream* had shown that Steve had the talent and temperament to write for an orchestra, then 2005's *Metamorpheus* album confirmed his position as a talent to be reckoned with in this sphere.

Touring with an orchestra, however, was to be cost prohibitive, so instead Steve went for his very own mini orchestra consisting of his brother John, Roger King and himself for a tour of the UK and subsequently an extensive tour of the USA, bringing the magic of the small orchestra to concert halls once more. Even here Steve managed to take us by surprise with the inclusion of among other things an acoustic version of 'After the Ordeal', which went down a treat.

This trend continued into 2007 with Steve and the trio performing a variety of gigs in Europe where even more Genesis material was exhumed for the delectation of the fans. Once again, a *Live Archive* album documents these performances quite nicely and if you are not satisfied with that, numerous private recordings are also available.

CARNGLAZE CAVERNS, LISKEARD, CORNWALL, ENGLAND, 8 APRIL 2005

Set List: Classical Jazz/Metamorpheus Medley/Black Light/Tales of the Riverbank/Segovia Tribute/Brand New/The Barren Land/Skye Boat Song/ Horizons/Jacuzzi-Overnight Sleeper-Bacchus/Firth of Fifth/Whole Tone Jam/The Red Flower of Taichi Blooms Everywhere/ Hands of the Priestess/After the Ordeal/Hairless Heart/M3/Imagining/Second Chance/Jazz on a Summer's Night/Next Time Around/ Kim/Idylle-Aubade-Meditation/The Journey/Ace of Wands/Waling Away From Rainbows/Gnossienne #1//
Source: Audience Recording.

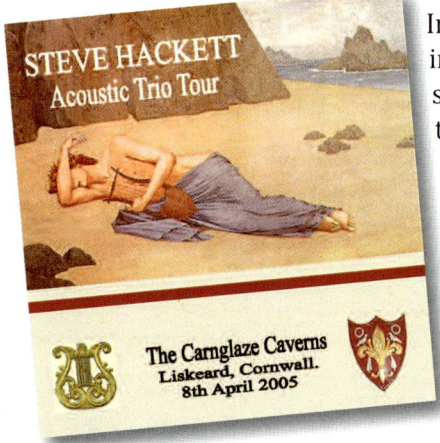

In my time I have seen Steve play in churches and tram sheds but never before in a slate quarry! The Caverns are exactly that a series of caves from which slate and other minerals have been mined for many years – in the last war they were even used to store the Royal Navy's reserves of rum!

It was certainly a rum do tonight as the trio took the stage for another acoustic performance which fortunately has been captured by this excellent quality audience recording. Opening with Steve's homage to the late Mason Williams we get 'Classical Jazz' and a medley of bits and pieces from the new orchestral album that Steve is ostensibly promoting. 'Black Light' and 'Tales of the Riverbank' are performed flawlessly and Steve dedicates the latter to his two hamsters, "both of them worked."

As has always been Steve's wont, the acoustic shows are an opportunity to revisit some of the tracks from his established rock oeuvre in a different setting, so tonight we get acoustic renditions of 'Jacuzzi' and 'Overnight Sleeper', but the real surprises are the inclusion of 'Firth of Fifth' and that "contentious little number", 'After the Ordeal', both of which are captured in all their glory here.

There are even solo spots for both John and Roger and as usual Mr King has his moment of sarcasm, remarking that the "star of the show" is the only one with a heater (the caverns are at a constant 10 degrees Fahrenheit), so it was a cool gig in more ways than one! The trio are evidently in good humour and enjoying themselves and this is a relaxed and informal performance. I love the venue manager's challenge and offer of free beer to anyone who can get a signal on their mobile phone! All in all, this is a fantastic document of one of Steve's more unusual gigs.

XM PERFORMANCE THEATER, WASHINGTON DC, USA, 12 OCTOBER 2005

Set List: Horizons/Classical Jazz/Jacuzzi/Overnight Sleeper/Bacchus- Firth of Fifth-Bacchus/Tribute to Segovia/Jazz on a Summer's Night/Mexico City-Black Light-The Barren Land/Ace of Wands/Hands of the Priestess/The Journey//
Source: FM Radio Broadcast.

This is another rarity on two counts. First, it is a radio broadcast from the acoustic trio comprising of Steve, his brother John on flute, and Roger King on keyboards. Secondly, it is taken from Steve's first extensive US tour for many years.

As such, this is a truly delightful recording, opening with the evergreen 'Horizons' with Steve sounding relaxed as he introduces it. Clear and sharp as you would expect from a radio recording, this still has the warmth of the music running through it though. 'Classical Jazz', incorporating Mason Williams' 'Classical Gas', is next, with Steve executing a galloping series of arpeggios in a mesmerising performance, including a few passing nods to the "new" orchestral album, *Metamorpheus*, which the trio were ostensibly promoting on this tour.

Steve is joined onstage in what sounds like a tiny room, by John and Roger next for a jaunty performance of 'Jacuzzi', which bubbles and simmers just like its subject full of life and wry humour. 'Overnight Sleeper' segues nicely into the performance. This is a rich, Spanish-flavoured version, which is a treat for the ears.

'Bacchus' is as bright and breezy as a summer's day with Roger and John duelling away before Steve joins in the fray with some percussive guitar, with the three of them definitely getting carried away by the magic of the moment. This in turn segues into a magnificent flute-driven 'Firth of Fifth' before returning to the polite madness of 'Bacchus'.

'Tribute to Segovia' is a truly magnificent performance. Steve is in complete command of his instrument as he delivers a tasteful performance worthy of the great man whom it is a tribute to, and with no audience noise every note is there to savour to the full. 'Jazz on a Summer's Night' has been alive favourite in Steve's acoustic shows ever since he first embarked on acoustic tours back in 1983, and here it is again, every bit as jaunty and full of fun as it has always been. John puts in some almost Ian Anderson-styled playing on his flute, while Steve and Roger duet away like two flamenco players a truly lovely performance.

A medley next of a trio of pieces, one new and two others harking back to that 1983 album. 'Mexico City' (a place Steve and the trio were to play later on this tour, ironically enough) is first. Vibrant and full of colour, this is Steve at his very best, painting a scene in music. 'Black Light' and 'The Barren Land' are much more sedate and restrained, almost severe in form but truly wonderful to hear.

A humorous 'Ace of Wands' finds the trio in playful mood before 'Hands of the Priestess' takes us to a magical world peopled with some truly remarkable characters if the subject is anything to go by, stately, commanding and yet with an inherent warmth throughout.

'The Journey' concludes this frustratingly short recording and is without doubt a track worthy of the term "classical". Perfect in form and executed in a truly magnificent fashion by Steve and Roger, this proves beyond any doubt that Steve is imbued by the classical spirit of the great masters – listen to this one in awe.

CHAPTER THIRTY-FOUR
"OUT OF THE TUNNEL'S MOUTH" 2009-2011

Recent years have been traumatic for Steve to say the least. In 2006, he and his partner Kim Poor filed for divorce and the resulting acrimony was to keep Steve pre-occupied for the better part of three years.

Legal disputes and other problems delayed several projects by Steve and it wasn't until the spring of 2009 that he re-emerged for a handful of shows in Italy during which some of this new material gained its debut. The new album, *Out of the Tunnel's Mouth*, can in some respects be compared to Phil Collins' *Face Value* album but only in so far as it is a reflection of Steve's state of mind during the divorce process. Musically enthralling and lyrically deep as you would expect from Steve, this one challenges the fans at every turn.

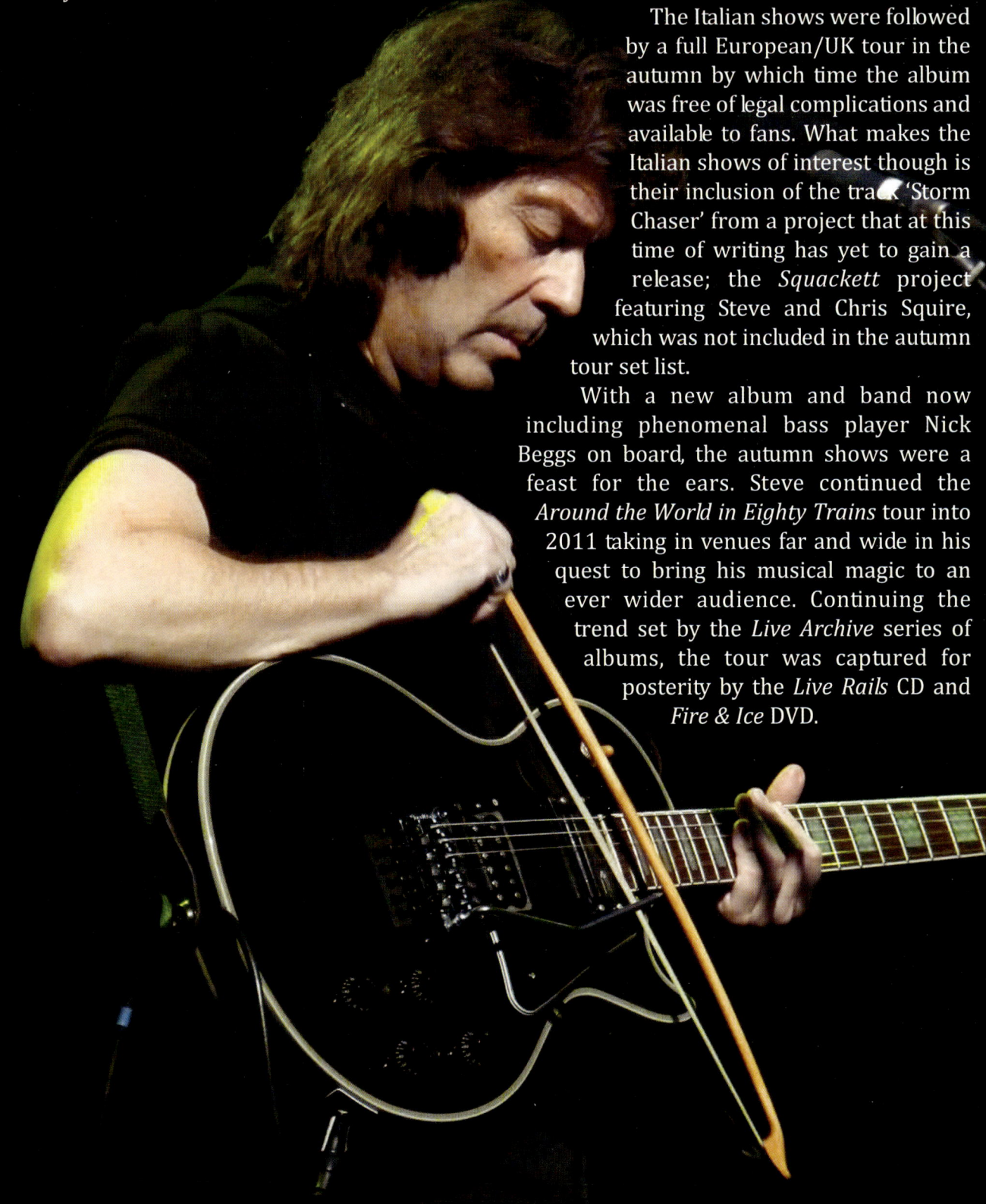

The Italian shows were followed by a full European/UK tour in the autumn by which time the album was free of legal complications and available to fans. What makes the Italian shows of interest though is their inclusion of the track 'Storm Chaser' from a project that at this time of writing has yet to gain a release; the *Squackett* project featuring Steve and Chris Squire, which was not included in the autumn tour set list.

With a new album and band now including phenomenal bass player Nick Beggs on board, the autumn shows were a feast for the ears. Steve continued the *Around the World in Eighty Trains* tour into 2011 taking in venues far and wide in his quest to bring his musical magic to an ever wider audience. Continuing the trend set by the *Live Archive* series of albums, the tour was captured for posterity by the *Live Rails* CD and *Fire & Ice* DVD.

DEPOSITO GIORDIANO, PORDENONE, ITALY, 13 MARCH 2009

Set List: Fire on the Moon/Every Day/Ace of Wands/Pollution B/The Steppes/Darktown/Slogans/Serpentine Song/Firth of Fifth/Walking Away From Rainbows/Blood on the Rooftops/Mechanical Bride/Spectral Mornings/The Wall of Knives/Fly on a Windshield/Broadway Melody of 1974/Please Don't Touch/A Tower Struck Down/In That Quiet Earth/Storm Chaser/Los Endos/Clocks//
Source: Audience Recording.

Back on the road again with a brand new band, Steve began what has since become an almost incessant round of touring, with a handful of shows in Italy in the spring of 2009. One of these early shows manages to capture the sheer exuberance of the new stage show to perfection.

From the opening track of 'Fire on the Moon', which was being road tested before being committed to what would later that year become Steve's twentieth solo album, *Out of the Tunnel's Mouth*, this recording is a superior stamp to many that have preceded it. Every note is crystal clear and I can attest that the acoustics in the building were excellent because I was there! 'Every Day' thunders along at a rapid rate of knots that does not diminish as they move on to 'Ace of Wands', which if anything picks the pace up even more.

'Pollution B' serves as a discordant link to 'The Steppes' where the kudos really lies with Roger King and Rob Townsend, who between them ably manage to assist Steve to magically evoke the spirit of a landscape that the track describes. On to happier things next with a truly delightful performance of the musical homage to Steve's father, which is 'Serpentine Song'; always emotional but given special resonance tonight by the presence of Steve's mum in the audience.

The next surprise comes with a *complete* performance of 'Firth of Fifth', in which Roger King perfectly recreates Tony Banks' part, while Gary O'Toole delivers a superb vocal free from any of the technical problems that had dogged his performance during the opening night's performance in Genoa. The pace slows down nicely next with the obligatory acoustic set including snippets from several classics leading up to the evergreen 'Horizons'. This is followed by 'Walking Away From Rainbows'; another song which takes on a special poignancy given Steve's then current matrimonial problems.

'Blood on the Rooftops' retains its place in the set, which I am delighted about. Here we have another marvellous performance of this underrated classic. Then it is back to rock & roll à la Hackett with the industrial grind of 'Mechanical Bride' and the always awesome 'Spectral Mornings', without which no show by Steve is complete. 'Fly on a Windshield' is preceded by 'The Wall of Knives' (a reference to the impression Peter Green made on the teenaged Hackett) and the former segues nicely into an extended version of 'Broadway Melody of 1974', which elicits a rousing cheer from the crowd.

'Please Don't Touch', 'A Tower Struck Down', and 'In That Quiet Earth' bring the show almost to a climax but not before we are treated to another new and as yet unrecorded track, 'Stormchaser', which has since found itself a home on the soon to be released *Squackett* album, by Steve and Chris Squire. This is a high octane number destined to become a stage favourite. The show proper finishes with what else but 'Los Endos' in Steve's own inimitable version, which gives the entire band (and audience) a chance to ladder their collective tights in fine style.

Of course, an encore wasn't long in coming and soon 'Clocks' rattled out of the traps bringing the show to a suitably emphatic conclusion. As bootlegs go, this is one of the finest I have ever heard and it is good enough to be an official release, in my opinion.

PICTURE DOME, HOLMFIRTH, ENGLAND, 22 NOVEMBER 2009

Set List: Mechanical Bride/Fire on the Moon/Every Day/Emerald & Ash/Ghost in the Glass/Ace of Wands/Pollution B/The Steppes/Slogans/Serpentine Song/Tubehead/Spectral Mornings/Firth of Fifth/Horizons/Blood on the Rooftops/Fly on a Windshield/Broadway Melody of 1974/Sleepers/The Darkness in Men's Hearts/Still Waters/Los Endos/Clocks//
Source: Audience Recording.

Steve's increased round of touring throughout 2009 finally brought him back to the UK in the autumn, and by the time we get to this mid tour show, the set had become a fairly standardised one. As usual, the show opens with the album intro from 'Last Train to Istanbul' before the power of 'Mechanical Bride' is unleashed. Here the entire band rampage through the song with new boy Nick Beggs and Rob Townsend in particular really letting their hair down. With a new set featuring almost the entire new album, *Out of the Tunnel's Mouth*, it isn't long before we get the first offering from it in the shape of 'Fire on the Moon', which is already established as a stage favourite since the Italian shows back in March. Here it has grown enormously and for sheer drama and intensity I think this one is hard to beat. Roger and Steve create just the right atmosphere, while the rest of the band join in on the hellish chorus, which threatens to tear the roof off.

'Every Day' is greeted like an old friend, which indeed it is. The harmonies here are greatly augmented by the presence of Amanda Lehmann who is a solid addition to the band throughout the show. Even the crowd get in on the act here, which is as it should be!

It's back to the new album next with a delightful pairing of tracks. First up is the real heart of the new album, 'Emerald and Ash', which simply gets better every time you hear it. 'Ghost in the Glass' is an unexpected delight with some fine playing from Roger and Steve – jazz on a winter's night indeed!

'Ace of Wands' takes us back to the glory days and unlike so many other things this one never seems to age. Once again, the entire band seems determined to pull the roof down on this one. 'Pollution B' still serves as a great segue into 'The Steppes', which certainly evoked the wintry conditions outside the Picturedome on the night in question! 'Slogans' also has all of the energy of its subject without any of the attendant falsehoods.

'Tubehead' proves once and for all that Steve can rock out with the best of them and he grabs the audience by the scruff of our necks for this one with some additional aural violence by Nick and Gary. 'Spectral Mornings' elicits the loudest cheer of the evening thus far. Difficult to credit that I first heard this thirty-one years ago – doesn't seem that long, I can tell you!

Of late Steve has begun to fully embrace his Genesis heritage and next we are treated to a quintet of Genesis classics, beginning with a truly magnificent 'Firth of Fifth', in which Steve and Roger share the honours, delivering their respective solos absolutely perfectly. 'Horizons' and the acoustic set were augmented by the appearance of Steve's brother John on stage for an impromptu acoustic version of 'Jacuzzi', which was followed by 'Blood on the Rooftops', which is every bit as emotional as ever.

'Fly on a Windshield' and 'Broadway Melody of 1974' also just seem to serve to show exactly how important Steve's contribution to that album had been and here they are truly magnificent with Steve aided and abetted by some damn fine ensemble playing by the rest of the band.

'Sleepers' is another number from the new album that really shines even more brightly in performance and it leads nicely to a solo spot for Nick Beggs, who demonstrates his exceptional skills on the Chapman "stick" bass, before he is re-joined by the rest of the band for the rampaging blues that is 'Still Waters', which really takes the breath away.

The band don't give themselves or their audience time to recover though, as the end of the show is heralded by 'Los Endos', which has replaced 'Clocks' as the band's finale. The supercharged, revamped version from *Genesis Revisited* has firmly established itself as the culmination of a Hackett gig and tonight the band really pull out all of the stops.

An encore is demanded and duly delivered, as Gary O'Toole's metronomic introduction leaves us in no doubt as to what is coming next – 'Clocks' and all its Hammer Horror glory leaves both audience and band breathless, but cheering for more is always a sign of a great night, which this show was.

PACIFIC ROAD ARTS CENTRE, BIRKENHEAD, ENGLAND, 27 NOVEMBER 2010

Set List: Valley of the Kings/Every Day/Emerald & Ash/The Golden Age of Steam/Watcher of the Skies/Carpet Crawlers/Fire on the Moon/Ace of Wands/Shadow of the Hierophant/Sierra Quemada/The Darkness in Men's Hearts/Acoustic Set/Blood on the Rooftops/Tubehead/Sleepers/Still Waters/Prairie Angel/Los Endos/Firth of Fifth/Clocks//
Source: Audience DVD Recording.

Another excellent recording, and unusually sourced from a complete film of the gig. 'Mechanical Bride' has now bitten the dust as the show opener and has been replaced by the much more appropriate 'Valley of the Kings', which gets the show off to a thunderous start. New boy Nick Beggs, resplendent in Child Catcher costume, drives the track along with some impeccable bass lines, while Steve delivers a blistering solo worthy of Ben Hur!

'Every Day' gets a knowing cheer from the crowd, and we are served up a piping hot version tonight. The addition of Amanda Lehmann and Nick to the band really comes out here with some superb harmony vocals and giving yours truly even more memories! 'Emerald & Ash' has already gained stage favourite status by now and here Steve, accompanied by Nick Beggs on Chapman "Stick", really go to town. Rob Townsend's mournful saxophone adds an element of bathos and once again Amanda's harmonies all add to a truly remarkable effort.

Steve's *Darktown* album is sadly underrepresented in terms of live performance and so 'The Golden Age of Steam' is a welcome surprise tonight. Roger King's locomotive keyboards and Gary O'Toole's military tattoo percussion managed to convey two of the central ideas of the piece whilst the lyrics delivered herein almost narrative style bring the child spy subject vividly to life in a magnificent performance.

Over the last few years Steve has gradually rehabilitated his Genesis past and tonight that rehabilitation took another step with a truly awesome 'Watcher of the Skies', in which Mr Roger King delivers one of Tony Banks's finest solos without even turning a hair, ably accompanied by some phenomenal bass playing from Nick Beggs and superlative drumming and vocals from Gary O'Toole. 'Carpet Crawlers' gets underway after some banter and Steve gets what he asks for as the Scouse choir carry this one along. Once again, Gary O'Toole puts in a fantastic performance whilst Steve's performance is guaranteed to send shivers up and down the spine. He is simply superb tonight.

The guitar howl of 'Fire on the Moon' brings us back to the new album quite emphatically. A firm favourite from its first outing in Italy back in 2009, the song has grown immeasurably in stature since then. Steve and Amanda intertwine their vocals and Nick Beggs joins in for the almost primal scream chorus. This is deeply personal and emotive song that gains enormously in the live context.

Back to where it all began for Steve next with a remarkable pairing of 'Ace of Wands' and 'Shadow of the Hierophant'. The former is all sound and fury, driven along by some wonderfully meaty bass lines from Nick and Steve looks to be in his element here. Roger, hunched over his keyboards, delivers the goods and even Rob Townsend's penny whistle gets in on the act! The latter had been a staple of Steve's earlier tours but hadn't seen the light of day for many years. Here it is restored to its rightful position within the set and adorned by a simply divine vocal performance from Amanda Lehmann, which takes the breath away.

'Sierra Quemada' lives up to its name (the 'Scorched Earth') next after Gary O'Toole sets up a delightful drum pattern. Sadly Steve's guitar has evidently gone severely wrong here and it sounds like someone with a sore throat. The gremlin is evicted before the end though, and the latter part of the track is delivered in truly awe inspiring fashion. New boy Nick Beggs gets his moment to shine next with a wonderfully jazzy solo piece from his *Stick Insect* album, entitled *The Darkness in Men's Hearts*, which showcases his complete command of fiendishly difficult to play Chapman "Stick" bass.

After a short interval, Steve and the band return to continue the show with some acoustic guitar, and as usual Steve romps through some snippets from his own and other people's repertoire, including Mason Williams' 'Classical Gas', although there is no 'Horizons' tonight. 'Blood on the Rooftops' more than makes up for it though with a truly wonderful version, in which Gary O'Toole delivers this underrated Genesis classic to perfection.

From the sublime to the outrageous next as Nick Beggs announces that Steve is about to perform a "death defying stunt with a bow" and invites the audience to take a few steps back for fear of being damaged. He is not exaggerating, as Steve lays into his Gold Top copy with a violin bow à la Jimmy Page before Gary and Nick get down and dirty with some ear splitting playing, and Steve himself lays down some damn fine rock licks!

An almost soporific 'Sleepers' calms things down with Roger laying down some particularly fine jazz chords and Steve and Amanda harmonise in fine style. Beggs' stick augments the performance whilst Townsend's tin whistle adds an edginess to an otherwise mellow performance. Always a frustrated blues player, Steve gets back to the blues next with a stonking version of 'Still Waters', which is Chicago style blues at its politically incorrect best. The smile on Steve's face gives the game away here. He's in his element. Amanda's harmony vocals add enormously to the song but when Hackett cuts loose with some really fiery riffs, I for one begin to wish that he would do a dedicated blues show if this is anything to go by.

Even now Steve likes to road test new stuff and so, the as yet unrecorded 'Prairie Angel' soars over the Pacific Road Arts Centre tonight, featuring a blistering guitar solo accompanied by the rest of the band, proving that Steve can still come up with musical landscapes like no other. The rest of the band also get down with some mean and moody licks with Townsend and O'Toole in particular duelling away throughout the track, which eventually segues into the now familiar Hackett version of 'Los Endos' and yet more excuses (if any were needed) for the band to get their licks out. The crowd love it and the band themselves are evidently having a real blast tonight.

Encores aren't long incoming and we get a superlative pairing tonight, as Roger King tickles the ivories for an amazing 'Firth of Fifth'. He doesn't put a foot wrong as he plays the piano introduction before he is joined by the rest of the band. Once again, O'Toole plays a blinder here with musical and vocal excellence on display throughout. Of course, it is Steve's solo that simply rips the hair off the back of your neck as you listen to it in a glorious performance.

We are saying goodbye to an old friend tonight as the metronomic percussion heralds the arrival of 'Clocks', which is soon to be dropped from the set into honourable retirement. There is still life in the old dog tonight though, as Steve and the band rip through a truly frightening version worthy of the Hammer Horror films that were the inspiration for the track.

PART THREE: STEVE HACKETT

CHAPTER THIRTY-FIVE
"MAKING TRACKS AROUND THE WORLD" 2011-2012

With the legal disputes firmly behind him by the end of 2009, Steve has since then entered an even more fruitful period of writing and performing.

The *Around the World in Eighty Trains* tour concluded in the autumn of 2011 and no sooner had it done so than the *Breaking Waves* tour started in the UK. With another brand new album – *Beyond the Shrouded Horizon* – having been released on 26 September 2011, Steve was evidently keen to get out and promote it and the resulting shows thus far are evidence that Steve's purple patch has shown no signs of dissipating just yet.

Steve's rehabilitation of his days with Genesis has continued with an increasing number of Genesis classics making their way into the set, including 'Watcher of the Skies' and 'Firth of Fifth', not to mention the magnificent 'Blood on the Rooftops', which has retained its place in the set after its introduction back in 2004. Oldies merge with new material seamlessly in Hackett shows and the existing recordings demonstrate the sheer exhilaration and enjoyment that is a Steve Hackett show.

With Steve having released the Squackett album with Chris Squire and more recently completed Genesis Revisited II his first album to gain a chart placing in the UK for many years, and for which he is (at time of writing this) about to undertake an extensive tour, one thing is certain, expect many more musical voyages from this particular acolyte!

FLORAL PAVILION, NEW BRIGHTON, ENGLAND, 20 FEBRUARY 2012
Set List: Loch Lomond/The Phoenix Flown/Prairie Angel/A Place Called Freedom/The Golden Age of Steam/Fire on the Moon/Every Day/Waking to Life/Carpet Crawlers/Firth of Fifth/Serpentine Song/Shadow of the Hierophant/Till These Eyes/Enter the Night/Walking Away From Rainbows/Blood on the Rooftops/Fly on a Windshield/Broadway Melody of 1974/Sleepers/Los Endos/Watcher of the Skies/Spectral Mornings//
Source: Audience DVD Recording.

This one is a marvellous treat, with an excellent recording on DVD no less, and on my birthday too! With another new album to promote, the audience are treated to a healthy dose of new stuff with the opening quartet of 'Loch Lomond', 'The Phoenix Flown', 'Prairie Angel', and 'A Place Called Freedom'. The latter two are a particularly magnificent examples of Steve's lyrical and musical storytelling. Mind you, he and the band conjure up more than misty Scottish lakes with 'Loch Lomond' too – stirring stuff!

'The Golden Age of Steam' has retained its place in the set and quite rightly too. This latter-day tale of child espionage and betrayal is driven along by a tattoo-like rhythm from Gary O'Toole and a suitably locomotive-like keyboard from Roger King. In fact, it sounds more like 'Murder on the Orient Express' to me, but just as much fun! 'Fire on the Moon' – one of the more raw and emotional tracks from 2009's *Out of the Tunnel's Mouth* – comes next. A 'Musical Box' intro and spoken lyrics give way to a raw and deeply primal scream therapy session for Steve and the band.

'Every Day' is prefaced by a little bit of audience banter (can't think who from!), but the song itself rattles along at a fair old pace and it is still a delight to hear the old warhorse in such fine form – and Steve wasn't too bad either! Here Amanda Lehmann's vocals add enormously to the harmonies between Steve, her, and Gary O'Toole. Speaking of Amanda, she really comes into her own on 'Waking to Life'; an oriental style song with tables and a sitar guitar accompaniment over which she lays down a superb vocal reminiscent to these ears of vintage Stevie Nicks.

As I have mentioned before, Steve has started to rehabilitate his career with Genesis and "that beat combo I used to be a member of …" 'Carpet Crawlers' opens with a rippling keyboard intro from Roger who has definitely given these older songs a new lease of life. Gary O'Toole's vocal is simply marvellous as well and Steve's solo still sends shivers down the spine. Whilst on the subject of shivers, well what else do you do when the introduction to 'Firth of Fifth' starts? Roger King even manages to pull off something Tony Banks had long since given up and delivers the piano intro faultlessly – bravo, Roger! Once again, Gary O'Toole manages the vocals superbly well whilst maintaining a rock solid rhythm. By the time we get to Steve's solo the audience (yours truly included) have been transported to another place – astonishing, really.

'Serpentine Song', that delightful homage to the London landscape that Steve grew up in and to his artist father, is another delightfully understated performance replete with gorgeous harmony vocals and between Steve, Gary, and Amanda. Rob Townsend's penny whistle adds an element of nostalgia without descending into sentimentality. As if the rehabilitation of his Genesis past wasn't enough, Steve has gone right back to where it all began with a truly glorious version of 'Shadow of the Hierophant', and cue Amanda Lehmann putting on one of the genuine highlights of the evening with a magnificent vocal.

We are brought kicking and screaming back to the new stuff next with 'Till These Eyes', a song that Steve and Amanda give an almost country feel to. Steve's vocals aren't the greatest here, not surprising as he was full of cold at the time, but Amanda puts in another great performance. 'Enter the Night', as most Hackett fans will know, has been through many changes and facelifts over the years. I always said that it should be a song and at last Steve has given the tune lyrics. A celebratory anthem of a track, Steve's guitar does most of the talking here in a stunning performance.

No Hackett show is complete without an acoustic moment and here we have "agnostic guitar" in excelsis with a breath taking performance of 'Walking Away From Rainbows', featuring Steve and Roger King in a performance that no one who was at this gig will ever forget, I am sure. The typical galloping acoustic figure next leading into snippets from 'Classical Gas' and 'The Pool of Memory, the Pool of Forgetfulness' from *Metamorpheus* morph (pun intended) into another remarkable performance, this time of 'Blood on the Rooftops'. Here it is Gary O'Toole who is the star, giving a truly impeccable vocal delivery.

From acoustic excellence to progressive magnificence next with 'Fly on a Windshield' and those Ben Hur rhythms, as Steve and the rest of the galley slaves pull for their lives. Here we can begin to truly appreciate exactly what Genesis lost when Steve left and this rips the hair off the back of your neck as Steve lets rip with some outrageously fiery playing, which leads into 'Broadway Melody of 1974' in which once again Gary O'Toole shines on vocals.

'Sleepers' takes us into the world of jazz for a brief interlude, a brittle, pungent piece in which Steve gives a sedate and restrained vocal augmented by some impeccably understated playing from Roger, Gary, and Rob. Back to the madhouse next though, as we get Steve's deranged version of 'Los Endos' an extended instrumental romp in which the entire band and especially the rhythm section of Gary O'Toole and Lee Pomeroy have a damn fine attempt at tearing the roof down, and indeed, this one brings the show proper to a suitably outrageous close.

Encores aren't long in coming and as the band return to the stage, it is Roger King who takes the lead with the sepulchral keyboard introduction to 'Watcher of the Skies', which gets a deserved cheer from the crowd. Driven along by Roger and the magnificent rhythms of Gary and Lee, the entire band appears to be in their element here and Steve has seldom sounded better. The band then take their well-deserved bows before some wag shouts out for 'Invisible Touch' and Steve obliges him with a few bars! 'Spectral Mornings' takes on special significance here, as Steve dedicates it to the author – nuff said as another magical night with Mr Hackett comes to an end.

VIPER THEATRE, FLORENCE, ITALY, 18 APRIL 2012

Set List: Loch Lomond/The Phoenix Flown/Prairie Angel/A Place Called Freedom/The Golden Age of Steam/Fire on the Moon/Every Day/Waking to Life/Carpet Crawlers/Firth of Fifth/Serpentine Song/Shadow of the Hierophant/Till These Eyes/Enter the Night/Blood on the Rooftops/Fly on a Windshield/Broadway Melody of 1974/Sleepers/Watcher of the Skies/Myopia Medley-Los Endos/Spectral Mornings//
Source: Audience Recording.

This is another "Italian Job" for Steve and the band. The annual visit to Italy took them to Florence recently for another gig on the *Breaking Waves* tour. Here we have another audience recording with a very flat and extremely bassy sound to it. Mind you, as the band launch into 'Loch Lomond', the bassiness adds something. Unusually for an Italian crowd, they are remarkably quiet here and the band gets on with the business of delivering the opening quartet of tracks in emphatic fashion. Steve sounds as if he means business during 'The Phoenix Flown'. His guitar playing is fiery and furious throughout whilst Lee Pomeroy's bass and Gary O'Toole's drumming are equally potent. Prairie Angel had already made its live debut last year but now expanded to encompass 'A Place Called Freedom', this one takes on a life of its own. Tonight the band pull out all the stops and the harmony vocals are beautiful and Steve's arpeggiated guitar reminds the listener of the keyboard figure of 'Carpet Crawlers' no less, but more of that later, folks!

'Fire on the Moon' became an instant stage favourite back in 2009 and time hasn't lessened its impact. Steve's plaintive but highly emotional spoken word intro gives way to a primal scream of anguish as the song lets rip with some raw emotion. Strangely enough on this recording Steve's introduction to 'Every Day' is followed by 'The Golden Age of Steam' … curious, but this has been an aspect on several other recordings available from this tour. Either way, a rollicking version of the latter is given here. Gary's percussion and Lee's bass in particular emulate the motion of a train whilst Rob Townsend's sax conjures up images of the Orient Express – lovely stuff!

'Every Day' comes next and a workmanlike performance is given here, although the harmonies are much better than in days of old. 'Waking to Life' is Amanda Lehmann's chance to shine and she grabs it with both hands tonight. An amazing vocal accompanied by some eastern-styled tabla percussion and a sitar effect laden guitar from Steve gives this a wonderfully atmospheric feel.

Being in Italy it was always a given that Steve would serve up some classics from the "beat combo" but as has been previously remarked, his choices this time round are inspired with 'Carpet Crawlers' leading the pack. Gary O'Toole once again puts in a marvellous vocal whilst Steve's guitar gently weeps behind him with some suitably ethereal playing. Whilst on the subject of things ethereal, Roger King's piano intro to 'Firth of Fifth' gets a cheer from the crowd and once again he nails the performance to perfection. By the time we get to Steve's own solo some six minutes later, the crowd are in ecstasy and no wonder – Steve puts in yet another truly remarkable effort here.

'Serpentine Song', that delightful homage to Steve's father comes next. This is a truly beautiful song given a thoughtful treatment tonight, with Gary delivering a particularly impressive vocal. 'Shadow of the Hierophant' takes us back to where it began for Steve and once again the star of the performance is Amanda Lehmann whose vocals are simply delightful. This is an ensemble classic tonight and a feast for the ears.

A pairing of two new tracks comes next, with 'Till These Eyes'. Steve's take on the Dorian Gray story gets a respectful treatment whilst 'Enter the Night', which we have known by a plethora of other titles, rocks the joint tonight with a bass heavy arrangement, over which Steve's guitar soars like an eagle and Amanda puts in her very best Stevie Nicks impression on vocals.

Some acoustic guitar follows next as Steve launches into 'Blood on the Rooftops'. This underrated Genesis classic simply gets better with age and here we have a truly delightful version. Steve's delicate glass-like guitar is joined by a haunting vocal from Gary and even Rob's jazzy sax generates an eerie atmosphere in a brilliant performance. Full speed ahead next with 'Fly on a Windshield' and 'Broadway Melody of 1974', and if proof were ever needed of exactly what it was that Genesis lost when Steve left, then here it is. A banshee-like wail is emitted from Steve's guitar whilst the rest of the band put in the galley slave-like rhythm, driven along by exceptional bass and drum playing from Gary and Lee.

'Sleepers' calms things down a little with its frost-like keyboards and haunted house vibe. It's a dreamscape in music as only Mr Hackett can pen them! Speaking of haunting, Roger's sepulchral intro to 'Watcher of the Skies' must have raised the hairs on the back of each and every member of the audience's necks, as it is simply perfect. Gary joins in with a Morse Code rhythm before the spaceship truly takes off with rest of the band in fine form. The Myopia medley first heard back in 1993 still kicks arse as Steve and his rhythm section cut loose with some ferocious playing, leading into an equally uptempo 'Los Endos' before the evening is brought to its close by what else? 'Spectral Mornings', of course. This is Steve's anthem and here it's a celebration of yet another magnificent night's entertainment.

CHAPTER THIRTY-SIX
"REVISITING OLD FRIENDS & SMOKING HOGWEED"
2013 -14

Steve had already taken his fans by surprise in many ways throughout the 1980's and 1990's but few were ready for the release in September 1997 of the first Genesis Revisited album for which he subsequently undertook a short series of gigs in Japan which were filmed and sound recorded and issued under the title of *The Tokyo Tapes*.

Having scratched that particular itch it was perhaps even more surprising when word leaked out in the latter part of 2012 that Steve was revisiting (pun intended) his Genesis past yet again. Who would have thought it? Upon its release on 22 October 2012, *Genesis Revisited II* not only proved the ongoing popularity of Genesis' music but also gave Steve a chart entry when the album reached the number-twenty four spot in the UK! Steve's highest UK chart position since 1983! A truly remarkable cast of musicians feature on the album including many names you would not necessarily associate with Progressive music such as Nik Kershaw and Phil Collins' son Simon alongside progressive alumni such as Steve Rothery and John Wetton.

As you may expect, an extensive bout of touring has been undertaken in support of this album with shows across the world wowing audiences as Steve revisits his old band's classic music. Many of the shows performed thus far have been recorded and a selection (pun intended) of these is examined here.

The tour, now re-titled as "Genesis Extended" continued well into 2014 and with several set changes, including 'Lilywhite Lilith', 'Squonk' and 'The Knife'. The resulting tour saw Steve and his band take the magic of the classic Genesis era material around the world for shows that were universally applauded for their musical and visual excellence. Such was the success of the tour, that it was eventually extended to cover even more territories and a change in personnel as Nick Beggs replaced Lee Pomeroy on bass, the tour was still in progress as this book went to print but even so, I have managed to include a couple of recordings from this leg of the tour here in order to give a flavour of what fans heard.

Nad Sylvan, Steve and Roger King relaxing pre-tour.

CRUISE TO THE EDGE, FORT LAUDERDALE, FLORIDA, USA, 25 MARCH 2013
Set List: Watcher of the Skies/Dancing with the Moonlit Knight/Fly on a Windshield/Broadway Melody of 1974/Cuckoo Cocoon/Chamber of 32 Doors/I Know What I Like/Musical Box/Supper's Ready//
Source: Audience Recording.

A novel idea: get a bunch of musicians together on a cruise ship to present performances. Well, that was the premise behind the *Cruise to the Edge* series of shows, which apart from Steve also featured Yes and many other rock alumni.

The recording featured here is the very first gig of the *Genesis Revisited II* tour and in keeping with the idea behind the cruise ethos it is a slightly truncated performance from what would become the show proper once Steve and the band made it back to dry land!

As you might expect with a first night, there are a few mistakes as the band open the show with 'Watcher of the Skies'. New vocalist Nad Sylvan does a creditable job of sounding like Gabriel here, but the real stars of the show are Messrs King, Pomeroy, and Hackett, who manage to breathe even more life into this classic.

Steve acknowledges the fact that this gig is the first of the tour and apologises for any lapses of memory that may occur before introducing 'Dancing with the Moonlit Knight'. Once again, the rhythm section of Gary O'Toole and Lee Pomeroy really get their teeth into this one whilst Steve's guitar does the talking with a virtuoso performance.

The Lamb Lies Down on Broadway is represented next as the ethereal chords of Roger King's keyboards usher in 'Fly on a Windshield'. Gary O'Toole puts in a creditable vocal on 'Broadway Melody of 1974', but even he is overwhelmed somewhat by the galley slave rhythm section of which he is a part, ironically enough! it is only a pity that the recording is a somewhat flat audience one because from the aural evidence, Steve really let rip here. The *Lamb* is the best represented album on this show with respectful versions of 'Cuckoo Cocoon' and 'The Chamber of 32 Doors', which follow along nicely, although I couldn't help expecting the incessant rhythms of the intro to either 'In the Cage' or 'Back in NYC' to appear before the latter, but instead Steve takes the opportunity to introduce the band, which spoils the flow somewhat. No matter, 'The Chamber of 32 Doors' gives the entire band a chance to flex their collective muscles and once again new boy Nad Sylvan gives a creditable performance.

We then move slightly further westward, agriculturally speaking (sorry I really must do something about that!), as the lawnmower heralds the arrival of 'I Know What I Like', which to these ears sounds as if there are still a few kinks to be ironed out of it but hey, it is the first gig! The new intro to 'Musical Box' comes next, leading into the familiar strains of Steve's guitar. Always a delight to hear, this performance is no exception and the entire band gets to grips with it in fine fashion.

With a shorter set time for these initial shows, the show comes to a suitably dramatic conclusion with 'Supper's Ready' – cue audience going ever so slightly nuts. I have lost count how many times I have heard this either on record or live but it still manages to send shivers up and down my spine. For once an American audience has learned how to behave and you can hear a pin drop during the performance, which as you would expect is a fitting ending to what was obviously an extremely enjoyable gig all round.

TEATRO DELLA LUNA, MILAN, ITALY, 23 APRIL 2013
Set List: Watcher of the Skies/Chamber of 32 Doors/Dancing with the Moonlit Knight/Fly on a Windshield/Broadway Melody of 1974/Carpet Crawlers (with Ray Wilson)/Firth of Fifth/Blood on the Rooftops/Unquiet Slumbers for the Sleepers/In That Quiet Earth/Afterglow/I Know What I Like/Dance on a Volcano/Entangled/Musical Box/Supper's Ready/Eleventh Earl of Mar/Los Endos//
Source: Audience Recording.

Moving on a few weeks from the previous recording, we have this one from the band's show in Milan.

'Watcher of the Skies' kicks things off with Roger King's majestic keyboards heralding the arrival of the band onstage. It isn't long before the rest of the band get their teeth stuck into this classic slice of Genesis, with new vocalist Nad Sylvan putting in another creditable performance and Steve himself is evidently in his element here.

With such a rich legacy of music to choose from, Steve and the band really are spoiled for choice and the audience too are treated to classic after classic, as the *Lamb* album gets a healthy serving, including excellent versions of 'Chamber of 32 Doors', which is preceded by Steve's dedication of the gig to Richie Havens who had died the day before. As if extra impetus was needed, the version of 'Chamber' that we get here is particularly fiery with Steve's guitar soaring like a soul in flight, and once again Sylvan's vocals sound incredibly similar to Gabriel's.

'Dancing with the Moonlit Knight' is greeted with applause from the partisan crowd and is a particularly fine version. Once again, kudos to Mr King whose performance on keyboards is one to cherish. Steve's guitar shimmers like sunlight on water – superb stuff! The ethereal keyboard and guitar intro to 'Fly on a Windshield' really need no introduction, so Steve doesn't bother. Here we have Gary O'Toole's dulcet tones on vocals in addition to his sterling work on percussion, which really drives this one along, while Steve puts in an incredible performance on guitar, which continues as the band tackle 'Broadway Melody of 1974' barely pausing for breath as they go.

'Carpet Crawlers' sees the arrival on stage of Ray Wilson, announced by Steve, which certainly brought back some happy memories of his time with Genesis for me. His vocal delivery here is impeccable and you can hear a pin drop as the crowd listen in respectful silence. Another classic next as once again Mr King doesn't put a foot wrong with the keyboard intro to 'Firth of Fifth' before the rest of the band jump in to deliver a truly amazing version.

An acoustic moment follows next as 'Blood on the Rooftops', perhaps the most underrated Genesis track ever, takes centre stage and it is a joy to behold. Steve's intro is as stately as a galleon moored on a calm sea, while Gary O'Toole once again gives a spine-tingling vocal augmented by some tasteful sax work from Rob Townsend.

The rest of the recording is taken up by what is probably the best Genesis set list ever put together for a live gig. Many so-called "purist" fans have snubbed both the *Genesis Revisited II* album and these shows but to those people I really do have to say that you are missing the point and cutting your own noses off to spite your faces. Here you have an answer to the vexed question of what it might have been like if Steve had been with Genesis in 2007, and in all honesty I have to say that recordings such as this simply emphasise what a mistake the band made by not enlisting Steve on their final tour.

ROYAL ALBERT HALL, LONDON, ENGLAND, 24 OCTOBER 2013

Set List: Dance on a Volcano/Dancing with the Moonlit Knight/Fly on a Windshield/Broadway Melody of 1974/Carpet Crawlers/The Return of the Giant Hogweed/Musical Box/Horizons/Unquiet Slumbers for the Sleepers/In That Quiet Earth/Afterglow/I Know What I Like/Firth of Fifth/Ripples/The Fountain of Salmacis/Supper's Ready/Watcher of the Skies/Los Endos//
Source: Audience Recording.

Steve's profile is higher now than it has been for many years and so a show at such a prestigious venue as this one comes as no surprise.

Several set changes had manifested themselves during the autumn leg of this tour and there were a couple more during the course of this star-studded performance.

First of these was the opening salvo, which tonight lived up to that with 'Dance on a Volcano' getting things off to a suitably frenetic start. Immediately the notoriously bad acoustics for which this venue is (in)famous are apparent, but that doesn't seem to spoil things for either Steve, the band, or the audience, who lap this one up. 'Dancing with the Moonlit Knight' and the remarkable triptych from the *Lamb*, comprising 'Fly on a Windshield', 'Broadway Melody of 1974', and 'Carpet Crawlers' showcase the growing confidence of Genesis as a band, and tonight's performances are delightful with the first of tonight's special guests, Ray Wilson putting in an excellent vocal delivery on the latter.

Another change to the earlier set comes next as 'The Return of the Giant Hogweed' – complete with another guest in the shape of Roine Stolt – rampages on to the stage. It's sod of a track to play apparently, but there are no such problems tonight, as the entire band, in particular the rhythm section of Gary O'Toole and Lee Pomeroy, make this one a winner. This is followed by 'Musical Box'; another classic that never fails to send shivers up and down my spine, but sadly the acoustics of the building let this one down, resulting in a particularly flat-sounding performance, which is a pity.

A spot of "agnostic" guitar next as Steve dons his acoustic guitar and leads us through 'Horizons' before the truly awesome triptych of tracks from *Wind & Wuthering*: 'Unquiet Slumbers for the Sleepers', 'In That Quiet Earth', and the magnificent 'Afterglow' are brought vividly to life buy some impeccable ensemble playing and a fine vocal performance from Nad Sylvan.

More special guests follow, as John Wetton is announced on stage and thankfully he doesn't manage to make a hash of 'Firth of Fifth' as he had done with 'Afterglow' during his previous appearance on stage with Steve at Hammersmith in May. The real stars of this one though are Steve himself and keyboards man Roger King, both of whom duel away incredibly throughout.

Amanda Lehmann makes a welcome return to the Hackett band fold for a delightful rendering of 'Ripples' in which she manages to bring a unique take to the performance and manages to make the song all her own – no mean feat!

From the passage of time and the coming of old age to the tale of a horny Greek Goddess next (well, this *is* Genesis's music after all!) and 'Fountain of Salmacis' takes us back to the days of patchouli oil, flares, and hair in abundance for what sounds like an impressive performance, or it would be if it weren't for the mediocre sound quality of this recording.

'Supper's Ready' is greeted with a massive cheer from the crowd and deservedly so. I can't think of any other song in the Progressive rock oeuvre that comes close to this one for sheer scale and magnificence and in such surroundings as the Albert Hall it must have taken on a truly awesome aspect. Sadly, once again the quality of this recording doesn't really match the spectacle but we can't have everything, can we?

Bows taken, the band aren't long in returning to the stage for the encores and Roger King kicks things off with the spine-tingling intro to 'Watcher of the Skies' and another magnificent slice of Genesis is served up piping hot for the audience's delectation before Steve's re-jigged (not to say revved up) version of 'Los Endos', bringing the evening to a suitably energetic close.

SCOTTISH RITE AUDITORIUM, COLLINGSWOOD, NEW JERSEY, USA, 27 MARCH 2014

Set List: Dance On A Volcano/Dancing With The Moonlit Knight*/Squonk/Fly On A Windshield/The Lamia/The Return Of The Giant Hogweed/The Musical Box/I Know What I Like/Horizons/Firth Of Fifth/Lilywhite Lilith/The Knife/The Fountain Of Salmacis/Supper's Ready */Watcher Of The Skies/Los Endos//
Source: Audience Recording.
* With Francis Dunnery on vocals.

One of the first recordings to appear from the 2014 tour is captured here in what is definitely an above average sounding audience recording. .

'Dance On a Volcano' gets us off to the usual fiery start and the band are evidently in fine form here. Steve's riffs are certainly hot enough to melt the seats in the theatre while Nick Beggs and Gary O'Toole do an equally impressive job in the rhythm department! 'Dancing with the Moonlit Knight' follows and here we have the first appearance of tonight's special guest: Francis Dunnery, cue audience going ever so slightly nuts. He sounds surprisingly like Mr Gabriel here and the entire performance is an extremely enjoyable one.

With the set being "revisited" there are a few changes from last year's outing and the first of these, 'Squonk', roars out from the stage next. Here once again, it is the rhythm section of Beggs and O'Toole, which bring this classic slice of rock 'n' roll Genesis to life. Nad Sylvan, who has done such an admirable job on most of the tracks sounds ever so slightly out of his depth on this one - opening night nerves perhaps?

Gary O'Toole gets his chance to shine vocally next with a sublime version of 'Fly On A Windshield' guaranteed to send shivers up and down all but the most hardened of spines! Here Steve really lets rip with some amazing playing while, the slaves in the galley (Messrs Beggs and O'Toole) keep this musical ship on an even keel. Nad returns to centre stage for 'The Lamia' accompanied impeccably by the keyboard work of Roger King for this underrated slice from The Lamb...

From the sublime to the... well, 'The Return Of The Giant Hogweed' really needs no introduction., does it?! Here the entire band grab this story of a rampaging garden plant by the scruff of the neck and take the audience along for the adventure - taking prisoners and surrendering are evidently not options tonight! Another slice of 1971 vintage comes next as the sound of a musical box heralds... what else but 'The Musical Box'. Here Nad Sylvan finally gets his mojo back and his delivery here is flawless to these ears while Steve is evidently having great fun shading the picture with some magnificent guitar playing.

The drone of Roger King's keyboards ushers in the arrival of the "cosmic lawnmower" and 'I Know What I Like' and a truly ensemble performance from everybody - audience included! Always a great stage number it is evident that Steve's slightly irreverent treatment of this one still goes down a treat and it is followed by some agnostic guitar as Steve treats the audience to snippets from a couple of tracks before 'Horizons' makes its well deserved entrance on to the stage . A slightly tentative performance here though as you might expect on opening night.

'Firth Of Fifth' gets under way with Roger King's superb keyboard playing - the man just impresses me more each time I hear him play this one but he is not the only one putting in a top notch performance tonight as Gary, Nad, Nick and Steve too all deliver 100% throughout with Steve's guitar wailing like a soul in torment at times, accompanied by Rob Townsend's equally soulful sax.

Another "new" track next: 'Lilywhite Lilith', and another enjoyable romp through this classic Lamb track. I have to admit though that going straight into it makes the end result sound a bit disjointed but there's no denying the sheer scale and power of the performance on show here, especially Nick Beggs' dirty bass sound! A minor quibble if I may, placing 'The Knife' at this point in the show really does spoilt the flow of the evening somewhat. Don't get me wrong, the performance here is another truly excellent one but 'The Knife' is really a bona fide set closer or final encore and it loses some of that magic here I think.

'The Fountain Of Salmacis' redresses the balance somewhat. Roger and Steve perform an exquisite ballet on their respective instruments while once again, Nick Beggs underpins the performance with some tasty bass lines before we reach the beating heart of these shows: 'Supper's Ready' where once again Francis Dunnery takes centre stage. I think this one has already had enough superlatives hurled at it but just one will suffice here - majestic!

The show is brought to a dramatic close by the encores: 'Watcher Of The Skies' has seldom sounded as impressive as it does in the hands of these musicians and tonight is no exception. Roger King has this one nailed to perfection whilst the entire band lets rip on the extended and jazzed up 'Los Endos' finally bringing what sounds like another excellent evening's entertainment to a close.

PUL XL (MARKANT), UDEN, NETHERLANDS, 17 May 2014

Set List: Dance On A Volcano/Dancing with the Moonlit Knight/Fly On A Windshield/Broadway Melody Of 1974/Squonk/The Return Of The Giant Hogweed/The Fountain Of Salmacis/The Musical Box/I Know What I Like/Horizons/Firth Of Fifth/Lilywhite Lilith/The Knife/Supper's Ready/Watcher Of The Skies/Los Endos//
Source: Audience Recording.

Moving a little further westward... we come to one of the recent crop of shows in Europe and what a little belter, the recording even has the intro music (from Metamorpheus no less!) before the band emerge on stage and unleash the raw power of 'Dance On A Volcano'. Even from the off, the band are evidently much more relaxed and confident with many shows under their belts leading up to this one and what you have here is a high octane performance from everyone. 'Dancing with the Moonlit Knight' is next and here Nad Sylvan's vocals sound a little bit strained not surprising given the demands he places on them daily performing this stuff - he is helped out by the crowd however who sing along remarkably in tune!

'Fly On A Windshield'/'Broadway Melody of 1974' serves as an apt demonstration of the sheer magic that the best of The Lamb... can generate. Once again Gary O'Toole takes vocal duties here and he does so exquisitely before proceeding to batter the living daylights out of his drum kit once more, aided and abetted in musical cruelty by Steve who wrings every last nuance of emotion from his guitar while once again Nick Beggs' bass threatens to lift the roof off!

'Squonk' evidently takes the audience by surprise, as there are cheers as this one starts. Rob Townsend is the surprise star of this one as his sax weaves its way between the battling rhythms of Messrs Beggs and O'Toole. Once again, Nad Sylvan sounds a little bit out of his depth on this one but he battles along gamely enough. 'The Return of The Giant Hogweed' redresses the balance in Nad's favour as he sounds much more at home performing this one. Roger King's keyboard and Steve's guitar eke out the story in truly magnificent fashion throughout.

A personal favourite next (as Steve introduces it). Roger King's sepulchral tones usher in 'The Fountain Of Salmacis' and here the combined talents of King, Beggs and O'Toole really bring this one musically to life with some truly remarkable playing.

'The Musical Box' too benefits enormously from the band being road fit and this is a much more confident reading than the previous show mentioned. Musically and vocally excellent throughout the entire band are obviously having a great time performing this one and Steve has seldom sounded better. 'I Know What I Like', featuring a spaced out intro which takes the audience a few seconds to recognise comes next. Once again, Steve has given this one his own unique take which some fans aren't too fond of but the audience tonight here seem to like it and they are in good voice throughout.

A few moments of acoustic guitar next as Steve rambles through an extended instrumental medley including extracts from 'Blood On The Rooftops', 'Bay Of Kings' and several others before 'Horizons' makes its appearance. 'Firth Of Fifth' follows and once again, it is Steve and keyboardist Roger King who take this one to new heights. I doubt if Tony Banks himself could play the intro better and that is saying something! The entire band are helped along by an enthusiastic crowd who are in fine voice once again.

Hearing 'Lilywhite Lilith' out on its own again merely serves to reinforce that this one should really have segued from another track. Once again, the performance is marvellous but its position here is somewhat jarring as is the next track: 'The Knife' which is once again a joyful romp but definitely in the wrong part of the set for my liking.

In fact, hearing 'Supper's Ready' again, after 'The Knife' merely reinforces my opinion that the former is in the wrong place but hey, you can't please everybody but the band come very close to it with tonight's performance of this, the real centrepiece of tonight's musical experience. Band and crowd are in unison here with a performance that grows in stature and magnificence throughout.

Anything after that might have been an anti climax but when you have the orchestral majesty of 'Watcher Of The Skies' still in your ammo locker then there are no such problems and once again the entire band serve this one up in truly impressive style leading to the finale: 'Los Endos' and Steve's tongue-in-cheek reworking of this classic brings another Genesis Extended evening to a close.

****

PART THREE: STEVE HACKETT

A Selection Of Shows: Genesis & Solo Live Guide 1976-2014

PART FOUR: PHIL COLLINS

PART FOUR: PHIL COLLINS

CHAPTER THIRTY-SEVEN
"BRAND LOYALTY WITH BRAND X" 1976-79

Phil's dissatisfaction with the situation within Genesis prior to Peter's decision to leave, led him to explore alternative musical avenues during the period between touring and recording. Initially these were in the form of a scratch band, Zox and the Radar Boys, which featured a revolving group of extremely talented musicians, including Bill Bruford who was soon to be such an important (if temporary) member of Genesis themselves.

As far as I am aware, there are no extant recordings from the handful of gigs that Zox and the Radar Boys performed, but we are more lucky when it comes to material from the band that grew out of their endeavours: Brand X. The first album by the band: *Unorthodox Behaviour* appeared on 18 June 1976 whilst Phil was otherwise occupied with the concluding shows of Genesis's highly successful *A Trick of the Tail* tour. Once that tour was over, however, Phil found time to flex his musical muscles with his "other band" and was to do so at varying intervals over the following few years when his duties with Genesis allowed.

Between 1976 and 1980 Brand X released a series of albums, not always featuring Phil, and they have continued to exist as a recording and gigging unit until the present day, although Phil's tenure with them had ended by 1982, which is where his solo touring story begins in earnest.

RONNIE SCOTT'S, LONDON, ENGLAND, 1 SEPTEMBER 1976
Set List: Unorthodox Behaviour/Malaga Virgen/Jam (AKA: Tito's Leg)//
Source: FM Radio broadcast.

Unusually for a musician of Phil's stature, this gig saw the fledgling Brand X as a support act for another artist, hence the somewhat truncated set list. However, what we do have here is an excellent FM broadcast made strangely enough for a radio station in Boston USA! No matter, after the DJ's introduction we are straight into the thick of things with the title track to the band's debut album, 'Unorthodox Behaviour'; a classic slice of the kind of fusion music that the band would soon become renowned for. If Phil was frustrated by the strictures of working in Genesis, then there are no such problems in evidence here, and the entire band seems perversely at home in the freeform extemporised style that this track represents.

'Malaga Virgen' comes next and is another delightful slice of fusion jazz. Some tasty percussion form Phil is overlaid by some wonderfully racy bass lines interwoven by some staccato keyboards and fluid guitar work, which elicits some polite applause from the cognoscenti in the audience. This sadly short recording is brought to an end by an extended jam opened by some incredibly funky effects laden guitar before the rest of the band take their cue and join in with what was evidently a heap of collective glee.

This stuff might not be everyone's cup of tea, and I do wonder what Genesis fans thought of it at the time, but as an example of just how varied Phil's musical tastes were even at this stage of his career, then this recording is a delight.

THE ROXY, WEST HOLLYWOOD, CALIFORNIA, USA, 22 SEPTEMBER 1979
Set List: Fanfare/Disco Suicide/Algon/Don't Make Waves/ Dance of the Illegal Aliens//Malaga Virgen/And So to F/Access to Data/ Nuclear Burn//
Source: Audience Recording.

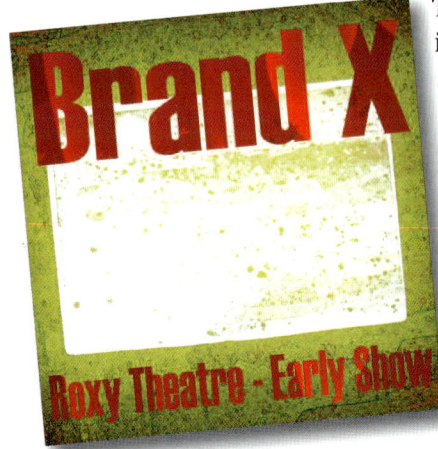

Three years on and a slightly bigger room sees Brand X in full swing (pun intended) at the scene of several of Genesis' earlier triumphs. A hilarious send-up of the movies gets the show under way and the opening track, 'Disco Suicide' sets the tone for tonight. This atmospheric track is driven along by Phil's drumming and some tasty guitar and bass from John Goodsall and Percy Jones.

'Algon' (I won't bother with its full title here) is next with a racy guitar riff set against some impeccable percussion from Phil and more driving bass lines from Jones. The audience are evidently enjoying themselves, but in a remarkably restrained way for an American audience, so the performance is not marred by too much by crowd noise.

Phil acknowledges the crowd in his best Maurice Chevalier voice sending up the crowd who couldn't get tickets for Abba! 'Don't Make Waves' stretches the band even further with some hard rocking guitar work and once again Phil sets to work giving his drum kit some serious abuse. A hilarious joke about car number plates (once you hear it, it will make sense, believe me!) leads into the wonderfully funky 'Dance of the Illegal Aliens' where Jones' bass and Peter Robinson's keyboards drive things along quite nicely whilst Phil's percussion underpins everything. In fact, if you listen carefully, you will hear the origins of one of Phil's later solo tracks in the keyboard refrain.

More hilarity from the band next before 'Malaga Virgen' erupts from the traps like a nightmare unleashed. A veritable virtuoso performance from the entire band here is given some deserved appreciation by the crowd but without doubt it is Jones' frantic bass lines that take the kudos on this one. 'And So to F' concludes the show proper with much on stage banter and what were obviously sight gags before the track itself gets underway. This is without doubt one of the band's best compositions and tonight the audience were treated to an astonishing performance.

The encores open with some wonderfully dirty bass playing from Jones leading into a cacophonous finale from the entire band. Band intros are next, leading into the appropriately titled 'Nuclear Burn'; a real fusion (geddit) number worthy of any late night jazz establishment and the combined extended bass and keyboard workout make this a truly delightful version.

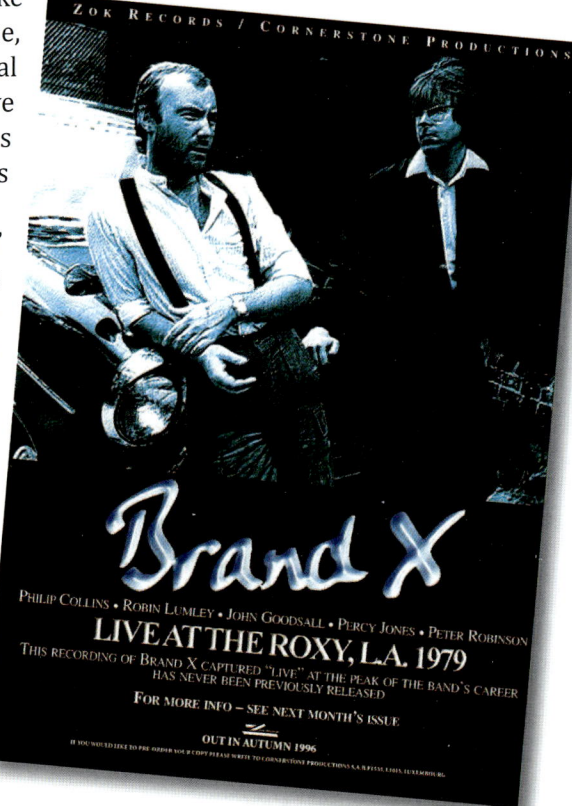

PART FOUR: PHIL COLLINS

CHAPTER THIRTY-EIGHT
"FOR PERVERTS ONLY" 1982-1983

Phil's decision to go solo proper was rather late in coming. Mike, Tony, Peter, and Steve had all flown the nest much earlier in terms of solo projects. Phil's first album, 1980s *Face Value*, was to prove his decision to wait to be a wise one.

The album erupted onto the scene in December 1980 and by February 1981, both it and the debut single, 'In the Air Tonight' had achieved enormous success the single only being held off the number one spot by Ultravox's 'Vienna'. With Phil's return to Genesis for the writing and recording of what became their *Abacab* album in September 1981, it was to be a further year before Phil was able to venture out on the road to promote both *Face Value* and its equally successful follow up, *Hello, I Must Be Going*.

Phil's first solo gig took place in Den Haag Holland on 21 November 1982 and he subsequently toured Europe, the UK, and the USA throughout the winter of 1982 and spring of 1983, bringing his very own brand of musical excellence to the concert stage. His first tour drew heavily on both his solo albums, along with a passing nod to his work with Jazz fusion group, Brand X, as well as his own upbeat cover of Genesis' 'Behind the Lines'. Thankfully, several of these shows were recorded and are easily available to fans among them, the ones mentioned here.

HAMMERSMITH ODEON, LONDON, ENGLAND, 28 NOVEMBER 1982

Set List: I Don't Care Anymore/Thunder & Lightning/I Cannot Believe it's True/This Must Be Love/Thru These Walls/I Missed Again/Behind the Lines/You Know What I Mean/The Roof is Leaking/Don't Let Him Steal Your Heart Away/The West Side/If Leaving Me is Easy/In the Air Tonight/Like China/You Can't Hurry Love/It Don't Matter to Me/Hand in Hand/And So to F.../Why Can't it Wait Till Morning/People Get Ready//
Source: Audience Recording.

Phil's first ever UK solo gig is captured here in a more than adequate audience recording. Opening with the driving rhythms of 'I Don't Care Anymore', the show gets off to a fast pace, which is kept up by 'Thunder & Lightning'. Both band and crowd sound in fine form here and Phil seems relaxed and comfortable and the banter is soon flowing between both Phil and the crowd.

'I Cannot Believe it's True' keeps the pace up and here the horn section really comes into its own with some fine ensemble playing. 'This Must Be Love' slows things down a bit giving everyone a chance to catch their collective breaths before the current single, the unlikely tale of a peeping Tom, and Phil dedicates it to all the perverts in the audience and from the comments from the audience there were a fair few in the room on the night! An unusual tale but 'Thru These Walls' manages to evoke just the right feeling of claustrophobic menace.

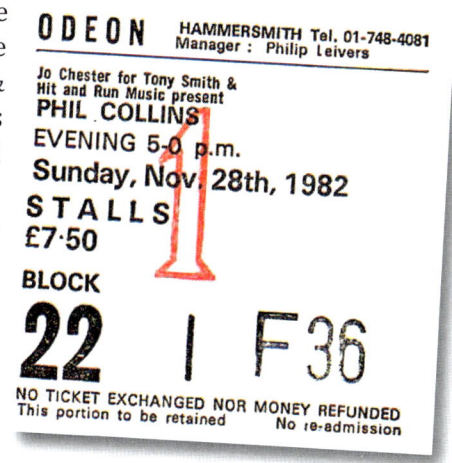

'I Missed Again' and 'Behind the Lines' further demonstrate Phil's Motown sensibilities, and difficult to credit as it is, the latter works rather well as an uptempo number. One of the best songs from Phil's first solo album, the story of pioneers of the Mid West that is the 'Roof is Leaking', is given a marvellous work out here and I wonder why this one didn't last longer in the live set. Daryl's banjo playing really sets an atmosphere, which gives this one an unexpected edge.

By the time we get to 'In the Air Tonight' it is obvious that Phil had the crowd in the palm of his hand and deservedly so. The performances on this tour were definitely among the best that I ever saw Phil give and this epic track still manages to send shivers up and down the spine. Once again, Daryl's playing takes this one to new heights.

'Like China' unfortunately never really cut the mustard to this listener's ears and in the live context it falls flat here with Phil's Mockney accent grating on the nerves. He redeems himself immediately, however, as the band start the party with 'You Can't Hurry Love' and you can hear the audience getting into the groove here, as they have done ever since when Phil plays this classic.

The band continues with their feet to the floor with 'It Don't Matter to Me', where the rhythm and horn sections battle away as if their very lives depended on it. 'Hand in Hand' gives Phil the opportunity to get some real audience participation going and it is obvious that the audience are definitely up for it.

'And So to F...' evidently takes at least one member of the audience by surprise of his exclamation of "Bloody hell" is anything to go by. This one simply races along at breakneck speed.

The pace is slowed down by 'Why Can't it Wait Till Morning'; one of Phil's more underrated songs, and the show is closed with the classic 'People Get Ready', which Phil delivers in marvellous fashion.

HILL AUDITORIUM, ANN ARBOR, MICHIGAN, USA 5 FEBRUARY 1983

Set List: I Don't Care Anymore/Thunder & Lighting/I Cannot Believe it's True/This Must Be Love/Thru These Walls/I Missed Again/You Know What I Mean/The Roof is Leaking/Don't Let Him Steal Your Heart Away/The West Side/If Leaving Me is Easy/In the Air Tonight/Like China/You Can't Hurry Love/It Don't Matter to Me//
Source: Soundboard Recording.

Phil's inaugural tour continued well into the spring of 1983 with a series of shows in the USA, out of which we are lucky to have this recording taken from the soundboard. Phil opens the show with the same salvo of tracks that he had done in Europe and 'I Don't Care Anymore' has seldom sounded more angry and dramatic than it does here. 'Thunder & Lightning' has also gained immeasurably since the debut gigs back in November '82 with Daryl putting in a storming performance on guitar here.

The crowd are relegated to the background here but from what you can hear of them it sounds like Phil had a large and very enthusiastic one here for this gig. Things calm down a bit for 'This Must Be Love', in which Phil delivers a particularly poignant vocal. The story behind 'Thru These Walls' hasn't improved with the telling, but it still gets a cheer from the crowd. The song itself still manages to convey the menace that makes it such an unusual song in Phil's canon but one that works extraordinarily well.

'I Missed Again' brings us back into the normal world and here the horn section take their cue to really let rip with some seriously funky playing. Then, "A couple of songs to get depressed to," as Phil introduces them. 'You Know What I Mean' is an unashamedly romantic song of the kind that Phil excels at writing, simple and effective, leading us to the much more grandiose mini epic that is the 'Roof is Leaking'; a cautionary tale of pioneers in the Old West and one of my favourites from Phil's catalogue, and tonight the band perform it with verve and gusto.

The rest of the set remains as it had been during the European shows, although sadly the encores are missing for some reason. Nonetheless, this is a delightful recording and one that should be in any fan's collection.

PART FOUR: PHIL COLLINS

CHAPTER THIRTY-NINE
"NO JACKET REQUIRED" 1985

With his solo career now well and truly on track, Phil soon found himself entering on the balancing act of maintaining both a rapidly growing solo career alongside the equally expanding success of Genesis. Having concluded touring and promotional duties for 'Hello, I Must Be Going', Phil was soon back in the studios with Genesis recording the follow up to 1981's *Abacab* album. The release of Genesis (or the *Shapes* album as it is more commonly known) in the summer of 1983 meant that Phil was locked into the touring and promotional duties that accompanied it for almost a year.

Having concluded those, however, he was soon back at work on what would become on its release in February 1985, his most successful album to date. He managed to raise his profile even higher before that with the smash hit single, 'Against all Odds', from the film of the same name, which reached the top of the UK charts in 1984.

Preceded by the catchy 'Sussudio' single in February 1985, Phil's third solo album, *No Jacket Required*, became the first of his albums to gain a release on the then new Compact Disc format. It entered the charts at the very top, proving that his previous success had been no flash in the pan. Replete with the kind of music that you would expect from Phil, the new stage show took on a life of its own with Phil's very own expanding band of musicians.

The tour began in the UK in February before wending its way across Europe, the USA, and further afield with shows in Australia and Japan, as well as Phil's now famous performances at *both* the Live Aid shows. Several shows are available to fans and it was even captured for posterity on the official video, *No Ticket Required*, which has sadly not yet gained official release on DVD.

APOLLO THEATRE, MANCHESTER, ENGLAND, 12 FEBRUARY 1985
Set List: I Don't Care Anymore/Only You & I Know/I Cannot Believe It's True/This Must Be Love/Against All Odds/Inside Out/Who Said I Would?/If Leaving Me is Easy/Sussudio/Behind the Lines/Don't Lose My Number/The West Side/One More Night/In the Air Tonight/House Muzak/Like China/You Can't Hurry Love/It Don't Matter to Me/Hand in Hand/Take Me Home/People Get Ready/It's Alright/And So to F...//
Source: Audience Recording.

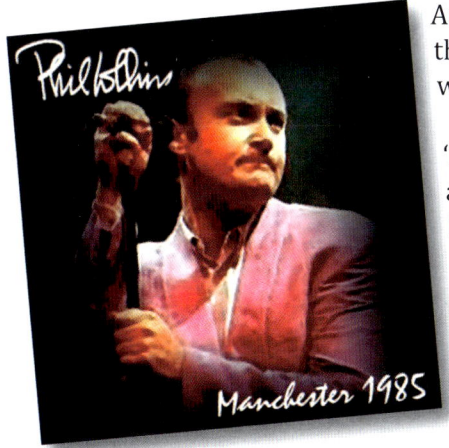

Aah, the memories! These were the days when you could still see an artist of the calibre of Phil in a theatre and it didn't cost an arm and a leg to do it! This was the fourth gig on what was to be Phil's most successful tour thus far.

Right from the start, Phil and the band set out to get the crowd on side and 'I Don't Care Anymore' thunders out of the traps like a greyhound. Chester and Daryl in particular set up some fantastic moods with their playing and Phil's vocal is particularly fiery tonight. An equally uptempo 'Only You and I Know' gets an airing next with the horns laying down some stabbing refrains accompanied by equally emphatic guitar and percussion.

'I Cannot Believe it's True' and 'This Must Be Love' come across like a couple of latter-day Motown classics whilst Phil admits to a "brown trousers Ville" moment next with only the fourth public performance of 'Against all Odds'. He needn't have worried, as the crowd give both him and the song an enthusiastic reception.

'Inside Out' with its marvellous guitar part and some equally tasty keyboards keeps the pace going along nicely, while 'Who Said I Would?' with its syncopated rhythms and rampaging horn playing keeps the party atmosphere in top gear before the pace slows to give Phil, the band, and the audience a chance to collect their breaths with 'If Leaving Me is Easy'; a late night jazz club gem of a song with a superb sax solo here.

'Sussudio', the current single, is next. Even though it has only been out a couple of weeks, the crowd evidently know it and sing along ... Prince? '1999'? Never heard of them! The crowd are evidently familiar with Phil's reworking of 'Behind the Lines', which in its new funky setting works incredibly well. The rest of this excellent quality recording is as you would expect from Phil. A mix of hits and excellent album tracks with a smattering of covers, including a superb rendering of Brand X's 'And So to F…' brings the show to a close.

NATIONAL TENNIS CENTRE, MELBOURNE, AUSTRALIA, 13 APRIL 1985
Set List: I Don't Care Anymore/Only You & I Know/I Cannot Believe It's True/This Must Be Love/Against all Odds/Inside Out/Who Said I Would?/You Know What I Mean/If Leaving Me is Easy/Sussudio/Behind the Lines/Don't Lose My Number/The West Side/One More Night/In the Air Tonight/Like China/You Can't Hurry Love/It Don't Matter to Me/Hand in Hand/Take Me Home/People Get Ready/It's Alright//
Source: Soundboard Recording.

With the massive success of *No Jacket Required*, demand to see Phil and his band took on truly mammoth proportions and he was to tour extensively throughout most of 1985, including his first visit to Australia for a series of highly successful shows, from which this excellent soundboard recording will serve as a document.

'I Don't Care Anymore' and 'Only You and I Know' set the pace for a fast and furious performance by Phil and the band. Daryl Stuermer lets rip with some ferocious licks during the latter and Phil's voice sounds raw and slightly strained at times.

Time for Phil to get the funk out next with a smooth and silky 'I Cannot Believe it's True', which the band perform to perfection, although once again Phil's voice betrays the strain that the demands of touring are taking on it. The pace is calmed down a bit for 'This Must Be Love' and 'Against all Odds', but no rest for the wicked, as 'Inside Out' and 'Who Said I Would?' pick it up again. Phil's extended band-cum-orchestra really sinks their teeth into this one, although once again the strain on Phil's voice means that the vocal is quite ragged at times.

Phil's joke about the "hot club tub and the nine warm jets" falls rather flat. In fact there is no audience reaction to it. Being a soundboard, the audience is *persona non grata* here. 'You Know What I Mean' and 'If Leaving Me is Easy' are accompanied by the string section required by Australian Musicians' Union rules and they certainly give both songs an added element of poignancy.

Party time arrives in the shape of 'Sussudio' and some damn fine bass playing from Leland Sklar. The horn section give some shit kicking rhythms too, leading nicely into 'Behind the Lines'; that rather natty little Genesis number that Phil has turned into a surprisingly good Motown-styled number.

Phil's banter with the audience before 'One More Night' gets an unexpectedly loud reaction from the crowd. Obviously the sound engineer remembered that there was actually an *audience* in the building. The song itself is a soulful performance as you would expect. 'In the Air Tonight' is marvellous too. Daryl's guitar intro threatens to tear the roof off and Leland's rumbling bass sounds like an earthquake. Nuff said.

'Like China' sounds surprisingly out of place here. For some reason I can't quite put my finger on it. It might be Phil's Mockney accent and that particular "joke" wearing a bit thin now, who knows? 'You Can't Hurry Love' is far better, however. Once again Leland Sklar's bass lifts this above the average and the harmonies are amazing here.

'It Don't Matter to Me' keeps the pace surprisingly high and one wonders how the band managed to generate such energy levels night after night. Phil has definitely got his second wind here and the rest of the band don't slacken the pace for a truly delightful instrumental work out on 'Hand in Hand' with Phil leading the chorus and getting the crowd worked up quite nicely.

'Take Me Home' hasn't quite got to its status as the final song in one of Phil's shows, but it does close the show proper in fine form with an extended workout, which would incorporate the audience normally but here you get the band sans-crowd, so every note can be heard clearly. Of course encores are expected and duly delivered in the shape of two classic slices of Soul and Motown. 'People Get Ready' is already a favourite from Phil's previous tour and it is just as emotional here and the performance is a marvel to hear. 'It's Alright' closes the show with a blood marvellous swinging performance, which it is evident Phil and the band have thoroughly enjoyed, making this an essential addition to any collection of Phil's recordings.

CHAPTER FORTY
"A SERIOUS BUSINESS" 1990

The ever busy Phil not only undertook his own touring and recording duties plus those with Genesis but also somehow managed to find time to not only produce but perform with the likes of Philip Bailey, Eric Clapton, and Robert Plant during the 1980s. The massive success of 1986's Genesis album *Invisible Touch* and its attendant tour, which lasted until the summer of 1987, ensured that Phil was unable to produce a further solo album until the end of 1987.

However, with a career burgeoning to include appearances in film and TV series, he did manage even more chart success with his contribution to the 1988 film *Buster*, in which he starred as well as having single success with two songs from that film's soundtrack.

1989 saw him release the album by which his career has since largely been measured. The enormously successful *But Seriously* brought his music into just about every household in the UK. A spate of successful singles, opening with the dramatic 'Another Day in Paradise', ensured that his profile both at home and elsewhere remained high during 1989 and 1990, and the ensuing tour also took him around the world on his biggest and most successful outing to date.

Never one to stint on either musical or visual excellence, the theme for the new show was a fairground carousel and the stage show reflected this to breathtaking effect as anyone who saw the shows will tell you. Musically, with four albums to draw from, the show expanded to almost three hours in length and covered just about every aspect of Phil's career.

Once again, the tour was captured for posterity officially by a live album and video and also by an increasing number of audio/video recordings by the fans, a couple of which have been selected here.

ENTERTAINMENT CENTRE, SYDNEY, AUSTRALIA, 15 MARCH 1990
Set List: Hand in Hand/Hang in Long Enough/Behind the Lines/Against all Odds/Doesn't Anybody Stay Together Anymore?/All of My Life/Don't Lose My Number/Do You Remember?/Something Happened on the Way to Heaven/Another Day in Paradise/Separate Lives/I Wish it Would Rain Down/Saturday Night and Sunday Morning/The West Side/That's Just the Way it Is/Heat on the Street/One More Night/Colours/Drum Thing/In the Air Tonight/You Can't Hurry Love/Two Hearts/Find A Way to My Heart/A Groovy Kind of Love/Easy Lover/Always/Take Me Home//
Source: Mix Desk Recording.

By the beginning of the 1990s Phil's star was definitely in the ascendant and his tour in support of the *But Seriously* album took him around the world in his most extensive tour to date. Thankfully not only was the performance captured by the subsequent *Serious Hits Live* album and VHS/DVD, but also by a number of excellent quality recordings, of which this one from Sydney during the first leg of the tour is one of the best.

Taken from a previously "hidden" soundboard recording, here we have Phil and his band in incredible form and sound quality from the opening salvo of 'Hand in Hand'; a marvellous instrumental warm-up for all and sundry, leading into the equally frantic 'Hang in Long Enough', driven along by the incessant horn section and a thumping percussion.

'Behind the Lines', that surprisingly good Motown-styled cover of a Genesis classic, still comes across as an extremely enjoyable romp for all concerned. A bit of audience banter leads us into 'Against all Odds', which once again, owing to Australian Musicians' Union rules is accompanied by a string section, which gives the song an added poignancy. The horn and rhythm section on 'Doesn't Anybody Stay Together Anymore?' make this a particularly tasty version of this underrated Collins classic.

'All of My Life' gets a wonderfully soulful sax introduction from Don Myrick. On this no-nonsense song, featuring Phil on piano and vocals, you can hear that he is already experiencing some problems with his voice, which sounds quite strained here but there is no doubting the emotion on display tonight. The pace is picked up by 'Don't Lose My Number', once again driven along by a superlative Chester Thompson whilst Daryl Stuermer cuts loose with some ferocious licks too. Pretty much every hit and classic album cut is here in superb quality in a show, which lasts well over two and a half hours. Other highlights including an emotion packed 'Another Day in Paradise' and a swaggering 'Heat on the Street' before the party really gets under way with 'Two Hearts', 'A Groovy Kind of Love', and 'Easy Lover' to name but a few – a superb recording and one which fans should definitely cherish.

CHAPTER FORTY-ONE
"BOTH SIDES AND FAR SIDES" 1994-1995

The early 1990s were traumatic for Phil. His second marriage to Jill Tavelman broke down amid a flurry of tabloid scuttlebutt and the associated tripe that passes for journalism these days.

Phil's swansong with Genesis, 1991's *We Can't Dance*, had eclipsed even its predecessor, 1986's *Invisible Touch*, selling over ten million copies. The subsequent tour had also seen Genesis performing to sell-out crowds at stadia in the USA, Europe, and the UK, with a live video and two live albums documenting his final performances with the band.

Phil's decision to leave Genesis was at this point unknown to the fan base and his next solo album, 1993's *Both Sides*, was a dark and angry reflection of the position Phil found himself in at the time. Written and recorded totally by Phil, this one is a completely different album to any that had gone before it.

This was reflected in the new stage show built to resemble a back street replete with scaffolding and oil drums disguising the drum kits on stage. Musically the show was divided into two halves, as well with the "dark" opening half and the "light" or "party" section after a short interval, which no doubt Phil and the band needed with a show nearing the three hour mark once more.

Phil's profile was such that several of the shows were recorded either in their entirety or in part by local TV stations and as the tour continued well into 1995. There is an abundance of both visual and audio material for fans to get their teeth into from this tour.

G-MEX CENTRE, MANCHESTER, ENGLAND, 29 NOVEMBER 1994
Set List: I Don't Care Anymore/Don't Lose My Number/Every Day/Survivors/Another Day in Paradise/I Wish it Would Rain Down/One More Night/A Groovy Kind of Love/We Wait & We Wonder/Separate Lives/Both Sides of the Story/In the Air Tonight/Hang in Long Enough/Find A Way to My Heart/It Don't Matter to Me/Easy Lover/Only You & I Know/Something Happened on the Way to Heaven/Knockin' on Heaven's Door/Two Hearts/Sussudio/Get Ready/My Girl/Take Me Home//
Source: Soundboard recording.

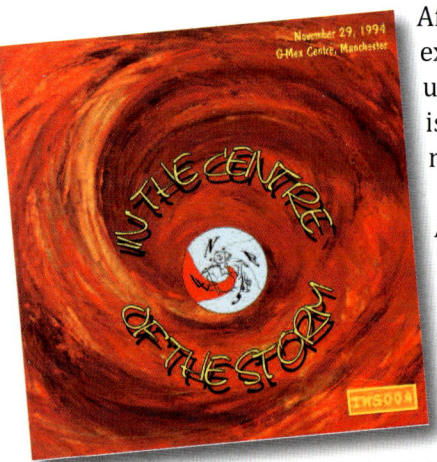

After an extensive tour of Europe and the US, Phil finally brought his new extravaganza to the UK in the winter of 1994 when we all needed warming up! There are many excellent recordings from this leg of the tour but this one is particularly significant being one of only a handful of Soundboard recordings from this tour.

An extended intro leads into the familiar drum pattern of 'I Don't Care Anymore', where Phil and new drummer Ricky Lawson battle away ferociously before Brad Cole's symphonic keyboard phrases get things going. Phil sounded as if he had a point to prove tonight, and with all the problems he'd had with the tabloid press, this is a fiery performance and a statement of intent to boot! 'Don't Lose My Number' thunders around the cavernous G-Mex, although once again Phil's voice betrays the evident strain that such lengthy shows are placing on it.

'Every Day' is introduced as a "barrel of laughs" and indeed, it certainly isn't the most cheerful of Phil's songs, but nevertheless it is a masterful performance here, restrained and thoughtful. 'Survivors' picks the pace up again with a syncopated drum rhythm, leading into a truly awesome song in which Phil really puts his poor old chords to the test. A little house muzak whilst Phil gets his in ear monitors attended to, and then the dilemma of giving to the homeless charity or buying a t shirt and all the humorous banter that accompanies that, leading into 'Another Day in Paradise', which tonight sounds incredible, helped no doubt by the hall's echoey acoustics. Daryl is magnificent here and the song is a masterpiece.

'I Wish it Would Rain Down', complete with amusing stories about exes comes next and Phil takes great delight in winding up the male members of the audience about their private lives, and once again Daryl really shines here with a stunning guitar solo – Clapton eat your heart out! 'One More Night' is equally emotional, although a lot simpler with Phil at the piano, no doubt getting his breath back. Harmony vocals are once again amazing here too.

This was a particularly emotional night, as Phil announced the death of his old friend "Buster" Edwards, which gives 'A Groovy Kind of Love' a particular emotional resonance and you can hear a pin drop as the band put in a wonderful performance of it – a nice tribute to the man himself. Smashing glass, police sirens, and bagpipes (which Phil actually *played* tonight) herald the start of 'We Wait & We Wonder', with Phil's raw vocal giving the song an added drama lacking from its recorded version.

'Separate Lives' glistens like polished glass, brilliantly simple but soaring above the average when you have such magnificent accompaniment as Amy Keys and Arnold McCuller, both of whom help Phil here with truly mesmerising results. 'Both Sides of the Story' brings the first half of this extended show to a dramatic close. Drum beats spatter like bullets while Phil's voice is as raw as a knife wound.

The drum machine pattern and Daryl's soaring guitar cut through the air to announce the band back onstage with 'In the Air Tonight'. Even after all these years and God alone knows how many times I have heard this one, it still brings the shivers to my spine and this recording is simply the best there is. A downright funky 'Hang in Long Enough' keeps things loose with the Vine St Horns driving everything along nicely.

Once again, Daryl kick starts the next song, aided and abetted by some impeccable percussion from Ricky Lawson as Phil exhorts us to 'Find A Way to My Heart', where he is accompanied by the awesome vocals of Amy Keys once again, and this is continued on the next song, 'It Don't Matter to Me'; another incredibly feisty performance driven along by the marvellous rhythms of Messrs Lawson and East.

Party time arrives with 'Easy Lover', and here Arnold McCuller gives Phil a run for his money in the vocal stakes. I can vouch for the fact that the band were having an absolute blast tonight and you can hear how relaxed they are here. Once again Daryl gives us some truly inspired guitar riffage. No rest for the wicked – or the audience either – as 'Only You & I Know' rattles along like an express train powered by the phenomenal guitar of Daryl Stuermer and drums of Ricky Lawson.

The impetus is retained by a celebratory rendition of 'Something Happened on the Way to Heaven', and then a truly delightfully funky 'Knockin' on Heaven's Door'. 'You Can't Hurry Love' indicates that it's time for the crowd to get up and boogie, which we did on the night, I can assure you. How could we possibly do otherwise while Phil and the band were putting this one down?! A swinging version of 'Two Hearts' segues nicely into the real heart of this part of the show: 'Sussudio'. I don't care if Prince reckons Phil lifted one of his riffs – this is a superb performance, which you can tell each and every member of the band is thoroughly enjoying – so were the crowd, I can tell you!

Phil gets soulful next with an uptempo 'Get Ready'. He is definitely in his element here with a relaxed and confident vocal. The entire band are on top of their game here too. This one swings with a capital S! The band then take things down a bit for a wonderful sauntering 'My Girl' before the evening's extravaganza is brought to a close by the now traditional 'Take Me Home'; an extended celebration in which band and audience take equal parts bringing this amazing recording to a brilliant close.

COLISEO NACIONAL, SANTIAGO, CHILE, 18 APRIL 1995

Set List: Drum Duet/I Don't Care Anymore/Don't Lose My Number/Every Day/Survivors/Another Day in Paradise/I Wish it Would Rain Down/One More Night/A Groovy Kind of Love/We Wait & We Wonder/Separate Lives/Both Sides of the Story/In the Air Tonight/Hang in Long Enough/Find a Way to My Heart/It Don't Matter to Me/Easy Lover/Only You & I Know/Something Happened on the Way to Heaven/Knockin' on Heaven's Door/Two Hearts/Sussudio/Take Me Home//
Source: TV/Radio Broadcast.

An unnecessarily long introduction by a TV/radio presenter who obviously likes the sound of his own voice precedes Phil's arrival onstage for the now standard duet with new drummer Ricky Lawson, which leads into a fiery version of 'I Don't Care Anymore', with some searing guitar riffs from Daryl to boot. As usual, the tempo remains high, as Daryl and Brad Cole lead the rest of the band into 'Don't Lose My Number'. Phil's voice sounds a little hoarse here, which isn't surprising given the demands he had placed on it throughout this, his most extensive tour ever.

Phil makes his usual phonetic intros next getting a cheer from the crowd. Interestingly enough, this is an edited recording as 'Every Day' is missing and Phil introduces 'Survivors' next; an emotional performance accompanied by some nifty percussion and an almost symphonic keyboard. 'Another Day in Paradise' opens with the usual synth drone and soaring guitar from Daryl, getting another cheer from the crowd, although the effect is

A Selection Of Shows: Genesis & Solo Live Guide 1976-2014

Birmingham 5 December 1995
Phil surprised everyone by playing the bagpipes during his final encore 'Amazing Grace'.

Phil Collins

spoilt somewhat by a pointless voiceover. Never mind, the rest of the song is here and in fine form too.

Another edit has obviously taken place as 'I Wish it Would Rain Down' comes next with Phil ably accompanied by the expanded team of vocalists. Ricky and Daryl really come up with the goods too, making this a particularly impressive performance. 'One More Night' calms the proceedings down a bit and Phil evidently sounds as if he is catching his breath during this one. We stay in the slightly sedate atmosphere next with 'A Groovy Kind of Love' with a beautiful vocal from Phil here who is obviously getting his second wind.

Breaking glass, sirens, and a tattoo-like drum rhythm and sampled bagpipes heralds the beginning of 'We Wait & We Wonder'; a superbly evocative song, in which Phil really outdoes himself in terms of emotional performance, even if the strain of the performance is beginning to tell. 'Separate Lives' gives Phil another chance to share the vocal burden and Amy Keys is astonishing here – and the crowd aren't too shabby either! 'Both Sides of the Story' finishes the first half of the show in emphatic style with a wonderfully feisty performance from Phil and Ricky Lawson.

'In the Air Tonight' has probably had enough superlatives thrown at it over the years, so I won't add any more here, apart from – marvellous! The party really gets under way with a barnstorming 'Hang in Long Enough', driven along at a frantic pace by the horn section, harmony vocals to die for, and some tasty percussion from young Mr Lawson.

A foghorn-like guitar intro heralds the arrival of 'Find a Way to My Heart', before the drums pick out a marvellously infectious rhythm, almost a samba but not quite. Phil puts in a restrained but effective vocal here – obviously saving himself for the exertions to come. 'It Don't Matter to Me'; an old friend rediscovered for this tour and despite the evident strain on his voice, Phil still manages to turn in a great vocal. Arnold McCuller and Amy Keys are equally prominent here.

Why Phil refers to 'Easy Lover' as, "something you don't see very often," is beyond me but hey, who cares? Our irritating voiceover is back again but otherwise the song is a damn fine and funky performance. 'Only You & I Know' keeps the pace up at as the band race through it at a breakneck rate of knots, which continues through a superb 'Something Happened on the Way to Heaven', which is a truly ensemble performance.

'Coversville' is next, with a suitably funky 'Knockin' on Heaven's Door', which the entire band seem to be having a blast playing. Phil in particular sounds in his element here. The drum pattern gives it away (oh, and the dark sunglasses too), as 'You Can't Hurry Love' takes us to the world of classic Motown – always a bright moment in any Phil Collins show, here it is bright as daylight. 'Two Hearts' keeps the party swinging whilst an extended version of 'Sussudio' (Prince? Never heard of him, Guv'nor) gets the crowd going. Daryl and bass player the inimitable Nathan East really cut the groove whilst the rest of the band simply have a blast. 'Take Me Home' signals the end of the show and is always the perfect closer. Here we have a truly emotional performance. Phil sounds genuinely touched by the evident enthusiasm from the massive crowd and it brings this superb recording to an emotional close.

CHAPTER FORTY-TWO
"BUSKING WITH THE BIG BAND & SEEING THE LIGHT" 1996-1998

Phil concluded his highly successful *Far Side of the World* tour in the summer of 1995, and he must have taken great satisfaction that despite his ongoing personal problems and the attendant negative coverage of these by the tabloid press, the shows were an enormous success.

Phil's next project was to take his fans completely by surprise, although why exactly is anyone's guess. Phil's love of Motown and Big Band Jazz has always been well known but his decision to embark upon a project that brought that love of the latter to the fore was viewed with a mixture of scepticism and scorn by fans and critics alike. The end result was a series of high profile shows in the summer of 1996, at which Phil was accompanied by a full size jazz ensemble and orchestra alongside the appearance on stage with him of the legendary Tony Bennett no less. The show at London's Royal Albert Hall was filmed and subsequently formed part of a documentary on the project for TV in the UK. Thankfully, there are a couple of excellent recordings documenting these shows and I have selected one of them here.

This project was in turn rapidly followed by Phil's next album, 1997's *Dance into the Light*, is once again a reflection of Phil's current state of mind, which found him in an altogether happier place and in a new relationship. The resulting album was a mixed bag and gained mixed reviews at the time of its release. That said, the resulting tours of the USA and Europe were nothing but a joy to behold. With the theme of the tour being a cruise liner, the stage was festooned with the appropriate paraphernalia, such as life buoys, etc., and with the show being performed "in the round" there wasn't a bad seat in the house if you attended any of the shows.

Fortunately once again there is a wide selection of recordings available to document the tour and I have selected a couple of the better ones here.

GRAND CASINO, MONTREUX, SWITZERLAND, 17 JULY 1996

Set List: Two Hearts/That's All/In the Air Tonight/Invisible Touch/The West Side/Against all Odds/Hand in Hand/Always/Do Nothing Till You Hear From Me/Sussudio/Watch What Happens*/Somewhere over the Rainbow*/People*/Old Devil Moon*/The Lady's in Love With You */From Now On*/Instrumental/Drum Thang/Los Endos//
Source: Soundboard Recording.
*Performed with Tony Bennett.

Phil's decision to finally indulge his long time love of big band jazz took most of his fans by surprise when he announced a short tour performing "jazzed up" versions of his own and Genesis' material alongside established jazz classics.

As this superb recording shows, the decision had mixed results. With a band/orchestra including such alumni as Tony Bennett, along with his own band and members of the WDR Orchestra, there was nothing wrong with the musicianship on stage. In fact, surprisingly enough many of the tracks here work extremely well in their new setting. The instrumentals 'The West Side' and 'Hand in Hand' in particular lend themselves quite easily to this treatment.

Some of the songs, like 'In the Air Tonight' and 'That's All', have an unexpected "swing", which is delightful to hear. Phil is joined on the second disc for a selection (pun intended) of classics by Tony Bennett and this works much better in terms of being convincing, but the overall result of this recording is to reappraise some of the material that we, as fans, are so familiar with.

NATIONAL EXHIBITION CENTRE, BIRMINGHAM, ENGLAND, 7 NOVEMBER 1997

Set List: Hand in Hand/Hang in Long Enough/Don't Lose My Number/River So Wide/Take Me Down/Find a Way to My Heart/Another Day in Paradise/Just Another Story/Against all Odds/Lorenzo/Separate Lives/Both Sides of the Story/Do You Remember?/Long, Long Way to Go/One More Night/In the Air Tonight/Timbantiocha/Easy Lover/Dance into the Light/Wear My Hat/You Can't Hurry Love/Two Hearts/Something Happened on the Way to Heaven/Sussudio/Take Me Home//
Source: Audience Recording.

The theme of this year's tour was that of an ocean liner and the circular stage was festooned with the paraphernalia associated with such things. Life belts, etc., were everywhere as Phil and his ever expanding band took to the stage tonight. Even the show itself was growing with a show that now verged on three hours in length.

The show opened with a marvellous version of the instrumental 'Hand in Hand' giving everyone in the band a chance to flex their musical muscles. This was in turn followed by a rampaging 'Hang in Long Enough'. 'Don't Lose My Number' continues the high energy delivery before we get to the new album with the paean to intolerance, 'River So Wide', which gave new boy Ricky Lawson chance to demonstrate his percussive skills, ably assisted by Phil who is obviously relishing the opportunity to bash the skins again. 'Take Me Down' is delivered here at breakneck pace, which makes me wonder how the band managed to keep this level of energy up night after night.

'Find a Way to My Heart' slows everything down a tad for one of Phil's more underrated ballads. He is in fine voice here and the performance is musically and vocally excellent. 'Another Day in Paradise' is preceded by Phil's spiel about homeless charities before Daryl's guitar rips the hairs off everyone's necks. Realistic storytelling has always been a forte of Phil's and 'Just Another Story' continues that trend here with some fine and sleazy playing by the horn section.

'Against all Odds' comes next and it's a fine version with an impeccable sax solo in the middle of it before another long-form song – Lorenzo – which works infinitely better here in the live context than it had done on the album where I had found it somewhat disjointed. 'Separate Lives' gives Phil a chance to duet with one of his other vocal cohorts in the band and Amy Keys' performance here is simply stellar. Surprisingly enough given the notoriously poor acoustics of the NEC, the show tonight is not dogged by any of the usual sound problems, and this recording is surprisingly clear for one made by a member of the audience.

The rest of the show is the usual mix of hits and a few surprises. 'Long, Long Way to Go' and 'One More Night' for instance are delivered by Phil at the piano, which gives them an added poignancy here. 'Both Sides' – one of the better efforts from the album of the same name – thunders along, as indeed does 'In the Air Tonight', which echoes around the NEC as it is delivered in suitably dramatic fashion.

'Easy Lover', 'You Can't Hurry Love' – you name it; just about every hit that Phil has in his repertoire is trundled out for the audience's delectation tonight and you can tell by the audience reaction to them that this was a show high on emotion and excitement and is represented here by an above average audience recording.

CHAPTER FORTY-THREE
"I WANT TO TESTIFY" 1998-2002

Phil returned to the world of the big band for his next project and in the summer of 1998 brought the show that had been so well received in Europe back in 1996 to the USA and finally to the UK as well. Once again, touring with an orchestra and restricting himself to drumming duties, Phil enlisted Oletta Adams to take on the vocal duties and the results can be heard on the subsequent live album, *A Hot Night in Paris*.

Unfortunately, Phil experienced health problems, which affected his hearing after these shows, were concluded and his touring activities have since become increasingly restricted. Phil has become more involved in the world of film music, composing several soundtracks for Disney films, including the award winning soundtrack for their animated *Tarzan* film. His last solo album, 2002's *Testify*, was followed by a handful of shows and the best of these has been included here.

MADISON SQUARE GARDEN, NEW YORK, USA, 1 NOVEMBER 1999
Set List: Against all Odds/You'll Be in My Heart/Separate Lives/Take Me Home/In the Air Tonight//
Source: Audience Recording.

Phil's shows after the conclusion of the big band tour in 1998 became increasingly sporadic with guest appearances being the norm and one-off gigs in aid of his recently created Little Dreams Foundation charity.

Phil had also entered the world of film music writing and his first effort, *Tarzan*, was released by the Disney Corporation in 1999 to great critical acclaim. In fact Phil won an Oscar for it. He also performed a handful of shows premiering music from it during the year including this one from New York's Madison Square Garden.

An average quality audience recording captures this performance and from the outset Phil is in fine humour, taking the mickey out of his health problems, before launching into a somewhat under rehearsed 'Against all Odds', where the band sound somewhat tentative in their playing. No matter, the audience know all the words and sing along throughout.

'You'll Be in My Heart' is stripped down to acoustic piano for tonight's performance and would work a lot better if the audience would sit and *listen* instead of chattering throughout because they are missing a particularly emotional version here.

'Separate Lives' is next with Phil paying respect to his friend and song writer Stephen Bishop. Either way it's a bona fide classic. It is a shame that the recording quality is mediocre at best because this sounds like a wonderful, acoustic version.

'Take Me Home' is greeted with shouts of "I love you Phil!" Once again, this marvellous classic has been stripped down to its acoustic components here but it still works remarkably well, and for once the audience's participation actually adds to the atmosphere – even the out of tune singing by the audience is somehow fitting.

'In the Air Tonight' closes off this somewhat short recording and Phil returns it to its acoustic roots, with solo piano and voice. It's almost like listening to Phil's demo but it is still an incredible song and he delivers it with just the right amount of passion.

THE SCALA CLUB, LONDON, ENGLAND, 6 NOVEMBER 2002
Set List: (Broadcast): In the Air Tonight/Something Happened on the Way to Heaven/Another Day in Paradise/I Can't Stop Loving You/I Missed Again/Against all Odds/You Can't Hurry Love/Two Hearts/Easy Lover/Lady Madonna/Sussudio/Take Me Home//
Source: Radio Broadcast.
Missing Tracks: Driving Me Crazy/One More Night/You'll Be in My Heart/Separate Lives/I Can't Dance/My Girl/Get Ready//

With Phil's hearing problems now restricting his performances, the 2002 *Testify* tour such as it was, was a short series of showcase gigs in various locations, including one at the Scala Club in London. Fortunately this one was recorded by the BBC, so the recording is, as you would expect, of excellent quality.

Phil and his band of merry men emerge on stage as Phil gave us "that bloody song again" only this time an acoustic piano-driven version of 'In the Air Tonight', which set the tone for the rest of what was to be a somewhat restrained night. This was followed by 'Something Happened on the Way to Heaven' and 'Another Day in Paradise', both of which were greeted by warm applause from the crowd. The stripped down acoustic version of the latter still sends shivers down my spine.

With a new album to promote, the first offering from it was the current single; a cover of Leo Sayer's 1978 hit, 'Can't Stop Loving You, which, in the hands of a master like Phil, manages to rise above the ordinary and sound a bit special here. Sadly the recording is minus several tracks edited out owing to programming restrictions, so we don't get to hear the other new offering 'Driving Me Crazy' here, but skip instead to a celebratory performance of 'I Missed Again'; a welcome addition to the set and one of Phil's better attempts at a Motown simulation.

'Against all Odds' has its face firmly set at all of the romantics in the crowd whilst 'You Can't Hurry Love' gives everyone a chance to let their hair down. The radio broadcast has its eye on the hits for its potential listening audience, so once again several classics are omitted, not least the encores of the *Mogtown* gems, 'My Girl' and 'Get Ready', but nevertheless, what you have here is a superb recording and a great addition to any collection.

CHAPTER FORTY-FOUR
"FAREWELL, ADIEU, AUF WIEDERSEHEN"
2004 - 2010

With Phil's health problems not getting any better, the prospect of shows became increasingly unlikely, yet Phil decided to bow out in style with the humorously titled *First Final Farewell Tour* in the summer of 2004. Effectively a "Greatest Hits" show, , the tour took in both Europe and the UK during the summer of 2004 extended into 2005 with visits further afield, including Phil's first visit to the Middle East. Once again, the tour has been well documented by live recordings and the magnificent *Finally... the First Farewell Tour* DVD, which was subsequently released.

Phil's subsequent reunion with Genesis is covered elsewhere in this book and his most recent solo activity thus far has been the excellent album of Motown covers, *Going Back*, which reached the top of the UK charts in 2010. Phil only performed a handful of shows in support of this album, including a string of gigs at the Roseland Ballroom in New York, which subsequently became the *Going Back – Live at Roseland Ballroom* DVD. Whether Phil is able or willing to indulge in any future touring activity remains to be seen, but as this book shows, his legacy as a performer is secure.

MEN ARENA, MANCHESTER, ENGLAND, 28 JUNE 2004
Set List: Drum Thang/Something Happened on the Way to Heaven/Against all Odds/Don't Lose my Number/You'll Be in My Heart/One More Night/Can't Stop Loving You/Hang in Long Enough/True Colours/Come with Me/A Groovy Kind of Love/I Missed Again/Another Day in Paradise/No Way Out/Separate Lives/In the Air Tonight/Dance into the Light/You Can't Hurry Love/Two Hearts/Wear My Hat/Easy Lover/Sussudio/It's Not Too Late/Drum Thang/Take Me Home//
Source: Audience Recording.

Phil pulled out all the stops for these, his final major shows, and with a set list that was a celebration of his music, this gig was an extremely enjoyable one – I know, because I was there!

The 'Drum Thang', originally aired back in '97, opened the proceedings here, segueing nicely into 'Something Happened on the Way to Heaven', which gets things off to a suitably raucous start with Chester fluffing the intro! He was having a bad day apparently. 'Against all Odds' and 'A Groovy Kind of Love' are delivered impeccably and the echoey acoustics of the massive arena give some idea of what it was like to be part of the show.

The tempo increases next with a surprise performance of 'Don't Lose My Number', which brought back memories for me of hearing it in Manchester almost nineteen years ago for the first time. 'You'll Be in My Heart' from Phil's *Tarzan* soundtrack fitted into the set nicely and even 'Can't Stop Loving You' and 'It's Not Too Late' demonstrated that *Testify* was a greatly underrated album. 'Come with Me' – a very sentimental song on record – comes across very well within the live context and is excellent here.

The party atmosphere is regained with fantastic versions of both 'A Groovy Kind of Love' and 'I Missed Again', before the serious message of 'Another Day in Paradise', with the screens behind the band delivering various statistics on homelessness. Okay, so you don't have the benefit of the visuals here, but the song gets its message across just as well here without them.

The rest of the show draws upon just about every hit that Phil has had in his amazing career, the band were on top form tonight and you can hear that in each and every performance in this above average audience recording.

GRAND CASINO, MONTREUX, SWITZERLAND, 10 JULY 2010
Set List: Signed, Sealed, Delivered/Ain't Too Proud to Beg/Girl (Why You Wanna Make Me Blue?)/Dancing in the Street/(Love is Like a) Heatwave/Papa Was a Rollin' Stone/Never Dreamed You'd Leave in Summer/Jimmy Mack/You've Been Cheatin'/Do I Love You?/Loving You is Sweeter Than Ever/Going to a Go-Go/Blame it on the Sun/Ain't That Peculiar/Too Many Fish in the Sea/You Really Got a Hold On Me/Something About You/Familiar Faces/Tears of a Clown/Nowhere to Run/In My Lonely Room/Take Me in Your Arms/ Uptight/Going Back/Talkin' 'Bout My Baby/You Can't Hurry Love/My Girl//
Source: Audience Recording.

Something of a rarity this one; a precursor to the shows at the Roseland Ballroom, which subsequently became the source for the official DVD from that venue. This recording sees the first outing for the Motown shows that have effectively become Phil's live swansong.

'Signed, Sealed, Delivered' gets things under way and it is a confident Mr Collins who takes the stage after a suitable introduction. He may not be 'Too Proud to Beg' but he should certainly be proud of the ensemble he has put together for this marvellous tribute to Motown.

With a catalogue as rich as this, Phil certainly has his pick of classics to choose from, and this is a recording full of them. 'Girl (Why You Wanna Make Me Blue?)' sings the Casino out, with Phil sounding in his element and his extended band/orchestra getting the audience in the mood from the get go. 'Dancing in the Street' needs no introduction and what you have here is a fun-packed rendition with a band obviously intent on having a good time and taking their audience with them. '(Love is Like a) Heatwave' is a delight to hear, and Phil gives it the full Collins treatment here. There are simply too many classic here to do all of them justice, but what isn't in doubt from this recording is that when he puts his mind to it, despite his current health issues, Phil is still a master of performance and this recording amply demonstrates that here.

****

CELEBS

▲ **RETIREMENT** Phil Collins

Phil Collins quits music to play dad

By STEVE MYALL

PHIL Collins last night announced his retirement from the music business.

The ex-Genesis frontman and drummer turned solo artist says he is quitting to bring up his two sons from his third marriage.

Collins, 60, shot down suggestions he was being forced to retire because of recent bad reviews.

The London-born singer of hits like Groovy Kind of Love, In the Air Tonight and Against All Odds (Take a Look at Me Now), used his website to explain his reasons "for calling it a day" in response to articles questioning his future.

Collins, who has sold more than 100 million solo albums told his fans: "I am stopping so I can be a full-time father to my two young sons on a daily basis."

Recent reports had claimed he was quitting due to health issues and even that a Texas clairvoyant had led Collins to believe he is the reincarnation of an Alamo survivor.

Mechanics play Sunrise: All tuned up, ready to go

By TOM MOON
Herald Music Writer

What can Mike and the Mechanics do after their two big hits *Silent Running* and *All I Need Is a Miracle*?

Plenty. They can create efficient, piston-popping instrumental settings that embrace current synthesizer technology as well as traditional rock arrangement — Genesis Lite, for the dance floor. They can deliver snappy, repetitive vocal hooks in *Hanging By A Thread* and *A Call to Arms*.

And once they've exhausted all the politely mechanical pop they've recorded, this six-piece outfit can actually get down and groove.

For their encore Thursday night at the half-full Sunrise Musical Theatre, Mike and the Mechanics covered the Spencer Davis Group classic *Gimme Some Lovin'*. Here Adrian Lee's reedy organ sound crested atop a big-beat bass and drum pulse, and vocalist Paul Carrack abandoned the strict vocal cadence to improvise on the pleading chorus. The crowd, which previously stood only when asked, erupted into a dancing mass as the intensity level on stage increased with every guitar-reinforced backbeat. This was clearly the show's peak moment.

The 75-minute show was Mike and the Mechanics' premiere live performance, the start of a nationwide summer tour. It came off surprisingly clean: Background vocals were tight and in tune, solos were taken with confidence, tricky ensemble sections were played without disruption.

The Mechanics have a number of instrumental options at their disposal. Drummer Peter Van

Music Review

Hooke uses Simmons electronic drums, and chooses from a variety of stored sounds — from harsh techno to the echoey crack of the old-time snare drum. Both leader Mike Rutherford, of Genesis, and guitarist Ashley Robert took turns playing bass. On *Silent Running* and others, Lee's sampling keyboards handled the bass parts, leaving Rutherford and Robert to develop a drone-heavy twin-guitar attack.

Vocals were split between ex-Squeeze man Carrack, who has more than a hint of Phil Collins affectation, and Paul (not the famous one) Young.

The Mechanics blasted through most of their currently hot album — including a hushed version of the drum machine-grounded ballad *Par Avion* — and re-interpreted Rutherford's *I Don't Think I Wanna Know* as a slow reggae-funk testimonial. Genesis material was avoided entirely.

Opening the show was the English band Keep It Dark. Their U.S. debut was distinguished by a collection of muscular, slightly imaginative rock songs sung poorly. The instrumental backing for too-long selections like *If You'll Be Mine Tonight* and *Don't Surrender* rang clean and competent, but exposed lead singer Jimmy Barrett as one who needs work on both pitch and delivery.

PART FIVE: MIKE RUTHERFORD

PART FIVE: MIKE RUTHERFORD

CHAPTER FORTY-FIVE
"THE MIRACLE TOUR" 1986

Mike and Tony had begun their solo careers at approximately the same time in a bid to give Phil a chance to sort out his marital problems back in 1979/80. Of the pair of them it was Mike who eventually took the plunge and decided to become a touring artist in his own right.

This wasn't before he had released a pair of solo albums under his own name, with 1980s *Smallcreep's Day* and 1982's *Acting Very Strange*; the latter featuring Mike doing the singing himself. It was as a result of the experience during the latter album that Mike realised that if he were to become a solo artist he would have to do so within the confines of another band of musicians with him as writer.

To this end he began to put together a group of musicians with the intention of recording material that he had written. He was fortunate early on to enlist the services of both Paul Carrack (ex-Ace, Squeeze) and Paul Young (ex-Sad Café), along with the writing and producing talents of both B. A. Robertson and Chris Neil. Out of this combination emerged Mike & the Mechanics whose eponymous debut was released in 1985. The band's first single, 'Silent Running', became an unexpected hit in the USA and as a result of its success and that of its successor, 'All I Need is a Miracle', Mike opted to indulge in a spot of touring in the USA in the summer of 1986, prior to returning to the Genesis fold for the recording of what would become the massive *Invisible Touch* album.

The new look band included Mike, both Carrack and Young and Ashley Mumford, who had been in Sad Café with Young, and Adrian Lee a well-known session keyboard player and Peter van Hooke on drums. With only one album to draw upon, the band nevertheless managed to put together a show that not only highlighted that album, but also brought in a few unexpected highlights, including a performance of 'Maxine', 'I Don't Wanna Know' and 'Halfway There' from *Acting Very Strange* – an album that Mike has not revisited in the live context since. The aptly titled *Miracle Tour* was a US-only affair but thankfully several of these shows were recorded and I have selected a couple of these here that document the tour quite nicely.

KIEL OPEN HOUSE, ST LOUIS, MISSOURI, USA, 10 JUNE 1986
Set List: Hanging by a Thread/Halfway There/Silent Running/Taken In/I Don't Wanna Know/Maxine/Par Avion/A Call to Arms/Tempted/I Get the Feeling/Take the Reins/All I Need is a Miracle/Gimme Some Lovin'//
Source: Audience Recording.

With only the time to promote the new album with a handful of shows, we are lucky that a few of them were recorded for posterity, including this audience recording from St Louis. Sadly the quality is not all that would be desired, nevertheless, it does manage to capture the essential spark of these early outings by the Mechanics.

The show opens with 'Hanging by a Thread' and immediately we are struck by just how good a choice Mike had made in enlisting Paul Young. This one is right up his street as a rabble rousing rocker and it is evident that he is in his element here. 'Halfway There' comes next, one of only two tracks from either of Mike's earlier solo albums to be given an outing at a Mechanics show. With its slightly reggae-ish rhythm it is Paul Young who takes on the vocal duties again and it has to be said, he brings an edginess to it that was definitely lacking on the album.

'Silent Running', the recent US hit, is next and even on this first tour, it is a bona fide classic. Sadly, as is often the case with US audiences, there is an excessive amount of chatter throughout, which spoils what sounds like an excellent performance of this awesome track, but at least it also serves to show that the audiences were enthusiastic about the new band! Adrian Lee and Peter van Hooke deliver a wonderful backing while we get to hear Paul Carrack's dulcet tones for the first time and he delivers in spades.

'Taken In' slows the pace down a bit with a tale of love lost served up in fine style by Paul Young, whose performance here reminds me of the heady days of his time in Sad Café. Sadly, once again the audience chatter is irritating here. It's back to *Acting Very Strange* next with 'I Don't Wanna Know', which the audience obviously don't know. This one works surprisingly well in the live context and sounds quite funky here, which definitely suits Paul Young's rough and ready vocals.

One of the tracks from the same album that had always been a favourite of mine is next, namely 'Maxine'. Once again, it is Young who takes on the vocal duties and he certainly seems to be relishing his new role within the band. Mike and Ashley Mumford put in some fine work on the guitar parts, while Peter van Hooke underpins everything with some fine percussive work.

'Par Avion' and 'A Call to Arms' give us an excellent contrast between the mellow and the rocky sides of the Mechanics. The former is performed with just the right tinge of bathos by Young who also brings one of Mike's most famous Genesis "bits" vividly to life augmented by excellent harmonies from Carrack and Mike himself.

Carrack gets to shine next with his Squeeze hit, 'Tempted', which he introduces as a "little foreigner"; an expression which I am sure the audience didn't understand. Never mind, they obviously know the song and not surprising really, as it is a little belter, and Paul is obviously having a great time performing it. By now the party is evidently in full swing, and 'I Get the Feeling' sets just the right atmosphere, and Carrack's soul man vocal does the song to a turn. The rest of the band put in an impeccable performance too, with Lee and Hooke in particular standing out here.

Paul Young gets the chance to rock out again next with 'Take the Reins' with its industrial grind and impatient rhythms threatening to tear down the roof. Audience participation is in full flow here and for once it actually adds to the atmosphere of the performance. By now the band have realised that they have definitely won over the St Louis audience and 'All I Need is a Miracle' is definitely something they don't need. The crowd love it and the party turns into a celebration, which is rounded off nicely by a slick performance of the Spencer Davis Group's classic, 'Gimme Some Lovin''.

TOWER THEATRE, UPPER DARBY, PENNSYLVANIA, USA, 19 JUNE 1986

Set List: Hanging by a Thread/Silent Running/Maxine/Taken In/A Call to Arms/Tempted/I Get the Feeling/All I Need is a Miracle//
Source: FM Radio Broadcast.

A few days after the St Louis show the band reached Upper Darby and the Tower Theatre; a scene of so many triumphs by Genesis in earlier years. Thankfully the legendary King Biscuit Flower Hour people recorded and broadcast this one, so at last we get to hear the real glories of the band's performance.

From the opening broadside of 'Hanging by a Thread', what we have here is a band evidently enjoying themselves and their new-found success. Mike puts in some excellent rhythm guitar work here and Paul Young's vocals are intense. Sadly this is an edited recording obviously done for with the constraints of broadcast time in mind. Never mind, what it lacks in quantity it more than makes up for in quality. 'Silent Running' is next and Mike acknowledges the theatre in his introduction. The crowd are high enough in the mix for you to realise that they were in the mood for a party tonight and here we get a chance to hear Paul Carrack at his best, soulful and full of emotion.

'Maxine' takes us back to Mike's pre-Mechanics days and Mr Young gets us in the groove with a particularly feisty performance here. The rest of the band get right behind him with some tasty and tight playing, especially the rhythm section and the harmony vocals are spot on too. 'Taken In' slows the pace down here and provides a nice contrast to the rock and roll excess that has gone before it. Unfortunately the radio announcer ruins it by his introduction of associate radio stations at the start. No matter, the song is a delight here with an impeccable performance all round.

The origins of 'A Call to Arms' are acknowledged by Mike, garnering a cheer from the crowd. Cue mini save the world lecture from Mike but before he gets too preachy the song begins with Adrian Lee's sepulchral keyboards melding into some fine guitar work from Mike and Ashley. Paul Young is evidently in his element here and this is a wonderfully theatrical (pun intended) performance.

Mr Carrack's other band's hit – 'Tempted' – comes next and the audience give it a rapturous reception. It's a great song, brilliantly delivered here, before the recording ends with the funky rhythms of 'I Get the Feeling' and you can tell that the band are enjoying themselves, and so are the crowd if their reaction to the final track – 'All I Need is a Miracle' – is anything to go by. A bona fide classic this one and the band tear through it, with Mr Young leading the rock and roll chorus, bringing this excellent recording to a suitably exhilarating climax.

PART FIVE: MIKE RUTHERFORD

CHAPTER FORTY-SIX
"A CALL TO ARMS" 1989

The massive success of Genesis' Invisible Touch album meant that for most of what remained of 1986 and 1987 Mike was fully occupied with writing, touring, and promotional duties with that band and it was not until the latter part of 1987 and early 1988 that he could begin to consider a follow up album to the first Mechanics project.

Retaining the services of the musicians that had been so integral to the success of that album, the second Mechanics album was destined to take the band to new heights on the back of a song that almost didn't get recorded. 'Living Years' is a song that Mike had written with B. A. Robertson as a tribute to their recently deceased fathers. It was released as the album's second single and it touched a chord with the public both at home and abroad and the band had an unexpected massive hit on their hands.

By the time the band began their first European tour in the spring of 1989, their profile was higher than any "part-time" band has a right to expect, and demand for the shows was high. With two albums to draw upon now, the resulting shows amply demonstrated the strengths of the band – great songs and marvellous singers. The show drew exclusively from the two Mechanics projects but that was more than enough to satisfy the capacity audiences, which filled out the theatres on the European and subsequent US legs of the tour.

CITY HALL, NEWCASTLE, ENGLAND, 18 MARCH 1989
Tracks; Nobody's Perfect/Seeing is Believing/Silent Running/Don't/Nobody Knows/Hanging by a Thread/Why Me/Taken In/Beautiful Day/Black and Blue/Par Avion/A Call to Arms/The Living Years/I Get the Feeling/Take the Reins/All I Need is a Miracle/Poor Boy Down//
Source: Audience Recording.

At last! The Mechanics make it to the UK for series of highly successful shows, of which this recording from Newcastle is one of the best – well, that's my opinion and I was there!

By the time of these gigs, the band were riding high on the success of the 'Living Years' single and audiences were keen to see Mike's new outfit and the band didn't disappoint. Opening with 'Nobody's Perfect' and 'Seeing is Believing' from the new record, the band grabbed the audience by the scruff of the neck with a rocking couple of openers. Paul Young is in his element here and the rest of the band aren't far behind him in the enjoyment stakes.

'Silent Running' opens with a suitably eerie keyboard phrase from Adrian Lee and some cheers of recognition from the crowd. This one's already established as a live favourite and the band take it to new heights tonight. Paul Carrack puts in an astonishing vocal performance underpinned by some tasteful percussion from Peter Van Hooke. Back to the new album next with 'Don't'; a feisty little number with some spiky guitar playing from Mike and a firm backbeat from Van Hooke. Paul Carrack's vocal is suitably impassioned giving the song a sharper edge than on the recorded version.

'Nobody Knows' calms things down for a while before the tempo increases again with a raucous 'Hanging by a Thread'. Paul Young is in best rabble rousing mode here and Mike delivers some blistering runs on his guitar brining the song to vivid life. 'Why Me?', with its symphonic keyboard opening, sounds like it belongs in a film soundtrack and is delivered in a suitably dramatic fashion by the band, with Carrack in particular putting in an excellent performance.

'Taken In' gives everyone a chance to get a breather and an infectious rhythm that finally got some of the unusually restrained audience out of their seats for a bit of a bop. The calm doesn't last long, however, as the band throw themselves into a storming version of 'Beautiful Day' and another superb vocal performance from Paul Young. Personally I think this one would have made a great choice as a single.

'Black and Blue' with its cod reggae rhythms gets the audience going again. I must admit that I hadn't like this one on the album but live it is catchy and really effective giving all of the band members a chance to jam around a bit and show off their talents.

'Par Avion' slowed things down again and gave the more enthusiastic members of the audience (yours truly included) a chance to get our breath back. 'A Call to Arms' and its tale of injustice picked the pace up again with Carrack and Young trading off vocal performances in a fine vocal duel.

Then the song came that finally woke the audience up, namely 'Living Years', although even Paul Carrack's beautifully impassioned vocal failed to lift the majority of the audience out of their seats. Throughout all of this I remember Mike looking quietly confident as if he knew that the band would eventually get the audience going. 'I Get the Feeling' and 'Take the Reins' firmly demonstrated that despite being a member of that progressive rock dinosaur that is Genesis, he can still write catchy and entertaining tunes and the band delivered them both with panache.

'All I Need is a Miracle' rounds off the show proper and the "miracle" finally happened as the audience began to actively participate in "their show". Once again, Paul Young took charge of this rock and roll party and turned what had seemed like a wake into a real celebration. Leaving the stage to deserved applause, the band return to deliver their encore. 'Poor Boy Down' is a strange song but with its punchy and infectious rhythms and a majestic vocal performance, once again from Mr Young, the recording closes on a suitable high point.

THE PAVILION CONCORD, WASHINGTON DC, USA, 24 AUGUST 1989
Set List: Nobody's Perfect/Seeing is Believing/Don't/Beautiful Day/Nobody Knows/Silent Running/Taken In/The Living Years/I Get the Feeling/Poor Boy Down/All I Need is a Miracle/Revolution//
Source: Audience Recording.

The Living Years album and single had catapulted the band's popularity and made it essential for them to return to the USA to capitalise on that success. An extensive series of shows was organised for the late summer of 1989 bringing the new look show to US audiences. The band had also recently contributed to the soundtrack of the latest film by US comedy duo, Cheech & Chong, and their contribution to the *Rude Awakenings* soundtrack was a cover of the Lennon/McCartney classic, 'Revolution', which was performed at several shows on this US tour and thankfully this recording is one of them.

Once again the staccato keyboards of Adrian Lee and a soaring guitar from Mr Rutherford himself take this track to new heights and unlike the Newcastle show, the audience are in fine voice from the very start, augmenting Paul Young's impassioned vocal. The rock and roll continues with 'Seeing is Believing' driven along by some marvellous drumming from Peter Van Hooke and Mike's guitar, over which Young once again gives us another magnificent rock and roll vocal.

Driving along nicely, we get the funky rhythms of 'Don't' next and a marvellous soulful vocal from Paul Carrack gliding over the incessant rhythms of Mike and the rest of the band. No rest for the wicked as 'Beautiful Day' keeps the pace up and the band's harmonies here are excellent, which is not surprising really with vocalists of this calibre, is it? 'Nobody Knows' and 'Silent Running' continue the tempo. Mike's guitar on the former has a jazziness, which was lacking in the UK shows. Both vocalists share the honours on the former with a soulful and at times raucous performance whilst the latter gets instant recognition from the crowd and the intro draws out the suspense before Lee's soaring keyboard ensures the song gets the necessary lift off. Once again, the rhythm section of Mike and Peter Van Hooke gives this one an added edge, over which Carrack's vocal cuts like a knife.

'Taken In' and its jazzy intro take things down a pace or two and Paul Young gives it one of his finest performances. It's just a shame that once again the audience seems more intent on chattering rather than listening. With its success both at home and elsewhere it isn't surprising that 'Living Years' elicits a cheer from the crowd. This is Carrack's masterpiece and he grabs the opportunity to shine with a truly impressive vocal performance.

'I Get the Feeling's' incessant rhythms give Carrack another chance to bring the goods home and he is evidently enjoying himself. Aided and abetted by some equally impressive playing from the rest of the band, this one is a sheer slice of musical fun.

Back to the rock & roll next with 'Poor Boy Down', elevated from encore status tonight, and if anyone had any doubts about Paul Young's rock credentials, then listen to this and you will soon revise that opinion. He delivers what is without one of the ballsiest vocals I have ever heard from him. He's not alone though, as the rest of the band get down and dirty with some fine licks too in an impressive performance.

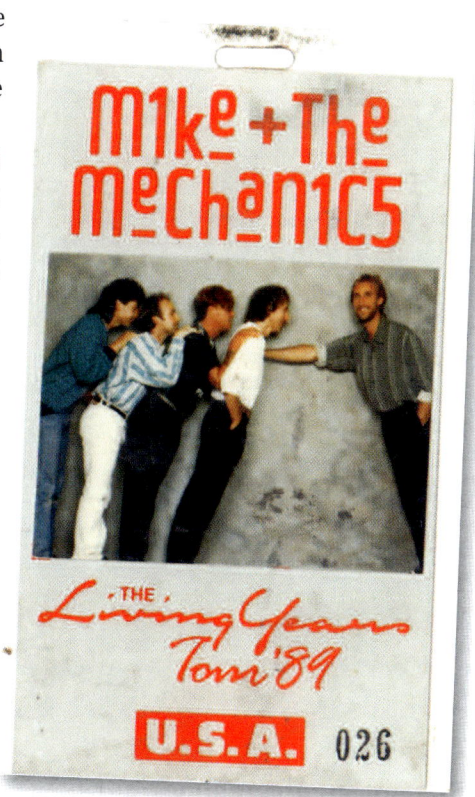

'All I Need is a Miracle' continues the rock and roll with another fine version of this classic Mechanics song ending the show on a suitably high point. That leaves the encore, and with 'Poor Boy Down' out of the running, the band's choice tonight makes this one a must for Mechanics collectors, as the band pull out a surprise performance of the classic Beatles' hit, 'Revolution', which the band had recently recorded for a film soundtrack. From this recording it is obvious that the band had swallowed the chance to perform this one with a heap of collective glee and the end result is a marvellous, fun way to conclude a show.

PART FIVE: MIKE RUTHERFORD

CHAPTER FORTY-SEVEN
"HITS ON A BEACH OF GOLD" 1995-1996

Once again, Mike reconvened with Tony and Phil for the recording of what was to prove to be Phil's last album with Genesis: 1991's *We Can't Dance* and the massive tour that followed it. Mike had found time to write and record the third Mechanics album prior to this but 1991's *Word of Mouth* was something of a lacklustre affair when compared to its predecessor, and with the constraints placed on him by duties with Genesis, there were no shows in support of the album.

With touring and promotional duties for the Genesis album over, Mike was able to put the Mechanics back together again in 1994 for what was to become their biggest album to date. *Beggar on a Beach of Gold* was released in February 1995, by which time several of its singles had ingrained themselves into the public consciousness. With another hit album on their hands, the band took to the highways and byways of the UK and Europe during the summer of 1995 with a new stage show, which contained just about everything any Mechanics fan could ask for, including a delightful medley of songs from the "other" bands that Mike and the two Pauls had been in.

Capitalising on this success, the band's record company put together a hits package in 1996 accompanied by a compilation of their promotional videos. With demand for the band still high, a second UK tour was organised and it was another great success with sell-out crowds at many of the venues that it took in. Fundamentally the set remained the same throughout both tours, although there were enough changes to keep it interesting for both the band and collectors and fortunately several excellent recordings from both tours are in general circulation, including those mentioned here.

SHEPHERD'S BUSH EMPIRE THEATRE, LONDON, ENGLAND, 18 JULY 1995

Set List: Interview/Get Up/You Really Got a Hold on Me/Over My Shoulder/Silent Running/Plain & Simple/Someone Always Hates Someone/Another Cup of Coffee/Web of Lies/Living Years/Word of Mouth//
Source: FM Radio Broadcast.

The Mechanics have been quite well served by radio recordings and this one, from the *Beggar on a Beach of Gold* tour, is no exception.

Opening the show with a stomping performance of 'Get Up', the band are evidently in great form and Paul Carrack in particular is in fine voice, augmented by the equally feisty harmonies from Paul Young. The band slow things down next for a fine rendition of the Smoky Robinson classic, 'You Really Got a Hold on Me', which suits Carrack's soulful voice to a tee. Mind you, Young is no slouch here either, while the rest of the band slip into a suitably laidback groove.

With an album chock full of hits in their hands, it is no surprise that we get several of them here, starting with a superb performance of 'Over My Shoulder', which will have you whistling the tune by the end of it! 'Silent Running' takes us back to where it began for the band. Keyboards and acoustic guitar strip the song back to the bare essentials for a surprisingly good acoustic version.

'Plain and Simple' and 'Someone Always Hates Someone' contrast the two sides of the band with the former giving Paul Young a chance to rock out with some rabble-rousing vocals and Mike gives the lie to anyone who thinks he can't write rock riffs with some marvellous meaty playing. The latter is an altogether more retrained and thought-provoking performance, which is a delight to hear.

'Another Cup of Coffee' lightens the mood somewhat with a marvellous soulful vocal from Carrack and Young. Simple but effective, bit like the Mechanics themselves, eh? Back to the dramatic stuff next, as a lush keyboard intro leads into a particularly fiery version of 'Web of Lies' with Mike and Tim Renwick trading off some superb riffs an excellent accompaniment to Carrack's impassioned vocal. No Mechanics concert would be complete without the 'Living Years' and it is delivered here in a superb version with Carrack catching just the right amount of emotion without descending into mawkishness. This excellent recording closes with a suitably upbeat 'Word of Mouth', in which the band and the audience take equal honours.

EMPIRE THEATRE, LIVERPOOL, ENGLAND, 14 APRIL 1996

Set List: Silent Running/Seeing is Believing/Get Up/A Beggar on a Beach of Gold/Someone Always Hates Someone/Another Cup of Coffee/Plain & Simple/Eyes of Blue/Nobody's Perfect/Every Day Hurts/How Long?/I Can't Dance/Living Years/All I Need is a Miracle/Word of Mouth/Over My Shoulder//
Source: Audience Recording.

The Mechanics in Liverpool at last! Another excellent audience recording documents the band's first visit to my home town and in above average quality too. The taper was evidently sitting in a good seat, as sound is well balanced throughout this one.

An extended intro leads into 'Silent Running' and the show is off to a top notch start. Even the echoey acoustics of the theatre bring an extra edginess to Paul Carrack's marvellously impassioned vocal. Mike's guitar rips the air with some stabbing riffs as the band launch into 'Seeing is Believing', giving a nice opportunity for Mr Young to indulge in some serious rabble rousing, while the bluesy 'Get Up' shows the magnificent harmony vocals of both Pauls,

'A Beggar on a Beach of Gold' rattles round the theatre with some neat playing from Mike and the ever solid Gary Wallis on percussion, while the poignant message of 'Someone Always Hates Someone' is brought vividly to life by one of Paul Young's best vocal performances of the night. It is a simple but thought provoking song and it's marvellous here.

'Another Cup of Coffee' lightens the mood somewhat with Paul Carrack taking on the vocal duties in this miniature soap opera of a song, which is upbeat and catchy with some understated playing from Mike and Tim Renwick. 'Plain & Simple' is another laidback rocker with some more excellent guitar playing from Mike and another laid back percussive delivery from Gary.

A solo spot for Mr Carrack comes next as he gets to plug his excellent new single/album 'Eyes of Blue'; a classic slice of the soulful performances that he is deservedly famous for. 'Nobody's Perfect' gets the mood up again with its jaunty keyboard intro and some searing guitar from Mike and Tim, over which Paul Young delivers yet another superb vocal.

The medley of material from the previous bands that the main incumbents have been in comes next, opening with a beautiful performance of the *Sad Café* classic, 'Every Day Hurts', which brought back so many memories for me then and now. This is followed by an equally superb performance of the Squeeze hit, 'How Long?' before the band get the crowd really in the mood to party with a down and dirty version of 'I Can't Dance', which sees Paul Young outdoing Mr Collins in the vocal stakes!

'Living Years' is delivered without descending into mawkishness with Carrack's brilliant vocal really getting the crowd going before the show proper ends with an equally emphatic performance by Paul Young on 'All I Ned is a Miracle'. Cue party time at the Empire as the crowd get up and boogie (yours truly included).

The encores aren't long in coming and 'Word of Mouth' with choirmaster Young leading the Scouse choir gets them started in typically upbeat fashion. Young is in his element here and the rest of the band give him his head as he and the crowd celebrate what has been an amazing night for the Mechanics. 'Over My Shoulder' keeps the atmosphere high with its infectious tune and another superb vocal from Carrack bringing the show to a marvellous close.

PART FIVE: MIKE RUTHERFORD

CHAPTER FORTY-EIGHT
"TRAVELLING ON THE M6" 1999

By the time Mike had undertaken the 1996 UK tour, Phil's departure from Genesis had been officially announced and as usual the obituaries were being written just as prematurely as they had been back in 1975. Genesis regrouped and bravely recruited relative unknown Ray Wilson for 1997's excellent *Calling all Stations* album and tour before effectively imploding.

Mike got the Mechanics back together again late in 1998 to begin work on their fifth studio album, which was to be confusingly titled *M6* upon its release on 31 May 1999. The tour to promote the album had already begun with a warm-up show at the Hanover Grand Theatre in London on 10 May and the UK tour proper commencing in York on 13 May. As usual, the new show drew heavily on the new album but with a healthy dose of older material guaranteed to keep the fans happy.

The tour was scheduled to continue into 2000 with festival shows in Europe pencilled in. These were cancelled in the light of Paul Young's untimely death on 15 July 2000 at the mere age of 53. As a result the band's last gig with Paul – a TV special for German TV on 19 September 1999 – takes on a special significance and is included here.

HANOVER GRAND CLUB, LONDON, ENGLAND, 10 MAY 1999
Set List: Ordinary Girl/Now That You've Gone/Another Cup of Coffee/Whenever I Stop/All the Light I Need/Every Day Hurts/How Long?/I Can't Dance/Living Years/All I Need is a Miracle/Over My Shoulder//
Source: FM Radio Broadcast.
Missing Tracks: A Beggar on a Beach of Gold/Get Up/My Little Island/Word of Mouth//

This was the final warm-up show before the tour proper commenced a few days later and an invited audience (including yours truly) crammed into the Grand Theatre for what was to be an extremely enjoyable evening. What we have here is the subsequent edited radio broadcast, so several tracks are missing, so we open with a superb performance of 'Ordinary Girl', with Paul Young giving his all in the vocal department. The new single, 'Now That You've Gone', is next and is delivered in a feisty manner by the band who sound relaxed and enjoying themselves almost as much as the crowd (but not quite!)

A mesmerising performance of 'Another Cup of Coffee' comes next with Paul Carrack getting the vocal plaudits. Always a magnificent performer, he sounds in his element here, while the rest of the band ably accompany him. Carrack continues to shine with the next number too, namely 'All the Light I Need', before we get to the band's medley of hits from their various "other bands", which runs us nicely through 'Every Day Hurts', 'How Long?', and 'I Can't Dance' respectively, all of which are served up piping hot and relished by the enthusiastic crowd which you can hear even on this radio broadcast.

An emotional (is there any other kind?) performance of the 'Living Years' gets full audience participation but we aren't allowed to get too maudlin, as the band next get the audience off their collective duffs with a stomping version of 'All I Need is a Miracle', with Paul Young fully in the driving seat for this high energy version and evidently feeding off the audience reaction. Only one of the encores is included here but it is one of the best Mechanics songs, the irritatingly catchy 'Over My Shoulder' with Carrack and Co. keeping the crowd on their toes. With Paul Young's sad death a few months later, this is an excellent tribute to the band he was such a big part of.

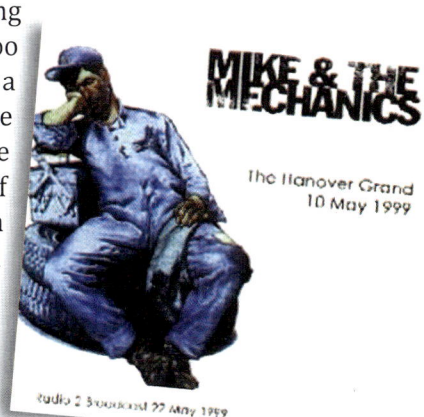

WDR TV STUDIOS, BADEN BADEN, GERMANY, SEPTEMBER 1999
Set List: Silent Running/Ordinary Girl/Now That You've Gone/Another Cup of Coffee/All the Light I Need/The Living Years/How Long?/ Every Day Hurts/I Can't Dance/All I Need is a Miracle/Over My Shoulder//
Source: TV Broadcast.

This one is a recording with particular historic significance and poignancy. This was to be Paul Young's last public performance with the Mechanics before his untimely death a year later and as such this one is an essential document in the band's story.

Fortunately, the good people at WDR's *Ohne Filter* TV show captured the proceedings for posterity and the end result is this superb TV broadcast, which means that unlike so many of the other recordings mentioned here, you can see what goes on for yourselves.

After the MC has his usual ramble, the band take the stage for the now standard restrained intro to 'Silent Running', with some fine acoustic picking from new boy Jamie Moses before Paul Carrack lets rip with those soulful vocals of his on a masterful performance, which is followed by the first of the new tracks tonight, 'Ordinary Girl', with Mr Young getting things moving whilst Mike puts in some nifty riffs himself.

Mike acknowledges the contribution that Germany has made to the Mechanics' success before the band launch into the new single, 'Now That You've Gone'; an uptempo delight with Carrack ably joined in the harmony vocals by Young and Moses. 'Another Cup of Coffee' is a classic slice of Mechanics and without doubt one of Paul Carrack's best vocal performances, although he and Youngie deliver superb harmonies, and it is in this department as well as his sheer larger than life character that Paul Young will be missed.

'All the Light I Need', an unabashed love song, gets the full Mechanics treatment here with Mike donning acoustic guitar for a laidback and soulful performance from the entire band. What can you say about 'Living Years' that hasn't already been said? Not a lot, so suffice to say that the performance you have here is another superb one, obviously taking on extra significance in the light of subsequent events.

Band intros follow and the now ubiquitous medley of their "other band hits" starting with 'Every Day Hurts' from Paul Young's Sad Café days; a peach of a song and he delivers a simply spine-tingling performance of it here; a worthy tribute to Paul. This is followed by an equally enjoyable rendition of 'How Long?' – Carracks' Squeeze classic social comment song – before the familiar drum rhythm and guitar riff of 'I Can't Dance' give Mr Yong another chance to rabble rouse and you can plainly see that he is having a real blast here. No crotch-grabbing or gurning though, thank goodness!

The party atmosphere continues with 'All I Need is a Miracle', and once again, Young is in complete control as he gets the crowd into the party mood. His face is lit up with a huge grin as he puts 110 per cent into another masterful performance ably assisted by a top notch effort from the rest of the band. The DVD concludes with 'Over My Shoulder' with Carrack taking centre stage to join in the fun – a delightful ending to a superb performance and a fitting tribute to the band and to the late, great Mr Paul Young in particular.

CHAPTER FORTY-NINE
"GETTING REWIRED" 2004

Paul Young's death in 2000 had effectively put paid to the Mechanics in many fans' eyes, but after a lengthy lay off Mike got back together with Paul Carrack to record *Rewired*; a much more experimental album, which was released to public indifference on 7 June 2004. With no single to help the album, it soon sank without a trace.

The new look band, however, did undertake a series of shows, ironically enough as opening act for Phil Collins on his *First Final Farewell Tour*. Restricted to Europe, these shows were the only promotion that the album received, although a Mechanics show proper at the Shepherds Bush Empire Theatre in London was subsequently organised and filmed for a live concert DVD.

AMSTERDAM ARENA, AMSTERDAM, NETHERLANDS, 19 JUNE 2004
Set List: Sooner Or Later/Now That You've Gone/Silent Running/If I Were You/One Left Standing/Living Years/Over My Shoulder/Word of Mouth//
Source: Audience Recording.

Supporting Phil Collins must have been a strange experience for Mike, but with the reception to the *Rewired* album being less than they might have hoped, it was perhaps better to showcase it this way than with a bona fide tour on their own.

I freely admitted at the time that I did not like the *Rewired* album, although in the live context it does come over better than one might expect. Sadly, the only recordings available are audience recordings of varying quality, of which this one from Amsterdam is the best I have heard. Opening with 'Sooner or Later' from the new album, Carrack is in fine form even in the enormous arena that they are evidently playing, if the echoey nature of the recording is anything to go by.

'Now That You've Gone' could perhaps be seen as a tacit acknowledgement of the absence of Paul Young. Either way, this one works much better. Mike gets into the groove here and the rest of the band give Carrack able support as he gives it his best shot. 'Silent Running' sees the band on much more familiar territory and a funkier version of this classic seems to blow the cobwebs away from both band and audience.

Back to the new album with a laidback version of 'If I Were You', and although it's a fine song, it loses much of its impact in the huge arena's echoing acoustics. 'One Left Standing' also doesn't benefit from the sheer size of the venue, although the performance is still much better than it had been on record.

Even 'Living Years' doesn't make much impact on a crowd who are obviously waiting for the main event, which is a shame, because they obviously miss out on witnessing what sounds like an above average performance of this classic Mechanics tune. 'Over My Shoulder' and 'Word of Mouth' only really serve to emphasise the sheer gap in the band left by Paul Young's death. Carrack's pipes are fine within their own element but he sounds embarrassingly out of his depth, especially on the latter, which really needs a rabble rousing vocal such as only Mr Young could deliver in order to make it work in a venue as big as this, and here the performance falls sadly flat.

CHAPTER FIFTY
"HITTING THE ROAD" 2010-13

Rewired saw the end of Paul Carracks' involvement with the Mechanics and many fans began to suspect that the band had run its course. The nay sayers were to be proven wrong, however, when in the autumn of 2010 Mike re-emerged with a new look Mechanics to promote a brand new Mechanics album with two brand new singers.

His choice once again proved to be inspired. Andrew Roachford was already a well-known name here in the UK at least and a fine artist in his own right. Canadian Tim Howar was not as well-known but had carved out a successful career in musicals and with his own band, Van Tramp, prior to joining the Mechanics. The resulting album, *The Road*, was released on 18 April 2011 and a UK/European tour was also organised.

Promoting the new album aside, the resulting show also highlighted many of the band's past glories to brilliant effect. There was even space for a couple of Roachford hits as well, which were well received by the crowds. Once again, the tour is well represented not only by audio recordings, but by several TV shows as well, some of which are mentioned here. The band have also returned to the concert stage both in the UK and Europe in 2012 and 2013 showcasing the new album and reintroducing audience to the Mechanics' unique brand of musical classics at the same time.

BAND ON THE WALL CLUB, MANCHESTER, ENGLAND, 25 NOVEMBER 2010
Set List: The Road/Get Up/Try to Save Me/Beggar on a Beach of Gold//
Source: FM Radio broadcast.

This was the first public appearance by the new look line up of the band. Thankfully, the performance was captured by local radio station, Smooth Radio, and this is the resulting broadcast. Opening with title track from the as yet unreleased new album, 'The Road', it is a suitably ramshackle performance with no gigs under their belts. Even so, the new vocalists, Andrew Roachford and Tim Howar, bring a zesty edginess to the performance, while Mike shows that he hasn't lost any of his magic touch in the guitar department.

'Get Up' takes us back a bit further with a classic slice of Mechanics history, which Paul Young had very much made his own. Here we have Roachford taking the reins and what a fine job he does of it too! The band still sound as if they are finding their feet musically, but old hand Gary Wallis keeps everything together with a rock steady percussive section and once again Mike rocks out in fine style.

'Try to Save Me' takes us back to the new album. Mike introduces it and acknowledges Paul's home town. Another excellent slice of Mechanics atmospheric writing and playing here. Once again, Roachford's soulful vocal puts you in mind of Paul Carrack without once trying to imitate the latter. A laidback but enjoyable performance all round.

The final track on this recording takes us back to the heady days of *Beggar on a Beach of Gold* and indeed that is the track played. Roachford introduces it with a humorous story about changing trades with his mum thinking he was going to become a mechanic! Once again, the band acknowledge Paul Young's legacy here with a magnificent performance of one of his classic songs. Roachford delivers it with just the right mixture of soul and rock – a credit to both himself and his predecessor rounding off this all too short recording in a fine way.

APOLLO THEATRE, MANCHESTER, ENGLAND, 20 MAY 2011
Set List: The Road/Beggar on a Beach of Gold/Get Up/Try to Save Me/Another Cup of Coffee/Nobody Knows/I Don't Do Love/If I Were You/Only to Be With You/Follow You Follow Me/I Can't Dance/Living Years/Over My Shoulder/All I Need is a Miracle/Cuddly Toy/Word of Mouth//
Source: Audience Recording.

With a new look band, Mike took the Mechanics out on the road (pun intended) again in the spring of 2011. With new vocalists, many fans (myself included) had reservations about the wisdom of this decision but the shows themselves proved that there was life in the old banger yet!

PART FIVE: MIKE RUTHERFORD

A Selection Of Shows: Genesis & Solo Live Guide 1976-2014

Andrew Roachford

Anthony Drennan

Gary Wallis

Mike Rutherford

Luke Juby

Tim Howar

Here we have an above average recording of the band's gig from Manchester, the late Paul Young's old stomping ground so no pressure then?! 'The Road' opens the show and definitely benefits from the live context, Roachford's vocals are excellent here and Mike and Anthony Drennnan put in some tasteful guitar work too getting things off to a good start. 'Beggar on a Beach of Gold' is next and what a pleasant surprise it is too. Tim Howar was an inspired choice for the band and he gives this one every ounce of magic that Paul Young had done before him.

'Get Up' also comes across far better than expected with both singers exhorting the evidently staid audience to "get up". It's difficult to believe that this one comes from that "problem" third album by the band – no problems here. It is a rocking version announcing that the Mechanics are most definitely back! New track 'Try to Save' merges seamlessly into the weave of the show, with another marvellous soulful vocal from Andrew Roachford and the vocal duties are shared equally between him and Tim Howar throughout the show, proving that Mike's decision to reconvene the band was a wise one.

The Mechanics have always been about moods and they give a laidback and polished performance throughout this excellent recording, which should be a delight for any Mechanics fans.

OSTSEEKANAL, KIEL, GERMANY, 24 JUNE 2012

Set List: A Beggar on a Beach of Gold/Get Up/Try to Save /Another Cup of Coffee/Throwing it all Away/Silent Running/I Get the Feeling/ This Generation/The Way You Look at Me/Cuddly Toy/Word of Mouth/Follow You Follow Me/I Can't Dance//
Source: TV/FM Radio Broadcast.

The Mechanics returned to the concert stage during the summer to consolidate the profile of the new look band. This recording, taken from either a TV or radio broadcast is an excellent example of their new live show, although there had been a few alterations from the show which the band had performed in 2011. Opening with the magnificent 'A Beggar on a Beach of Gold' we get to hear the awesome vocals of Tim Howar who does a superlative job taking on one of the late Paul Young's classic performances.

From the comments about keeping people warm and apologies for the rain, this was obviously an open air gig, so what better to lift the spirits than 'Get Up'? This is an altogether more soulful performance from the band, in which both Howar and Roachford give it some serious welly in the vocal department, while new boy Luke Juby lays down some impeccable keyboards. 'Try to Save' is the first offering from the new album, replete with some bum notes from Mike – well it was the first gig after all! Once the song gets under way though, there is nothing bum about the performance, which is faultless.

'Another Cup of Coffee' receives a fairly standard treatment here with some excellent harmonies. It is obvious that there is still some rustiness to be knocked off the band though, as there are occasional slips that can be heard, but no one seems to mind. There are several surprises in this set, though not least the inclusion of 'Throwing it all Away', in which Roachford tries to emulate Mr Collins with some participation from some of the crowd. This one falls rather flat for me, but then again I was never that keen on Genesis' version either, if I'm honest!

'Silent Running' reverts to the acoustic intro, but there is no mistaking this classic slice of Mechanics history that soon roars out of the traps with another impeccable vocal performance from Roachford, who does manage to fluff the lyrics at times, but otherwise this is every bit as enjoyable as it ever was, proving that the band have not lost out from not having Paul Carrack's involvement.

'I Get the Feeling' takes the band right back to their first album and here Tim Howar gives his utmost in a funky and downright raunchy performance. Funnily enough, Roachford had said when the author interviewed him last year that he might try and sneak in a few more of his own compositions into the set, so 'This Generation' does exactly that with a soulful and emotive performance, in which the entire band seem to be having a blast.

'(Something in the Way) You Look at Me' is preceded by Roachford asking the crowd for the score in the England football match, which is met with deafening silence as you might expect from a German crowd! It is interesting to see the underrated *Word of Mouth* album getting such a dominant slice of the set but this one is a bona fide classic, and despite the slip ups with the lyrics, it is perhaps even more enjoyable this time round.

Mr Roachford's biggest UK hit is next with 'Cuddly Toy', with some downright raunchy guitar playing from Mike and Anthony Drennan. Andy himself is obviously in his element and this one goes down surprisingly well. Not as well as 'Word of Mouth' though, which is given a truly marvellous workout tonight and it has to be said, Mike's decision to employ Tim Howar and Andrew Roachford has evidently paid off in spades, as this is a genuinely impressive rendition and a worthy tribute to the late Paul Young, who was definitely with the band in spirit tonight.

'Follow You Follow Me' gets off to a somewhat hesitant start as if the band are unfamiliar with it, but once Mike's guitar kicks in there are no more problems and Andy puts in a marvellous vocal performance, which probably brought out the goose bumps among the crowd before the show, which is now evidently subject to more than a bit of rain (well, the old equation of Genesis gig + open air = rain obviously still holds true), so 'I Can't Dance' gives the chance to shake off their blues and join in whilst the band, led by an impressive Tim Howar vocal, bring the show to a suitably uptempo close.

CHAPTER FIFTY-ONE
"REVISITING THE LIVING YEARS"
LIVING YEARS 25TH ANNIVERSARY TOUR 2014

Since The Mechanics reconvened with a new line up in 2011, the band have continued to re-establish the Mechanics "brand" with regular touring both in the UK and Europe and sometimes further afield too.

2014 has proven to be an incredibly busy year for Mike Rutherford, and Mike & The Mechanics. Mike became the first member of Genesis to publish his own autobiography and in addition to that, two compilation albums have also been released celebrating the success that the band has achieved since its inception back in 1985. In addition to this, 2013/14 witnesses the 25th anniversary of the iconic Living Years album and said album was re-issued as a deluxe edition in January 2014 featuring a re-working of the title track and a second disc of live material from the 1989 tours.

The band also undertook an extensive tour of the UK in celebration of that album with a set which focussed on the Living Years material but also drew upon material from most of the rest of the band's back catalogue as well as a nod in the direction of Mike's "other" band and a brace of tracks by vocalist Andrew Roachford as well. The shows were very well received and a new track was aired during the set too, which augurs well for a future album release from the band.

FLORAL PAVILION, NEW BRIGHTON, ENGLAND, 22 FEBRUARY 2014

Set List: A Beggar On A Beach Of Gold/Another Cup of Coffee/Get Up/Try To Save Me/Seeing Is Believing/Silent Running/Don't/My Generation/Turn It On Again/When My Feet Don't Touch The Ground/Nobody's Perfect (fuck up)/Everybody Gets A Second Chance/Cuddly Toy/I Can't Dance/Living Years/All I Need Is A Miracle/Over My Shoulder/Word Of Mouth//
Source: Audience Recording.

With the UK being battered by severe storms at the time of the beginning of this tour, it was a wonder that several of these gigs were not cancelled. Fortunately, this one was unaffected and we have a typical audience recording documenting the evening's performance.

From the outset, the new look band were enjoying themselves as were the audience (yours truly included) and they get things off to a flying start with 'A Beggar On A Beach Of Gold' and 'Another Cup Of Coffee, both of which re-emphasised (if that were necessary) the immense vocal talents of Andrew Roachford and Tim Howar, both of whom have slotted into the vocal seats left vacant by Messrs Carrack and Young. The rest of the band are no slouches either as you can hear as the recording progresses.

Okay, for the audiophiles out there, this one will probably not be their cup of tea (or coffee?) but it does manage to capture something of the atmosphere of the gig especially where the band really let rip such as on 'Nobody's Perfect' and 'All I Need Is A Miracle' which Howar in particular delivers in a fashion which would make his predecessor quite proud.

Mike's day job also gets a look in with a raunchy 'Turn It On Again' and 'I Can't Dance' which falls curiously flat tonight but hey, you can't have everything. What we do get here is a well balanced set drawing on the all too evident strengths of the Mechanics; back catalogue and the resulting recording is an enjoyable if not perfect result.

****

A Selection Of Shows: Genesis & Solo Live Guide 1976-2014

PART SIX: RAY WILSON

CHAPTER FIFTY-TWO
"Not Necessarily Acoustic" 1999 -2003

Ray had already had success with Stiltskin in the mid-1990s and had set about putting together a new band after its demise. He was in the process of doing this when he got the call to join Genesis. Putting his solo career on hold for what proved to be the final recording incarnation of Genesis. Following the one album, *Calling All Stations* and one tour, once it became obvious that Genesis were not about to resume recording and/or touring activities, Ray was free to pick up the threads of his solo career which he duly did, first of all with Cut, the band he had been in the process of setting up when he got the call from Tony Smith to join Genesis.

Cut were very much in a similar vein musically to Ray's earlier band: Stiltskin and secured a record deal with Virgin Records in Germany and the resulting album, *Millionairhead*, was released that year. The new look band undertook a tour in the summer of 1999 promoting that album and things look set fair for Ray to pick up the solo career he had left off. Cut were to prove to be a short-lived affair, mainly owing to the logistics of band members who lived as far apart as Scotland, Norway, and New York – not easy to keep such a disparate group together – and Cut imploded after that tour.

With the failure of Virgin Records to take up the option on a second album by the band, Ray opted to re-evaluate his musical career and went back to basics recording and releasing a handful of acoustically driven albums and with performances mainly reduced to acoustic ones featuring himself, his brother Steve and female vocalist Amanda Lyon. Fortunately there are several excellent quality recordings from this period and I have selected a couple of them here.

Since then, Ray has reconvened his solo career with a string of albums including a resurrected Stiltskin who thus far have released two albums.

ROCK CAFÉ RADIO, SWR3 CLUB, GERMANY, 1999
Set List: Young Ones/Reason for Running/Dark/Another Day/Millionairhead/Not About Us/Inside/Sarah/Space Oddity/Ghost//Squonk (Spock's Beard)//
Source: FM Radio Broadcast.

Ray had already put together a band before he joined Genesis and it is this band, Cut, that we get to hear here in an all too rare radio broadcast that brilliantly captures one of these performances.

From the sound of the recording, this is a large crowd, possibly a festival, but wherever it is from, this is a superb recording, opening with a stomping 'Young Ones' from the debut album. Ray is definitely establishing his credentials as a rock musician but one with a strong penchant for observant lyrics as well as a musical punch.

Ray and his brother Steve rock things up with some ferocious riffs at the start of 'Reason for Running', before the pace calms down for 'Dark'; a haunting performance with another impassioned vocal from Ray.

'Another Day', a reflection on the situation that Ray had found himself in during his time in Stiltskin, is another emotional song, aided here by the sound of Ray's voice, which is betraying some strain, but that simply gives the performance an extra edginess. 'Millionairhead' – another bitterly reflective song – gets a suitably dramatic performance here with Nir Z. putting in a great percussive background and Steve Wilson's guitar buzzes around like an angry wasp.

'Not about Us' slows the tempo down for a marvellous acoustic performance of this sadly underrated Genesis classic. Stripped down to acoustic guitar, voice, and some claps from the audience, this one is a great contrast to the rock that has preceded it and once again, Ray's slightly strained vocal gives it added atmosphere. Inside is given a choral intro before it threatens the roof off the room. 'Dark' – menacing and totally brilliant – is driven along by a superb performance with John Haimes Nir Z. really getting to grips with a fantastic rock song.

'Sarah' is an altogether different beast, catchy infectious and delivered in a suitably jaunty fashion by Ray on acoustic guitar. Ray's homage to David Bowie is next, with 'Space Oddity', which works incredibly well. Ray sounds eerily like Bowie at times here and his harmonies with brother Steve are excellent. The recording is closed by a superb performance of 'Ghost'; Ray's reflection on the situation within Genesis at the time of the cancellation of the US tour. Darkly emotional and thought-provoking, it is followed, ironically enough, by a performance of 'Squonk' by US prog rockers, Spock's Beard, and what it is doing on this recording is anyone's guess, but there you go!

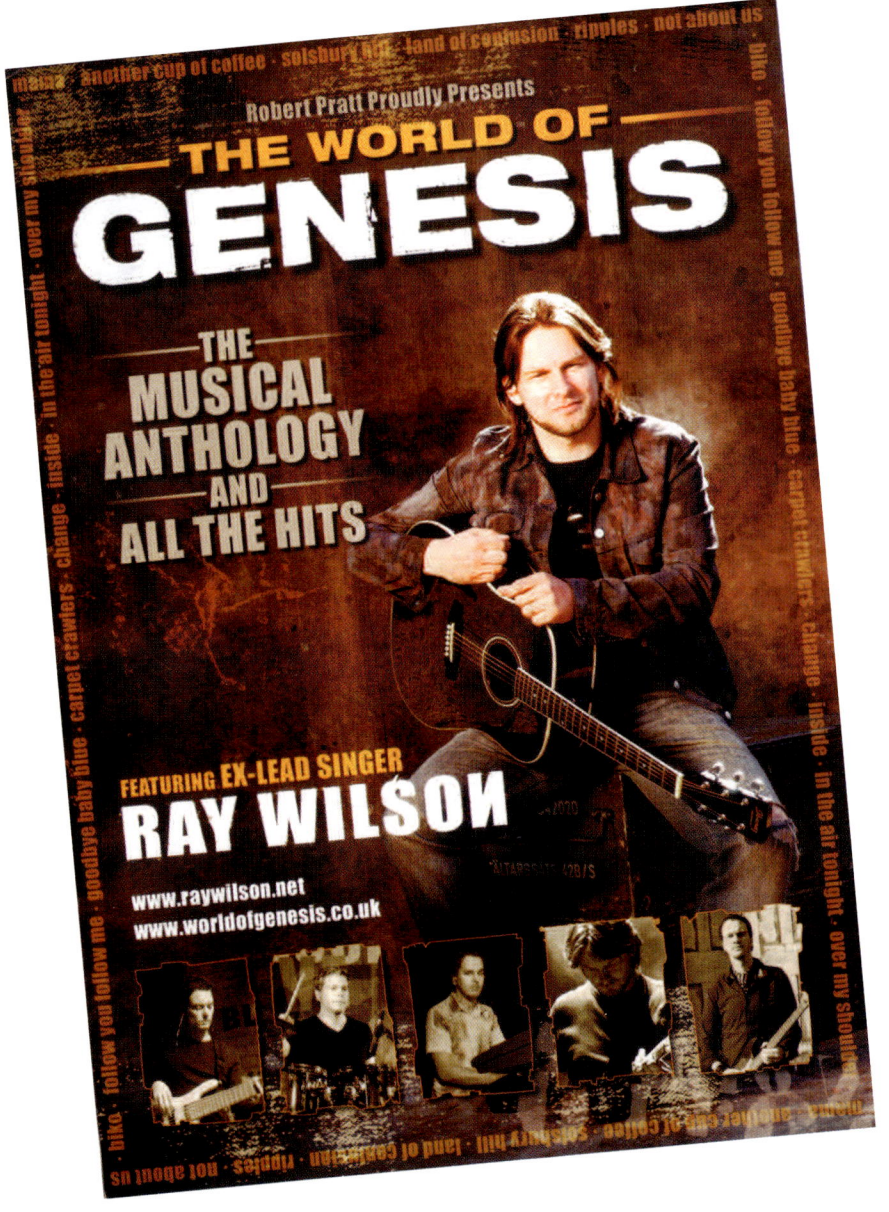

PART SIX: RAY WILSON

CHAPTER FIFTY-THREE
"Visiting The World Of Genesis" 2003 - 2006

By 2003 Ray had re-established his own brand of music with a series of accomplished albums and further extensive touring throughout Europe and with occasional forays back into the UK as well.

Ray has toured incessantly since he began his solo career and thankfully there are many recordings that document the various facets that those tours have taken and I have selected a few of the more interesting ones here.

BURG SATZVEY, MECHERNICH, GERMANY, 23 JULY 2003
Set List: Follow You Follow Me/In the Air Tonight/Change/She Fades Away/No Son of Mine/Believe/Inside/Beach/I Can't Dance/Along the Way/Heroes/Born to Run/Yesterday/Woke Up This Morning/You Don't Bring Me Flowers/The Airport Song/Shipwrecked/Mama/Forever Young/Knocking on Heaven's Door/Hey Hey/Carpet Crawlers/Another Day//
Source: Audience DVD Recording.

A delightful audience recording here captures Ray in fine form, opening with 'Follow You Follow Me'; an acoustic performance that will surely bring back memories for anyone who was lucky enough to catch any of the *Calling all Stations* tour performances of this classic. Ray is in fine form bantering about playing Genesis songs first because they need the royalties, before launching into a stripped down 'In the Air Tonight', which still retains the spirit of the original.

Back to the solo stuff next with 'Change'; the title track to Ray's current solo album. A bitter sweet look at the vagaries of life, delivered with just voice and acoustic guitar, this one still packs a mighty punch. The rest of this excellent recording features a healthy mix of Genesis material and Ray's solo stuff, as well as a good helping of Ray's humorous banter and stories making it an extremely enjoyable offering, and the added bonus here is that it is a DVD recording so you can actually *watch* it as well as listen to it!

UNDERGROUND CLUB, COLOGNE, GERMANY, 23 SEPTEMBER 2003
Set List: Change/Along the Way/Inside/ Gyspy/Shipwrecked/Not about Us/Goodbye Baby Blue/Footsteps//
Source: TV Broadcast.

A magnificent TV broadcast from Germany's Rockpalast series captures Ray performing a set drawn from his solo albums opening with 'Change'. Performing here with a full band it is interesting to compare this performance with the acoustic performance mentioned earlier. Accompanied by his brother, Steve and Amanda Lyon on vocals, the harmonies are much more poignant then when Ray handles this one on his own.

An enthusiastic crowd greet 'Along the Way'. A slightly jazzy rhythm gives this one an altogether warmer feel than is characteristic of so much of Ray's material. Having a female vocalist certainly gives a broader depth to the performance here. Ray's hit with Stiltskin is next. 'Inside' gets the full rock and roll treatment here with some excellent bass playing from Lawrie MacMillan and Ray puts in a superb vocal performance. 'Gypsy', from Ray's only album with Cut, is next. This haunting song is given a laidback performance, which leads to a suitably dramatic climax in which Ray's vocal will send shivers up your spine when you hear it. Ray revisits his time with Genesis next with a marvellous version of the underrated 'Not about Us'. Even Brian McAlpine's accordion sounds totally in place here and this is a gem of a performance.

'Goodbye Baby Blue's' acoustic treatment contrasts nicely with the souped-up version of Stiltskin's 'Footsteps', with which this all too brief recording finishes. This is an excellent document of an extremely enjoyable performance.

BURGERHAUS, WELKERS, GERMANY, 29 MAY 2004
Set List: Follow You Follow Me/Carpet Crawlers/Ghost/Sunshine & Butterflies/Alone/Ever the Reason/Fading Lights/Gypsy/Along the Way/The Actor/Another Cup of Coffee/Biko/Sometimes/Adolescent Breakdown/No Son of Mine/Not About Us/Shipwrecked/Yesterday/Goodbye Baby Blue/Change/Beach/Lover's Leap/Ripples//
Source: Soundboard recording.

An excellent Soundboard recording here of the first night of the German Genesis unofficial fan club's "Ray Vent" in 2004. Ray announces it as if it is a show in his living room before making a sarcastic remark about Mike Rutherford's living room, and then we get the campfire music of 'Follow You Follow Me', which is a beautiful relaxed version getting things off to a nice start. 'Carpet Crawlers' opens with a marvellous keyboard intro from new boy Irvin Duguid and Ray's vocal is uncannily similar to Peter's here.

'Ghost' takes us back to Ray's band Cut. This is a highly emotional song and one that comes across superbly well stripped down to its acoustic elements. 'Sunshine and Butterflies' is a deceptive title for what is another deeply emotional song. Even here in acoustic form it still manages to send shivers up the spine. The show proves to be a healthy mix of Ray's solo material and Genesis classics, which is as it should be, and there are several surprises among the set, not least a brilliant version of 'Fading Lights', in which Irvin really shines as he puts in a great rendition of Tony's keyboard part. Ray's vocal here manages to capture the sheer emotion of the song to perfection too.

The second set also has some memorable moments, not least Ray's interpretations of such latter-day classics as 'Another Cup of Coffee', 'Biko', and 'Ripples', as well as a contrasting mix of more of his own material, all of which is here in superb sound quality making this one of the most enjoyable Ray Wilson recordings around.

CHAPTER FIFTY-FOUR

"Stiltskin and other stories" 2006 - 2011

Ray evidently had unfinished business from his Stiltskin days as he reformed the band and released the She album. With albums now varying from acoustic to full on rock Ray was now able to expand his performing palette and shows during this period were to draw up on all these facets.

With other solo albums such as Propaganda Man also demonstrating Ray's fine line in song writing, his shows were an excellent mix as the recordings selected here show.

His decision to begin to include material not only from Genesis but also songs by several of the solo members took many by surprise as he had previously distanced himself from his involvement with the band. Not that it mattered to the fans who were lucky enough to see him perform his very own "World Of Genesis" shows, although attendance numbers in the UK were disappointing he nevertheless continued to tour increasingly in Europe and even took the show to South America.

Once again, there is a wealth of audio and video material available from these various shows available to collectors as is demonstrated by the selections I have made here.

THE ASSEMBLY, LEAMINGTON SPA, ENGLAND, 26 JUNE 2006
Set List: Calling all Stations/The Lamb Lies Down on Broadway/Land of Confusion/The Actor/Carpet Crawlers/Ghost/Games without Frontiers/Change/In the Air Tonight/Follow You Follow Me/Ripples/Not About Us/Alone/Entangled/Lemon Yellow Sun/She/Inside/I Can't Dance/Turn it on Again/Shipwrecked/Mama//
Source: Audience DVD Recording.

A tour that caused a certain amount of controversy among the Genesis fan base at the time, 2006's *World of Genesis* shows saw Ray giving the fans a healthy mix of songs from his time with Genesis along with classics by the band, and even some by the various solo members, leading to accusations in some quarters of Ray becoming in effect a "Genesis tribute band".

Of course, nothing could be further from the truth, as Ray has every right to perform these songs, and as you will hear (and see if you have the DVD of this gig), he puts in an amazing performance throughout. Opening with 'Calling all Stations', a dark and angsty version is driven along by some fine musicianship and a superbly emotional vocal from Ray himself. This still makes me wonder why the band didn't give it another go. No time for pondering, however, as the band follow that with the 'Lamb Lies Down on Broadway' and 'Land of Confusion', giving a nice contrast between the prog and the pop elements that made Genesis the success that they were.

'The Actor' from Ray's debut solo album *Change* gives us a chance to hear his own work in a wonderfully observant song, replete with emotion and delivered in fine fashion here. 'Carpet Crawlers' and 'Ghost' contrast just as nicely, with the latter being a thought-provoking song from Ray's only album with Cut. 'Games without Frontiers' is given the Ray Wilson treatment here, and it has to be said, his voice suits this kind of material to a tee, and it is evident that both he and the band are having a great time performing it.

The evening proves to be one of enormous contrasts as the emotional complexity of 'Change' rubs shoulders with the raw emotion of 'In the Air Tonight' and the simplicity of 'Solsbury Hill', all of which are given respectful and yet enjoyable performances tonight. 'Follow You Follow Me' and 'Not about Us' sandwich the glorious 'Ripples' like the two sides of a particularly wonderful musical sandwich, which is evidently relished by both the musicians and the audience.

Further contrasts are to be found in the rockier performances of some of Ray's Stiltskin material, which contrast with the pristine delicacy of 'Entangled', before the show closes with a trio of Genesis songs including a raucous 'I Can't Dance', which gets the crowd going and in the mood for 'Turn it on Again', which still rates as one of the best songs Genesis ever wrote, in my opinion, and Ray and his band more than do it justice before closing the show with an impressive version of the underrated 'Shipwrecked'.

THE YARD, ROSYTH, SCOTLAND, 8 JUNE 2007

Set List: Sunshine & Butterflies/Taking Time/Fly High/Shipwrecked/Follow You Follow Me/Change/Alone/Goodbye Baby Blue/Hey Hey/Sarah/Footsteps/Inside/Fame/ Ghost//
Source: Audience DVD Recording?

Sadly Ray has to compete with an incredibly ignorant audience tonight who seem determined to talk all the way through this performance, which opens with 'Sunshine & Butterflies'; a mournful and dark song with Ray in fine voice throughout. 'She' too has to compete with the bloody audience, which if irritating me watching the DVD, it must have been even more galling for Ray on the evening!

Ray seems surprisingly good-natured and indeed 'Taking Time' is a suitably laidback performance with some tasty bass lines. 'Fly High' gives the new Stiltskin album its first airing tonight. This is a melodic rocker with a harder edge as you would expect from Ray and at last he manages to win the battle with the audience noise.

Ray's first mention of Genesis is next with 'Shipwrecked' once again the crowd seem indifferent, except for one idiot who keeps on screeching throughout, which completely spoils what is otherwise an impressive rendering of this underrated track. 'Follow You Follow Me' garners only slight attention from the crowd again, although Ray appears relaxed and comfortable throughout what must have been an increasingly frustrating evening.

Ray's introduction to 'Change' is completely wasted on the crowd again, and indeed as the lyric says he is "making the most of it" with a brilliant performance with great harmony vocals, which once again goes right over the audience's heads. 'Alone' dedicated to Michelle who can be heard screeching her head off like a harpy throughout, which is a shame because she is missing a wonderfully laidback effort here.

Intriguingly the DVD artwork lists several songs that do not appear on the version here but what remains of the performance gives an interesting glimpse into the world of Ray Wilson circa 2007.

ARENA IM FREIZEITHAUS, BUXTEHUDE, GERMANY, 16 NOVEMBER 2007

Set List: She/Space Oddity/Another Day/Lemon Yellow Sun/Calling all Stations/Hey Hey/Sarah/Constantly Reminded/In the Air Tonight/The Actor/Follow You Follow Me/Change/Carpet Crawl/Alone/The Airport Song/Goodbye Baby Blue/Show Me the Way/Taking Time/Sick and Tired/Footsteps/Inside/Sunshine & Butterflies/Knockin' on Heaven's Door/No Woman, No Cry//
Source: Audience DVD Recording.

After the irritation of the Rosyth gig mentioned above, it is refreshing to get another recording from later in the same year where the audience seem much more attentive!

Once again, taken from a single camera shot, the show opens with 'She' from the new Stiltskin album. This is a haunting yet rocky number with Ray in fine voice. 'Space Oddity' gets Ray's own inimitable version, in which he sounds uncannily like Bowie, it has to be said.

'Another Day' is a marvellously thought-provoking song about drugs and depression is delivered in a suitably plaintive style by Ray and the band whilst 'Lemon Yellow Sun' sees Ray relaxed and evidently enjoying himself. We are then treated to the first amusing story about Ray's time with Genesis, which precedes a blistering version of 'Calling all Stations', which is a genuine delight, and his band give it a balls to the wall treatment, which is superb.

'Hey, Hey' and 'Sarah' take us back to the days of Cut; the band Ray put on hold effectively to join Genesis. These are a pairing of underrated songs with the former almost folky in its delivery whilst the latter gets the funk out with a driving rock rhythm. 'Constantly Reminded' is a story of a broken relationship (personal or perhaps a reflection of the one Ray had with Genesis). Either way, the performance here is laden with angst and emotion.

Ray as always has been prepared to cover other people's material and the solo members of Genesis have given him plenty to get his teeth into, including this marvellously atmospheric acoustic performance of 'In the Air Tonight'. 'The Actor' is another wonderful wistful reflection on life's might have beens, listened to in rapt attention by the crowd. 'Follow You Follow Me' is preceded by a hilarious story about Genesis betraying the inherent sense of bitterness that Ray obviously still has about the situation following the *Calling all Stations* debacle. No bitterness in the song itself, however, which is a delightful campfire styled acoustic performance. The mood is kept light with a marvellous laidback performance of 'Change' which closes Ray's first set.

The second set is a much more mixed bag opening with 'Carpet Crawlers' stripped down to its acoustic essentials but marvellous just the same. Other highlights from this half include the wonderfully tongue-in-cheek 'Airport Song', an emotional 'Goodbye Baby Blue', and a couple of equally enjoyable covers of 'Knockin' on Heaven's Door' and the Bob Marley classic, 'No Woman, No Cry', making this an altogether much more enjoyable performance all round.

BULL & GATE, LONDON, ENGLAND, 9 OCTOBER 2009
Set List: Bless Me/Lemon Yellow Sun/Another Day/Not About Us/Propaganda Man/Constantly Reminded/Show Me the Way/Change/ Follow You Follow Me/Along the Way/Solsbury Hill/Sarah/Razorlite/The Actor/Shipwrecked/Sunshine & Butterflies/She/ Footsteps/ Inside/Taking Time/In the Air Tonight//
Source: Audience DVD Recording.

An all too rare appearance by Ray in the UK opens with the first track off Ray's current *Propaganda Man* album, which is a suitably dark song that suits Ray's soulful vocal to perfection. 'Lemon Yellow Sun' from Ray's first Stiltskin album gets an uptempo rocking performance here. Once again, there is plenty of relaxed banter throughout the evening and some of Ray's hilarious stories about his time with Genesis, although there is still an element of bitterness in some of his comments but the stories are very amusing.

'Not about Us' still gets me wondering why it wasn't a hit. This is a peach of a song and Ray really gets it across perfectly on this recording. 'Propaganda Man' is evidently unfamiliar to most of the crowd but once again Ray's biting lyrics are a delight to hear. 'Constantly Reminded', a wry look back on divorce, gets a suitably almost country setting here.

With Ray's performances in the UK becoming rarer, it is a treat to hear the usual mix of solo and Genesis material, along with some Genesis solo moments too, including excellent versions of 'Solsbury Hill', which gets the crowd going. Other highlights are blistering performances of 'She', 'Footsteps', and 'Inside', proving that Ray can still rock out with the best of 'em.

RYNEK MIASTA, GNIEZNO, POLAND, 23 APRIL 2010
Set List: No Son of Mine/Land of Confusion/That's All/Not About Us/Carpet Crawlers/Another Cup of Coffee/Ripples/ Shipwrecked/ Follow You Follow Me/Change//
Source: Audience Recording.

This is a fascinating recording here of the highlights from one of Ray's "Genesis Klassik" shows with the Berlin Symphony Ensemble and a full band. Taken from the audience, this one is above average and it is evident from the tape that it was quite close to the stage.

A blistering 'No Son of Mine' opens the recording and the ensemble manage to give it a new twist with the end result being extremely enjoyable. Ray's vocal is every bit as emotional and dramatic as it had been on the *Calling all Stations* tour all those years ago.
'Land of Confusion' is one of those songs you either love or hate, and here it is obvious that the audience love it a tad too much, as the taper has to move out of the way of someone clapping a little bit *too* hard! 'That's All' falls a little bit flat here and Ray doesn't sound too comfortable and the ensemble are quite hesitant too but they manage manfully enough.

'Not about Us' is given a delightful piano introduction, which is a new and unexpected element in this underrated song, with almost a little touch of jazz before Ray's acoustic guitar gets a cheer of recognition from the crowd. This is definitely a delightful performance, with Ray's delivery spot on. 'Carpet Crawlers' was one of those songs that convinced Genesis fans that Ray could do the job and here it is again; a spine-tingling performance with the pianist laying down Tony's arpeggios to perfection for a stately and serene performance of this classic.

'Another Cup of Coffee' is stripped down to bare acoustic guitar and voice for an extremely enjoyable performance before Ray treats the audience to another Genesis classic, namely 'Ripples', which was one of the songs that he was trying to persuade the band to perform back in '98. Here it is simply amazing and the harmony vocals are to die for – a magnificent performance.

Contrasting that with 'Shipwrecked' works well too. In fact the latter sounds better here than it ever did with Genesis if truth be told! The plaintive violins augment an equally emotional vocal from Ray, giving the song an added emotion which has previously been lacking. Some campfire music comes next with a countrified version of 'Follow You Follow Me', which is always a delight and here it is obvious that Ray is enjoying himself, and so are the crowd! 'Change' is the only representative from Ray's solo career on this recording and it is here that the taper has problems with his recording equipment. Sadly there are several dropouts on sound, but the performance is evidently a strong one, which closes this short but nifty recording.

ESKULAP, POZNAN, POLAND, 19 OCTOBER 2011
Set List: Bless Me/Another Day/Goodbye Baby Blue/Propaganda Man/First Day of Change/Lemon Yellow Sun/Congo/Calling all Stations/More Than Just A Memory/Shipwrecked/Razorlite/Fly High/Accidents Will Happen/Voice of Disbelief/Change/ Sarah/Tales From A Small Town/Not About Us/The Airport Song/Constantly Reminded/Guns of God/Footsteps/Inside/American Beauty/The Seventh Day//
Source: Audience Recording.

With Ray's increasing touring schedule being mainly centred around shows in Poland and Germany, here we have one of his most recent shows with the revamped Stiltskin promoting the *Unfulfilment* album. The show opens with an uptempo version of 'Bless Me', which unfortunately suffers from some drop outs as if the taper has had to cover their recording equipment, which is a shame. 'Another Day' is much better. This dark and emotional song is given a suitably emphatic performance here.

'Propaganda Man' is a brilliant observation of the cynical manipulation of people by politicians and those in power with superbly bitter and emotional lyrics, which contrast quite superbly with the mainly acoustic treatment it is given here tonight. By the time we get to the first of the Genesis offerings a few songs later, with an upbeat 'Congo' replete with drums whistles and an infectious keyboard riff, we find a relaxed and confident Mr Wilson, especially when it comes to the hard rocking 'Calling all Stations', which is delivered here in a blistering performance. Ray's band takes this latter-day classic and rock it out fit to bust and it is superb to hear!

The contrast between tracks like this and 'Fly High' only serves to emphasise Ray's rock credentials. Here his band are tight and there are some superb performances from Ashley MacMillan on drums and Lawrie MacMillan on bass.

The angst and incredibly ironic 'Voice of Disbelief' sends up the vagaries of the world of rock and roll to perfection and Ray is obviously in his element here. It isn't all doom and gloom though, as we have the marvellous tongue-in-cheek 'Airport Song', but the emphasis is firmly on rock and the closing series of tracks that are taken from the first incarnation of Stiltskin, including a hard rocking 'Inside' and 'Footsteps', and equally hard hitting 'American Beauty', with the awesome 'Seventh Day' ending the show in a truly dramatic fashion.

KOLOSSEUM, LÜBECK, GERMANY, 30 MARCH 2012
Set List: Follow You Follow Me/Sarah/Another Day in Paradise/More than Just a Memory/Carpet Crawlers/No Son of Mine/Lemon Yellow Sun/That's All/One/Shipwrecked/Mama/Land of Confusion/Invisible Touch/Tale From a Small Town/Change/Four Seasons Medley/Ripples/Entangled/Not About Us/First Day of Change/Solsbury Hill/In the Air Tonight/The Airport Song/Inside/Knockin' on Heaven's Door//
Source: Soundboard Recording?

One of the most recent recordings by Ray to surface and another delight it is too. From the sound of the acoustics this was a small theatre but that only adds to the atmosphere. This show was another featuring the "Genesis Klassik Quartet" as well as members of his regular band. The recording opens with a particularly lovely 'Follow You Follow Me' with a crisp clear sound, in which the strings contribute enormously to the cheerfulness of the song. As usual Ray mixes things up, so we get 'Sarah' next from the Cut album, which is a nice contrast to its predecessor.

'Another Day in Paradise' is next. Stripped back to piano, acoustic guitar, and voice, this is another delightful offering and Ray's voice if anything manages to capture even more emotion than Mr Collins. What is impressive from the start is the overall quality of this recording, which leads me to suspect that it is taken from the mixing desk. Audience noise is restricted to polite between songs applause, which means that the actual performance can be enjoyed even more than usual. 'More Than Just a Memory' and the 'Carpet Crawlers' contrast classic slices of Ray's own song writing skill and that of his erstwhile bandmates with two superb performances. The piano playing on the latter is absolutely superb.

'No Son of Mine' is delivered as if Ray wrote it, such is his command of the song and the atmospheric nuances it generates, while 'Lemon Yellow Sun' has his own unique stamp written all over it. Party time arrives with a fantastic 'That's All'. The audience finally get in on the act here with clapping throughout and the string quartet really add zest to the performance. One features Ray's brother Steve on vocals and this is another incredibly strong performance.

'Shipwrecked' and 'Mama' bookend two different facets of Genesis' music. The former opens with a sparse piano introduction before the strings take up the slack and put some meat on the bones of the performance. This is so much better than the recorded version, in my opinion. Perhaps the band should have used a string section? Oh, well … 'Mama' is driven along by piano before Ray starts in with the vocal. Hearing this one in an acoustic setting really gives it a completely different vibe to its more usual, although the manic "laugh" sounds as if Ray is throwing up much to the evident amusement of the audience!

'Land of Confusion' is one of those songs you can either take or leave if you are a Genesis fan. I am not too enamoured of it and tonight the ensemble strings and acoustic guitar-driven version falls rather flat to my ears, but the band redeem themselves with a storming version of 'Invisible Touch', which Ray really seems to be enjoying, and once again the piano gives it a totally different slant, which is every bit as enjoyable.

'Tales from a Small Town' from Ray's latest Stiltskin album is another brilliantly observed song, which demonstrates once again just how strong a song writer Ray is. His vocal performance here is a master class in emotion. 'Change' also benefits enormously from the addition of the strings that provide a lovely warmth to an already delightful song. A snippet from Vivaldi's *The Four Seasons* follows, which remarkably doesn't sound out of place here and the string section are superb, and this makes for quite an unexpected change of pace.

A rather savage edit leads us into 'Ripples'; a song which I am sure most Genesis fans would have loved to hear Ray sing back on the *Calling all Stations* tour. There is no denying it, as here he nails it to perfection. Vocally and musically this is another stunning arrangement that leads into the equally impressive 'Entangled'. Piano and strings lead the way here in a delightful ballet of sound with the audience evidently listening in rapt attention to every note. It's truly beautiful and is another Genesis classic that Ray comfortably makes his own.

Steve Wilson takes the vocal lead with 'All I Need is a Miracle' and it is surprising how much he sounds like the late, great Paul Young here. Sadly the string accompaniment, which is so strong on other tracks, doesn't really cut it here. This one needs a rock band to get the real emotion of the performance out. That said, the strings do put in some remarkable playing and once again the sound is nicely balanced and crystal clear.

'Not about Us' is another of those Genesis songs that to my mind never got a fair hearing from most fans at the time of *Calling all Stations*. Maybe this version by Ray might make them re-evaluate it. Personally I loved the original and this version is, if anything, even better. Piano and strings provide a lovely background to a fine vocal from Ray. 'First Day of Change' is equally emphatic' It is a brilliantly emotive song brought even more vividly to life by a superlative string and piano accompaniment.

'Solsbury Hill' needs no introduction and the audience take their chance to participate with evident relish. You can almost see the smile on Ray's face as he belts this one out and the ensemble aren't far behind him – simply joyous stuff. A superb contrast comes next with 'In the Air Tonight'. Once again the audience take their cue and Ray actively encourages it.

'The Airport Song' is a superbly hilarious observation of the trials and tribulations of travel with a rock band or simply as a tourist. There is an element of 'Living Next Door to Alice' about this one but the sheer wry humour of it will bring a smile to the most hardened of rock fans. Who said Ray doesn't do humour?!

'Inside' – Ray's first big hit – gets an acoustic treatment as you would expect tonight. Staccato strings and piano manage to generate some of the sheer dynamism of the original but without the thundering bass line this one doesn't manage to get the same feel, but nevertheless Ray and the band give it a good go. 'Knockin' on Heaven's Door' works much better and the show closes with the entire band and audience getting in on the act in a relaxed and enjoyable version.

COLOS-SAAL, ASCHAFFENBURG, GERMANY, 6 APRIL 2013

Set List: American Beauty/That's All/Easier That Way/Lemon Yellow Sun/Follow the Lie/The Lamb Lies Down on Broadway/Another Day in Paradise/Another Day/Bless Me/Saxophone-Piano Duet/Mama/Inside/Tales from a Small Town/She's A Queen/Sarah/Carpet Crawlers/Stay Another Day/Shipwrecked/Ripples/Horizons/Entangled/Excerpt from Vivaldi's Four Seasons/Solsbury Hill/Calling all Stations/Congo/The Airport Song/Knockin' on Heaven's Door//
Source: Audience Recording.

One thing you can never accuse Ray of is short-changing his fans! This lengthy recording taken from one of Ray's most recent shows is clear evidence of that.

Throughout the course of this excellent quality audience recording we are treated to a healthy mix of old and new material from Ray's expanding back catalogue including several cuts from the soon to be released new album (soon at time of writing at least).

Ray's skill as an observant lyric writer is on display from the first track, namely 'American Beauty', which is a wry look at the fascination with looks and where it can lead. Contrasting this with a humorous romp through the country & western-tinged 'That's All' gives a fine example of the contrasting styles of music that are to feature during tonight's performance.

From a personal standpoint, I am somewhat surprised to see the emphasis of the show is still placed heavily upon the Genesis material with respectful nods to the solo material of Messrs Collins and Gabriel too. Some of this stuff works better than others. 'The Lamb', for example, is delivered here with every bit as much bite as it had been by Ray back in the days of the *Calling all Stations* tour. 'Mama' and 'Calling all Stations' both amply demonstrate the sheer power of Ray's voice too, augmented by the considerable talents of the rest of his band.

The extract from Vivaldi's masterpiece *The Four Seasons* and the violin-led 'Ripples' and 'Horizons' give an extra element to what was evidently an extremely enjoyable evening for all concerned and the remaining mix of material makes this another worthy addition to any collection.

STUDIO POLSKIE, WARSAW RADIO 3, POLAND, 18 APRIL 2013

Set List: Another Day/Easier That Way/Show Me the Way/Lemon Yellow Sun/That's All/Piano/Saxophone Duet/The Actor/No Son of Mine/American Beauty/Carpet Crawlers//
Source: Radio Broadcast.

Another excellent if all too short radio broadcast from one of Ray's most recent shows gets under way with a superb version of the Cut song, 'Another Day'. This superbly emotional song is given just the right amount of angst by Ray and the band here and gets things off to a great start.

With a new album to promote, Ray gets straight down to business next with 'Easier That Way'; a slightly more upbeat number with an infectious chorus augmented by some superb harmony vocals from several members of the band. Once again, the mix of old and new material here works extremely well. I have no doubt that there were many highlights omitted from the actual performance but what we have here serves as another extremely enjoyable item.

****

PART SEVEN: AFTERGLOW

PART SEVEN: AFTERGLOW

CHAPTER FIFTY-FIVE
WHAT THEY SAID...

I thought it might prove interesting to hear what the band members have said about the various tours/albums covered by this book, so I have selected extracts from interviews given by the band both to my own magazine/web site, *The Waiting Room*, and contemporaneously via radio/TV and in the press.

Allowing Phil to "wiggle his bum" and take on the singer's role in the band:
"Funnily enough, one of the first people to suggest that Phil should be the singer was Jon Anderson who came to Phil's wedding at the time ... and I was talking to him and said, 'Phil has a wonderful range,' and he said, 'Why don't you get in extra instrumentalists and make the band stronger? Phil's got a nice voice. You seem to be aware of that already.' And I said, 'Really, Jon, I don't think the band will wear that one really because they see him as the drummer.' So, eventually we did take somebody into the studio and record and he sang a version of 'Squonk' and he had considerable trouble with the melody line because it was written by instrumentalists where the line was weaving up and down and all over the place; not an easy melody for a singer to sing, and he found it difficult to respond to ... So I remember Mike and Tony saying to Phil, 'What do you think, Phil?' and he said, 'I think it sounds fucking average. Let me have a go...'
(Steve Hackett "The Genesis of a Guitarist" Issue 37 of The Waiting Room Magazine)

Recruiting Bill Bruford for the *A Trick of the Tail* tour:
"Well, Bill was an easy person to get along with; he is still a friend of mine in fact and he is obviously a very versatile drummer. I wouldn't say that everything we did came naturally to him, really. He is very much a thinking drummer; he counts everything whereas we had never really counted, so all these things came out in a different place where he would count two instead of our usual one ... He gave us so much, really, because he was quite a name in his own right. When we got on stage there would be calls of 'Bruford!' I think he helped us through what was obviously quite a difficult period trying to establish ourselves without Peter ..."
(Tony Banks "The A to Z of Genesis" Issue 30 of The Waiting Room Magazine)

Recording *Wind & Wuthering* in Holland and Steve's departure:
"It was down to financial reasons. I mean, it was very stupid but if you recorded at home at that time the tax situation was such that if you recorded your album outside of the country it was regarded as foreign earnings. Now, we are not particularly mercenarily motivated but it didn't worry us going to Holland. In fact we were quite happy going there and recording it. It didn't make that much

difference to us and it was quite good too in a way; getting away from all the distractions and that helped give the album a strong identity..."

"I think at the time I was anxious to do a string of solo albums and this was something that worried Tony and Mike. Phil wasn't worried in the least, as he had been operating with Brand X for quite some time, but I think that wasn't regarded as quite such a threat because he wasn't pushing it out under his own name ... Nonetheless, I felt that I was coming up with far too many ideas for the band to exploit – explore is perhaps a better word – and in order to do that I had to work with other people ... It was perceived as a threat, however, and it was basically a two-year decision. I didn't make it lightly and it didn't happen overnight. I think, perhaps, I underestimated how difficult it was going to be but even now I think it was the right decision because otherwise I would have had to say goodbye to a lot of great music ..."
(Sketches of Hackett, the authorised biography 2009)

Going solo (Phil):
"It was just a complete shock – a solo album done under those circumstances – so lazily. I was very intense obviously when I was doing it. It wasn't, 'Okay, I want to make a record,' it was just suddenly there was a record and suddenly people liked it ..."
(Record Mirror interview 1980)

Going solo with the Mechanics (Mike):
"Looking back on it, it was a bit like Genesis. I wanted to be a songwriter, so I got together with Chris Neil and B. A. Robertson and we tried to get people to do our songs. I always believed in that but it didn't really happen. I suppose making a version of 'Silent Running' didn't seem a good song to cover, so once again history was repeating itself ..."

Going solo (Peter):
"I wanted to make it sound varied and I wanted it to sound different from Genesis. You see, Genesis have since reappeared sounding much the same as before and I had been written off simply as a performer rather than as a musical figure. I think I will approach the next album the same way and maybe after that I will try to establish a definite Peter Gabriel 'sound'..."
(NME interview 1977)

Touring solo for the first time (Steve):
"I realised after several months after swearing that I wouldn't tour I realised that I missed touring. The trouble is if you are not touring an album all you have got is the critical response, and the professional critics will obviously give you the benefit of

the doubt first time round, but the next time round it is so much more difficult it is because more of yourself you commit to it, the less 'new' it is. People started saying perhaps you need to promote it, perhaps you need to get out there and start doing it ..."
(BBC Radio Hallam interview 1978)

Coming back to group writing for the *Duke* album:
"Well, Mike and I had just done solo albums and we were dry on material, and so we had to write more on the spot, so something like 'Turn it on Again' came out of a bit that Mike had discarded from his solo record and a bit that I had discarded from mine, and we just put the two together. Originally it was a link, a tentative link on a longer piece after 'Duchess' and before 'Guide Vocal', and we recorded it and it sounded so good we thought let's do it twice and then put a vocal on the riff and see what happens, and we put it down with no lyrics or anything, and then Mike went away and wrote a lyric and a melody for it and it sounded great ... The most group track on that album was 'Duchess', where we used the drum machine for the first time on an album and we tried all sorts of things on that with heavy compression on the song and simple chords, and I wrote a melody and the lyrics for it, and I thought that it was at that point on the album on that song that Phil became the singer. He just got this edge to his voice and it took off from there really ..."
(Tony Banks: "The A to Z of Genesis" Issue 31 of The Waiting Room Magazine)

The way songs are put together (Peter):
"My initial ideas come at any time and I write them down in a notebook or diary or on a cassette if it is a musical idea. The hard part is working through all these ideas, sifting out the good ideas from the rubbish, and turning them into songs ..."

The origins of 'Abacab' the track and people's reactions to it:
"The song is in three bits – bit A, bit B, and bit C. When we were putting it together we were trying different orders from 'Abacab' to 'Cabba' and so on. 'Abacab' wasn't the order used in the end, but it was a nice sounding word, so it stuck for the working title. When we came to give it a final title we had all grown fond of it and used to the word and so it stayed ..."

"When People heard that song ('Abacab') they tore their hair out because it was almost like Genesis playing punk – they didn't like that at all ..."
(Mike and Phil unknown radio interview 1981)

Tony's perverse liking for 'Who-dunnit?' and the famous booing incident in Leiden:
"I listened to that album recently and one of my favourite tracks was the one everybody hates: 'Who-dunnit?' I thought that's a great track. Why didn't we do more like that? I remember playing that and trying to get this sort of computer noise and Mike and Phil were listening and they said, 'You've got something there.' So we put it down on tape with this drum music that Phil was playing and we improvised on it for thirty minutes, and there is a thirty-minute version of that song, for people who really like that song! (laughter) And we cut it down and it was a great result. I liked it because it was very extreme, as I am a kind of perverse person and I like to explore different areas...

Some of the other songs didn't quite match that and I think it is great. We used to get booed when we played it. We played Leiden in Holland and we got booed, and so we went back and played there again. There was this reaction against songs like that and 'Man on the Corner' because it was simple and that was seen as being wrong and yet that has always been a part of Genesis..."
(Tony Banks "The A to Z of Genesis" Issue 35 of The Waiting Room Magazine)

The origins of 'Mama':

"It's about this old... It's a personal story of Phil's (laughs). There was Phil in this Cuban brothel and there was this big old hooker (Phil does the manic laugh) and they went upstairs... Basically there is this young guy who was keen on this old hooker and she gave him a hard time, really, and that's basically what it's about. Our manager Tony thought it was... and if you listen to it, an anti-abortion song. You can apply that to it. We describe it as 'surgical rock'..."

(US syndicated radio interview with Phil, Mike, and Tony 1983)

The way the band write:

"On 'No Son of Mine', that to me was a great little song, because it just happened and we wrote it by deciding we will try it out for the album and it will be great; or if it doesn't work then we will throw it away and Phil had lyrics and it just happened in the morning, and then Tony had the elephant noise and I tried to get two or three chords under it and the atmosphere was just great. 'Dreaming While You Sleep' started with just the drum machine; that's why its working title was 'Rolling Toms'. A lot of the songs began around the drum machine and then we would get the chords ..."

(Mike Rutherford Issue 37 of The Waiting Room Magazine)

The stage set up:

"A lot more in terms of what you see; once we had decided to use the screens – if we were going to use the screens; if we were going to do open air shows. So we decided that we wanted to use them as a special effect like we had tried to do with *The Lamb* but now we had the technology to do it properly. So we got a bloke in and we went through all the possible things.

The trouble was that once things got started it became a *very* expensive operation and very time consuming, so what we decided to do was incorporate a lot of stock footage. Some of that stuff is very easy to do and looks very effective and because people had never seen it before in this kind of situation I felt that we could get away with some of the very simple ideas, the most obvious being the '2001' effect, and I thought why not? It is a very simple thing to do. It is all computer generated and all the lines come towards you and you get the effect of travelling into a thing and I had always thought that that effect would look great in 'Domino', and so the guy came up with the stuff that looked like '2001' and it worked on the big screen, and then there was the idea of sticking Phil up in the middle of it and suddenly he was where you weren't expecting him and it worked ..."

(Tony Banks "The A to Z of Genesis" The Waiting Room Magazine)

The strains of touring:

"We want to do a tour for a week, and then our manager wants us to do one for a year, so we compromise and do one for about four months. We want this time around instead of flogging ourselves into the ground to try and keep it to the level where we are still interested and excited when we do the last gig and we feel by keeping it down a bit we will do that ..."

"Night after night after night and then a break. I mean, four shows on the run are about all my voice can take these days ...When we start we'll just keep going. It'll be big shows though; stadiums, which is what we would like to do, although we are not committing ourselves. We would like to think about doing a theatre tour because that's what we would like to do, but of course, you can't do that otherwise you are going to have to be on the road for two or three years at a time to fulfil the demand for tickets ..."

"What has made it hard for us over the years is the balance of actual writing and recording and touring, the promotion side – things have grown a lot. We have to try and find a balance between what they want us to do and what *we* want to do ..."
(Tony, Phil, and Mike in conversation with Chris Tarrant GLR Radio 1 January 1992)

The reaction to Ray getting the Genesis job:
(SW): "He actually told me. I was doing a gig in Edinburgh at the time and he came up to me at the gig and said, 'You are never going to believe this one ...' and Tim who is Ray's manager was on the phone and he said that Tony Smith had been on and that they wanted him to audition for the Genesis job, and I said, 'What are you doing carrying amps around?' or something ..." (laughter)
(PH): "We were all genuinely behind him and I thought instantly that he should do it because offers like that don't come around that often ..."
(Steve Wilson and Paul Haimes "Cutting Talk" interview #39 of The Waiting Room Magazine)

The failure of *Calling all Stations* to make a dent in the US market and fans' reaction to the new look band:
"Genesis this time round is a little underdog-ish. Phil has gone and quite frankly even if Phil was still here it would be quite difficult because the mood in America has changed towards more established artists... and we are struggling like fuck in America; really struggling... I think with this album we are caught somewhere between what the band has done recently and what it has done in the past. When it came to singing Mike's songs I had a freer rein than when I was singing Tony's and that's because he doesn't know what he wants until he hears it, whereas Tony knows what he wants in the first place... The American thing is obviously very disappointing but we will play them (the US shows) if we have to play smaller shows, then fuck it – we will play smaller shows but we will play them. All they give a fuck about is that the places we play are busy – they don't want to play a half empty arena , stadium, or anything. The way we look at it is, if we have to do theatres in America, then let's do *full* theatres rather than half empty arenas..."

"A lot of people are having problems in America. The turnover of certain artists has been down and they can't find a niche, so to speak. But we are going to battle on. We have to get a vibe going. We're a bit cold at the moment. The trouble is until they hear something, until they hear Ray, they can't get excited about it and it's all hearsay ..."

"The cancellation of the US tour was a disaster and I believe that it ended Genesis. I didn't want to do another album after the tour, nor did Mike. Tony did. We should have listened to him. Not only older but wiser too ..."
(Ray Wilson and Mike Rutherford "Another Chiddingfold Afternoon" interview in issue 36 of The Waiting Room magazine and "There Must Be Some Other Way to do an interview" Issue 42 of The Waiting Room Magazine)

The problems of making a band look and sound good on stage:
"The vocals we have to work on every day really. You know, the singer's voice is probably the most delicate instrument in rock and roll, really, and when Ray has had to do three or four gigs in a row and it has been a really shitty room and he has had to be barking and the next night he might be suffering a bit ..."

"There are a couple of tracks that do run fine but some of the older tunes just because of the way they play them they are slightly different each evening, so I am literally editing live to what they are playing and sometimes I get caught out, and so every day they play it slightly differently and I have to react to that, and it is the most challenging work I have done in ages ... What went wrong last night was the strobe and then the bulb blew in the next one ... it was one of those nights last night and then the aircraft light bulb went down. You have those occasionally and it is usually in London, so I am pleased to say that this time it was Birmingham. The systems have

been very good generally and the crews are fantastic. They keep on top of it ..."
(Interviews with Chris "Privet" Hedges and David Hill sound and lighting engineers for the Calling all Stations tour in Issue 47 of The Waiting Room Magazine)

The 5.1 remastering process and the recent live official bootlegs: "The original multitrack is baked in an oven for ... I don't know how many hours ... twenty-four and that makes the glue re-stick to the plastic. Then you play it on to a 2-inch tape and then into a Pro Tools system that is running at 24 Bit 192K, and we record the multi-track into that, and then I mix from that format and through the desk into 5.1. I haven't got the original track sheets, which is a bit of a pain in the arse. I had some photocopies because at some stage they had been photocopied and they are nearly up to date but they are missing things, so when I start each track I have to sit and listen through everything and find out what is on each track, and that doesn't always correspond to what is on the sheet. And then just try and work out which parts they used ..."

"They are recorded onto a little Pro Tools 003 system by Geoff Callingham. He takes the front of house mix and adds a bit of audience. They sound great."
(Interviews with Nick Davis in Issues 48 and 66 of The Waiting Room Magazine)

Putting together the set list for the *Turn it on Again* tour and the vagaries of the weather:
"In many ways it was just like putting together a set as if we had a new record but instead of doing songs from the 'new' album we were able to put in some earlier things that we hadn't played for a while. Listening to *Three Sides Live* we particularly liked the 'Cage/Afterglow' medley but wanted to make it a little different, so we replaced 'Colony of Slippermen' with a bit of 'Duke's Travels', which both Phil and I were keen to do. I also wanted to do one song that we hadn't played for a very long time, so I suggested 'Ripples' amongst one or two other possibilities. The other earlier songs – 'Follow You Follow Me', 'Carpet Crawlers', etc. – helped to balance the show to stop it becoming too heavy for what would, after all, be a pretty mixed crowd ... The strangest moment for me was looking across early during the Katowice show and seeing Mike and Daryl wearing caps and raincoats with rain pouring on them and lightning flashing behind them, especially when we had been told that if there was lightning they would take us off the stage ..."

"On this last European tour the one that stood out for me was in Katowice, Poland. It was one of the most difficult but rewarding shows on the tour. It was storming all day before the show. The audience had to endure the wind and the rain from the moment they arrived before the show. We had a strong plastic-type covering over the stage. Once we started, the wind was blowing the rain into the stage. It was covering our pedal boards and keyboards. Tony's keyboard went out halfway through the second song. He had to put up a spare for the rest of the show. I thought we would be taken off stage after the third song because it was starting to get dangerous. Lightning was lighting up the sky and here we were with electric instruments in our hands. We were wearing rain

jackets and caps – which we never have. It continued to rain for the whole show. It was amazing to see these people out there with smiles on their faces in spite of the weather. They were standing out there in pouring rain for hours before we even started and all through the two and a half-hour show ..."
(Tony Banks and Daryl Stuermer interviews in Issue 66 of The Waiting Room Magazine)

Reconvening the Mechanics after Paul Young's death and the recent changes in line up:
"Well, there was no sort of master plan. I think, looking back, I think really when Paul Young died, something changed. The chemistry changed and both myself and Paul (Carrack) felt it, actually. We did one more album, *Rewired*, which was a bit of ... but I don't think we should have done it. It was a nice thought, actually, but the album was a bit odd. Anyway, in my mind when Paul died we came to the end of an era really and the chemistry had changed and I put it away in my mind. Then it was a guy called Brian Rawlings who said, 'Why not go back to the first thing? The name and the sound are there; just see what happens. Write some songs, get some new writers, some might come on board writing-wise.' The first time we did it I had written all these songs and I didn't know who was going to sing them! It was the same process this time round but it was kind of easier because Andrew (Roachford) came down earlier on and I sort of let it happen ..."
("One More for the Road" TWR interview with Mike Rutherford and Andrew Roachford in Issue 77 of TWR Online).

Phil's farewell tour:
"The reason for that is a little bit of English humour. I could easily have called it "The Farewell Tour" but that is a little bit to the point and a little bit sentimental, so we thought. Me and Smithy (Tony Smith) started thinking what can we call it? And it is taken from *Monty Python*; a sort of nod in their direction. It is meant to be funny but at the same time it is a way of saying it is a joke but with a serious message. There *won't* be a second one. This really is the last tour as far as I am concerned ..."
("In Conversation" TWR interview with Phil in Issue 51 of TWR Online)

Working with an orchestra (Peter):
"The orchestra does provide different dimensions to the music that weren't there originally. A lot of rock artists work slowly in the studio, building up layer by layer. One of the powerful advantages of the orchestra is that you have this number of musicians playing at the same time at one moment with all these colours and personalities that either blend or don't ... Here the idea was to strip away the rock band so you had to use the colours only available to the orchestra ..."
(Blood Donors EPK)

The risk of becoming his own Genesis tribute band with Genesis Revisited II (Steve):
"I Tell you what, if I were to answer you with regard to any criticism that might be aimed at me with regard to that, all I can say is since I left Genesis I have been involved in so many different kinds of music and after I have spent a year doing this, which is what I am going to do, I am going to become an individual again. I have always said that there is always a danger of wearing a curator's cap in a museum of your own making but I do think those exhibits are worth looking at again, because they are pretty fine and if I weren't a proud exhibitor or curator and I do feel some sense of responsibility to these songs, which I feel have not exactly been disowned by the majority of the other perpetrators, then certainly I feel that often disparaging statements are made about them ... All I know is that since I started to do this there has been massive interest and the tickets have been selling massively well and so there is a huge interest in it!
(Genesis Re-Evaluated Issue 81 of TWR Online)

****

ACKNOWLEDGEMENTS

None of this would have been possible without the help of a great many fans. The following in particular are to be thanked for their help and encouragement: Mike Jackson, Phil Myland, Peter Gozzard, David Howarth, Ted Sayers, Ronnie Pepl, and Weel Smeets, without whom my own collection would never have got off the ground in the first place. Grateful thanks to the band members and road crews for writing the music and staging the shows. My grateful thanks to Carol Willis, Dale Newman, Geoff and Annie Callingham, and Nick Davis for all their help and assistance. Thanks to Simon Funnell and David Dunnington, Mike Carzo and Tom Morgenstein for their sterling work documenting so many different aspects of the band's live and studio output and Simon's web site – www.Genesis-TheMovement.org – is an indispensable source of material on the band and every solo member. And to Paul Russell, Jeff Kaa and Yashima Tsukamoto and Mario Giammetti whose previous works inspired this one.

My grateful thanks also to the fans who have contributed material of one sort or another to this and my previous projects. It couldn't have been written without you and I hope you enjoy the finished results!

This book is dedicated to the memory of my father who, while not a Genesis convert, certainly got to know more about them than many a fan over the years! Even to the extent of being referred to as "The Boss" by one of the founder members of the band. This one's for you, Dad, with love and gratitude.

PHOTO CREDITS

The Publisher would like to take this opportunity to thank the following for the use of their work within this book: Mike Ainscoe, Atlantic Records, Stuart Barnes, David Birtwell, Camino Records, Charisma Records, Paul Cox, Richard Davies, Martin Dean, Mike Ellison, EMI Records, Albert Gouder, Jonathan Guntrip, Jo Hackett (p192), Anthony Hobkinson, Stuart Holmes, Stefan Hummel, Ulrich Klemt, Kurt Lambert Newgord (p179), Wesley McDowell, Richard Mills (p172), Lee Millward, Andrew Nagy, Alan Perry, Shirley Powell, Sylvia Pistel, Real World Records, Roger Salem, Ted Sayers, Ina Schneider, Pauline Thompson, Guido Truffer, Virgin Records, Voiceprint Records, Jill Walker.

We have been unable to trace the photographers who took some of the images used. If you recognise your work within, please contact us. All memorabilia within this book is from the author's own personal collection unless otherwise stated.

ABOUT THE AUTHOR

Alan Hewitt has been a fan of Genesis and all of its solo protagonists for the better part of thirty-six years and has travelled extensively following the band and the various solo members, even working for one of them in the capacity of merchandiser on several tours.

In addition to this, he has also been the driving force behind *The Waiting Room*, which was established as an informal information service/forum for fans back in August 1987, making it the longest established source of information about the band anywhere in the world. *The Waiting Room*, or *TWR* as it has since become abbreviated, went online as an Internet Magazine in 1998; preceding the band's own official web site by several months, and 2015 marks the twenty-eighth anniversary of the establishment of *TWR*. The author has also written several books on the subject of the band, including 2000s *Opening the Musical Box – A Genesis Chronicle*, 2007's *Genesis Revisited*, and 2009's *Sketches of Hackett - The Official Steve Hackett Biography* (updated in 2011). His expertise has also been called upon for several TV projects on the band, including 2000's *Genesis Songbook* and the BBC's long-running quiz show, *Mastermind*.

When not indulging his passion for all things Genesis, the author has a wide-ranging interest in music from rock to classical. He also has a passion for history and gardening as well as active involvement with several charitable organisations.

A Selection Of Shows: Genesis & Solo Live Guide 1976-2014